Introduction to Qualitative Research Methods

ABOUT THE AUTHORS

Steven J. Taylor, Ph.D.
Steve Taylor is Professor of Cultural Foundations of Education and Sociology and Director of the Center on Human Policy, a disability research and policy institute, at Syracuse University. He has published widely on qualitative sociology, social and cultural aspects of disability, and disability policy. He currently serves as editor of *Mental Retardation*, a journal published by the American Association on Mental Retardation (AAMR), and was the recipient of AAMR's 1997 Research Award.

Robert Bogdan, Ph.D.
Bob Bogdan is Professor of Cultural Foundations of Education and Sociology at Syracuse University. He also serves as director of the Social Sciences Doctoral Program and is a long time associate of the Center on Human Policy. He has published numerous books and articles on qualitative research methods, disability studies, and the sociology of education. He is the author of the widely acclaimed book *Freak Show*.

Introduction to Qualitative Research Methods

A GUIDEBOOK AND RESOURCE

THIRD EDITION

STEVEN J. TAYLOR

ROBERT BOGDAN

JOHN WILEY & SONS, INC.

New York • Chichester • Weinheim • Brisbane • Singapore • Toronto

Copyright © 1998 by John Wiley & Sons, Inc.
Published by John Wiley & Sons, Inc.

Library of Congress Cataloging-in-Publication Data:
Taylor, Steven J., 1949–
     Introduction to qualitative research methods : a guidebook and
resource / by Steven J. Taylor, Robert Bogdan. — 3rd ed.
          p.   cm.
     Includes bibliogrpahical references and index.
     ISBN 0-471-16868-8 (cloth : alk. paper)
     1. Social sciences—Research—Methodology.   2. Sociology—
Research—Methodology.   I. Title.
     H61.T385   1997
     301'.072—dc21   97-30083
                                                               CIP

Printed in the United States of America

10 9 8 7 6

Contents

PART ONE:

AMONG THE PEOPLE: HOW TO CONDUCT QUALITATIVE RESEARCH

PART TWO:
WRITING QUALITATIVE STUDIES 165

Preface

THIS IS THE third edition of *Introduction to Qualitative Research*. When the first edition was published in 1975, qualitative research was struggling for respect in a research scene dominated by quantitative approaches. People were just beginning to take seriously the subjective side of social life—how people view themselves and their world—and methods that are descriptive and holistic.

As we write this edition, we can say with conviction that qualitative research has come of age. New journals devoted to qualitative research appear regularly, book series have been developed, and handbooks and encyclopedias have been published. Courses in qualitative research are a regular part of social science and education curricula. Funders of research are looking for qualitative studies or at least research with a qualitative component.

It was not until the early 1970s that the phrase *qualitative research* came into wide use to refer to the research approaches discussed in this book. Prior to that, these methods were mainly lodged in the disciplines of anthropology and sociology and referred to by such terms as fieldwork, participant observation, ethnography, and the Chicago school approach. The phrase *qualitative research* both heralded the beginning of an interdisciplinary approach and served to forge it. During the late 1970s and most of the 1980s, qualitative research rose in popularity in other social science disciplines and became a strong influence in interdisciplinary and professional fields such as women's studies, disability studies, education, social work, information studies, management, nursing, and human services.

Toward the end of the 1980s and now into the 1990s, tensions have developed among those who identify with qualitative research. Many people who first embraced qualitative research in the 1980s had been trained in quantitative approaches. They saw the potential of qualitative research, but worried about its uncodified procedures, its lack of concern with reliability, and its imprecise modes of data analysis. They aimed to fix it. The servants to these interests were the development of software that could manage, sort, and count unwieldy mountains of descriptive data and codified procedures for collecting and analyzing the research materials.

During the early 1990s, qualitative research had another visitor: postmodernism. People who practice this brand of theory and method were critical of researchers who sought to produce factual accounts of culture and social life. Having been born in literary criticism, postmodernism dismissed inductive reasoning and careful collection of data in the empirical world and championed writing that was interpretive, political, and personal.

Thus we find ourselves in the midst of a period in which the qualitative research tradition is being pulled in at least two different directions. It is in this climate that we have revised this book. There is a temptation to drift from our original purpose and write more about the state of qualitative methods and inquiry and the debates. Although we cannot ignore the tenor of the times, and we comment on this when it is relevant, we have remained true to our original purpose: to provide those unfamiliar with qualitative research with an introduction to the range of different approaches and with guidance on how to actually conduct a qualitative study.

The book is based on our own research experience; our theoretical perspective, which informs how we think about interacting with people in our society; our cultural knowledge of how to act in everyday life; and our sense of ethics. We have drawn extensively on the firsthand accounts of other researchers and several of the recently published writings that challenge traditional conceptions of fieldwork. We also draw heavily on the specific qualitative research tradition we were taught in graduate school, an approach referred to as the Chicago school tradition. We are particularly grateful to the late Blanche Geer, who was an exemplary Chicago school sociologist and an outstanding mentor. We dedicate this third edition to her.

Steven J. Taylor
Robert Bogdan
Syracuse, New York
May 1997

Acknowledgments

M ANY PEOPLE HAVE contributed directly or indirectly to this book, and we want to take this opportunity to acknowledge their contributions.

We owe a special debt of gratitude to staff, students, and faculty colleagues who have worked with us on qualitative research projects at the Center on Human Policy. Some have called us their professors, but they have taught us much. In fear of leaving someone out, we will not try to list the names of all of those who helped us learn about both qualitative research and the nature of the social world. To all of those who have supported us and our work, thank you.

During the preparation of this third edition, we have enjoyed outstanding assistance from loyal and dedicated support staff. This edition of the book would have been much more difficult and stressful to write without the excellent support from Rachael Zubal (special thanks for helping us with style), Cyndy Colavita, and Debbie Simms. What would we have done without you?

Since the publication of the last edition of this book, the Center on Human Policy has benefited from significant funding from the National Institute on Disability and Rehabilitation Research (NIDRR), the U.S. Department of Education (Contract No. G0085C03503, Cooperative Agreement H133B00003-90, Cooperative Agreement H133B80048, Contract No. H133D50037, and Contract No. H133B30072). Projects funded by NIDRR have supported much of the research described in this book and reported in the chapters in Part 2. Of course, the opinions expressed in this book are solely our own, and no endorsement by NIDRR or the U.S. Department of Education should be inferred. We want to thank NIDRR Project Officers Roseann Rafferty, David Esquith, and Naomi Karp for supporting our work over the years.

We also want to express our sincere appreciation to Charlie Lakin of the University on Minnesota, with whom we have collaborated on projects funded by NIDRR. Rare is the expert "numbers cruncher" who genuinely values the qualitative approach to social life.

Like many others, we first learned qualitative methods through the oral tradition handed down by outstanding teachers and mentors. We stand in what has become a long line of researchers operating within the Chicago school tradition. Bob Bogdan was taught qualitative methods by Irwin Deutscher and Blanche Geer and, in turn, passed on this tradition to Steve Taylor. We acknowledge the contributions of all those who came before us and dedicate this edition of the book to the late Blanche Geer.

Thanks also to Jo Ann Miller, Executive Editor at John Wiley & Sons, Inc., who initiated the third edition of this book and has supported the project throughout.

Finally, no acknowledgement would be complete without some words of thanks, appreciation, and love to those with whom we share our lives. So, thanks and love to Betsy, Jeff, and Lea and to Janet, Yinka, Meg, Chet, and Jono. Loved ones sometimes make work easier and sometimes make it harder, but they always remind us that there are other things in life than writing books.

Introduction to Qualitative Research Methods

PART ONE

AMONG THE PEOPLE: HOW TO CONDUCT QUALITATIVE RESEARCH

CHAPTER 1

Introduction: Go to the People

THE TERM *methodology* refers to the way in which we approach problems and seek answers. In the social sciences, the term applies to how research is conducted. Our assumptions, interests, and purposes shape which methodology we choose. When stripped to their essentials, debates over methodology are debates over assumptions and purposes, over theory and perspective.

Two major theoretical perspectives have dominated the social science scene[1] (Bruyn 1966; Deutscher 1973). The first, *positivism*, traces its origins in the social sciences to the great theorists of the nineteenth and early twentieth centuries and especially to Auguste Comte (1896) and Emile Durkheim (1938, 1951). The positivist seeks the *facts* or *causes* of social phenomena apart from the subjective states of individuals. Durkheim (1938, 14) told the social scientist to consider social facts, or social phenomena, as "things" that exercise an external influence on people.

The second major theoretical perspective, which, following the lead of Deutscher (1973), we describe as phenomenological,[2] has a long history in philosophy and sociology (Berger and Luckmann 1967; Bruyn 1966; Husserl 1962; Psathas 1973; Schutz 1962, 1967). The phenomenologist, or interpretivist (Ferguson, Ferguson, and Taylor 1992), is committed to understanding social phenomena from the actor's own perspective and examining how the world is experienced. The important reality is what people perceive it to be. Jack Douglas (1970b, ix) writes, "The 'forces' that move human beings, as

3

human beings rather than simply as human bodies . . . are 'meaningful stuff.' They are internal ideas, feelings, and motives."

Since positivists and phenomenologists take on different kinds of problems and seek different kinds of answers, their research requires different methodologies. Adopting a natural science model of research, the positivist searches for causes through methods, such as questionnaires, inventories, and demography, that produce data amenable to statistical analysis. The phenomenologist seeks understanding through qualitative methods, such as participant observation, in-depth interviewing, and others, that yield descriptive data. In contrast to practitioners of a natural science approach, phenomenologists strive for what Max Weber (1968) called *verstehen*, understanding on a personal level the motives and beliefs behind people's actions.

This book is about qualitative methodology—how to collect descriptive data, people's own words, and people's behavior. It is also a book on how to study social life phenomenologically.

We are not saying that positivists cannot use qualitative methods to address their own research interests: Durkheim (1915) used rich descriptive data collected by anthropologists as the basis for his treatise *The Elementary Forms of Religious Life*. We are saying that the search for social causes is neither what this book is about nor where our own research interests lie.

We return to the phenomenological or interpretivist perspective later in this chapter, for it is at the heart of this work. It is the perspective that guides our research.

A NOTE ON THE HISTORY OF QUALITATIVE METHODS

Descriptive observation, interviewing, and other qualitative methods are as old as recorded history (Wax 1971). Wax points out that the origins of fieldwork can be traced to historians, travelers, and writers ranging from the Greek Herodotus to Marco Polo. It was not until the nineteenth and early twentieth centuries, however, that what we now call qualitative methods were consciously employed in social research.

Frederick LePlay's 1855 study of European families and communities stands as one of the first genuine pieces of participant observation research (Bruyn 1966). Robert Nisbet (1966) writes that LePlay's research represents the first scientific sociological research:

> But *The European Working Classes* is a work squarely in the field of sociology, the first genuinely scientific sociological work in the century. . . . Durkheim's *Suicide* is commonly regarded as the first "scientific" work in sociology, but it takes

nothing away from Durkheim's achievement to observe that it was in LePlay's studies of kinship and community types in Europe that a much earlier effort is to be found in European sociology to combine empirical observation with the drawing of crucial inference—and to do this acknowledgedly within the criteria of science.

In anthropology, field research came into its own around the turn of the century. Boas (1911) and Malinowski (1932) can be credited with establishing fieldwork as a legitimate anthropological endeavor. As Wax (1971, 35–36) notes, Malinowski was the first professional anthropologist to provide a description of his research approach and a picture of what fieldwork was like. Perhaps due to the influence of Boas and Malinowski, in academic circles field research or participant observation has continued to be associated with anthropology.

We can only speculate on the reasons why qualitative methods have been so readily accepted by anthropologists and so easily ignored by sociologists. Durkheim's *Suicide* (1951), which equated statistical analysis with scientific sociology, has been extremely influential and has provided a model of research for several generations of sociologists. It would be difficult for anthropologists to employ the research techniques, such as survey questionnaires and demographics, that Durkheim and his predecessors developed: We obviously cannot enter a preindustrial culture and ask to see the police blotter or administer a questionnaire. Further, whereas anthropologists are unfamiliar with and hence deeply concerned with everyday life in the cultures they study, sociologists probably take it for granted that they already know enough about the daily lives of people in their own societies to decide what to look at and which questions to ask.

Yet qualitative methods have a rich history in American sociology. The use of qualitative methods first became popular in the studies of the Chicago school in the period from approximately 1910 to 1940. During this period, researchers associated with the University of Chicago produced detailed participant observation studies of urban life (Anderson, *The Hobo*, 1923; Cressey, *The Taxi-Dance Hall*, 1932; Thrasher, *The Gang*, 1927; Wirth, *The Ghetto*, 1928; Zorbaugh, *The Gold Coast and the Slum*, 1929); rich life histories of juvenile delinquents and criminals (Shaw, *The Jack Roller*, 1966; Shaw, *The Natural History of a Delinquent Career*, 1931; Shaw, McKay, and McDonald, *Brothers in Crime*, 1938; Sutherland, *The Professional Thief*, 1937); and a classic study of the life of immigrants and their families in Poland and America based on personal documents (Thomas and Znaniecki, *The Polish Peasant in Europe and America*, 1927). Up until the 1940s, people who called themselves students of society were familiar with participant observation, in-depth interviewing, and personal documents.

As important as these early studies were, interest in qualitative methodology waned toward the end of the 1940s and beginning of the 1950s with the growth in prominence of *grand theories* (e.g., Parsons 1951) and quantitative methods. With the exception of Whyte's (1943, 1955, 1981, 1993) *Street Corner Society,* few qualitative studies were taught and read in social science departments during this era.

Since the 1960s there has been a reemergence in the use of qualitative methods. So many powerful, insightful, and influential studies have been published based on these methods (e.g., Anderson 1990; Becker 1963; Erikson 1976; Goffman 1961; Liebow 1967; Thorne 1983; West and Zimmerman 1987) that they have been impossible to discount. What was once an oral tradition of qualitative research has been recorded in monographs (Emerson, Fretz, and Shaw 1995; Lincoln and Guba 1985; Lofland 1971, 1976; Lofland and Lofland 1995; Schatzman and Strauss 1973; Spradley 1979, 1980; Van Maanen, Dabbs, and Faulker 1982; Whyte 1984) and edited volumes (Emerson 1983; Filstead 1970; Glazer 1972; McCall and Simmons 1969; Van Maanen 1995). There also have been books published that examine the philosophical underpinnings of qualitative research (Bruyn 1966; Denzin and Lincoln 1994), relate qualitative methods to theory development (Glaser and Strauss 1967; Prus 1996; Strauss and Corbin 1990), describe writing strategies for reporting qualitative research (Richardson 1990; Van Maanen 1988; Wolcott 1990b), and contain personal accounts of researchers' experiences in the field (Douglas 1976; Johnson 1975; Shaffir and Stebbins 1991; Shaffir, Stebbins, and Turowetz 1980; Wax 1971). In sociology alone, there are journals devoted to publishing qualitative studies (*Journal of Contemporary Ethnography, Qualitative Sociology*) and to qualitative inquiry generally (*Qualitative Inquiry*). Sage Publications continues to produce short monographs on different slices of qualitative research (edited by Van Maanen, Manning, and Miller), and by now the number surpasses 40.

Paralleling the growing interest in qualitative research in the social sciences has been an increased acceptance of these methods in applied fields. Qualitative methods are increasingly used for program evaluation and policy research (Bogdan and Taylor 1990; Guba and Lincoln 1989; Patton 1990; Rist 1994). Journals and texts on qualitative research can be found in such diverse applied areas of inquiry as health research (*Journal of Qualitative Health Research*), education (Bogdan and Biklen 1992; *International Journal of Qualitative Studies in Education*), disability studies (Ferguson, Ferguson, and Taylor 1992), social work (Sherman and Reid 1994), and special education (Stainback and Stainback 1988).

Just as significant as the increasing interest in qualitative research methods has been the proliferation of theoretical perspectives rooted in the phenomenological tradition underlying this form of inquiry. We consider the relationship between theory and methodology more fully later in this chapter.

QUALITATIVE METHODOLOGY

The phrase *qualitative methodology* refers in the broadest sense to research that produces descriptive data—people's own written or spoken words and observable behavior. As Ray Rist (1977) points out, qualitative methodology, like quantitative methodology, is more than a set of data-gathering techniques. It is a way of approaching the empirical world. In this section we present our notion of qualitative research.

1. *Qualitative researchers are concerned with the meanings people attach to things in their lives.* Central to the phenomenological perspective and hence qualitative research is understanding people from their own frames of reference and experiencing reality as they experience it. Qualitative researchers empathize and identify with the people they study in order to understand how those people see things. Herbert Blumer (1969) explains it this way:

> To try to catch the interpretative process by remaining aloof as a so-called "objective" observer and refusing to take the role of the acting unit is to risk the worst kind of subjectivism—the objective observer is likely to fill in the process of interpretation with his own [sic][3] surmises in place of catching the process as it occurs in the experience of the acting unit which uses it. (p. 86)

As suggested by Blumer's quote, qualitative researchers must attempt to suspend, or set aside, their own perspectives and taken-for-granted views of the world. Bruyn (1966) advises the qualitative researcher to view things as though they were happening for the first time. Nothing is taken for granted. Psathas (1973) writes:

> For the sociologist, a phenomenological approach to observing the social world requires that he break out of the natural attitude and examine the very assumptions that structure the experience of actors in the world of everyday life. A method that provides assistance in this is "bracketing" the assumptions of everyday life. This does not involve denying the existence of the world or even doubting it (it is not the same as Cartesian doubt). Bracketing changes my attitude toward the world, allowing me to see with clearer vision. I set aside preconceptions and presuppositions, what I already "know" about the social world, in order to discover it with clarity of vision. (pp. 14–15)

2. *Qualitative research is inductive.* Qualitative researchers develop concepts, insights, and understandings from patterns in the data rather than collecting data to assess preconceived models, hypotheses, or theories. Glaser and Strauss (1967) coined the phrase "grounded theory" to refer to the inductive theorizing process involved in qualitative research. A theory may be said to be grounded to the extent that it is derived from and based on the data

themselves. Lofland (1995) describes this type of theorizing as "emergent analysis" and points out that the process is creative and intuitive as opposed to mechanical.

In qualitative studies, researchers follow a flexible research design. We begin our studies with only vaguely formulated research questions. We do not know what to look for or what specific questions to ask until we have spent some time in a setting. As we learn about a setting and how participants view their experiences, we can make decisions regarding additional data to collect on the basis of what we have already learned.

Of course, qualitative researchers operate within theoretical frameworks. Pure induction is impossible. We can never escape all of our assumptions about the world. Even an interest in social meanings directs our attention to some aspects of how people think and act in a setting and not to others. Within a broad theoretical framework, the goal of qualitative research is to make sure the theory fits the data and not vice versa.

DeVault (1995) cautions against taking Glaser and Strauss's grounded theory approach too literally. As she points out, what is missing from the data may be just as important for theorizing as what is there. For the purposes of inductive reasoning, it is important to be sensitive to unstated assumptions and unarticulated meanings.

3. *In qualitative methodology the researcher looks at settings and people holistically; people, settings, or groups are not reduced to variables, but are viewed as a whole.* The qualitative researcher studies people in the context of their pasts and the situations in which they find themselves.

When we reduce people's words and acts to statistical equations, we can lose sight of the human side of social life. When we study people qualitatively, we get to know them personally and experience what they experience in their daily struggles in society. We learn about concepts such as beauty, pain, faith, suffering, frustration, and love, whose essence is lost through other research approaches. We learn about ". . . the inner life of the person, his moral struggles, his successes and failures in securing this destiny in a world too often at variance with his hopes and ideals" (Burgess, as quoted by Shaw [1966, 4]).

4. *Qualitative researchers are concerned with how people think and act in their everyday lives.* Qualitative research has been described as naturalistic (Lincoln and Guba 1985). This means that researchers adopt strategies that parallel how people act in the course of daily life, typically interacting with informants in a natural and unobtrusive manner. In participant observation, most researchers try to "blend into the woodwork," at least until they have grasped an understanding of a setting. In qualitative interviewing, researchers model their interviews after a normal conversation rather than a formal question-and-answer exchange. Although qualitative researchers cannot eliminate their effects on the people they study, they attempt to mini-

mize or control those effects or at least understand them when interpreting data (Emerson 1983).

5. *For the qualitative researcher, all perspectives are worthy of study.* The qualitative researcher rejects what Howard Becker (1966, 67) refers to as the "hierarchy of credibility"; namely, the assumption that the perspectives of powerful people are more valid than those of the powerless. The goal of qualitative research is to examine how things look from different vantage points. The student's perspective is just as important as the teacher's; the juvenile delinquent's as important as the judge's; the paranoid's as important as the psychiatrist's; the homemaker's as important as the breadwinner's; that of the African-American (Puerto Rican, Mexican, Vietnamese-American, Haudenosaunee, etc.) as important as that of the European-American (English, Swedish, Italian, Irish, Polish, etc.); that of the researched as important as the researcher's.

In qualitative studies, those whom society ignores—the poor and the deviant—often receive a forum for their views. Oscar Lewis (1965, xii), famous for his studies of the poor in Latin America, writes, "I have tried to give a voice to a people who are rarely heard."

6. *Qualitative researchers emphasize the meaningfulness of their research.* Qualitative methods allow us to stay close to the empirical world (Blumer 1969). They are designed to ensure a close fit between the data and what people actually say and do. By observing people in their everyday lives, listening to them talk about what is on their minds, and looking at the documents they produce, the qualitative researcher obtains firsthand knowledge of social life unfiltered through operational definitions or rating scales.

Whereas qualitative researchers emphasize the meaningfulness of their studies—or what some people term *validity* (Deutscher, Pestello, and Pestello 1993)—quantitative researchers emphasize reliability and replicability in research (Rist 1977). As Deutscher, Pestello, and Pestello (1993, 25) write, reliability has been overemphasized in social research: "We concentrate on whether we are consistently right or wrong. As a consequence we may have been learning a great deal about how to pursue an incorrect course with a maximum of precision."

This is not to say that qualitative researchers are unconcerned about the accuracy of their data. A qualitative study is not an impressionistic, off-the-cuff analysis based on a superficial look at a setting or people. It is a piece of systematic research conducted with demanding, though not necessarily standardized, procedures. In the chapters that follow, we discuss some of the checks researchers can place on their data recording and interpretations. However, it is not possible to achieve perfect reliability if we are to produce meaningful studies of the real world. LaPiere (quoted in Deutscher, Pestello, and Pestello 1993) writes:

The study of human behavior is time consuming, intellectually fatiguing, and depends for its success upon the ability of the investigator. . . . Quantitative measurements are quantitatively accurate; qualitative evaluations are always subject to the errors of human judgment. Yet it would seem far more worthwhile to make a shrewd guess regarding that which is essential than to accurately measure that which is likely to prove irrelevant. (p. 19)

7. *For the qualitative researcher, there is something to be learned in all settings and groups.* No aspect of social life is too mundane or trivial to be studied. All settings and people are at once similar and unique. They are similar in the sense that some general social processes may be found in any setting or among any group of people. They are unique in that some aspect of social life can best be studied in each setting or through each informant because there it is best illuminated (Hughes 1958, 49). Some social processes that appear in bold relief under some circumstances appear only faintly under others. Of course, the researcher's own purposes will determine which settings and groups will be the most interesting and yield the most insights.

8. *Qualitative research is a craft.* Qualitative methods have not been as refined and standardized as other research approaches. This is in part an historical artifact that is changing with the establishment of conventions for collecting and analyzing data and in part a reflection of the nature of the methods themselves. Qualitative researchers are flexible in how they go about conducting their studies. The researcher is a craftsperson. The qualitative social scientist is encouraged to be his or her own methodologist (Mills 1959). There are guidelines to be followed, but never rules. The methods serve the researcher; never is the researcher a slave to procedure and technique.

If a choice were possible, I would naturally prefer simple, rapid, and infallible methods. If I could find such methods, I would avoid the time-consuming, difficult and suspect variants of "participant observation" with which I have become associated. (Dalton 1964, 60)

THEORY AND METHODOLOGY

The phenomenological perspective is central to our conception of qualitative methodology. What qualitative methodologists study, how they study it, and how they interpret it all depend upon their theoretical perspective.

Phenomenological Perspectives

The phenomenologist views human behavior, what people say and do, as a product of how people define their world. The task of the phenomenologist, and of qualitative methodologists like us, is to capture how people construct their realities (Berger and Luckmann 1967). As we have emphasized, the phenomenologist attempts to see things from other people's points of view.

The phenomenological perspective is tied to a broad range of theoretical frameworks and schools of thought in the social sciences.[4]

We identify with a theoretical perspective known as symbolic interactionism, and we treat this perspective as a point of departure for the discussion of more recent frameworks.

Symbolic Interactionism

Symbolic interactionism stems from the works of Charles Horton Cooley (1902), John Dewey (1930), George Herbert Mead (1934, 1938), Robert Park (1915), W. I. Thomas (1931), and others. Mead's (1934) formulation in *Mind, Self, and Society* was the clearest and most influential presentation of this perspective. Mead's followers, including Howard Becker (Becker, Geer, and Hughes 1968; Becker et al. 1961), Herbert Blumer (1969), and Everett Hughes (1958), have applied his insightful analyses of the processes of interaction to everyday life.

The symbolic interactionist places primary importance on the *social meanings* people attach to the world around them. Blumer (1969) states that symbolic interactionism rests on three basic premises. The first is that people act toward things, including other people, on the basis of the meanings these things have for them. Thus people do not simply respond to stimuli or act out cultural scripts. It is the meaning that determines action.

Blumer's second premise is that meanings are not inherent in objects, but are social products that arise during interaction: "The meaning of a thing for a person grows out of the ways in which other persons act toward the person with regard to the thing" (Blumer 1969, 4). People learn how to see the world from other people. As social actors, we develop shared meanings of objects and people in our lives.

The third fundamental premise of symbolic interactionism, according to Blumer, is that social actors attach meanings to situations, others, things, and themselves through a process of interpretation. Blumer (1969) writes:

> This process has two distinct steps. First, the actor indicates to himself the things toward which he is acting; he has to point out to himself the things that have meaning. Second, by virtue of this process of communicating with himself, interpretation becomes a matter of handling meanings. The actor selects, checks, suspends, regroups, and transforms the meanings in the light of the situation in which he is placed and the direction of his action. (p. 5)

This process of interpretation acts as an intermediary between meanings or predispositions to act in a certain way and the action itself. People are constantly interpreting and defining things as they move through different situations.

We can see why different people say and do different things. One reason is that people have had different experiences and have learned different social meanings. For instance, people holding different positions within an organization have learned to see things in different ways. Take the example of a student who breaks a window in a school cafeteria. The principal might define the situation as a behavior control problem; the counselor, as a family problem; the janitor, as a clean-up problem; and the school nurse, as a potential health problem; the student who broke the window does not see it as a problem at all (unless and until he or she gets caught). Further, the race, gender, or class of any of the participants may influence how the participants view the situation and define each other.

A second reason why people act differently is that they find themselves in different situations. If we want to understand why some adolescents become delinquents and others do not, we cannot simply examine their demographic characteristics, but we must look at the situations they confront.

Finally, the process of interpretation is a dynamic process. How a person interprets something will depend on the meanings available and how he or she sizes up a situation. Something as seemingly unambiguous as the flick of an eyelid can be interpreted as a sexual advance, recognition of shared understanding, expression of superiority, or an involuntary tic.

From a symbolic interactionist perspective, all organizations, cultures, and groups consist of actors who are involved in a constant process of interpreting the world around them. Although people may act within the framework of an organization, culture, or group, it is their interpretations and definitions of the situation that determine action, not their norms, values, roles, or goals.

Many years after the articulation of symbolic interactionism by Blumer, this perspective and variants such as labeling theory (Becker 1963; Kitsuse 1962; Lemert 1951) and Goffman's (1959, 1961, 1963, 1967, 1971) dramaturgy ("all the world is a stage") remain influential among qualitative researchers. Symbolic interactionism is not alone, however.

Since the late 1960s, a large number of theoretical perspectives rooted in the phenomenological tradition have achieved visibility in the social sciences. Here we review some of the major perspectives—ethnomethodology, feminist research, and postmodernism.

Ethnomethodology

Ethnomethodology was developed by Harold Garfinkel and was first articulated in his widely read book *Studies in Ethnomethodology* (1967). Although interest in ethnomethodology peaked in the 1970s and early 1980s, this perspective remains influential in the social sciences today (Coulon 1995).

Ethnomethodology refers not to research methods but rather to the subject matter of study: how (the methodology by which) people maintain a sense of an external reality (Mehan and Wood 1975, 5). For the ethnomethodologists, the meanings of actions are always ambiguous and problematic. Their task is to examine the ways people apply abstract cultural rules and commonsense understandings in concrete situations to make actions appear routine, explicable, and unambiguous. Meanings, then, are practical accomplishments on the part of members of society.

A study by D. Lawrence Wieder (1974) illustrates the ethnomethodological perspective. Wieder explores how addicts in a halfway house use a "convict code" (axioms such as "do not snitch" and "help other residents") to explain, justify, and account for their behavior. He shows how residents "tell the code" (apply maxims to specific situations) when they are called upon to account for their actions:

> The code, then, is much more a method of moral persuasion and justification than it is a substantive account of an organized way of life. It is a way, or set of ways, of causing activities to be seen as morally, repetitively, and constrainedly organized (Wieder 1974, 158).

Consistent with the European phenomenology of Alfred Schutz (1962), the ethnomethodologists bracket or suspend their own belief in reality to study the reality of everyday life. Garfinkel (1967) has studied the commonsense or taken-for-granted rules of interaction in everyday life through a variety of mischievous experiments he calls "breaching procedures" (see Chapter 5). Through an examination of common sense, the ethnomethodologists seek to understand how people "go about the task of seeing, describing, and explaining order in the world in which they live" (Zimmerman and Wieder 1970, 289).

One of the most productive areas of study in ethnomethodology is conversational analysis (Coulon 1995). By closely observing and recording conversations, ethnomethodologists have examined how people negotiate and jointly construct meanings in conversation (Psathas 1995; Sacks 1992).

Ever since the publication of Garfinkel's influential book on ethnomethodology, social scientists have debated the place of ethnomethodology within social theory. For some, ethnomethodology falls squarely within the symbolic interactionist perspective (Denzin 1970). For others, it represents a radical departure from other sociological traditions (Coulon 1995; Zimmerman and Wieder 1970). Mehan and Wood (1975) characterize ethnomethodology as a separate enterprise from sociology. In any case, researchers writing from different theoretical perspectives, including symbolic interactionism, have incorporated concepts and insights developed by the ethnomethodologists into their studies.

Feminist Research

Perhaps the most significant development in qualitative research over the past decade has been the growing prominence of feminist research perspectives (DeVault 1990; Gilligan 1982; Reinharz 1992; Smith 1990a). As Olesen (1994) notes, feminist research is not a single activity; there are many feminisms and many varieties of feminist research.

One variant of feminist research builds on what is known as critical ethnography (Clifford 1988) and postmodernism. From this perspective, qualitative research must be conducted with an understanding of how the broader social order oppresses different categories of people by race, gender, or class. Dorothy Smith (1987), for example, applies phenomonological and Marxist theories to examine how male-dominated (patriarchal) structures and modes of conversation (discourses) shape women's experiences.

More generally, feminist research takes as subject matter for study issues of potential importance to women and uses women's standpoint as a point of departure for research. A legitimate criticism of many of the classic sociological and anthropological studies in the qualitative tradition is that women are missing from them. For example, Whyte's (1943, 1955, 1981, 1993) *Street Corner Society* and Liebow's (1967) *Tally's Corner* attempt to analyze the social organization of poor urban communities by a nearly exclusive focus on male members of street-corner groups. As Richardson (1992) notes, a look at urban life from the vantage point of women would yield a very different picture.

A solid contribution of feminist research in the 1990s has been the publication of studies rooted in the qualitative tradition but undertaken from a woman's standpoint. In her book *Feeding the Family*, DeVault (1991) examines the gendered nature of the invisible work that goes into the preparation of food. DeVault (1991) provides insights into not only women's household work but the construct of family itself:

> I have argued that the feeding work traditionally undertaken by women is both produced by and produces "family" as we have known it—the work itself "feeds" not only household members but also "the family," as ideological construct. Thus, taken-for-granted, largely unarticulated understandings of family stand in the way of equity. (p. 236)

Thorne's (1983) participant observation study *Gender Play* analyzes scenes that will seem familiar to practically any reader. Through interactions with "kids" (as Thorne notes, how children define themselves) and close observation of school playgrounds, Thorne explores the social construction of gender and how different contexts shape gender-related patterns in children's play. Building on the work of other feminist researchers, Traustadottir (1991a, b, 1995; see also Chapter 10 in this volume) studies the nature of caregiving among family members, friends, and human service workers of people with disabilities. She shows how the concept of caring obscures the difference between affective attachments ("caring about") and the day-to-day work involved in supporting people with disabilities ("caring for").

As demonstrated by feminist researchers, gender is not only a fruitful area for study, theorizing, and writing, but a factor that warrants methodological attention as well. Women may face special problems conducting research in male-dominated settings (Easterday et al. 1977; Warren and Rasmussen 1977). DeVault (1990) also points out that interviewing with women may require special attention to the nuances of language and experiences that are not easily captured by conventional linguistic forms (for example, the distinction reflected in the terminology of *work* and *leisure* may not adequately reflect many of women's activities).

Postmodernism

The postmodern perspective rejects the Enlightenment's faith in reason and rationality and the belief in progress (what Richardson [1990b] describes as the oxymoronic label "postmodernism" derives from it being "post" or after the philosophical era of modernism). It challenges the authority of science and examines the ideological underpinnings behind what we call scientific. Postmodernism comes from the field of literary criticism and streams within philosophy (for example, Foucault 1980). Within departments of English, literature, or "textual studies," debates rage over how the great works of Western literature should be read. Should they be read in terms of conventional qualities such as plot, drama, mode of exposition, and literary technique, or should they instead be interpreted in terms of the social position and subterranean ideology of the authors?

Interest in postmodernism and related schools of thought such as poststructuralism in qualitative research coincided with the emergence of critical ethnography (Denzin and Lincoln 1994; Thomas 1993). Attention has increasingly focused on how the researcher's race, class, gender, and social position structure the production of ethnographic accounts or "texts." Postmodernist scholars deconstruct social science writing and hence strip the social scientist, whether quantitative or qualitative, of any claims to authority as an all-knowing observer of the social scene. Thomas (1993) offers a useful description of the postmodernist's process of deconstruction by comparing it to taking a building apart and examining its underlying structure (in the case of social science writing, assumptions, ideologies, and literary devices).

Some postmodernists reject the distinction between fiction and nonfiction (Atkinson 1992; Denzin 1996). From this perspective, both fiction and nonfiction (ethnography, social science writing) are narratives and are based on literary devices such as metaphors and synedoches (Richardson 1990b). As Denzin (1996, 238) writes, "... the discourses of the postmodern world involve the constant commingling of literary, journalistic, fictional, factual, and ethnographic writing. No form is privileged over the other."

A series of exchanges between William F. Whyte and Norman Denzin in the *Journal of Contemporary Ethnography* (or *JCE;* 1992) and *Qualitative Inquiry* (1996) highlight the differences between traditional ethnography or qualitative research and the postmodern perspective.[5] An entire issue of *JCE* (1992) was devoted to a reconsideration of Whyte's (1943, 1955, 1981, 1993) *Street Corner Society*. Widely considered a sociological classic in participant observation, Whyte's study made important contributions to our understanding of the social organization of lower-class urban areas and the social structure of small groups. Many years later, Marianne Boelen visited Cornerville, the site of Whyte's study, over an extended period of time and subsequently published a devastating critique of Whyte's study in *JCE,* challenging his interpretations, conclusions, and ethics. Boelen's critique in *JCE* is followed by a rebuttal by Whyte, a strongly worded defense of Whyte by Angelo Ralph Orlandella, one of his original informants, and commentaries by sociologists Arthur Vidich, Laurel Richardson, and Norman Denzin.

The specifics of Boelen's charges against Whyte are less important than the issues raised in some of the commentaries in this exchange. As Richardson points out in her commentary, Boelen's critique consists of a long series of "ho-hum" indictments. If Boelen were not taking on a sociological icon such as Whyte, her article would never have seen the light of day. Richardson refers to Boelen's critique as the trashing of *Street Corner Society* and states that the purpose of publishing it seems to have been to teach a lesson about "the epistemological questions about how sociological knowledge is created" (Adler, Adler, and Johnson 1992, 6), or postmodernism, at Whyte's expense.

Denzin's commentary on the Whyte-Boelen exchange is most instructive for understanding the postmodern stance. For Denzin, Whyte and Boelen are engaged in a hopelessly naive and outdated debate about who got the facts about Cornerville straight. Denzin (1992) writes:

> It is the hegemonic version that must be challenged, and Whyte and Boelen refuse to take up the challenge. They still want a world out there that proves their theory right or wrong. But how do they find that world and bring it into existence? How do they record what it does when they push against it? Unfortunately, they never answer these questions. Hence the poverty of their respective statements, for social realism will not produce the kinds of definitive statements they seek, nor will social realism furnish the political foundations for the projects they pursue. (p. 126)

In concluding his commentary, Denzin (1992) equates ethnographic reporting with positivism and questions:

As the 20th century is now in its last decade, it is appropriate to ask if we any longer want this kind of social science. Do we want the kind of classic sociology that Whyte produced and Boelen, in her own negative way, endorses? (p. 131)

Whyte continues the discussion in the appendixes of the fourth edition of *Street Corner Society* (1993) and an article in *Qualitative Inquiry* (1996b) to which Richardson and Denzin respond. Whyte's 1996 article revisits the debate with Boelen and responds to the postmodern, or "postfoundational," critique of his research. According to Whyte, some social phenomena are real. Whyte believes that Denzin fails to recognize the difference between description of facts and interpretation. Conceding that interpretations can be wrong, Whyte maintains that social and physical facts exist.

In an extended response to Whyte, Denzin (1996) argues that not only postmodernists but non-postmodern social constructionists have rejected Whyte's assumptions about the objective reality of social facts.[6] Denzin proceeds to review the work of the "New Journalists," which challenges the traditional distinctions between fact and fiction. In a terse rebuttal, Whyte (1996b) dismisses Denzin's treatise:

If I were to undertake a serious study of the evolution of qualitative sociology in relation to journalism and deconstructionism, I would find the Denzin essay and footnotes an invaluable resource. Because I continue to believe that deconstructionism is a fad, which will pass as behavioral scientists come to recognize that it leads nowhere, I am not inclined to participate in that line of research. (p. 242)

Some well-known qualitative researchers express discomfort over what Van Maanen (1995) refers to as this "new ethnographic turn" in the direction of the postmodern stance (also see Lofland 1995). Some who defend postmodernism decry attempts to marginalize or politicize postmodern versions of qualitative research methods, yet call for a "colonization" of other versions of qualitative research:

The constructionists in the subfield believe that their methods will do the interpretation for them, yielding up empirical materials that will allow them to produce true and faithful accountings of this socially constructed world. . . . These are the tough-minded empiricists. They like closed and realist texts, certainly, foundational criteria, substantive theory, single-voiced texts, and good science canons. It is this version of QRM that we think should be colonized. (Denzin and Lincoln 1995, 353)

And some (Snow and Morrill 1993, 1995) seem to recognize the value of having multiple voices on qualitative methods and perspectives.

MAKING SENSE OF THEORETICAL DEBATES

Novices to qualitative research—and even some old-timers—can be confused by the array of theoretical perspectives available within the qualitative tradition. Just learning the language associated with certain perspectives can be a daunting task.[7] Even more intimidating are polarized debates that pop up from time to time, forcing practitioners to believe that they have to declare allegiance to one camp or another.

Although we identify with the traditions of the Chicago school and symbolic interactionism, we believe that much can be learned from other theoretical perspectives without sacrificing the core tenets of this perspective (Blumer's three premises). The experience of ethnomethodology is instructive in this regard. Soon after the development of this perspective by Harold Garfinkel (1967), proponents sought to establish ethnomethodology as distinctive from all hitherto established sociology; thus ethnomethodology was incompatible with symbolic interactionism. Yet, over 20 years later, we find ethnomethodological approaches and concepts appearing in studies rooted in other traditions. For example, West and Zimmerman's (1987) analysis of "doing gender" finds its way into works identified with feminist research and symbolic interactionism. The triumph of ethnomethodology was represented not by its domination but through its incorporation into other ways of theorizing about the world. So, too, we believe, will postmodern notions such as deconstruction and the questioning of voice and authority leave a mark on the qualitative research scene by bringing these questions to the forefront.

That said, there *are* differences among the various theoretical perspectives that exist today. An appreciation of the differences, and where these differences lead, can be realized by addressing three questions: What is the relationship between the observer and the observed? Whose side are we on? Who cares about the research?

What Is the Relationship between the Observer and the Observed?
Depending on their theoretical allegiances, qualitative researchers differ on the relationship between the observer (the subject or knowner) and the observed (the object or what is known). At one extreme are those qualitative researchers who share with the positivists a belief that reality exists and can be more or less objectively known by an unbiased observer. In the exchange between Whyte and Denzin discussed previously, for example, Whyte holds firm to the belief that social and physical facts can be objectively discovered and reported on by a conscientious researcher. At the other extreme are some postmodernists who believe that objective reality does not exist and that all knowledge is subjective and *only* subjective. Thus Denzin takes the position that there is no difference between fact and fiction. From this perspective, ethnographic reporting has no greater claim to truth than any other version of reality. Ethnography becomes autobiography.

The views of most qualitative researchers fall somewhere between these two positions. Within phenomenological, symbolic interactionist, and ethnomethodological perspectives, it is taken for granted that reality is socially constructed. Take the example of food and its preparation. Food seems, at first glance, to be a fairly objective thing. If you do not eat and meet certain of the body's nutritional requirements, you die, no matter what your definition of the situation. Subjectivity becomes, in this instance, a luxury of your bereaved. Yet food, food preparation, and mealtimes are social constructions and phenomena. Religious belief systems revolve around what food can be eaten and how it can be prepared. Cultural definitions of health and beauty influence what people eat and how they think about food. Social customs surround how food is eaten and the proper behavior at mealtimes. Gender relations structure roles and responsibilities for feeding others (DeVault 1991).

Now, everything we just said about the social construction of food and mealtimes is itself a social construction. It is one version of food told from one point of view and reflecting one set of interests. What we term *social constructions* might alternatively be viewed as conforming to God's will, good manners and proper etiquette, or the natural order of relations between women and men. Our definition of the situation is one out of many, but this does not mean that we cannot somewhat faithfully record and report on the cultural beliefs and practices surrounding food.

This is the phenomenological puzzle: As qualitative researchers, we develop social constructions of social constructions (and sometimes others come along and deconstruct our social constructions). The ethnomethodologists refer to this as *reflexivity*; the process is captured by Mehan and Wood (1975), who reprint Escher's famous *Drawing Hands* (in which two hands are shown, each drawing the other) in their ethnomethodology text.

Merging the postmodernists' skepticism of the authority of the researcher's version of reality with a progressive impulse, Richardson (1990b) provides a useful analysis of the nature of qualitative knowledge:

> Sociological discovery, generally, happens through finding out about people's lives from the people themselves—listening to how people experience their lives and frame their worlds, working inductively, rather than deductively. Qualitative researchers, generally, learn about other people through interaction in specified roles, such as participant observer/informant, interviewee/interviewer, and so on. As a result, their knowledge of people's lives is always historically and temporally grounded. Most ethnographers are keenly aware that knowledge of the world they enter is partial, situated, and subjective knowledge. (p. 28)

Whose Side Are We On?

Qualitative research methods are ideally suited to examining the world from different points of view. As we have noted, there is no inherent hierarchy of credibility in qualitative research. All perspectives are valuable in the sense that there is something to be learned from them. For this reason, qualitative research and ethnography have been accused of being apolitical and upholding the status quo (Thomas 1993).

Recent theoretical perspectives such as critical ethnography and feminist research highlight the importance of analyzing and presenting reality from the vantage point of powerless people in society. Feminist research develops theory, or tells the research story, from the historically neglected perspective of women. Critical ethnography and certain versions of postmodernism do not merely present the points of view of powerless people—the marginalized or oppressed—but challenge traditional authority structures.

Research can never be values-free (Gouldner 1970). Values determine what we study, how we understand our data, and how we present our findings. Although qualitative researchers must seek to understand all perspectives, they must eventually decide from whose vantage point to write their studies. To refuse to give greater weight to one vantage point over another is, in fact, to leave the prevailing point of view unchallenged. This is a values position and a political decision in itself.

Within the qualitative tradition, the idea that researchers should side with powerless members of society is not new. Becker's (1966–1967) essay, "Whose Side Are We On?," presented a compelling rationale for presenting the perspectives of certain groups of people. According to Becker, we must necessarily present reality from someone's point of view. Becker argues that since powerful people have many means at their disposal to present their versions of reality, we should side with society's underdogs, the powerless.

In a similar vein, C. Wright Mills (1959) admonished social scientists to accept their political responsibility to help people understand their "personal troubles," problems experienced as individual and ideosyncratic, as social issues confronting others. Mills (1959) writes:

> Whether or not they are aware of them, men in mass society are gripped by personal troubles which they are not able to turn into social issues. They do not understand the interplay of these personal troubles of their milieux with problems of social structure. . . .
>   It is the political task of the social scientist . . . continually to translate personal troubles into public issues, and public issues into the terms of their human meaning for a variety of individuals. (p. 187)

Who Cares about the Research?

The final question, "Who cares?" relates to the purpose of research and theorizing. As sociologists, we are interested in understanding social life and developing sociological concepts that illuminate aspects of society and culture. Yet much of our research has been conducted in the applied fields of education, human services, and disability studies. How can our theories and research improve the human condition, if only on a small scale? The most elegant and liberating theory does not interest us if it can only be understood by a small group of like-speaking people and cannot be translated into terms meaningful to people confronting problems in their everyday lives.

The divide between so-called basic and applied research is not insurmountable. Qualitative research sometimes finds its way to broader audiences. Richardson's (1985, 1990b) feminist research has been published not only in sociological journals, but in a trade book written for a popular audience. Even theories developed for a sociological audience can have a profound influence in applied fields and practice. In the field of disability studies generally and mental retardation specifically, for example, Becker's (1963) labeling theory of deviance and Goffman's (1961, 1963) analyses of total institutions and stigma not only have inspired research in these areas but have been extremely influential in the evolution of policy and practice. The trend of deinstitutionalization is due, in no small part, to an understanding of the social construction of disability, stereotyping and the stigma of the disability label, and the devastating effects on the self of confinement in total institutions. Conversely, research conducted for applied or evaluation purposes can sometimes yield sociological insights and understandings (Bogdan and Taylor 1990).

In this book we describe qualitative research methods from the vantage point of the tradition of this approach in sociology and related social science disciplines. We are also interested in how research and theories can be applied to issues and problems experienced by people outside of the social sciences.

In this chapter we have attempted to give a sense of some of the methodological and theoretical dimensions of qualitative research. The remainder of this book covers data collection, data analysis, and writing in qualitative research. Part 1 deals with how to conduct qualitative research. We discuss participant observation, in-depth interviewing, and a host of creative qualitative approaches. Our intent here is not to offer recipes for conducting qualitative research. Rather, our purpose is to present some conventions that qualitative researchers have developed and to discuss how some researchers have dealt with the issues and dilemmas that arise in qualitative research. In a sense, we present an ethnomethodology of qualitative research, a description of the methodology of some people who conduct qualitative research, based on certain traditions as well as our own experience and that of the students and others with whom we have worked.

In Part 2 we consider the presentation of findings in qualitative research and offer a series of articles based on qualitative data. After a concluding note in Chapter 13, we include samples of field notes in the appendix, as well as an extensive bibliography on qualitative research.

NOTES

1. It is probably an oversimplification to classify all theories in terms of either positivism or phenomenology. There are many variations. Other theoretical perspectives (ethnomethodology, postmodernism, poststructuralism, postpositivism) have attempted to push themselves onto the social science scene as equal in stature and significance to positivism and phenomenology. Yet none of these has withstood the test of time. For now, at least, the distinction we have made will suffice.

2. Like Deutscher (1973), we use the term *phenomenology* broadly to refer to a tradition within the social sciences concerned with understanding the social actor's frame of reference. Psathas (1973) and Bruyn (1966) provide a good overview of origins of this tradition. Some sociologists use the term more narrowly to refer to the European school of thought in philosophy represented by the writings of Alfred Schutz (1967). Heap and Roth (1973) argue that the original meaning of phenomenology has been lost.

3. *Sic! Sic!* Throughout this book we quote authors who, writing in a different era, used masculine pronouns and male-dominated language. We are confident, or at least hopeful, that these authors would use different language if writing today. So as not to disrupt the flow of the quote, we have decided not to use *sic* each time male-dominated language is quoted. Further, we have resisted the temptation to change male-dominated language in quotations, since this language serves as a reminder of who was doing the writing and their assumptions about the world.

4. Even a cursory review of the qualitative research literature over the past 25 years yields an incredible number of new theories and theoretical perspectives: a sociology of the absurd, reflexive sociology, poststructuralism, postfoundationalism, dramaturgy, labeling theory, critical ethnography, critical realism, emerging relational constructionism, analytic ethnography, interpretative biography, cultural theory, standpoint research, feminist empiricism, deconstructionism, ethnic modeling, critical hermeneutics, resistance postmodernism, and so on.

   A review of all of these perspectives is beyond our interests and the scope of this book. For our purposes, a discussion of symbolic interactionism, ethnomethodology, feminist research, and postmodernism captures the flavor of recent theorizing related to qualitative research.

5. Richardson is also a participant, albeit a somewhat reluctant one, in both of these discussions. In sympathetic commentaries on *Street Corner Society* and Whyte's reactions to criticisms, Richardson (1992,

1996a) questions Whyte's failure to engage in contemporary discussions of ethnographic authority, the invisibility of women in his account, and the ethical implications of his having caused potential harm or discomfort to some of his key informants. These seem to be legitimate points. Although Richardson critiques Whyte's work from a postfoundational stance, among others, she does not take a hammer to his head to try to teach him postmodernist thinking.

6. Denzin is correct on this point. Although a classic in participant observation, Whyte's *Street Corner Society* does not fall squarely in the phenomenological tradition. Most phenomenologists, interpretivists, ethnomethodologists, symbolic interactionists, or constructionists view the nature of reality as more complex than Whyte did. Yet this should not detract from the importance of Whyte's contributions.

   In a recent issue of the *American Journal of Sociology*, Denzin (1997) and Huber and Mirowsky (1997) debate the nature of sociological knowledge. Huber and Mirowsky take Denzin to task for his extreme relativism and for dismissing Whyte's attempt to get the facts straight. In this connection, it should be noted that most phenomenologists, symbolic interactionists, and the like, stop short of endorsing the position that there is no difference between sociological reporting and fiction.

7. The ethnomethodoligists used to be blamed for obscurantist language ("indexicality," reflexivity," etc.). Now it is the postmodernists who tend to use inaccessible language: "hegemony," "privileged discourse," and so on. Certainly, anyone identifying with the postmodernist stance must be embarrassed by Alan Sokal's spoof in the postmodernist journal *Social Text*. Sokal, a physicist, wrote a nonsensical article filled with meaningless jargon and submitted it to *Social Text* as a genuine work, and the journal published it (Begley and Rogers 1996). The danger here is that the obscurantist language will be used as grounds for dismissal of the whole phenomenological/interpretivist/feminist enterprise.

CHAPTER 2

Participant Observation: Pre-Fieldwork

IN THIS AND the following chapters we discuss participant observation, the mainstay of qualitative methodology. The phrase *participant observation* is used here to refer to research that involves social interaction between the researcher and informants in the milieu of the latter, during which data are systematically and unobtrusively collected. We begin discussion of participant observation with the pre-fieldwork stage of research: locating and getting into the setting one wishes to study. The next chapter deals with participant observation fieldwork.

RESEARCH DESIGN

In contrast to most methods in which researchers' hypotheses and procedures are determined a priori, the research design in participant observation remains flexible both before and throughout the actual research. Although participant observers have a methodology to follow and perhaps some general research interests, the specifics of their approach evolve as they proceed.

Until we enter the field, we do not know what questions to ask or how to ask them. In other words, the preconceived image we have of the settings and people we intend to study may be naive, misleading, or downright false. Most participant observers attempt to enter the field without specific hypotheses or preconceptions. As Melville Dalton (1964) writes:

> (1) I never feel sure what is relevant for hypothesizing until I have some intimacy with the situation—I think of a hypothesis as a well-founded conjecture; (2) once uttered, a hypothesis becomes obligatory to a degree; (3) there is a danger that the hypothesis will be esteemed for itself and work as an abused symbol of science.

One of the authors was involved with a large-scale structured interviewing project that highlights the dangers of beginning a study with a rigid research design. This study's research design revolved around the distinction between one- and two-parent families, a common distinction in social science research. Both the sampling and analytical procedures were designed around this distinction. When field researchers entered families' homes, however, they found that the differentiation between one- and two-parent families is a gross oversimplification of the living situation of families today. For example, in "two-parent" families the researchers found couples where one spouse accepted no responsibility for the child and where one spouse, while trying to fulfill the parental role, spent weeks at a time away from home. In "one-parent" families, researchers came across couples living together where the nonparent accepted equal responsibility for the child; divorced couples who had reunited, sometimes permanently and sometimes for only a night; couples living together where the nonparent ignored the child; and a host of other relationships. Further, the field researchers learned that living together, for married and unmarried couples alike, can be a fluid situation; living circumstances change regularly. Complicating the study even more, some families, especially those receiving public assistance, tried to conceal their living situation from the researchers. Despite these findings, the study was locked into the commonsense distinction between one- and two-parent families and proceeded according to the assumption that this corresponded to the actual nature of family relationships.

Most researchers do, of course, have some general questions in mind when they enter the field. These typically fall into one of two broad categories—substantive and formal (Glaser and Strauss 1967).

The first category includes questions related to specific issues in a particular type of setting. For instance, one might be interested in studying a mental hospital, school, bar, or juvenile gang. The second category is more closely

formal

tied to basic sociological issues such as socialization, deviance, and social control. For example, Goffman's stated purpose in studying a mental hospital was to develop a sociological version of the self by analyzing situations in which the self is assaulted.

These two categories are interrelated. A good qualitative study combines an in-depth understanding of the particular setting investigated with general theoretical insights that transcend that particular type of setting.

After entering the field, qualitative researchers often find that their areas of interest do not fit their settings. Their questions may not be relevant to the perspectives and behaviors of informants. In a study of institutional wards for the "severely and profoundly retarded," Taylor (1977, 1987a, b) began with the intention of studying residents' perspectives on the institution, only to find that many residents were nonverbal and others were reluctant to speak openly. Taylor then shifted his attention to staff perspectives, which proved to be a fruitful line of inquiry. The same occurred in a study of a "hard-core unemployed" job training program (Bogdan 1971). The researchers hoped to study "resocialization" in the program, but soon learned that other factors were far more important to understanding the experiences of the people involved.

Once you begin your study, do not be surprised if things are not what you thought them to be (Geer 1964). This is likely to be especially frustrating for researchers who enter their studies with well-formulated interests and ideas. For example, one of our students conducted a study of a teenager with learning disabilities. She was interested in how the teenager "coped" and managed her learning disability. To the researcher's dismay, the teenager's learning disability played an insignificant role in her life. Disappointed, the researcher wanted to give up the study and find a person who matched her preconceptions. Yet, if one wishes to understand people with learning disabilities, then one has to be open to the range of ways people in this category experience and view their lives. The experience of the person who is unaffected by the learning disability is just as fruitful for theorizing as that of the person who is consumed by it. Our advice is to not hold too tightly to any specific interest, but to explore phenomena as they emerge during your study. All people and settings are intrinsically interesting and raise important issues for understanding and theorizing.

Just as participant observers begin a study with general research questions and interests, they usually do not predefine the nature and number of cases—settings or informants to be studied. In traditional quantitative studies, researchers select cases on the basis of statistical probability. Random sampling, stratified sampling, and other probability techniques are designed to ensure that cases studied are representative of a larger population in which the researcher is interested.

Qualitative researchers typically define their samples on an ongoing basis as the study progresses. Glaser and Strauss (1967) use the phrase *theoretical*

theoretical sampling

sampling to refer to a procedure whereby researchers consciously select additional cases to be studied according to the potential for developing new insights or expanding and refining those already gained. Through this procedure, researchers examine whether and to what extent findings in one setting apply to others. According to Glaser and Strauss, the researcher should maximize variation in additional cases selected in order to broaden the applicability of theoretical insights.

In participant observation, the best advice is to "get your feet wet": enter the field, understand a single setting, and only then decide upon other settings to study. Any study suggests almost limitless additional lines of inquiry. Until you are actually engaged in the study, you do not know which of these lines will be most fruitful.

In the state institution study, Taylor spent the first year conducting participant observation on a single ward. By the end of that year, he had acquired an in-depth understanding of the perspectives and routines of the attendants on this ward. In the words of Glaser and Strauss (1967), he had reached the theoretical saturation point. Additional observations did not yield additional insights. Once deciding to continue his study, the researcher was faced with selecting other settings to observe. He could pursue either substantive (e.g., attendants on other wards or other institutions; other staff at institutions) or theoretical (lower-level staff at other types of organizations) interests. Since he had developed a specific interest in this type of institution, he continued his study by observing in institutions that varied according to different characteristics (size, age, locale).

SELECTING SETTINGS

The ideal research setting is one in which the observer obtains easy access, establishes immediate rapport with informants, and gathers data directly related to the research interests. Such settings seldom exist. Getting into a setting is often hard work. It may require diligence and patience. The researcher must negotiate access, gradually win trust, and slowly collect data that only sometimes fit his or her interests. It is not uncommon for researchers to "spin their wheels" for weeks, even months, trying to break into a setting.

You cannot always determine beforehand whether you will be able to get into a setting and pursue your interests. If you encounter difficulties, keep trying. There are no guidelines for determining when you should give up on a setting. However, if you cannot give your best effort to obtain access to a setting, it is unlikely that you will be able to deal effectively with the problems that inevitably arise in the course of fieldwork.

We usually recommend that people who are new to qualitative methods stay away from settings in which they have a direct personal or professional stake. There is a tendency for novice observers to want to study friends and familiar surroundings, places where they are accepted and feel at home. When one is directly involved in a setting, one is likely to see things from only one point of view. In everyday life, people take their ways of seeing things for granted. They equate their views with an objective reality. As a researcher, you must learn to see their version of reality as only one out of many possible ways of viewing the world. If you are an active participant in a setting, you also have a preexisting identity. People know you and see you in a certain way, and this may affect how they act and what they say around you.

Although we generally advise students and novices to steer clear of settings to which they are closely connected, this is a guideline and not a rule. There have been outstanding qualitative studies written by participants of the settings they observed (Riemer 1977). Becker's (1963) study of jazz musicians and Roth's (1963) study of a TB hospital are good examples. Some researchers have also used their personal experiences as a resource for understanding the perspectives and experiences of others (see Chapter 5). For example, Karp's (1996) insightful study of the social meaning of depression uses his long-term efforts to struggle with his own depression as a point of departure for his interviews with others.

Those who are steeped in professional disciplines in applied fields face special problems when they conduct qualitative studies in their professional domains. It is difficult for people trained in an area of professional expertise to hold their own perspectives and feelings in abeyance. They will tend to share commonsense assumptions with other professionals in a setting. For example, teachers, social workers, health care workers, and other professionals may bring perspectives to a study that prevent them from viewing the world qualitatively. As a result, they may impose preconceived frameworks on people's experiences, rather than examining how people construct their worlds. We know one observer of a behavior modification program who characterized clients' behavior as "appropriate" and "inappropriate" and was unable to understand how the clients viewed their situations. If one has already formulated all of the questions to ask in a setting, there are probably simpler and more efficient methods to use than participant observation and other forms of qualitative research.

Conventional wisdom among qualitative researchers traditionally advised against studying areas and issues in which the researchers had a political or ideological interest. Douglas (1976) has argued that researchers should stay away from areas in which they have deeply felt commitments. It is probably wise to stay away from issues in which one merely has an ax to grind. However, research is never "values-free" (Becker 1966–1967; Gouldner 1970; Mills 1959), and current thinking among qualitative researchers acknowledges that it is not only impossible but also sometimes undesirable to adopt a neutral stance in research (Richardson 1990b). What is more important than neutrality is awareness of one's own perspective and honesty about where one stands when research findings are reported.

ACCESS TO ORGANIZATIONS

Participant observers usually gain access to organizations by requesting permission from those in charge. These persons are usually referred to as *gatekeepers* (Becker 1970; Burgess 1991). Getting into a setting involves a process of managing your identity and projecting an image of yourself that will maximize your chances of gaining access (Kotarba 1980). You want to convince gatekeepers that you are a nonthreatening person who will not harm their organization in any way.

Students are likely to put gatekeepers at ease. Most people expect students to have class assignments or program requirements. The naive, eager student can often attract sympathy and help. Gatekeepers will probably assume that students want to learn concrete facts and tasks from "experts."

In many organizations a straightforward approach will work. People are usually surprised at how accessible many organizations are. Bogdan (1972) conducted a study of door-to-door salespersons in two companies. Although these companies trained prospective salespersons in the techniques of calculated misrepresentation, the heads of the branch offices opened their doors to the researcher within minutes of his request to observe. In fact, one of the branch heads gave permission over the phone after the researcher responded to a "come-on" in the newspaper to lure trainees into the program.

Not all organizations are studied so easily. The upper echelons of corporations (Dalton 1964), hospitals (Haas and Shaffir 1980), and large government agencies are notoriously difficult to infiltrate. Officials at organizations that have been subjected to public criticism or scrutiny, such as psychiatric hospitals and other total institutions, have become increasingly adept at imposing obstacles to being studied. The researcher can expect to "get the runaround" or to be turned down outright. Prior to his study of door-to-door salespersons, Bogdan tried first to observe a U.S. Air Force fire fighter training program. Officials at each of a number of levels wanted to interview the researcher personally. After each interview, they told him that they would have to get written permission from someone else before granting him access. By the time he finally received tentative permission to conduct the study, Bogdan had given up hope and turned to the study of salespersons.

When a straightforward approach does not work, you can use other tactics to gain access to a setting. Many researchers have gotten into organizations by having someone else vouch for them. As Hoffmann (1980) notes, most researchers have friends, relatives, and acquaintances who have contacts within organizations. These people can be enlisted to help win over reluctant gatekeepers. Similarly, a mentor or colleague can write a supportive letter on official letterhead to prospective gatekeepers (Gurney 1991; Johnson 1975).

If all else fails, you can try to get into an organization "through the back door." For example, we have observed institutions by tagging along with family members and staff from other agencies. In one instance, one of us obtained official permission to visit and then negotiated regular access with lower-level staff. Although being a volunteer at a setting can interfere with research, some observers have gained their initial entrées into a setting by assuming this role and proving themselves trustworthy.

One of the ironies of observing organizations is that once access has been obtained from gatekeepers, researchers often must disassociate from them (Van Maanen 1982). Many organizations are characterized by tension, if not conflict, between the upper and lower levels of the hierarchy. If researchers are interested in studying people at the lower levels, they must go out of their way to avoid the appearance of collaborating or siding with gatekeepers or officials. They must also be alert to the possibility that gatekeepers may request reports on what the researchers observe. When negotiating access, most observers are only prepared to provide gatekeepers with a very general report, a report so general that no one can be identified.

As should be apparent, there can be a significant lapse of time between the initial attempt to gain access and the beginning of observations. In some cases you will be unable to obtain access to an organization and will have to start all over again somewhere else. Keep this in mind when you design your study. It is not unusual for inexperienced researchers, especially students working on theses and dissertations, to leave insufficient time to gain an entrée and complete a study.

ACCESS TO PUBLIC AND QUASI-PUBLIC SETTINGS

Many studies are conducted in public (parks, government buildings, airports, train and bus stations, beaches, street corners, public restrooms, etc.) and semipublic (bars, restaurants, pool halls, theaters, stores, etc.) settings. In these settings, researchers do not ordinarily have to negotiate access with gatekeepers. Anyone can go to these places. Of course, in quasipublic settings—private establishments—the researcher may have to obtain permission from the owner to continue observations.

Although obtaining access to these settings does not present a problem, the participant observer, as a participant versus a passive observer, does have to develop strategies to learn about the setting and to interact with informants. One of the first orders of business is to figure out where to spend time in the setting. If you "hang out" long enough in the right position, sooner or later something will happen. Prus (1980) recommends that observers situate themselves in high-action spots in public places. In other words, go to where the people are and try to engage someone in casual conversation.

Liebow (1967) describes how he met Tally, the key informant in his study of black street-corner men, while discussing a puppy in the street in front of a carry-out restaurant. Liebow spent four hours with Tally that day, drinking coffee and lounging around in the carry-out. After he met Tally, Liebow's study blossomed. Before long, Tally was introducing him to others and vouching for him as a friend.

However, if you are going to stay in a single location for a long time, you had better find an acceptable role to play. Although it is acceptable for strangers to engage each other in casual conversation, people suspect the motivations of someone who acts too interested in others or asks too many questions. The participant observer is easily confused with the mugger, voyeur, flirt, or, in certain circles, undercover agent (Karp 1980). William Foote Whyte (1943, 1955, 1981, 1993) recounts his first efforts at locating an informant in his study of Cornerville. Acting on the advice of a colleague who suggested that he go to a bar, buy a woman a drink, and encourage her to tell him her life history, Whyte found himself in an awkward situation. Whyte (1955) writes:

> I looked around me again and now noticed a threesome: one man and two women. It occurred to me that here was a maldistribution of females which I might be able to rectify. I approached the group and opened with something like this: "Pardon me. Would you mind if I joined you?" There was a moment of silence while the man stared at me. He then offered to throw me down the stairs. I assured him that this would not be necessary and demonstrated as much by walking right out of there without any assistance. (p. 289)

Some researchers who have conducted successful studies of public and quasipublic settings have adopted an acceptable participant role. In a study of hustlers and criminals, Polsky spent hours playing pool. According to Polsky, if you want to study criminals, go to where they spend their leisure time and win the trust of a few of them. Laud Humphreys (1975), whose study generated criticism on ethical grounds, but who has demonstrated enormous sensitivity to the people he studied, played the role of "voyeur-lookout" and "waiter" in a study of impersonal sex in public restrooms.

Although it is not necessary for observers in these settings to introduce themselves as researchers and explain their purposes to people with whom they will have only fleeting contact, they should explain themselves to people with whom they will have a sustained relationship. Identify yourself before people begin to doubt your intentions, especially if they are involved in illegal or marginal activities. Thus Liebow explained his intentions to informants after his first or second contact with them, whereas Polsky advises researchers to identify themselves to criminals shortly after meeting them.

ACCESS TO PRIVATE SETTINGS

The task of the participant observer in gaining access to private settings (homes) and situations (some activities take place in a range of settings) is similar to the interviewer's in locating informants. Settings and individuals must be tracked down; consent for the study must be negotiated with each individual.

The basic approach in obtaining access to private settings is the "snowball" technique: start with one person or a small number of people, win their trust, and ask them to introduce you to others. Polsky (1969) writes:

> In my experience the most feasible technique for building one's sample is "snowballing"; get an introduction to one criminal who will vouch for you with others, who in turn will vouch for you with still others. (It is of course best to start at the top if possible, that is, with an introduction to the most prestigious person in the group you want to study.) (p. 124)

There are several places to start. First of all, check with friends, relatives, and personal contacts. People are usually surprised at the number of different persons their personal contacts know. In an experiment conducted with a class of students, Polsky reports that a third of the students found that friends and relatives could arrange a personal introduction to a career criminal.

Second, involve yourself with the community of people you wish to study. For his study of an inner-city ethnic neighborhood in Boston, Herbert Gans (1962) moved into the neighborhood and became a member of the community. He made friends with neighbors, used local stores and facilities, and attended public meetings. Through these activities, he eventually received invitations to homes, parties, and informal gatherings in the neighborhood.

Third, go to agencies and social organizations that serve the people in whom you are interested. For example, depending on your interests, you might go to local churches, neighborhood centers, self-help groups, day care centers, schools, or fraternal associations. Bercovici (1981) conducted a participant observation study of boarding homes and other settings for the mentally retarded by accompanying a team of occupational therapists who visited the facilities. Whyte's (1993) study got off the ground when he was introduced to Doc, who turned out to be his key informant and sponsor, by a social worker at a neighborhood settlement house. In contrast to the time when Whyte's study was begun—the late 1930s—researchers today can expect organizations to set up hurdles in their path in the form of confidentiality and privacy.

A final tactic researchers have used to locate private settings and informants is advertising (Karp 1996; Kotarba 1980). Researchers have placed ads in local papers, made appearances on local talk shows, and prepared handouts describing their studies for distribution among local groups. Internet newsgroups and listservs are another possible source of possible informants.

WHAT DO YOU TELL GATEKEEPERS AND INFORMANTS?

Explaining your research procedures and interests to gatekeepers and informants can be a difficult and sensitive task. Our own approach is to be truthful, but vague and imprecise. We take this position not only on ethical grounds, but pragmatic ones as well. If you deliberately misrepresent your intentions, you have to live with the fear and anxiety of getting caught. There is also the real possibility of having your cover blown and either being booted out of the setting or shattering your relationship with informants. Perhaps the greatest disadvantage of covert research is the limitations it places on the researcher. The overt researcher can transcend the narrow roles people in a setting play and engage in actual research activities. Further, many people will be more open and willing to share their perspectives with a researcher than with a coworker or fellow participant.

It is generally unwise to give details concerning your research and the precision with which notes will be taken. If they knew how closely they were going to be watched, most people would feel self-conscious in your presence. In the unlikely case that you are pressed on the matter, you can tell people that you jot down some notes afterward or keep a diary.

What exactly you say to people about your research interests should reflect your research design and purposes. One way we have explained our research interests is to let people know that we are not necessarily interested in that particular organization or the specific people there. In all studies, the researcher's interests are broader than a particular setting and concern the general type of organization. If you are seeking access to a school, for example, you should suggest that you are interested in understanding what *a school is like*, rather than in the nature of *that specific* school.

In some studies, however, it is useful to explain to people that you are interested in them because of their unique or special characteristics. Researchers in applied fields such as education, social work, and human services sometimes select settings for study because of their reputations. For example, many of our students in special education have been interested in understanding the process of integration or inclusion of students with disabilities and have sought out schools and teachers with reputations for successful efforts. Some of our own research (Taylor, Bogdan, and Racino 1991) has focused on community agencies that have developed creative ways of supporting people with disabilities in the community. If people take pride in their efforts or view themselves as unique or innovative, then it makes sense to tell them that you want to study them because they stand out from others. We have always been greeted with open arms by administrators and others in such situations (Bogdan and Taylor, 1994); some agencies have actually lobbied to have us study them.

It is a common experience among field researchers in large organizations for informants to assume that they are there to learn about people at another level. In Taylor's institutional study, attendants naturally assumed that the observer was there to observe the behavior patterns of the "severely and profoundly retarded" and to learn about the retarded from attendants. Whether or not researchers should cultivate false impressions, as Douglas (1976) suggests, there is no need to correct such misunderstandings.

Some gatekeepers will demand an elaborate explanation and defense of the research. Participant observers can get bogged down in extended discussions of research methodology trying to get into an organization. The standard objections to participant observation include: "We have to protect the privacy and confidentiality of our clients"; "We're too busy to answer a bunch of questions"; "You'll interfere with what we're trying to do"; "You won't find much interesting here anyway"; and "Your study doesn't sound scientific."

Anticipate the objections and have your responses ready. We are usually prepared to make certain guarantees to gatekeepers. This is sometimes called the *bargain*. Observers should emphasize the fact that their research will not disrupt the setting. Gatekeepers often assume that research involves questionnaires, structured interviews, clipboards, and other obtrusive methods. In contrast to these approaches, participant observation involves nondisruptive and unobtrusive activities. In fact, it is as important to most researchers to minimize disruption as it is to gatekeepers.

You should also guarantee the confidentiality and privacy of the people you study. We go out of our way to let informants know that any articles, books, or reports we write, or for that matter any notes we take, will not contain the names of or identifying information about individuals or the organization and that we are as bound to confidentiality as the people in the organization.

How you respond to questions about your research design should be based on how you size up the people in the organization or setting. Critical questions about the research design usually reflect concerns about the potential findings (Haas and Shaffir 1980). For instance, gatekeepers at institutions sometimes use client confidentiality and privacy to hide substandard conditions (Taylor and Bogdan 1980).

In the institutional study, Taylor spent hours defending the integrity of his research to officials at one institution who happened to be trained in psychology and wanted to know about the reliability of his research instruments. It was not until he stumbled upon the phrase *unobtrusive measures* that the officials finally granted him permission to observe. Johnson (1975) reports that his fumbling performance explaining his research to a group of social workers was a key factor in gaining access to a social service agency. The social workers concluded that they had nothing to fear from someone who had such difficulty explaining his aims.

Douglas (1976) advocates "playing the boob" or the "hare-brained academic ploy" when people seem afraid of the research. That is, the researcher tries to convince gatekeepers that the study is so academic and abstract that it could not possibly threaten anyone. Douglas (1976) gives an example:

> It is especially effective to tell them in some detail how, "We're doing a phenomenological-ethnomethodological reduction of your natural attitude in order to display and document the invariant interpretative procedures which are constitutive of the transcendental-ego and hence of intersubjective cognition." (p. 170)

Assuming this kind of ploy works, you will have to live for a while with this identity. We know one observer who identified himself to informants as an ethnographer. He later heard one person whisper to another, "Don't make any racial jokes in front of that guy. He's an ethnographer."

It is not uncommon today for gatekeepers at formal organizations to ask participant observers to prepare a written proposal or to submit their research design to a "protection of human subjects committee." The same general guidelines apply to written documents: be honest, but you do not have to volunteer specific details about your interests or theoretical perspective.

COLLECTING DATA

Detailed field notes should be kept during the process of identifying potential settings and gaining entry. As in later research, notes should be recorded after both face-to-face encounters and telephone conversations. The data collected during this time may prove extremely valuable at a later date. During the getting-in stage of the institutional study, Taylor spent time with the director of the facility. In addition to setting the ground rules, the director offered her perspective on the institution: "Nobody's perfect"; "We are overcrowded"; "We could use more money from the state." After concluding his study of attendants, Taylor analyzed the perspectives of officials. The statements by the director helped him understand how institutional officials try to project a favorable image of themselves to the outside world.

The process of gaining access to a setting also lends insight into how people relate to one another and how they process others. One good way to learn about the structure and hierarchy of an organization is to be handed around through it. Finally, the notes collected at this time will help the observer later understand how he or she is viewed by people in the organization.

COVERT RESEARCH

Throughout this chapter we have emphasized overt research, that is, studies in which researchers communicate their research interests to prospective gatekeepers and informants. Yet many successful and important participant observation studies have been conducted using a covert approach (Festinger, Riecken, and Schacter 1956; Humphreys 1975; Rosenhan 1973; Roy 1952a). Quite apart from pragmatic considerations, there are serious ethical issues raised by covert research.

Ethical decisions necessarily involve one's personal sense of what is right. One must choose among a number of moral alternatives and responsibilities. Social scientists such as Kai Erikson (1967, 254; 1995) take the position that undercover research and deception jeopardize the goodwill of potential research subjects and the general public on whom researchers depend: "It probably goes without saying that research of this sort is liable to damage the reputation of sociology in the larger society and close off promising areas of research for future investigators." In a similar vein, Warwick (1975) warns that a "public-be-damned" attitude among field workers has already created a societal backlash against social research.

Consistent with this position, the Code of Ethics of the American Sociological Association (1989, 3), which is currently under revision, reads, ". . . irresponsible actions by a single researcher or research team can eliminate or reduce future access to a category of respondents by the entire profession and its allied fields." The ASA's Code of Ethics also requires "informed consent" when "the risks of research are greater than the risks of everyday life" (1989, 3).

Some researchers have argued that the scientific knowledge gained through research justifies otherwise distasteful practices.[1] Glazer (1972, 133) reports that Arthur Vidich justified deceptive assurances about the protection of identities as the price inherent in contributing to knowledge. Denzin (1978) takes the position that each researcher should decide on what is ethical behavior. Denzin (1978, 331) argues for ". . . the absolute freedom to pursue one's activities as one sees fit." Jack Douglas (1976) characterizes society as a dog-eat-dog world. Since lies, evasions, and deceptions are part of everyday social life, according to Douglas, researchers must lie to, evade, and deceive their informants if they are to get the "truth."

Still other social scientists subscribe to situation ethics (Humphreys 1975). In other words, the practical social benefits of research may justify deceptive practices. For Rainwater and Pittman (1967), social science research enhances the accountability of public officials.

Finally, there are those who categorically condemn the deception of people and advocate a "right not to be researched" (Sagarin 1973). Thus some social scientists argue that researchers never have a right to harm people and that the only ones who can judge whether research might cause harm, even if that harm only takes the form of exposure of group secrets, are informants themselves (Spradley 1980).

In matters of ethics, then, researchers must counterbalance their multiple responsibilities to their profession, the pursuit of knowledge, the society, their informants, and, ultimately, themselves.

Our own view is that there are situations in which covert research is both necessary and ethically justified. It depends on what you are studying and what you intend to do with the results. Since powerful groups in our society are the least likely to grant access to researchers, social science research tends to concentrate on the powerless (Hertz and Imber 1993). We have far more studies of workers than corporate managers, poor people than politicians, and deviants than judges. Researchers expose the faults of the powerless while the powerful remain unscathed. To study powerful groups covertly, therefore, may well be warranted morally and ethically. However, we find it difficult to justify outright deception of anyone merely for the sake of completing degree requirements or adding a publication in an obscure journal to a vita.

It is also true, as Roth (1962) points out, that the distinction between overt and covert research is an oversimplification. That is, all research is to some extent secret in the sense that researchers never tell their informants everything (Punch 1986). What of researchers who observe in public places? Must they inform a crowd of people that they are being observed? Should researchers be compelled to give informants a blow-by-blow account of their emerging hypotheses and hunches?

There are no hard-and-fast rules in the realm of ethics. Research in the field must involve the researcher in a great deal of soul-searching. Whatever ethical decisions researchers make, they should not be cavalier or casual about deceiving people. Further, even if some measure of deception is justifiable, the researcher has a responsibility to take appropriate steps to minimize potential risks or harm to people under study (Goode 1996; Punch 1986).

NEGOTIATING WITH INSTITUTIONAL REVIEW BOARDS

Quite apart from the ethical issues raised by research, most American universities and organizations receiving public funds are required to maintain institutional review boards to review biomedical and behavioral research involving human subjects (Stanley, Sieber, and Melton, 1996). Federal requirements for procedures to protect human subjects grow out of public horror at the biomedical experiments conducted on inmates of Nazi concentration camps as well as exposés of ethically problematic research in the United States (National Commission for the Protection of Human Subjects of Biomedical and Behavioral Research 1978). For example, in the 1940s, the Tuskegee syphilis study followed the untreated course of this disease without informing poor, rural African-American men that they were infected. From the late 1950s to the early 1970s, award-winning medical research directed by Dr. Saul Krugman sought a vaccine for hepatitis B at the infamous Willowbrook State School by infecting children with mental retardation there with a live virus (Rothman and Rothman 1984).

In accord with federal regulations, institutional review boards require researchers to conduct an assessment of risks and benefits of research and to ensure that subjects grant informed consent to participate in the research. Special protections must be employed for potentially vulnerable populations, including children, prisoners, and persons with cognitive impairments.

As part of the institutional review board process, researchers must submit written protocols describing the purposes of the research; the methods to be used; procedures used to select subjects; assessments of risks and benefits; mechanisms to minimize risks; and procedures to obtain written or oral informed consent from either subjects or, in some cases, parents or guardians. A committee of researchers and community members must review and approve research protocols, although in certain cases the committee chairperson can grant expedited approval.

Although no one can reasonably dispute the need for safeguards and protections for subjects of biomedical and intrusive psychological research, most forms of qualitative research do not seem to fit the institutional review board process (Klockars 1977; Wax 1983). Informants or participants in qualitative research are not, strictly speaking, human subjects[2]; no invasive procedures or interventions are conducted on them. Seemingly innocuous safeguards such as informed consent can wreck havoc for the qualitative researcher. Take, for example, the researcher studying teacher routines and classroom management strategies or interaction patterns between students with and without disabilities in school settings. Must a researcher in these instances obtain written informed consent from the parents of each child who might appear in field notes? If an individual parent fails to provide consent, does that mean that the research must be halted or that the researcher cannot record observations of that parent's child?

Despite all this, in our experience most universities and funders do not exempt qualitative researchers from institutional review board requirements.

Even students completing field research requirements for qualitative methods courses may be expected to undergo formal review. Complicating the matter for qualitative researchers is that institutional review committee members may be trained in medical or experimental design research and may not have the faintest understanding about the nature of qualitative methods. As a result, they may try to impose procedures that are foreign to qualitative research. For instance, some review boards want to see all of the questions that might be asked during the course of the research.

So, how should a qualitative researcher approach the institutional review board? First of all, do not assume that board members have any knowledge or understanding of qualitative research methods. In describing your methods, emphasize that qualitative methods such as participant observation and in-depth interviewing have long histories in the social sciences and cite references to support this position. Demonstrate that you are not "winging it," but following an established tradition of research. Refer to the qualitative tradition in your description of your research methods, sample selection, and other matters.

Second, you should expect to be required to obtain informed consent from subjects. For most adults, oral consent will probably be sufficient (although institutional review boards usually want to see a written copy of what you will say). For children and certain vulnerable populations, you will be required to obtain formal written consent, often from parents or guardians.

Although we believe in the general principle that people should have the right to decide whether or not to be involved in any form of research, formal informed consent procedures can create the wrong impression among people and can make qualitative research projects appear much more structured and obtrusive than they actually are. Most people associate research with formal instruments and experimental procedures. When obtaining consent for research, we like to use everyday, straightforward language ("we will be observing unobtrusively and talking informally with people").

You will need to decide from whom you will request consent. As we have noted, it is simply not practical to obtain consent from any or all persons who might be observed or who might appear in data. You should be prepared to obtain consent from any person who will be the focus of your research. If you are observing a classroom on a regular basis, for example, you should obtain consent from the teacher. But how about all of the students? We do not think that it is ethically required or consistent with the spirit of informed consent to obtain permission from the parents of each and every student who may appear in field notes or with whom you may have casual conversations. If, however, you plan to conduct formal interviews with the students or to concentrate on selected students (for example, to follow individual students around to different classrooms or activities), then you should be prepared to observe formal consent procedures. Your chances of obtaining institutional review board approval for your research will be strengthened if you submit a letter of cooperation from a gatekeeper or key informant along with your application; some boards may require this.

Third, as part of the review process, you will be expected to describe the risks to subjects and the steps to be taken to minimize or eliminate these risks. Never claim that there are no risks to subjects; institutional review boards will not accept this and may interpret it as an indication that you are insensitive to the protection of human subjects. Be explicit about the potential risks and how you will minimize them: participant observation may interfere with people's usual activities and routines, so you will conduct yourself in an unobtrusive manner and inform people that you do not want to interfere with their everyday activities; qualitative research may threaten people's privacy and confidentiality, so you will take all steps necessary to eliminate this risk by using pseudonyms and omitting identifying information in your data and written products, maintaining all data in a secure location, and destroying video or audio recordings after they are transcribed and analyzed.

Finally, if the institutional review board wants to know exactly what questions you will ask or what you will look for during your observations, you can prepare an interview or observation guide that will be used in your research. You will need to explain, however, that in qualitative research the researcher him- or herself is the research instrument, and that an interview or observation guide should be regarded as flexible and open to change as the research proceeds.

It is easy to be cynical about institutional review boards. Procedures for the protection of human subjects are required by the federal government in the United States and have the potential to be a bureaucratic impediment to free inquiry. However, the institutional review board has become a fact of life confronting researchers today. Our approach is to try to relate to these boards openly and honestly and, if necessary, to meet with them personally to explain the nature and purposes of our research. The majority of the members of these boards are themselves academics and researchers, and, although they may not understand qualitative research, they are generally sympathetic with the goals of research. If you treat board members as though they are the enemy, they just might act that way.

Of course, you can always take the position that your research does not fall under the purview of institutional review boards and ignore this process, but you do so at your own risk. No one wants to be accused of unethical conduct or violating clearly established procedures for protecting the subjects of research. Further, many universities expect students to submit evidence of review board approval in completing dissertations and program requirements, and some professional journals require all published articles to have formal institutional review board approval.

WRITING PROPOSALS

Students working on theses or dissertations or researchers seeking external funding usually have to prepare formal written proposals reviewing relevant literature, specifying research questions, and describing the research design in detail. This can seem foreign to the nature of qualitative research. Qualitative researchers do not know exactly what questions to ask or how to ask them until they actually enter the field; the literature that will be relevant to any particular study will not be clear until at least some research has been conducted. Yet no one ever had a dissertation proposal approved or a research project funded by simply asserting: "I'm a qualitative researcher and will follow a flexible research design; trust me."

Our best advice for people working on theses or dissertations or seeking grants is to conduct some initial research *prior to* submitting formal proposals. Once you have collected and analyzed some data, you will be in a much better position to specify research questions, identify relevant literature, and present an initial research design. When you prepare your proposal, you can state that you have based your proposal on a pilot study; this might even enhance the credibility of your proposed research.

What exactly you put in a proposal will depend on the standards and conventions associated with your academic program, if you are a student, or your funder, if you are a researcher seeking funds. If you are writing a thesis or dissertation proposal, you should be able to find examples of accepted proposals written by other students in your program. Funders usually specify review criteria for grant proposals and assign points for different criteria (for example, the importance of the research question, the quality of research design, the qualifications of the researcher, and the adequacy of resources); be sure you address each of these.

Whether written to satisfy academic requirements or to obtain funding, proposals usually need to address the following issues.

REVIEW OF LITERATURE

In a qualitative study, you cannot be sure what literature might be relevant to your study until you have completed your research. In our research at institutions for people labeled mentally retarded, for example, the most useful literature came from research on other types of organizations, including prisons and factories. If you have already conducted some preliminary research, you should be in a better position to identify potentially useful sources of literature.

Students pursuing degrees in professional fields (education, social work, and so on) or researchers applying for funding from specific federal agencies (e.g., the U.S. Department of Education) should be prepared to review literature relevant to these fields or agencies. You should review the conclusions obtained in previous studies, but show the gaps that exist in current knowledge in the field. For instance, in our recent funded research we examined the experiences of people with mental retardation living in the community. In reviewing the literature for grant proposals, we showed how prior research had documented the exclusion and rejection of people with disabilities in society but had not devoted sufficient attention to processes that might lead to accommodations and acceptance. Thus we used the literature review to demonstrate the need for qualitative studies of examples of community acceptance.

STATEMENT OF RESEARCH QUESTIONS

As suggested above, your research questions should flow from your literature review, and, specifically, from questions that have not been satisfactorily answered in previous studies. Be sure to frame your research questions in ways that can be answered through qualitative methods. Qualitative methods are poorly suited for answering questions about the causes of social behavior. Frame your research questions in terms of social processes and understanding the meanings underlying what people say and do.

THEORY AND METHODOLOGY

Depending on who will review and approve your proposal, you will need to say more or less about your theoretical perspective and qualitative methodology in general. If, for example, you are preparing a proposal for a dissertation committee composed of faculty knowledgeable about the qualitative tradition, you will not have to explain the assumptions underlying qualitative research. For readers relatively unsophisticated about qualitative research, you should provide a definition of qualitative methods and their characteristics and explain the theoretical perspective (e.g., symbolic interactionism) that will underlie your research.

RESEARCH DESIGN

The first thing you need to explain is that qualitative researchers follow a flexible research design; the design of the research is based on the ongoing data collection and analysis. However, it is useful to provide a general road map of how you will conduct your study. Here are some specifics to address.

1.   The techniques you will use: for example, participant observation or open-ended interviewing. Explain what you mean by these methods.

2. Strategies for identifying and obtaining access to settings or informants.
3. The approximate number of settings or people you will study. Although this is difficult to specify in advance of a study, reviewers generally want to know the nature and size of your sample.
4. Data collection and recording procedures. Describe the nature of the data you will collect and your recording methods. Participant observers generally record their data as field notes; interviewers prepare transcripts based on either tape recording or notes taken during the interviews.
5. Data analysis procedures. Specify your analytical procedures (e.g., grounded theory or analytical induction; see Chapter 6) and how you will code and organize your data.
6. Timelines for the completion of the research, including identification of settings or people, data collection, data analysis, and the final writing of the study.

If you are successful in getting your proposal approved, then you can look forward to the hard work of actually conducting a qualitative study.

This chapter has dealt with the pre-fieldwork stage of participant observation research. More specifically, we have focused on matters related to the decisions observers must make before they enter the field and the initial contacts they must make to conduct their research. The following chapter shifts to the issues and dilemmas the observer faces in the field: "Now that you're in, where do you go from here?"

NOTES

1. Apparently, few social scientists would carry this belief to its logical extension. Lofland (1971, 301), who justifies his own covert research among Alcoholics Anonymous groups, writes, "The 'research' activities of Nazi Germany taught us (or should have) very well that there are definite moral limits on what can be done in the name of science." See also Lofland 1961.
2. Klockars (1977, 217) quotes a marvelous statement from Margaret Mead made in reference to federal research guidelines: "Anthropological research does not have subjects. We work with informants in an atmosphere of mutual trust and respect."

CHAPTER 3

Participant Observation: In the Field

IN THIS CHAPTER we consider the fieldwork phase of participant observation. Fieldwork involves three major activities. The first relates to inoffensive social interaction—putting informants at ease and gaining their acceptance. The second deals with ways to elicit data—field strategies and tactics. The final aspect involves recording data in the form of written field notes. We discuss these and other issues that arise in the field in this chapter.

ENTERING THE FIELD

Participant observers enter the field with the hope of establishing open relationships with informants. They conduct themselves in such a way that they become an unobtrusive part of the scene, people the participants take for granted. Ideally, informants forget that the observer is there to do research. Many of the techniques used in participant observation correspond to everyday rules about inoffensive social interaction; the researcher's personal attributes are critical in determining whether or not people cooperate with the research (Shaffir 1991).

Observers remain relatively passive throughout the course of the fieldwork, but especially during the first days in the field[1] (Geer 1964). Participant observers "feel out the situation," "come on slow," "play it by ear" (Johnson 1975), and "learn the ropes" (Geer 1964; Shaffir and Stebbins 1991). The first days in the field are a period in which observers try to put people at ease, dispelling notions of obtrusive research approaches; establish their identities as "OK" persons; and learn how to act appropriately in the setting. What clothes should I wear? Who looks too busy to talk to me? Where can I sit without being in the way? Can I walk around? What can I do to avoid sticking out like a sore thumb? Can I talk to the clients? Who looks approachable?

During the initial period, collecting data is secondary to getting to know the setting and people. Questions are designed to help break the ice. Since some people may ask you what you want to know, it is a good idea to jot down some general questions before you enter the field. Questions such as "Could you give me an overview of this place?" and "How did you come to work here?" are usually good openers.

Different people will probably exhibit different degrees of receptivity to you. Although the gatekeeper may have consented to your study, others may resent your presence (Burgess 1991). Sue Smith-Cunnien, on the first day of a participant observation study, overheard one person ask another: "What's she going to do—stand around and watch us all the time?" As Johnson (1975) notes, it is not uncommon for observers to find themselves in the middle of a power struggle over their presence. It is important to explain who you are to all people in the setting. In a study of teachers' use of the media, for example, Bogdan and colleagues (1975) interviewed each teacher individually to explain the study and obtain permission to observe in each classroom, even though this had been granted by administrators.

You should also try to let people know in subtle ways that what they say to you will not be reported to others. (Of course, you do not introduce yourself by saying that you are a researcher and ethically bound not to violate their confidentiality.) On the second observation in Taylor's institutional study, one of the attendants asked the researcher, "Did you tell (the director) about the boys here on this ward?" The researcher responded with something like: "No, I didn't even tell him where I was. I don't tell people outside of here about the institution, so why should I tell him about all of you?" In Smith-Cunnien's study, she seized on the opportunity to explain the confidentiality of her research during the following exchange:

Observer: Would you want to be editor-in-chief next year?
Informant: Who are you going to tell all of this to anyway?
Observer: I'm sorry, I should have told you from the start that everything you tell me is confidential. I won't be repeating any of this around here.

During the first days in the field, researchers usually feel uncomfortable. Many of us shun unnecessary interaction with strangers. It is natural to feel awkward in a new setting with no definable role to play.

All observers are faced with embarrassing situations in the field. Although it is true, as Shaffir, Stebbins, and Turowetz (1980) write, that fieldwork is characterized by feelings of self-doubt, uncertainty, and frustration, take comfort in the fact that you will feel more comfortable in the setting as the study progresses.

When first entering the field, observers are often overwhelmed by the amount of information they receive. For this reason, we generally advise people to try to limit the amount of time spent in the setting during each observation. An hour is usually enough time. As you become more familiar with a setting and adept at observation skills, you can increase the length of time in the setting.

Field research can be especially exciting early in a study. Some observers are inclined to stay in a setting so long that they leave the field drained and filled with so much information that they never record it. Observations are useful only to the extent that they can be remembered and recorded. Do not stay in the field if you will forget much of the data or if you will not have the time to write your field notes.

NEGOTIATING YOUR ROLE

The conditions of field research—what, when, and whom you observe— must be negotiated continually (Gubrium 1991). You must strike a balance between conducting your research as you see fit and going along with informants for the sake of rapport.

The first problem you are likely to face is being forced into a role incompatible with conducting research. People often do not understand participant observation, even when it has been explained to them. In many settings, gatekeepers and informants will place observers into roles commonly performed by outsiders. The personnel in schools, mental hospitals, and other institutions often try to force observers into a volunteer role, especially in the case of women and students. Observers may be expected to sign the volunteer book, work with certain clients, and report to the volunteer supervisor. We know one observer who was pushed into a tutoring relationship with a boy in a detention home, despite the fact that he had explained his interests to the institution's director. Similarly, Easterday et al. (1977) report that female researchers in male-dominated settings often get put in the role of "gofer," among others.

There are sometimes advantages to being placed in a familiar role in a setting. Access is more easily obtained; the observer has something to do; people are not as self-conscious in the researcher's presence; and some data are more accessible—we are familiar with one observer who, in a study of a charitable organization, was given a volunteer assignment to record information on donors. As a study progresses, however, the researcher may lose control of the study and have limitations imposed on collecting data if he or she is confined to a narrow organizational role.

A second problem encountered by field researchers is being told what and when to observe. All people attempt to present themselves in the best possible light to outsiders (Goffman 1959). Informants will share those aspects of their lives and work in which they are seen in a favorable light and hide, or at least downplay, those in which they are not. Many organizations appoint tour guides to give tours to outsiders. Although these tours are valuable in certain respects, they tend to give a selective view of the setting. At total institutions, for example, tour guides will often show visitors the best living units and model programs and discourage visitors from seeing other parts of the institution (Goffman 1961; Taylor and Bogdan 1980).

In many organizations, people also try to structure the times at which observers can visit. Total institutions are notorious for denying visits on weekends, since this is when the least programming occurs and most staff members have days off. Typically, organizational officials and staff will try to limit observers to special events, such as a holiday party or open house.

Women sometimes face special problems in having informants limit their research (Easterday et al. 1977; Warren and Rasmussen 1977). For example, Easterday et al. note that older males often act paternalistically with younger women; in a study of a morgue, a medical examiner attempted to "protect" a young woman researcher from seeing the "bad cases."

You should try to resist attempts of informants to control your research. Ideally, researchers should select their own places and times to observe. As observers establish some level of rapport, they usually find they can gain access to more places and people.

ESTABLISHING RAPPORT

Establishing rapport with informants is the goal of every field researcher. It is an exciting and fulfilling feeling when you begin to establish rapport with those you are studying. *Rapport* is not an easily defined concept. It means many things:

- Communicating a feeling of empathy for informants and having them accept it as sincere
- Penetrating people's "defenses against the outsider" (Argyris 1952)
- Having people "open up" about their feelings about the setting and others
- Being seen as an "okay" person
- Breaking through the "fronts" (Goffman 1959) people impose in everyday life
- Sharing in informants' symbolic world, their language, and their perspectives (Denzin 1978)

Rapport comes slowly in most field research. Even then, it may be tentative and fragile. It is doubtful whether anyone completely trusts anyone else at all times and under all circumstances. As John Johnson (1975) tells us, rapport and trust may wax and wane in the course of fieldwork. With some informants, the researcher may never develop true rapport. Johnson (1975) writes:

> Near the end of the welfare investigations I finally concluded that it is not a realistic possibility to develop relations of trust as such. This was especially true in a setting that included a radical leftist, a militant women's liberationist, older people, younger people, mods and squares, Republicans, Democrats, third-party members, Navy chiefs and commanders, Reserve Army majors, pacifists, conscientious objectors, and so on. . . . During the final months of the field research I gradually developed a notion of "sufficient trust" to replace the earlier presuppositions gained from a reading of the traditional literature. Sufficient trust involves a personal, common-sense judgment about what is accomplishable with a given person. (pp. 141–142)

Although there are no hard-and-fast rules for establishing rapport with informants, a number of general guidelines can be offered.

PAYING HOMAGE TO THEIR ROUTINES

Observers can only establish rapport with informants if they accommodate themselves to informants' routines and ways of doing things. All people like to do things in certain ways and at certain times. Observers must "stay out of their hair." Polsky (1969, 129) offers advice on how to observe criminals that applies to observing anyone: "If he wants to sit in front of his TV set and drink beer and watch a ball game for a couple of hours, so do you; if he wants to walk the streets or go barhopping, so do you; if he wants to go to the race-track, so do you; if he indicates (for whatever reason) that it's time for you to get lost, you get lost." We know one observer who, in a study of a hospital, came late to two staff meetings and then asked the physicians, who felt pressed for time themselves, to reschedule the meetings to suit his schedule. These kinds of people turn out to be poor researchers.

Establishing What You Have in Common with People

Probably the easiest way to build relationships with people is to establish what you have in common with them. The casual exchange of information is often the vehicle through which observers can break the ice. In Bogdan's study of the unemployed training program, he got to know many of his informants through conversations about fishing, children, sickness, past jobs, and food. It is natural for people to want to know about the observer's interests and pastimes.

In Taylor's study of the Duke family, it seemed important for Winnie and Bill, the parents, to establish common interests with the researcher; commonality of interests helped bridge the gap in social status separating Taylor, as a university professor, and the Dukes, a family receiving public assistance and labeled as disabled. Bill tutored Taylor on car mechanics and educated him on the personalities in professional wrestling. Winnie acted toward him as an experienced parent and lectured him on child development and child rearing regarding his youngsters. Taylor eagerly accepted Bill's and Winnie's tutorials and advice.

Helping People Out

One of the best ways to begin to gain people's trust is to do favors for them. Johnson (1975) reports that during his fieldwork he served as a driver, reader, luggage porter, baby-sitter, moneylender, ticket-taker at a local conference, note taker, phone receptionist when business was heavy, book reader, book lender, adviser on the purchase of used automobiles, bodyguard for a female worker, letter writer, and messenger, among other things. We know one researcher studying an understaffed institutional unit for 40 young children with severe disabilities who was having a terrible time relating to the staff. The attendants were abrupt with him and did their best to ignore him totally. The situation became increasingly uncomfortable until the observer offered to help the two attendants feed the children one day. As he began to feed the first child, the attendants opened up and started to share their concerns and complaints. For the first time, they invited him to join them for a break in the staff lounge.

The Duke family's social network was characterized by mutual support and reciprocal relations among kin and friends. People expected help from family and friends when in need and were prepared to offer support when able. An understanding of the nature of relations within this network was critical for Taylor in establishing a solid relationship with the Dukes. Prior to meeting the Dukes, Taylor had been informed that the family was always on the lookout for donated clothes, old appliances, and junk metal. He used the excuse of having an old television and other appliances to get rid of as a way to meet and visit the Dukes. When, several visits later, he told the family he was writing a book and wanted to include the Dukes in it, they enthusiastically agreed. As Bill put it, "Oh, so we'd be helping *you* out." Throughout the Duke study, Taylor has continued to do favors for the family: lending them money ($20 or so, and sometimes being paid back), giving them rides, being their "lawyer" and helping them with government paperwork, and taking pictures and videotaping at family gatherings.

BEING HUMBLE

It is important for people to know that the researcher is the type of person to whom they can express themselves without fear of disclosure or negative evaluation. Many observers, ourselves included, try "to appear as a humble person who would be a regular guy and do no one any dirt" (Johnson 1975, 95).

Observers frequently become the people with the most knowledge and understanding of what everyone in the setting thinks. Keep this knowledge to yourself. Researchers should be careful not to reveal certain things that informants have said, even if they were not related in private. To display too much knowledge makes the observer threatening and potentially dangerous.

Informants may also be reluctant to express their feelings if the observer acts too knowledgeable. Let people speak freely. You will find that many people hold beliefs that are inaccurate if not patently absurd. There is no need to correct these beliefs. You will only make people self-conscious in your presence.

In some situations, people may say things that the researcher finds offensive. For example, Griffin (1991) notes that people may make sexist or racist remarks in the researcher's presence and that silence can be taken as tacit agreement. How you respond in such situations is not just a research issue; it will depend on your personal priorities. You will need to decide whether it is worth jeopardizing rapport with informants by challenging their remarks. Further, will it change their minds if you express disagreement with their opinions?

ACTING INTERESTED

It should go without saying that you should act interested in what people have to say. Yet it is sometimes easy to act bored in the field, especially if you find yourself in a situation with someone who monopolizes the conversation about seemingly irrelevant or trivial matters. There are ways to channel a conversation and to subtly avoid people. We cover some of these later in this chapter and in our discussion of interviewing.

PARTICIPATION

When active involvement in people's activities is essential to acceptance, then by all means participate, but know where to draw the line. In some settings, you may be exposed to morally or legally problematic activities. Van Maanen (1982, 114), who witnessed many instances of police brutality, writes, "Only practical tests will demonstrate one's trustworthiness."

The attendants in Taylor's institutional study often cruelly teased and abused their charges: beat them, threw buckets of water on them, forced them to engage in fellatio, encouraged some to hit others, forced them to swallow burning cigarettes, and tied them to beds spread-eagle (the attendants' folk wisdom included ways to do these things without leaving marks). Although the attendants subtly encouraged the observer to participate in these abuses, they never exerted strong pressures on him to join. However, they did watch him closely for signs of disapproval. For his part, he tried to ignore these acts as best he could.[2]

Fine (1980) reports that he was tested by children in his study of Little League baseball. For example, kids would engage in rowdiness and roughhousing in his presence as a way of sizing him up. Given the difficulties of overcoming generational differences, it was important for Fine to distance himself from an adult role of supervising in order to gain the kids' trust. Thorne (1994) describes a similar approach in her study of gender relations in elementary schools:

> I avoided positions of authority and rarely intervened in a managerial way, and I went through the days with or near the kids rather than along the paths of teachers and aides. Like others who have done participant-observation with children, I felt a little elated when kids violated rules in my presence, like swearing or openly blowing bubble gum where these acts were forbidden, or swapping stories about recent acts of shoplifting. These incidents reassured me that I had shed at least some of the trappings of adult authority and gained access to kids' more private worlds. (pp. 18–19)

The participant observer walks a thin line between being an active participant—"participant as observer"—and a passive observer—"observer as participant" (Gold 1958; Junker 1960). There are clearly times in which it is best not to be accepted as a genuine member of the setting or group.

Where involvement places you in a competitive situation with informants, it is best to withdraw. It is sometimes difficult to set aside your own ego. Like other people, observers have a self-concept to defend and want to be thought of as witty, bright, and sexually attractive. In a study of a newsroom, Rasmussen found that although the "cute young datable guy" approach worked in winning over some female reporters, this alienated the male reporters (Warren and Rasmussen 1977).

You should also avoid acting and talking in ways that do not fit your own personality. For example, although you should dress in such a way as to blend into the setting (if people dress casually, dress casually; if they dress formally, do the same; if people dress in different ways, try to find a neutral form of dress), you should not wear anything in which you feel unnatural or uncomfortable. Similarly, it is wise not to use people's vocabulary and speech patterns until you have mastered them and they come naturally. Whyte (1955, 304) learned this lesson when he was walking down the street with a street-corner group and, entering the spirit of the small talk, let loose with a string of obscenities. Whyte reports what happened: "Doc shook his head and said: 'Bill, you're not supposed to talk like that. That doesn't sound like you.' "

"Rapping" was a common pastime among trainees in Bogdan's study of a job training program. Here, rapping, also called "playing the dirty dozen" and "joking," refers to a competitive verbal exchange the object of which is to put down another person by the clever use of phrases with double meanings (Hannerz 1969; Horton 1967). Bogdan found himself to be the object of trainees' jokes and, after a few days of observation, was encouraged by them to engage in verbal exchanges about his potency as a lover and his capacity as a drinker. Although he gradually began to participate in these exchanges, he soon realized that he lacked the ability to perform well on this level. At first, he saw this inability to rap as a barrier. As the study progressed, however, he found this inability to be an asset. Since he was not adept at rapping, he was not forced into these exchanges, which had become progressively repetitive, and could concentrate on collecting data.

There are also situations in which you want to go out of your way to point out the differences between yourself and informants. Polsky (1969) discusses the tightrope field researchers walk trying to blend into the social scenery without pretending to be something they are not. In studying heroin users, Polsky made a point of wearing short-sleeved shirts and an expensive watch, both of which let any newcomer know that he was not a junkie.

Any participation that interferes with the researcher's ability to collect data should be avoided. In their rush to be accepted by informants, some observers get drawn into active participation. We know an observer who, on his first day at a school, overheard teachers express a desire to have a sensitivity training workshop. Since he had led a number of such workshops previously, he immediately offered to help them. He ended up abandoning his research.

Field researchers also have to guard against being exploited by informants. There is a difference between establishing rapport and being treated as a stooge. Polsky suggests that researchers have to know where to draw the line with informants. Polsky (1969, 128) offers this example: "I have heard of one social worker with violent gangs who was so insecure, so unable to 'draw the line' for fear of being put down, that he got flattered into holding and hiding guns that had been used in murders."

No discussion of rapport would be complete without a mention of over-rapport or "going native" (Miller 1952). Conventional wisdom in qualitative research warned of the dangers of going native—joining the groups under study—and overidentification with informants. More recent postmodernist and standpoint perspectives challenge the notions of overrapport and going native as the last vestiges of a naive belief in scientific objectivity (Denzin and Lincoln 1994). Certainly, the traditional concept of going native had a colonial ring and positioned the researcher as an all-knowing figure above the unwashed masses. Yet the potential problems of overrapport should not be dismissed out of hand.

As a qualitative researcher, your role is to try to capture how people define their world or construct their reality. What you produce as a qualitative account of people's definitions, constructions, and perspectives has no absolute claim to scientific truth or to being the only version of the ways things are. Given this indisputable fact, however, personal relationships or ideological allegiances should not prevent you from telling the story as you see it and from your point of view (of course, acknowledging that this is your point of view). Miller's (1952) cautions about being co-opted by friendships in the field to the point of giving up embarrassing lines of inquiry or, worse, confusing people's preferred ways of presenting themselves with truth are well taken. Just as ethnographic texts can and should be subjected to critical inquiry (Atkinson 1992), so too should the perspectives of people under study. When, for example, institutional attendants assert that their charges "don't get hurt like you and me" (Taylor 1987b), a researcher needs to distance him- or herself from this perspective in order to understand it *as* a perspective with profound social implications.

KEY INFORMANTS

Ideally, participant observers develop close and open relationships with all informants. However, as mentioned previously, rapport and trust come slowly in field research. The researcher will never develop rapport with some informants.

Field researchers usually try to cultivate close relationships with one or two respected and knowledgeable people in the early stages of the research. These people are called *key informants*. In the folklore of participant observation, key informants are almost heroic figures. A key informant is the researcher's best friend in the field. Whyte's (1993) Doc and Liebow's (1967) Tally are notable examples.

Key informants are the researcher's sponsor in the setting and primary sources of information (Fine 1980). During the first days in the field especially, observers try to find people who will "take them under their wing": show them around, introduce them to others, vouch for them, tell them how to act, and let them know how they are seen by others. Whyte (1955) recounts Doc's words to him at their first meeting:

> . . . You tell me what you want to see, and we'll arrange it. When you want some information, I'll ask for it, and you listen. When you want to find out their philosophy of life, I'll start an argument and get it for you. If there's something else you want to get, I'll stage an act for you . . . You won't have any trouble. You come in as my friend. . . . There's just one thing to watch out for. Don't spring (treat) people. Don't be too free with your money. (p. 292)

Participant observers also look to key informants to provide them with a deep understanding of the setting. Since field research is limited in time and scope, key informants can give the history of the setting and fill in the researcher on what happens when he or she is not there. Zelditch (1962) calls the informant the "observer's observer." In some studies, participant observers have used key informants to check out emerging themes, hunches, and working hypotheses. Whyte reports that Doc became a collaborator in the research by reacting to Whyte's interpretations and offering his own (although subsequent accounts make it clear that Whyte and Doc had a complex relationship).

Although researchers are always on the lookout for good informants and sponsors, it is generally wise to hold back from developing close relationships until you have developed a good feel for the setting. In the initial phase of the research, there is a tendency to latch onto anyone who seems open and friendly in a strange situation. Yet the most outgoing and friendly people in a setting may be marginal members themselves. It is often difficult to know initially who is or is not respected in a setting. If researchers attach themselves to an unpopular person, they are likely to be regarded by others as an arm or ally of that person.

It is also important to avoid concentrating exclusively on one or a handful of people. Do not assume that all informants share the same perspective or have the same depth of knowledge (Van Maanen 1991). They seldom do.

In the institutional study, Bill, the "ward charge" or supervising attendant, tended to monopolize Taylor's time. He took Taylor on long coffee breaks in the staff room, during which he freely expressed his perspectives on the institution, residents, his supervisors, and life in general. As the study progressed, Bill began to repeat himself, telling the same stories and expressing the same views on every observation session. It was not until Taylor scheduled his visits on Bill's days off that he began to talk at length with other attendants and learn about their perspectives. In his study of the job training program, Bogdan encountered similar problems with a staff member who was particularly friendly. Although it helped to have a sponsor and informant in the setting, the staff member kept him from interacting with other staff and the trainees. The observer withdrew from the relationship and only reestablished it after he had gotten to know others.

Close relationships are essential in field research. The right key informant can make or break a study. However, you have to be prepared to stand back from relationships formed early in a study if and when circumstances demand it.

DIFFICULT FIELD RELATIONS

Fieldwork is characterized by all of the elements of human drama found in social life: conflict, hostility, rivalry, seduction, racial tension, and jealousy. Observers often find themselves in the middle of difficult and sensitive situations in the field.

Age, gender, race, and other features of personal identity can have a powerful influence on how informants react to the observer (Warren and Rasmussen 1977). Liebow (1967) conducted his study of black street-corner men as a white researcher. Although he developed strong and friendly relationships with his informants, Liebow (1967, 248) does not pretend to have overcome the barriers to insider status imposed by race: "In my opinion, this brute fact of color, as they understood it in their experience and I understood in mine, irrevocably and absolutely relegated me to the status of outsider."

In some situations women enjoy certain advantages in conducting field research (Easterday et al. 1977; Warren and Rasmussen 1977). Obviously, women stand a better chance than men of being accepted as insiders in female-dominated settings. Warren and Rasmussen (1977) also point out that male and female researchers alike can use sexual attraction to gain information.

However, female researchers are often confronted with problems in the field that men usually do not face. In the large-scale family study with which Taylor was involved, female interviewers occasionally found themselves to be the objects of husbands' sexual advances and, consequently, wives' jealousy. Easterday et al. (1977) describe being hustled as a common problem of young female researchers in male-dominated settings. They recount the following exchange during an interview:

I was in the midst of industriously questioning the attendant about his job at the morgue and he came back with, "Are you married?"

Observer: No. How long have you worked here?
Attendant: Three years. Do you have a steady boyfriend?
Observer: No. Do you find this work difficult?
Attendant: No. Do you date?
Observer: Yes. Why isn't this work difficult for you?
Attendant: You get used to it. What do you do in your spare time?

And so our interview went on for over an hour, each of us working at our separate purposes. I doubt whether either of us got any "usable data." (p. 339)

As Easterday et al. note, in these situations every encounter can become a balancing act between cordiality and distance.

Gurney (1991) similarly reminds us that female researchers need to recognize that instances of sexism, sexual hustling, and sexual harassment occur in the field, just like anywhere else. Gurney advises female researchers to give some thought to how to respond to hypothetical situations before the fieldwork begins (Gurney's advice is to speak to the person privately first, and then try to find allies in the setting to intervene).

Hostile informants can be just as troublesome as overly attentive ones. In many settings—almost surely in large organizations—observers come across people who seem to resent their very presence. Van Maanen (1982) offers the following quote as an example of unambiguous rejection in his study of the police:

Sociologists? Shit. You're supposed to know what's going on out there. Christ, you come around here asking questions like we're the fucking problem. Why don't you go study the goddamn niggers and find out what's wrong with them. They're the fucking problem, not us. I haven't met a sociologist yet who'd make a pimple on a street cop's ass. (pp. 111–112)

Johnson (1975) uses the term *freeze-out* to refer to an informant who expresses an unwillingness to aid the research. In his study of a social service agency, Johnson encountered 2 freeze-outs out of 13 case workers. What he eventually discovered was that both of the freeze-outs padded their case loads, meaning that they kept files on people to whom no services were provided.

Although some people may never accept you, do not assume that hostile informants will remain hostile forever. People often soften over time. In Taylor's institutional study, one attendant, Sam, avoided him for over six months. Although other attendants seemed to accept the observer, Sam remained very guarded in his presence. Taylor visited the ward one evening when only Sam and one other attendant were on duty. Sam, who was in charge, was sitting in the staff office. Taylor stopped by the office and asked Sam if it was all right for him to hang around for a while. Suddenly, Sam went off on a long monologue on why it was necessary to maintain strict discipline on the ward. He explained why he thought attendants had to hit and scream at the residents. It seems that Sam had not trusted Taylor up until that point. He was afraid that Taylor was some kind of a spy. After that visit, Sam, although never overly friendly, was cordial and appeared at ease.

You should try to provide hostile informants with opportunities to change their minds. Continue to be friendly without pushing them into interaction. Even if you cannot win their acceptance, you might avoid making them your enemies and allowing them to turn others against you. Observers can find themselves torn by conflict and organizational power struggles (Roy 1965). People on both sides of a controversy may vie for their allegiance. Support for one side may be expected as the quid pro quo, or exchange, for information. Johnson (1975) found himself being manipulated for information by a supervisor who was trying to build a case against one social worker.

Probably the best way to deal with conflict is to lend a sympathetic ear to both sides. The strategy is to make both sides believe that you are secretly agreeing with them without actually taking a position or giving either side ammunition. Observers often walk a tightrope and have to be able to sense when they are off balance.

FORMING RELATIONSHIPS

When you become involved with people in their everyday lives, you sometimes become attached to them. Unlike researchers who use most other methods, participant observers and qualitative interviewers often develop strong feelings toward their subjects, and subjects often develop feelings toward the researchers. You should be prepared to deal with the feelings, emotions, and attachments that arise in this kind of research (Asher and Fine 1991; Kleinman 1991).

Researchers who use survey, experimental design, and other methodologies are usually trained to maintain a professional distance with subjects, much like a physician or therapist. This is not possible in many qualitative studies. Qualitative researchers spend time with people in their day-to-day lives and work hard to establish a level of rapport with them, and so cannot always put up barriers to the feelings that come any time people spend a significant amount of time together. You will like some people and dislike others.

It is not necessarily undesirable to form friendships and relationships with people under study. The researcher is first and foremost a human being. In Taylor's study of the Duke family, he liked family members right away and continues to be close to them. Further, like many people studied by qualitative researchers, the Dukes are poor and powerless, and Taylor continues to help the family out when he can, even though this is no longer necessary for establishing rapport or learning about their lives. For example, Taylor continues to help the family negotiate with the Social Security office on their entitlement benefits, even though he has already learned everything of interest about the functioning of this office. As researchers, we gain many benefits from being allowed into people's lives. We earn degrees, publish books, gain tenure, and realize many other advantages. If we can reciprocate in small ways, we probably should—not because research ethics requires this, but because this is the way people should act toward each other.

Of course, in many studies, the researcher may not like or respect the people under study. If you are successful as a qualitative researcher, however, you will act as though you do and convince these people that you like them and are interested in them. This can create strong feelings of being false, manipulative, and inauthentic (Taylor 1991).

FIELD TACTICS

Establishing and maintaining rapport with informants is an ongoing activity throughout field research. As fieldwork moves beyond the first days in the field, however, observers devote increasing attention to finding ways to broaden their knowledge of settings and informants. Here are some tactics.

ACTING NAIVE

Many observers find that presenting themselves as naive but interested outsiders is an effective way of eliciting data (Lofland 1971; Sanders 1980). Sanders (1980, 164) notes that presenting him- or herself as an "acceptable incompetent" enables the researcher to ask questions about "what everyone knows." Outsiders are expected to possess a degree of naiveté about a setting. For example, an observer at a school would not be expected to know about educational curricula and standardized testing. In Taylor's institutional study, he developed a strategy to get access to ward records by asking naive questions about residents' IQs and ward events, questions he knew attendants could not answer without consulting the files.

BEING AT THE RIGHT PLACE AT THE RIGHT TIME

Perhaps the most effective field tactic to use is placing yourself in situations likely to yield the data in which you are interested. You can tag along, wrangle invitations to go places or see things, show up unexpectedly, or "play both sides against the middle" (Johnson 1975). The latter is a variation of the tactic children use to get permission to do things from their parents: imply to both parents that it's okay with the other without specifically saying so, thereby leaving yourself an out if you get caught. At the institution Taylor developed a number of ways to gain information in an unobtrusive manner and stumbled upon others.

1. He frequently visited the ward late at night, after residents had been sent to bed and when the attendants had the time to engage in long conversations, and at shift changes, when accounts of the day's events and most recent institutional rumors were given to one set of attendants by another.

2. On the first day of his study, Taylor hung around with attendants at the conclusion of their shift as they were talking about going out for a drink. By placing himself in this awkward position, he wangled an invitation to go to a local bar frequented by attendants.

3. Taylor broke down Sam's resistance by happening to visit the ward on an evening when only Sam and another attendant were working and finding Sam alone in the staff office.

Most observers catch themselves eavesdropping on conversations and peeking at memos and other documents. The subtle eavesdropper sometimes gains important data that would not otherwise have been obtained. Of course, the discovered eavesdropper faces embarrassment (Johnson 1975).

RUNNING ERRANDS AND DOING FAVORS

Building rapport in the field and giving something back to informants are not the only reasons to do favors for people or to help them out; this can also be an effective way to get access to information that would not otherwise be available. Throughout Taylor's study of the Duke family, he has played the roles of family driver, photographer, and, as Winnie puts it, "lawyer."

In contrast to Bill's broken-down cars and trucks, Taylor has always had a vehicle that runs. The family often has called upon him for rides to one place or another. One of the most fruitful trips was a visit to Bill's sister's family and his mother's home outside of Capital City, 150 miles or so away. As Bill explained, his truck at the time would never make it to Capital City, and he wanted to visit his family. So, Taylor offered to take him. The Dukes' family relations have been a strong area of interest during this study, and the visit to Bill's sister's family and especially his mother filled in important parts of the story.

Early on in the study, Taylor brought a camera along to family events and celebrations. The Dukes, and others in their network, were delighted to get pictures of events such as anniversary or birthday parties. For Taylor, of course, the camera (and later a camcorder) captured details of settings and people that usually go unnoticed in everyday life. Over time, the Dukes started to invite Taylor to events for the explicit purpose of having him take pictures. For example, he was invited to end-of-the-year school events for Cindy and got a glimpse of how teachers related to Cindy and her mother.

Perhaps the most important role Taylor has played with the Dukes, in their eyes, has been that of family "lawyer" (Winnie once asked, "Now, are you a *lawyer* lawyer, or another kind?"). As recipients of public assistance in one form or another, the Dukes are literally flooded with often confusing and contradictory forms, letters, and paperwork. Even someone who is literate can have a difficult time deciphering the bureaucratic language contained in correspondence from government agencies and understanding rules and regulations governing entitlement programs. Winnie takes care of the family's business with public and other agencies and is often at a total loss to understand much of the paperwork she receives. Taylor tries to help Winnie interpret correspondence from agencies, fills out forms for her, maintains copies of past letters and paperwork, and accompanies her on visits to government offices to clarify family members' benefits. From a research perspective, this has yielded information about the family's actual income and has provided insight into how government programs are experienced by those on the receiving end (Winnie has used the term "stupidness" to refer to how government agencies operate, and this seems like an apt description at times).

YOU DO NOT HAVE TO LET INFORMANTS KNOW EXACTLY WHAT YOU ARE STUDYING

It is usually unwise to let informants know what you want to learn about or see (if you know yourself). In the first place, as Hoffmann (1980) notes, it is sometimes useful to camouflage the real research questions to reduce self-consciousness and the perceived threat. Hoffmann (1980) reports:

> Many of my respondents became reticent when they perceived themselves to be the object of study—that is, when I told them that I was interested in how the old elite system worked. I found, however, that they were prepared to offer their views more freely on "external" topics, such as reorganization policy or problems of the new membership. With respondents who appeared defensive about the old system . . . or who countered direct questions with front work, I presented myself as being interested in the consequences of reorganization or organizational problems rather than in the board as a social group or in board work as an elite social institution. (p. 51)

In the second place, when informants know too much about the research, they are likely either to hide things from the observer or to stage events for his or her benefit. The design of the large-scale family study described earlier called for a series of interviews with the parents and home observations, including observations of the bedtime routines of children. The fieldworkers observed dramatic differences in how some parents acted during the interviews and the prescheduled observations. In most families, children were better dressed and had more toys around on the days of the observations. During evening interviews, the fieldworkers found that in many families there is no bedtime routine per se. Children fall asleep in front of a television sometime after early evening. When the fieldworkers returned to conduct the preannounced bedtime observations, some parents actually staged bedtime routines for them to observe (telling the child to get ready for bed at an early hour, tucking the child in, etc.). By informing parents what they wanted to see, the fieldworkers unwittingly encouraged some parents to fabricate events because they wanted either to look like "good parents" or to be cooperative and give the researchers what they wanted.

You Can Use Aggressive Field Tactics Once You Have Developed an Understanding of the Setting

Early in a study, you conduct yourself in such a way as to minimize so-called reactive effects (Webb et al. 1966); your goal is for people to act as naturally as possible in your presence (knowing that you have some effect by virtue of being there). For instance, participant observers do not walk around with clipboards or questionnaires, take notes, or ask a lot of structured questions. As Jack Douglas (1976) argues, the more controlled the research—the further it departs from natural interaction—the greater the likelihood that one will end up studying the effects of research procedures.

At a later stage of research, you can employ obtrusive or aggressive tactics, knowing enough about the setting to gauge how these tactics affect what people say and do. Some observers conduct structured interviews toward the end of their research. Altheide (1980) reports that as he was about to exit the field, he became much more aggressive in his questioning, probing sensitive political issues.

ASKING QUESTIONS

Although participant observers enter the field with broad questions on their minds, they allow themes to emerge before pursuing specific lines of inquiry. Initially, field researchers ask questions in such a way as to enable people to talk about what is on their minds and what is of concern to them without forcing them to respond to the observers' interests, concerns, or preconceptions. The observer's stance should be: "I don't know what questions to ask or how to ask them until I have spent some time in the setting."

Early in a study, observers ask nondirective and nonjudgmental questions. Use the phrases with which you usually initiate conversations: "How's it going?" "How do you like it here?" "Can you tell me a little about this place?" These kinds of questions allow people to respond in their own ways and with their own perspectives. Another good way of getting people to talk initially is to wait for something to happen and then ask about it. As discussed earlier, newcomers are expected to be naive and to ask questions about things they have not seen before.

Knowing what *not* to ask can be just as important as knowing what to ask. Sanders (1980) points out that when a researcher is studying people who are engaged in legally questionable activities, inappropriate questions can reasonably be interpreted as an indication that the researcher is an informer. Van Maanen (1982) argues that any form of sustained questioning implies evaluation. In the institutional study, Taylor directly questioned only one attendant about abuse (and this was after a few beers at a bar), even though this was a major focus of the research. The subject was too sensitive and explosive to explore in a straightforward way. This was a risky line of questioning, and the only reason Taylor got away with it was that this particular attendant liked to complain that the others were too harsh with residents (although he engaged in many of the same behaviors as the rest).

We know of one group of observers who, on a tour of a mental hospital, questioned a supervisor about a ward's "time-out," or isolation rooms: "Are they allowed to go to the bathroom?" "Do they still get meals when they're in there?" The supervisor was infuriated by the questions and shot back: "What do you think we are here—sadists?"

It is also important to know how to phrase questions. Questions should be phrased in sympathetic terms that support informants' definitions of themselves. One researcher referred to the "funeral business" during her first visit to a funeral home. The funeral director was taken aback. This seemingly innocuous phrase contradicted his view of his work as a profession and not merely a business.

The meaning of disability has been a major theme in Taylor's study of the Duke family. Bill and Winnie and their two children, as well as many of their kin and friends, have been labeled as mentally retarded or handicapped by schools, human service agencies, and government programs. Yet none of the members of the family seem to define themselves as mentally retarded or disabled. Winnie refers to her family's "medical problems," and Bill talks about being "on disability" as opposed to being "on welfare." The term "handicapped" is used synonymously with "crippled" and reserved for people with physical disabilities who use wheelchairs. As in other social circles, "retard" and "crazy" are used casually as general epithets by people within the Dukes' social network.

This poses an interesting tactical question: if people do not define themselves as retarded or handicapped or relate to disability labels, how can we learn who has and has not been labeled as being disabled? As an indirect way of learning about whether people had ever been labeled as disabled, Taylor has asked questions about people's source of income (specifically, Supplemental Security Income and Social Security Disability, both disability entitlement programs) and their experience with special education, sheltered workshops, and other disability agencies. By asking these kinds of indirect questions, Taylor could chart members of Bill's and Winnie's extended families who had been defined as disabled by one agency or another and then compare these labels with how people define themselves and each other.

In the institutional study, it was not uncommon for attendants to straitjacket or tie residents. Taylor was always careful to ask questions that would not intimidate the attendants or challenge their perspectives: "Does he always give you problems?" "How long do you have to keep him in there?" There is no doubt that if Taylor had asked questions requiring the attendants to justify their actions—"How often do you let them out?" "What's the institution's policy on restraint?"—he would have been frozen out.

Once informants start talking, you can encourage them to say more about topics in which you are interested. Encouraging words, cues, and gestures that indicate your interest are usually sufficient to keep someone on track: "That's interesting." "Is that right?" "I always wondered about that." Small signs of sympathy demonstrate support and encourage people to continue: "I know what you mean." "That's rough."

You should ask for clarification of informants' remarks. Do not assume that you understand what people mean. Use phrases like "What do you mean by that?," "I don't follow you exactly," and "Explain that again." You can also restate what informants say and ask them to confirm your understanding.

As observers acquire knowledge and understanding of a setting, questioning becomes more focused and directive (Denzin 1978; Spradley 1980). Once themes and perspectives have emerged, researchers begin to round out their knowledge of the setting and check out information previously gathered.

In participant observation, data analysis is an ongoing activity. Observers move back and forth between the field and data already collected. What they try to observe and ask about in the field depends on what they think they have learned. It is a good idea to keep a running record of themes to explore and questions to ask (as described later, we use observer's comments to do this).

After they have developed some working hypotheses, observers round out their knowledge by asking informants to elaborate on subjects mentioned previously and by following up with informants on things mentioned by others. In the institutional study, after talking to several attendants about previous jobs and relatives, Taylor had a hunch that attendants' work careers (previous jobs) and personal networks (family members and friends who worked at the institution) played a role in shaping their perspectives on work. Over the next couple of months, Taylor made a point of casually asking other attendants what they did before they worked at the institution and whether they had friends and relatives there.

Jack Douglas (1976, 147) stresses the importance of checking out informants' accounts and stories: "Checking out consists essentially of comparing what one is told by others against what can be experienced or observed more directly, and therefore more reliably, or against more trustworthy accounts." Accounts that the researcher suspects early in the study can be checked out after he or she has a sense of who can and cannot be believed and to what extent.

Most observers also employ more aggressive questioning tactics once they have developed a feel for a setting and informants. Especially toward the end of a study, observers pose "devil's advocate" questions (Strauss et al. 1964), confront informants with falsehoods, probe taboo subjects (Altheide 1980), and ask informants to react to their interpretations and conclusions (Strauss et al. 1964).

The observer who has spent some time in a setting can use knowledge already gained to obtain more information. The idea is to act as if you already know about something to get people to talk about it in depth. Douglas (1976) calls this the *phased-assertion* tactic. Hoffmann (1980) describes how she used inside information when people seemed reluctant to talk too freely:

> First, respondents learned that I was "in the know," that I had penetrated through the public veneer to the underlying social reality. Front work was discouraged because they knew that I could distinguish it from backstage information and because it might look as if they were covering something up. Second, the use of insider details possibly acted to reassure reticent informants. I often had the impression that respondents felt relieved by the knowledge that they were not the only persons to make such disclosures, that initial responsibility lay with someone else, and that this person must have had reason to trust me in the first place. (p. 53)

Hoffmann also notes that by dropping inside information the researcher discourages informants from going over familiar points and encourages them to make responses relevant to his or her interests.

LEARNING THE LANGUAGE

An important aspect of participant observation is learning how people use language (Becker and Geer 1957; Spradley 1980). Field researchers must start with the premise that words and symbols used in their own worlds may have different meanings in the worlds of their informants. They must also be attuned to and explore the meanings of words with which they are not familiar.

Observers almost always come across new words and symbols. Any group, especially one cut off from the broader society, develops its own special vocabulary. For example, Wallace (1968) provides a glossary of terms used on skid row: *beanery,* a cheap restaurant; *dead one,* a retired hobo; *dingbat,* the lowest type of tramp; *jack,* money; *slave market,* street corner employment office. Similarly, Giallombardo (1966) offers the argot (special language) of a women's prison: *bug house,* institution for the "mentally insane" or "defective"; *butcher,* a prison doctor; *flagging,* an older inmate attempting to involve a younger one in sex.

The vocabulary used in a setting usually provides important clues to how people define situations and classify their world and thus suggests lines of inquiry and questioning. In Bogdan's job training program, the staff and trainees used special terms to refer to each other that indicated the distrust in the setting. Some of the staff used the phrase *professional trainee* to refer to people who had been involved in other training programs. Some trainees, on the other hand, referred to staff members as *poverty pimps,* a phrase that suggested that they were living off of the plight of others.

Certain assumptions may be built into a vocabulary. In institutions for the so-called mentally retarded, for example, mundane activities are referred to as *therapy* and *programming; motivation training* and *recreation therapy* refer to going for walks, coloring, and similar activities (Taylor and Bogdan 1980).

Some observers are unable to cut through professional jargon and vocabularies. They uncritically accept the assumptions behind professional categories. Terms like *schizoid, paranoid,* and *psychotic* have little concrete meaning and are based on psychiatric ideologies rather than scientific knowledge (Szasz 1970). Likewise, the vocabulary used in many educational settings reflects class and racial bias (Cicourel and Kitsuse 1963). Lower-class children who cannot read or are disruptive are labeled "educable retarded," "culturally deprived," and "emotionally disturbed," whereas middle-class children with the same behavior are likely to be called "learning disabled" or "minimally brain-damaged."

People use a special vocabulary to build lines of action in some settings. Calling a person "profoundly retarded" or "severely handicapped" can be used to keep that person institutionalized. Calling a child "emotionally disturbed" may allow the child to be excluded from school.

You must learn to examine vocabularies as a function of the assumptions and purposes of the users rather than an objective characterization of the people or objects of reference. This applies even to clear-cut words. A person described as "nonambulatory" might be thought of as someone who cannot walk at all. Yet in understaffed nursing homes and institutions the term might be used to refer to people who could walk if they had minimal assistance.

The meaning and significance of people's verbal and nonverbal symbols can only be determined in the context of what they actually do and after an extended period of time. There is a danger of imputing meanings that people did not intend. Polsky (1969) warns against assuming that a person's vocabulary reflects deep-seated feelings:

> I have seen it seriously argued, for example, that heroin addicts must unconsciously feel guilty about their habit because they refer to heroin by such terms as "shit," "junk," and "garbage." Actually, the use of any such term by a heroin addict indicates, in itself, nothing whatever about his guilt feelings or the lack thereof, but merely that he is using a term for heroin traditional in his group. (pp. 123–124)

Although the words people use lend insight into the meanings they attach to things, it is naive to presume that the intricacies of a social setting or situation can be revealed by vocabulary alone.

DeVault (1990, 97) argues that conventional language does not adequately capture the experiences and realities of women:

> The names of experiences often do not fit for women. For an example that is simple and immediate, consider the difficulties that arise in an attempt to apply the terms "work" and "leisure" to most women's lives. Many of the household activities so prominent in women's lives do not fit comfortably into either category (see e.g., Smith 1987, p. 68), and many of women's activities, such as family, community, and volunteer work, are best described as "invisible work" (Daniels, 1987).

According to DeVault, researchers who are trying to understand the experience of women, as well as other subordinate groups, must "translate" language by drawing on an understanding of the deeper meanings behind common speech. DeVault (1990, 102) writes, "As an interviewer who is also a woman—who has also learned to translate—I can listen 'as a woman,' filling in from experience to help me understand the things that are incompletely said."

FIELD NOTES

As an analytic research method, participant observation depends upon the recording of complete and detailed field notes. You should record field notes after each observation, as well as after more casual contacts with informants such as chance encounters and phone conversations. As noted earlier, field notes should be recorded during the pre-fieldwork stage of the research.

Since field notes provide the raw data of participant observation, you should strive to write the most complete and comprehensive field notes possible. This requires a tremendous amount of self-discipline, if not compulsiveness. It is not uncommon for observers to spend four to six hours recording field notes for every hour of observation. Those who want to use qualitative methods because they seem easier than statistics are in for a rude awakening. Anyone who has carried out a participant observation study knows that recording field notes can be drudgery.

Many beginning observers try to cut corners by writing sketchy summaries, omitting details, or postponing recording the notes. "Nothing much happened" is a common rationalization. Yet the observer's frame of mind should be such that everything that occurs in the field is a potentially important source of data. You do not know what is important until you have been in the setting for a while. Even small talk can lend insight into people's perspectives when viewed in context at a later time. A common experience in participant observation is to go back to your initial notes when you begin to analyze your data to look for something you vaguely remember being said or done, only to find that you never wrote the information down. Of course, as you get to know the setting and people and focus your research interests, you can be more selective in what you record. We have found that we can spend half as much time recording notes in the latter stages of fieldwork than in the early ones.

Try to find a mentor or colleague to read your field notes. This is probably the best way to get the motivation to record field notes session after session over a period of time. By virtue of their distance from the dynamics of a setting, readers can also point out emerging themes that escape the observer.

The field notes should include descriptions of people, events, and conversations as well as the observer's actions, feelings, and hunches or working hypotheses. The sequence and duration of events and conversations are noted as precisely as possible. The fabric of the setting is described in detail. In short, the field notes represent an attempt to record on paper everything that can possibly be recalled about the observation. A good rule to remember is that if it is not written down, it never happened.

HINTS FOR RECALLING WORDS AND ACTIONS

Participant observers must strive for a level of concentration sufficient to enable them to remember most of what they see, hear, feel, smell, and think while in the field (they can also "cheat" by using mechanical recording devices and potentially threaten rapport, as we discuss later). Although precise recall is impossible, most observers are amazed at the accuracy with which they can recall details by virtue of training, experience, and concentration. Some observers use the analogy of a switch to describe the ability they have developed to remember things; they can turn on the concentration needed to observe and recall. This analogy is a good one, if only for the reason that it sets the tone for the goal of observation skills.

People vary in the amount they can remember and in the techniques that enable them to recall things. We have found the following techniques useful to aid in recalling details in a broad range of settings.

1. *Pay attention.*　The reason most people do not recall all things in everyday life is that they never notice things to begin with. As Spradley (1980) remarks, participant observers must overcome years of selective inattention. Watch; listen; concentrate. As Yogi Berra is said to have remarked, "You can see a lot by just looking."

2. *Shift focus from a "wide-angle" to a "narrow-angle" lens.*　In busy places, observers are usually overwhelmed by the sheer number of activities and conversations occurring at the same time. It is literally impossible to concentrate on, let alone remember, everything that is happening. One especially effective recall technique that can be perfected with practice is to focus on a specific person, interaction, or activity while mentally blocking out all the others.

In Taylor's study, over 70 residents and anywhere from 1 to 10 attendants could be in one large dayroom at a single time. The number of activities occurring simultaneously seemed infinite: several residents rocking on benches, one removing his clothes, another urinating on the floor, two cleaning up feces and urine with a rag and bucket, a handful sitting in front of the television, three lying on the floor, several pacing back and forth, two hugging each other, two in strait jackets; one attendant scolding a resident, two other attendants reading a newspaper, another attendant preparing to dispense tranquilizers and seizure control drugs, and so on.

When first entering the room, Taylor observed with a wide-angle focus for a few minutes, noting the various activities occurring. After that, however, he would shift focus to a single activity or corner of the room, ignoring everything else. By concentrating on specific activities one at a time, Taylor could later reconstruct specific scenes and events; over time, the general picture became complete.

3. *Look for key words in people's remarks.*　Although you should strive for accuracy in your field notes, it is not possible to remember every word that people say. However, you can concentrate on and commit to memory key words or phrases in every conversation—speech that reveals what is meaningful and important to people.

You will find that certain words and phrases stand out in your mind. In Bogdan's (Bogdan, Brown, and Foster 1982) study of a hospital neonatal unit, doctors and nurses used special, easy-to-remember terms to refer to infants, for example, *feeders and growers, nonviable,* and *chronics.* Other, more familiar words or phrases, such as *very sick baby* and *good baby,* although less striking, were easily recalled once the researchers were attuned to how medical staff defined the infants.

4. *Concentrate on the first and last remarks in each conversation.*　Conversations usually follow an orderly sequence. A certain question elicits a certain response; one remark provokes another; one topic leads into a related subject. If you can remember how a conversation started, you can often follow it

through to the end in your own mind. Even when conversations do not follow a logical or orderly sequence, remarks that come out of nowhere should not be difficult to recall. You should find that the substance of long monologues, which usually confuse the novice observer, is retrievable.

5. *Play back remarks and scenes in your mind.*   After you see or hear something, repeat it to yourself mentally. Try to visualize the scene or remark. It is also a good idea to take a break from talking or observing every once in a while during a session to play back in your mind what has already happened.

6. *Leave the setting as soon as you have observed as much as you can remember.* Although this point has been made already, it bears repeating. In a new setting, you probably should not spend more than an hour observing unless something important is happening. As you get to know a setting and learn to remember things, you can spend more time in the field.

7. *Record your field notes as soon as possible after observing.*   The longer you wait between observing and recording the data, the more you will forget. Try to schedule your observations in such a way that you will have the time and energy to record your notes.

8. *Draw a diagram of the setting and trace your movements through it.*   In a sense, walk through your experience. Doing this is a valuable aid in recalling events and people. A seating chart can similarly be helpful. The diagram or chart will help you in recalling who did what and in remembering less conspicuous people.

9. *Once you have drawn a diagram and traced your own movements, outline specific events and conversations that occurred at each point in time before you record your field notes.*   The outline will help you recall additional details and approximate the sequence in which events occurred. The outline does not have to be elaborate—it only needs to contain key words, scenes, and events that stand out in your mind; the first and last remarks in conversations; and other reminders. The time you take to construct an outline will be well spent in terms of the accuracy and clarity added to your notes.

10. *If there is a time lag between observing and recording the field notes, tape-record a summary or outline of the observation.*   One of the institutions Taylor studied was located an hour's drive away. Taylor taped a detailed summary of the observation on the way home. He let conversations and events flow freely from his mind during this time. Later, after arriving home, he transcribed the summary, organizing events according to the sequence in which they occurred. From this summary, Taylor wrote up a detailed account of the day's events. Between observations in his study of impersonal sex in public restrooms, Humphreys (1975) occasionally went to his car to tape-record what he had just observed.

11. *Pick up pieces of lost data after you have recorded your field notes.* Observers often recall things days or even weeks after an observation. Some-

times events and conversations are remembered after the next observation. These pieces of data should be incorporated into the field notes.

TAPING AND TAKING NOTES IN THE FIELD

Although most participant observers rely on their memories to record data, some researchers take notes in the field or use mechanical recording devices for data collection. Indeed, there is a growing number of qualitative studies in which researchers use tape recorders, videotape machines, and time-lapse photography (Dabbs 1982; Whyte 1980).

Participant observers seem divided on the pros and cons of recording notes and using mechanical recording devices in the field. Some researchers take the position that obtrusive recording devices draw unnecessary attention to the observer and disrupt the natural flow of events and conversations in the setting. Douglas (1976, 53) writes, ". . . there is every reason to believe that obtrusive recording devices have fundamental effects in determining what actors think and feel about the researcher (mainly, it makes them terribly suspicious and on guard) and what they do in his presence." Other researchers, especially those interested in conversational analysis, question whether the observer can accurately remember and subsequently record the important details of what happens in the setting (Schwartz and Jacobs 1979).

Our view is that researchers should refrain from taping and taking notes in the field at least until they have developed a feel for the setting and can understand the effects of recording on informants. In our experience, mechanical recording devices have untoward effects on people. In the large-scale family study, Taylor used a tape recorder during an initial interview with the mother of a young child. In the warmup prior to the interview, he casually mentioned that he previously lived in her neighborhood and asked her how she liked living there. She proceeded to complain about how many blacks had recently moved into the neighborhood and how they had "taken over" the parks and playgrounds. Then came the interview, which included questions on likes and dislikes about the neighborhood. As Taylor questioned the mother with the tape recorder playing, she gave bland responses to questions about what she liked about the neighborhood and what changes had occurred since she had been living there. Never was race mentioned. After the interview had been completed and the tape recorder turned off, the interviewer again struck up a conversation about the neighborhood and again the mother complained about the number of blacks who had moved there. The conclusion: few people want to be a racist for the record. In other words, it is naive to assume that filming or taping will not alter what some people may say or do.

There are situations and settings in which observers can use mechanical recording devices without dramatically altering the research. Whyte's (1980) excellent photographic study of small urban places demonstrates that a camera can be an effective research tool in public places. Similarly, Frederick Wiseman and others have produced many insightful documentaries filmed by camera operators who captured an incredible amount of people's private lives (although one is left wondering to what extent the people put on performances for the cameras). In our interviewing, we have found that over a period of time people seem to forget about a tape recorder and speak relatively freely while it is recording.

It is also true that there are some social patterns that cannot be studied and analyzed without audio or video recording devices. Thus observers are not likely to recall, or even notice, all of the minute details of interactional patterns and conversations sufficient for ethnomethodological analysis and certain other lines of inquiry.

In most symbolic interactionist studies, researchers do not need to rely on mechanical recording devices to collect important data. Through training and experience, researchers can develop sufficient recall to remember events and conversations necessary to understand people's meanings, perspectives, and definitions. In fact, the accuracy a tape recorder gains for the experienced observer interested in this level of analysis is probably illusory.

There are few instances when it is advisable to take notes in the field. More so than recording, note-taking reminds people that they are under constant surveillance and tips them off to areas in which the researcher is interested. As mentioned earlier, in many situations the observer wants to deflect informants' attention from the research concerns. One of the few times notes can be taken unobtrusively is when other people are also taking notes, as in a classroom or formal meeting. Even in these situations, the researcher should be discreet.

Some observers go to a private place such as a bathroom to jot down key words and phrases that will later help them recall events that transpire during long observation sessions. You can buy a small reporter's notebook that will fit easily and inconspicuously into a pocket. If this helps you remember things and can be done secretly, so much the better.

THE FORM OF THE NOTES

Everybody develops his or her own way of writing up field notes (Emerson, Fretz, and Shaw 1995). Although the form varies from observer to observer, the field notes should he written in such a way as to allow you to retrieve data easily and to code (and sort) themes or topics. Here are some guidelines we try to follow.

1. *Start each set of notes as a separate file with a title page.* The title page should include the date, time, and place of observation and the day and time the notes were recorded. Some observers title each set of notes with a quotation or descriptive phrase. Such titles serve as reminders of the general contents in the event the researcher needs to consult the notes to check on something.

2. *Include a diagram of the setting at the beginning of the notes.* Trace your movements and indicate on which page of your notes each movement is described. This will serve as an easy reference when you want to check specific events. For those who are fortunate enough to have someone read their notes, a diagram provides a useful point of reference for the reader.

3. *Leave margins wide enough for your own and others' comments.* Wide margins also enable you to add forgotten items at a later time and to code or comment on your notes in the analysis stage of your research.

4. *Begin new paragraphs often.* When you analyze your data, you will find it helpful if you have used separate paragraphs for every quotation, event, thought, or topic.

5. *Use quotation marks to record remarks as often as possible.* It is not necessary to have a flawless reproduction of what was said. What is important is capturing the meaning and approximate wording of remarks. If you cannot recall the wording, paraphrase: "John said something like—I've got to go home. Bill agreed and John walked out." Strauss et al. (1964) recommend that the researcher use quotation marks for exact recall, apostrophes to signify less precision in wording, and no marks to indicate reasonable recall.

6. *Use pseudonyms for the names of people and places.* More than a few participant observers have fretted over what would happen if their data fell into the wrong hands (Humphreys 1975; Johnson 1975; Van Maanen 1982, 1983). You never know what you might see or hear that would jeopardize the people you are studying if someone else found out. You also do not know whether readers of your notes might have relationships with the people described in your notes. Nothing is lost by using pseudonyms for people and places.

7. *Make copies of your notes or data disks.* Accidents might happen. A fire, theft, or hard drive crash—or simply misplacing your field notes or disk—can cause you to lose your data forever. As soon as you record your notes, make hard copies or a backup disk.

OBSERVER'S COMMENTS

The field notes should include not only descriptions of what occurs in a setting, but also a record of the observer's feelings, interpretations, hunches, preconceptions, and future areas of inquiry. These personal comments should be clearly distinguished from descriptive data through the use of parentheses and the designation *O.C.* for *observer's comment.*

It may be difficult for those trained in objective research to accept the observer's own feelings and interpretations as an important source of understanding. Yet, as a participant in the setting and a member of the general society and culture, the researcher is likely to share many feelings and perspectives with the people in a setting. Indeed, participant observers must learn to empathize with informants, to experience their experiences vicariously, and to share their sufferings and joys. To distance yourself from personal feelings is to refuse to take the role of the other person and see things from his or her point of view (Blumer 1969).

What you feel may be what informants feel or may have felt in the past. You should use your own feelings, beliefs, preconceptions, understandings, and assumptions to develop potential insights into others' perspectives (DeVault 1990; Kleinman 1991). By recording these in observer's comments, you identify areas for future investigation and analysis. The following comments are excerpted from field notes in Taylor's institutional study:

> (O.C. I feel quite bored and depressed on the ward tonight. I wonder if this has anything to do with the fact that there are only two attendants working now. With only two attendants on, there are fewer diversions and less bantering. Perhaps this is why the attendants always complain about there not being enough of them. After all, there is never more work here than enough to occupy two attendants' time so it's not the fact that they can't get their work done that bothers them.)
>
> (O.C. Although I don't show it, I tense up when the residents approach me when they are covered with food or excrement. Maybe this is what the attendants feel and why they often treat the residents as lepers.)

In the following excerpt from Bogdan's job training study, he reflects upon one of his first contacts with a trainee after having spent the initial stages of the research with staff:

> I approached the two trainees who were working on assembling the radio. The male trainee looked up. I said, "Hi." He said, "Hi" and went back to doing what he had been doing. I said, "Have you built that (the radio) right from scratch?" (O.C. After I said this I thought that that was a dumb thing to say or perhaps a very revealing thing to say. Thinking back over the phrase, it came across as perhaps condescending. Asking if he had built it right from scratch might imply that I thought he didn't have the ability. He didn't react in that way but maybe that's the way people think of the "hard core" unemployed out at the center. Doing well is treated with surprise rather than as standard procedure. Perhaps rather than expecting that they are going to produce and treating them as if they are going to produce, you treat doing well as a special event.)

Bogdan thus gained a possible insight into how staff members define trainees by reflecting on his own remark.

The participant observer also records emerging ideas and interpretations in the observer's comments. These comments provide a running record of the observer's attempts to understand the setting and become extremely valuable during the analysis phase of the research. The following comment is taken from the field notes in the institutional study: "(O.C. Many residents on this ward collect and hoard seemingly insignificant things. This is similar to what Goffman writes about in institutions of this kind. I'll have to start looking into this.)"

Some observers also find it useful to write a brief analytic memo identifying themes and summarizing an observation when they record their field notes.

DESCRIPTIONS OF SETTINGS AND ACTIVITIES

The research setting and people's activities should be described in the field notes. When writing field notes, you should force yourself to describe the setting and activities in sufficient detail to paint a mental picture of the place and what occurred there. Some researchers strive to write their field notes in such a way as to present narratively what a camera would capture in film.

You should be careful to use descriptive and not evaluative words when you write your field notes. For example, you would not describe a room simply as *depressing;* rather, you would write something like the following: "The room was relatively dark, with dust and cobwebs in the corners and on the windowsills and chipped paint on the walls." Similarly, you would not say that people were receiving *occupational therapy;* you would record the activities in descriptive terms: "The three women were sitting at the table. One was caning a chair, while the other two were crayoning in coloring books. The staff member in charge referred to these activities as 'occupational therapy.' "

Your own feelings, evaluations, or interpretations should be included in the observer's comments. By doing this, you can identify possible areas for investigation or analysis without assuming that everyone sees things exactly the same way that you do. The following excerpt comes from the notes in the institutional study:

> A strong smell of feces and urine mixed with antiseptic permeated the air as I entered the smaller dormitory. (O.C. I find the smell to be repulsive, so much so that I immediately want to leave. Yet the attendants do not seem to mind the smell. Some claim to have gotten used to it. Others never mention it. I wonder if this reflects the difference between myself and them or the fact that I am a newcomer to the ward compared to them.)

You will find that a detailed description of the setting and people's positions within it can give you important insights into the nature of participants' activities, interaction patterns, perspectives, and ways of presenting themselves to others. At many total institutions, the front regions—areas visible to outsiders—are arranged to present an appearance of benign, idyllic retreats where residents receive appropriate care and treatment (Goffman 1961; Taylor 1977; Taylor and Bogdan 1980). Thus the grounds of most institutions are filled with tall trees, meticulously maintained gardens, and stately buildings. The administration building is likely to be an old Victorian or colonial structure with carefully polished woodwork and floors on the inside. Institutions sometimes have special rooms set aside for family visits. As Goffman (1961) notes, the furnishings and decor of these rooms more closely approximate outside standards than residents' actual living quarters.

In dramatic contrast to these front regions, institutional back regions, where residents actually live, are designed to facilitate the staff's control over residents and efficient maintenance of ward order and cleanliness (Taylor 1977). The following were common features on the institutional wards Taylor studied:

- Locked doors and areas within the ward
- Televisions and stereos located high on the walls out of residents' reach
- Heavy, destruction-proof furniture
- Wire mesh on windows
- Light switches and temperature controls inaccessible to residents
- Bathrooms lacking toilet paper, soap, towels, and mirrors
- Clothing and personal objects stored in locked rooms
- Staff offices and nursing stations positioned in such a way as to maximize staff surveillance of residents
- Sparse furnishings and decorations (wall paintings, curtains)

Not all aspects of a setting will be significant. However, you should note and question the meaning of everything you observe.

When you are new to a setting, it is difficult to take everything in at once. Develop a picture of the setting over time. On each visit, concentrate on a new aspect. For example, in a school classroom you might focus on notices on a bulletin board on one visit and decorations on the walls on another. Once you have captured the setting, you should be attuned to changes that occur. These changes may reflect changes in how people see themselves or others. For example, a change in the seating pattern in a teachers' lunchroom may reflect a change in social relationships in the school.

DESCRIPTIONS OF PEOPLE

Like settings and activities, people should be carefully described in the notes. People convey important things about themselves and make assumptions about others on the basis of clothing, hair styles, jewelry, accessories, demeanor, and general appearance. Goffman (1959, 1963, 1971) uses the phrase *impression management* to describe how people actively try to influence how others think about them through their looks and actions.

You should note those features of people that lend insight into how they view themselves or want to be viewed by others. What kinds of clothing do they wear—casual or formal dress? Do men have long hair and beards or short haircuts? What is the condition of their teeth and what might this tell you about them? How do people walk?[3] What kind of glasses are they wearing? Are people wearing jewelry? Do women have handbags and do men carry briefcases? These and other features should be described in the field notes.

People, as settings, should be described in specific and nonevaluative terms. Words like *shy, flashy, aggressive,* and *fancy* are interpretative, not descriptive words. Your own impressions and assumptions about people based on their appearance should be relegated to observer's comments. The following excerpt comes from the field notes of Bogdan's study of door-to-door salespeople:

> The door leading from the corridor opened and a man paused for a moment and tiptoed in. (O.C. He looked surprised when he opened the door, like he didn't expect to see all the people. His tiptoeing seemed to be an attempt not to cause any excess noise. His carriage was one of "I'm imposing.") He was approximately 5'7" and had a deep brown suntan. (O.C. It looked like he was tan from working outside.) His skin was leathery. His hair was black and combed back. It had a few streaks of gray and he was slightly bald in front. He was maybe 45 years old. He was thin. His clothes were cleaned and well-pressed and fit him well. A set of keys was hanging from his belt on a key ring in back. He had on dark brown flannel straight-leg trousers with a light tan stretch belt with the buckle worn on his hip. He had on a dark brown plaid sport shirt with a button down. He was wearing well-polished loafers and had on black horn-rimmed glasses.

In many settings, especially organizations, dress and appearance differentiate people according to their position and status. Sometimes the signs of status are obvious; for example, some people wear work clothes or uniforms, whereas others wear dresses or coats and ties; hats and nameplates also may indicate a person's status. In other settings, signs that indicate status are subtle and will strike the observer only after a period of time in the field. One researcher noticed that female employees in an organization carried their handbags with them wherever they went. It took the researcher a while to realize that the women held subordinate positions in the organization and were not provided with lockers. At many total institutions, staff members have heavy key rings hanging from their belts. It is not uncommon to observe residents copying the staff by hanging keys on strings from their belts.

RECORD DIALOGUE ACCESSORIES

People's gestures, nonverbal communications, tone of voice, and speed of speaking help the observer to interpret the meaning of their words (DeVault 1990). These dialogue accessories are important for understanding interaction and should be included in the field notes. The following excerpts are examples of the kinds of gestures that should be recorded in your notes:

> Joe loosened his tie and said, " . . ."
> As Pete spoke, the sound of his voice got louder and louder and he began pointing his finger at Paul. Paul stepped back and his face turned red.
> Bill raised his eyes to the ceiling as Mike walked past. (O.C. I interpret this as a ridiculing gesture.)

You should also try to capture accents and speech patterns when these might be significant; that is, when they tell something important about the person or how others are likely to view him or her.

RECORD YOUR OWN REMARKS AND ACTIONS

Participant observers should record their own behavior in the field. People's words and actions can only be understood if they are examined in the context in which they are said or done. You, as a participant observer, are part of that context. For instance, you will usually find that comments made in response to a question must be interpreted differently than volunteered remarks or that certain remarks are meaningless when viewed apart from the questions that elicited them. Further, recording and reflecting upon your own actions will help you revise your field tactics or develop new ones.

RECORD WHAT YOU DO NOT UNDERSTAND

Participant observers often hear phrases and conversations that they do not fully understand. Since these comments are difficult to recall precisely, there is a tendency to omit them from the notes. However, even the most incomprehensible remarks may become understandable when viewed in light of later conversations or events. In Taylor's institutional study attendants made frequent reference to *bung hole,* which sometimes sounded like *bungle.* Although he didn't understand the word, Taylor included these references in the field notes. It was only later that he learned that *bung holing* was an institutional term for anal intercourse.

There are also remarks the observer overhears that seem inappropriate or out of context. Such data should be recorded as is. Do not try to reconstruct what you heard to make it read better.

BOUNDARIES OF A STUDY

As noted in the last chapter, the research design is flexible in participant observation and other qualitative research. That is, qualitative researchers usually start modestly; they enter the field, understand a single setting, and then decide upon other settings to study.

Sooner or later, you will have to set some boundaries for your research in terms of the number and types of settings studied. The selection of additional settings or informants will hinge on what you have learned and your own research interests. In the institutional study, Taylor could have pursued a large number of different lines of investigation, ranging from attendant training programs to other types of organizations. Because he had developed a strong substantive interest in total institutions, however, he proceeded to study attendants and officials at other institutions for people labeled retarded.

It is difficult to set limits on a study. There are always more people and places to study. However, many excellent studies have been conducted that were based on a single setting, whether a classroom, a hospital ward, or a street corner. What is important is that, no matter how many settings you study, you develop an understanding of something that was not understood before.

Many observers prefer to take a break from fieldwork after they have spent some time in a setting. Doing this will allow you time to clear your mind, review and analyze your data, set priorities, develop field strategies and tactics, and decide whether to move on to other areas or settings. A respite from the intensive observation the research requires will also give you a second breath and the endurance needed to continue the study. When you take a break from the field, it will usually be helpful to write an analytic memo (see Chapter 6) summarizing what you have learned to date and outlining possible courses of future data collection.

LEAVING THE FIELD

Participant observers almost never reach a point when they feel that their studies are complete. There is always one more person to interview, one more loose end to tie up, one more hunch to check out, or one more area to pursue. Yet most field researchers arrive at a stage when the long hours spent in the field yield diminishing returns. Glaser and Strauss (1967) use the phrase *theoretical saturation* to refer to the point in field research at which the data become repetitive and no major new insights are gained. This is the time to leave the field.

Field studies last anywhere from a few months to well over a year. In fact, Bogdan's study of door-to-door salespersons lasted only three weeks. However, he observed daily and focused on a narrow aspect of the sales training program. In the institutional study, Taylor made weekly or biweekly visits to a single ward for approximately one year. During the last two months he learned relatively few new things about attendants and institutional life, although he was able to round out his understanding of the setting and confirm many hunches and working hypotheses. After completing his research at this institution, Taylor spent the next couple of years focusing on other institutions.

In most instances researchers should spend at least several months in a setting regardless of the frequency of their visits. It is common for field researchers to develop a deeper understanding of a setting and to reject or revise working hypotheses after the first several months. One often stumbles across some insight that ties everything together only after a prolonged period of time in the field. Sometimes it takes quite a while for informants to let down their guard around the observer.

A common way of leaving the field is "easing out" (Junker 1960) or "drifting off" (Glaser and Strauss 1967), that is, gradually cutting down on the frequency of visits and letting people know that the research is coming to an end. It is a good idea not to cut off contacts with informants too abruptly, although this is easy to do. Miller and Humphreys (1980) point out that there are sound reasons for concluding the research on good terms with informants and leaving the door open to future contacts. Thus they have been able to study people over a long period of time, learning about changes in people's lives and their definitions of themselves. On a more human level, Miller and Humphreys have been able to assess the impact of the research on informants by sending out copies of publications and maintaining phone and mail contact.

Leaving the field can be a difficult time personally for participant observers (Shaffir and Stebbins 1991; Snow 1980; Taylor 1991). It may mean breaking attachments and sometimes even offending those one has studied, leaving them feeling betrayed and used (Maines et al. 1980). Perhaps for this reason, many observers end up staying in the field longer than they need to for the purposes of the research (Wax 1971).

It is not uncommon for participant observers to maintain contact with informants after they have concluded their studies. When you become intimately involved with people through this kind of research, you can find it difficult, even undesirable, to sever your personal relationships with them. Even though Taylor has finished conducting intensive and frequent observations of the Duke family, he continues to remain in touch with them, as much for personal reasons as anything else.

In those relatively rare instances in which informants actually read a book or article based on studies of them, they may develop deep resentments. After the publication of Whyte's *Street Corner Society*, for example, Whyte's key informant, Doc, apparently become estranged from him and eventually cut off all contact. Although Whyte is at a loss to understand why Doc may have felt alienated from him, Richardson (1992) speculates that Doc resented the fact that he did not share in the "fame" and "fortune" Whyte achieved by publishing this classic study.

Ellis (1995a) reflects on the emotional and ethical dilemmas encountered when she returned to Fishneck, a small isolated fishing village on which she had published a qualitative study several years earlier. Like many successful participant observers, Ellis came to be accepted by the Fisher Folk to the point where most had forgotten that she had been conducting a study on their community. After her realist ethnographic book on the Fisher Folk had been published (Ellis 1986), a sociologist with ties to the community made a point of showing members what they interpreted as unflattering accounts of their lives and lifestyles. Ellis describes her dismay when confronted by some of the Fisher Folk regarding her description of such intimate details of their lives as their personal hygiene and sexual experiences. Reflecting on the hurt inadvertently caused by her study, Ellis considers how she will conduct research differently in the future by regarding her informants as a potential audience and reading her texts through their eyes.

As in the case of other aspects of participant observation and qualitative research generally, leaving the field is seldom a cut-and-dried process. It involves reflection, negotiation, and sometimes soul-searching.

TRIANGULATION

In the literature on participant observation, the term *triangulation* refers to the combination of methods or sources of data in a single study (Denzin 1978; Patton 1980). Although field notes based on first-hand experience in a setting provide the key data in participant observation, other methods and approaches can and should be used in conjunction with fieldwork. Triangulation is often thought of as a way of checking out insights gleaned from different informants or different sources of data. By drawing on other types and sources of data, observers also gain a deeper and clearer understanding of the setting and people being studied.

Practically all participant observers conduct interviews and analyze written documents during or at the conclusion of their field research. Especially toward the end of the research, after the observer has established relationships with people and has gained insider knowledge, open-ended interviews with informants can be relatively focused and specific. Altheide (1980) reports that as he was about to leave the field, he conducted aggressive interviews, probing areas that were too sensitive to explore earlier in the research. Of course, you can also interview new people toward the end of the study to obtain background information relevant to the research or to check out different people's perspectives.

Written documents such as official reports, memos, correspondence, contracts, salary schedules, files, evaluation forms, and diaries provide a potentially important source of data. As emphasized in later chapters, these documents should be examined not as objective data, but rather to lend insight into organizational processes and the perspectives of the people who write and use them as well as to alert the researcher to fruitful lines of inquiry. Since written documents are sometimes regarded as private or sensitive, it is usually wise to wait until you have been in the field for a while before asking to see them.

Researchers can also analyze historical and public documents to gain a broader perspective on a setting. Newspapers, organizational archives, and local historical societies may be valuable repositories of information. In the training program for the hard-core unemployed, Bogdan analyzed these kinds of data in great depth in his research. He not only reviewed materials relevant to the formation of that particular program, but also researched materials on the local and national history of poverty programs. Through an historical perspective, researchers can view a setting in the context of its past and in relation to other settings.

Another form of triangulation is team research: two or more field workers studying the same or similar settings (see Becker et al. 1961, 1968; Bogdan et al. 1974; Geer et al. 1966; Strauss et al. 1964; Taylor, Bogdan, and Lutfiyya 1995). In most team research, the basic techniques of participant observation remain the same, with the exception that field tactics and areas of inquiry are developed in collaboration with others.

Jack Douglas (1976) makes a convincing case in favor of team research as an alternative to the traditional "Lone Ranger" approach in fieldwork. As Douglas notes, the research team can develop an in-depth understanding typical of participant observation while grasping the broader picture by studying different settings or different people within the same setting. Team research also permits a high degree of flexibility in research strategies and tactics. Since researchers differ in social skills and ability to relate to different people, they can play different roles in the field and study different perspectives. For example, in team research, one observer can be aggressive while another is passive within a setting; male and female researchers will be viewed and reacted to differently and hence can pursue different areas of study.

As in many cooperative endeavors, it is a good idea to establish clear ground rules regarding each person's responsibilities and to be sure people can work together prior to entering into team research. Haas and Shaffir (1980, 250) report how personal pressures and professional competition led to the destruction of a three-member research team: "Differences of opinion about research roles, methods of collecting and analyzing data, and the publication and authorship of findings created strains among the researchers and threatened the veneer of collegiality."

Team research also raises the danger of a "hired hand" relationship between a research director, often a senior professor, and research assistants, usually graduate students, in which field workers are reduced to the status of data collectors who have no say in research design and analysis and, therefore, no stake in the research (Roth 1966). People treated as hired hands can be expected to fudge data or otherwise subvert the research. The only way to avoid a hired hand mentality, as Roth so persuasively argues, is for each researcher to be actively involved in the process of formulating the research questions, deciding on field strategies, and making sense of the data.

ETHICS IN THE FIELD

In the last chapter we discussed the ethical issues raised by covert research. The choice between overt as opposed to covert research is only one of of the many difficult ethical dilemmas in field research. As a research method that involves you in people's day-to-day lives, participant observation reveals both the best and the worst of others and very often places you in unresolvable morally and ethically problematic situations.

Getting into a setting usually involves some sort of bargain—explicit or implicit assurances that you will not violate informants' privacy or confidentiality, expose them to harm, or interfere in their activities. Once you are in the field, you try to establish rapport with informants, to gain a certain level of trust and openness, and to be accepted as a nonjudgmental and nonthreatening person. So what do you do when informants engage in acts you consider distasteful, illegal, or immoral?

Published field studies are filled with reports of researchers having witnessed a broad range of illegal and, more important, immoral acts. Thus Van Maanen (1982, 1983) observed police brutality firsthand. Johnson (1975) observed numerous illegal acts committed by caseworkers in his study of social service agencies. Humphreys (1975), whose research has become synonymous with ethical controversy in many commentators' eyes, was accused of being an accomplice to over 200 acts of fellatio.[4]

In the institutional study, Taylor (1987a, b) regularly observed acts of beating, brutality, and abuse of residents by attendants. Complicating the situation, how attendants define and account for abuse was a major focus of the study.

The literature on research ethics generally supports a noninterventionist position in fieldwork. Most researchers owe their loyalty to the pursuit of research goals or to their informants. Any involvement that would interfere with their research or their commitments to informants is to be avoided. We know one observer who, while studying a juvenile gang, witnessed the brutal beating of a young girl by a gang member. The researcher admitted that he had difficulty sleeping that night, but argued, "What could I do? I was just an observer. It wasn't my place to intervene."

After observing illegal behavior, Humphreys, Johnson, and Van Maanen all state that they would go to jail before they would violate the confidentiality of informants. Van Maanen went so far as to refuse to turn over subpoenaed materials in a case of alleged police brutality on the dubious legal grounds of research confidentiality.[5] Similar claims were made by Brajuha, who faced jail when he refused to turn over his field notes from a study of a restaurant when the notes were subpoenaed during an arson investigation (see Brajuha and Hallowell 1986).

Yet researchers are not absolved of moral and ethical responsibility for their actions or inactions merely because they are conducting research. To act or fail to act *is* to make an ethical and political choice. It is to say that research goals and attachments to informants outweigh other considerations.

The field researcher is also faced with the possibility that his or her presence may encourage people to engage in immoral or illegal activities. Van Maanen strongly suspected that police officers were showing off for his benefit when they beat one suspect. In Taylor's institutional study, attendants frequently teased residents or forced them to do certain things such as swallowing burning cigarettes to amuse themselves and the observer. Even when observers do not provoke certain behavior, a strong case can be made that to do nothing, to stand by passively, is to condone behavior and hence perpetuate it.

Participant observers are not unlike reporters who wittingly or unwittingly create news events through their presence. An incident involving two camera operators created an uproar in television circles. The camera operators passively filmed a man as he covered himself with flammable liquid and set himself on fire, even though they could have stopped him easily. In fact, it was apparent that the man staged the incident for the cameras. In a television interview shortly afterward, one of the camera operators awkwardly attempted to account for his and his colleague's role in the incident: "It's my job to report what happened." Of course, this is the same rationale used by fieldworkers to justify nonintervention. The pursuit of the good story, like the pursuit of the good study, it is claimed, excuses otherwise amoral or immoral actions.

So we return to the question: What do you do when you observe people engaging in immoral acts? What do you do when your informants, the people on whom you depend for information and with whom you have worked hard to establish rapport, harm other people? There is no simple or correct answer to this question. The institutional study illustrates this quite well.

In that study, Taylor could have intervened directly or reported the attendants to their supervisors when residents were mistreated. That he chose not to do so did not reflect any commitment to uphold the research bargain or to protect the interests of informants. As in most fieldwork, the research bargain was struck with institutional gatekeepers—the administrators. Although Taylor suggested to attendants that he could be trusted with information, he did not make any formal guarantees to that effect. Further, although the research literature presents informants' interests as unitary, people in the setting, and perhaps in most settings, had competing interests. Thus the administrators, attendants, and residents each had different interests. Whereas it is possible to take the position that a researcher would not have the right to harm attendants by violating their confidentiality, it could also be argued that residents' interests would be harmed by this cloak of secrecy. Rather, the decision not to do anything in the setting at the time reflected Taylor's own uncertainty about how to deal with the situation and his estimation of the effect of intervention. It would not have done much good.

As Taylor spent time in the setting, he learned that attendants used a number of evasion strategies to conceal their activities from supervisors and outsiders. For example, they placed a resident—a so-called watchdog—by the door to warn of the arrival of visitors, and they were careful not to leave marks when they hit or tied residents. If Taylor had attempted to intervene in their actions or had even expressed outward disapproval, the attendants simply would have treated him as an outsider, closing off opportunities for truly understanding the setting.

An event that occurred toward the conclusion of the research also illustrated the futility of reporting abusive attendants to administrators or others. As a result of a parent's complaint, the state police placed an undercover agent at the institution to pose as an attendant and uncover abuse. The scam resulted in the arrests of 24 attendants on abuse charges. All of the 24 attendants were suspended amid proclamations by the director of the institution that "There are a few rotten apples in every barrel." Yet not one of these was an attendant in the study although each of these routinely abused residents. Eventually the 24 attendants were cleared of abuse charges on the basis of insufficient evidence and reinstated in their jobs. Any attempt by Taylor to blow the whistle on attendants might have met the same fate.

None of this should be taken as a justification for turning your back on the suffering of fellow human beings. To the contrary, we believe that researchers have a strong moral obligation to act on the basis of what they observe, even though the choices in the specific situation may be severely limited. Over the course of the institutional study, Taylor came to see abuse and dehumanization as being rooted in the nature of total institutions (Goffman 1961; Taylor 1977; Taylor and Bogdan 1980). Attendant abuse was rampant at the institution. However, the attendants were not sadistic or brutal individuals otherwise. They were not so much bad people as they were good people (or at least people as good as most of us) in a bad place. In a real sense they were dehumanized by the institution just as the residents were. Further, although the attendants might be condemned for blatant physical abuse, professionals at the institution sanctioned and prescribed control measures, such as drugging residents into oblivion and placing them in straitjackets, that were equally abusive and dehumanizing. Attendants are often scapegoats for an abusive system. Little would be served by scapegoating them further.

What you learn through your research and what you do with your findings may at least partially absolve you from the moral responsibility for standing by as people are harmed. It is doubtful whether publishing findings in professional journals can justify participating in immoral actions. However, you can use your findings to try to change the circumstances that lead to abuse.

There is a long tradition of qualitative researchers engaging in social action as a result of their studies. Becker was an early leader in the National Organization for the Reform of Marijuana Laws; Goffman was a founder of the Committee to End Involuntary Institutionalization; Humphreys has been active in the gay rights movement. Less than two years after completing his initial study, Taylor led a half dozen television and newspaper reporters through the institution in a widely publicized exposé. Subsequently he has been involved in exposés in many other states and has served as an expert in deinstitutionalization law suits because of his knowledge of institutional conditions and abuse.

Not all researchers will find themselves in the difficult moral and ethical situations we describe in this section. We suspect, though, that these situations occur more commonly than reported by researchers. Before you get too involved in a study, too close to informants, and too sympathetic to their perspectives, it is wise to know where you will draw the line.

As Van Maanen (1983) notes, there are no easy stances to be taken by the observer in field situations. Clearly, there are situations in which researchers can and should intervene on behalf of other people. However, people who cannot tolerate some moral ambiguity probably should not do fieldwork or should at least have the good sense to know when to get out of certain situations.

As researchers, we recognize the fact that to withdraw from all morally problematic situations would prevent us from understanding and, indeed, changing many things in the world in which we live. In Van Maanen's (1983, 279) words, "The hope, of course, is that in the end the truth, when it is depicted fully, will help us all out."

The last two chapters dealt with learning about the world firsthand. In the next chapter we turn to a discussion of learning about the world through secondhand accounts—in-depth interviewing.

NOTES

1. An increasing number of field researchers emphasize the importance of understanding your effects on a setting rather than trying to eliminate them altogether (see Emerson 1981). Some researchers also advocate active involvement in the field as a means of revealing social processes that would otherwise remain hidden (Bodemann 1978). Although these points make sense, we still feel that it is essential to "come on slow" in the field until you have developed an understanding of the setting and the people within it.

2. See the *Ethics in the Field* section in this chapter for a discussion of the ethical issues raised by this research.

3. Ryave and Schenkein (1974) have conducted an ethnomethodological study of how people "do walking." As they demonstrate, walking is a practical accomplishment in which people produce and recognize appearances to navigate in public places.

4. Humphreys' research has generally been criticized on the grounds of violating people's privacy and confidentiality. Although the charge of being an accomplice to acts of fellatio seems frivolous today, this demonstrates how researchers place themselves in jeopardy by observing acts others consider illegal or immoral.

5. As Van Maanen (1983, 276–277) points out, there is no legal protection guaranteed to social scientists on the grounds of research confidentiality (also see Nejelski and Lerman 1971). Researchers are not legally bound to report criminal acts, but they are legally obligated to testify and turn over data in court proceedings.

CHAPTER 4

In-Depth Interviewing

IN THE PRECEDING CHAPTERS we described the methodology of participant observation (field research in natural settings). This chapter deals with in-depth qualitative interviewing, a research approach that is related but different in many ways. After a discussion of the types of interviewing and the strengths and limitations of this method, we discuss specific strategies and tactics for qualitative interviewing.

As Benney and Hughes (1970) point out, the interview is the "favored digging tool" of social researchers (see also Kvale 1996). Social scientists rely largely on verbal accounts to learn about social life. When most people hear the term *interviewing*, they think of structured research tools such as attitude surveys, opinion polls, and questionnaires. These interviews are typically administered to a large group of respondents or subjects (Benney and Hughes 1970). People may be asked to rate their feelings along a scale, select the most appropriate answer from among forced-choice responses, or respond to a predetermined set of open-ended questions in their own words. Although these research approaches differ in many respects, they all adopt a standardized format: the researcher has the questions and the research subject has the answers. In fact, in most structured interviewing each person is supposed to be asked identically worded questions to assure comparable findings. The interviewer serves as a cheerful data collector; the role involves getting people to relax enough to answer the predefined series of questions completely.

In stark contrast to structured interviewing, qualitative interviewing is flexible and dynamic. Qualitative interviewing has been referred to as nondirective, unstructured, nonstandardized, and open-ended interviewing. We use the phrase *in-depth interviewing* to refer to this qualitative research method. By in-depth qualitative interviewing, we mean repeated face-to-face encounters between the researcher and informants directed toward understanding informants' perspectives on their lives, experiences, or situations as expressed in their own words. The in-depth interview is modeled after a conversation between equals rather than a formal question-and-answer exchange. Far from being an impersonal data collector, the interviewer, and not an interview schedule or protocol, is the research tool. The role entails not merely obtaining answers but learning what questions to ask and how to ask them. As a qualitative research approach, in-depth interviewing has much in common with participant observation. Like observers, interviewers "come on slow" initially. They try to establish rapport with informants, ask nondirective questions early in the research, and learn what is important to informants before focusing the research interests.

The primary difference between participant observation and in-depth interviewing lies in the settings and situations in which the research takes place. Whereas participant observers conduct their studies in natural field situations, interviewers conduct theirs in situations specifically arranged for the purposes of the research. The participant observer gains firsthand knowledge of what people say and do in their everyday lives. The interviewer relies extensively on verbal accounts of how people act and what they feel.

TYPES OF INTERVIEW STUDIES

Three closely related types of qualitative interview studies can be distinguished. The first is the life history or sociological autobiography.[1] In the life history, the researcher attempts to capture the salient experiences in a person's life and that person's definitions of those experiences. The life history presents people's views on their lives in their own words, much the same as a common autobiography. E. W. Burgess (in Shaw 1966) explains the importance of life histories:

> In the life history is revealed as in no other way the inner life of the person, his moral struggles, his successes and failures in securing his destiny in a world too often at variance with his hopes and ideals. (p. 4)

Becker (1966) notes that life histories provide a touchstone by which to evaluate theories of social life.

What distinguishes the life history from popular autobiographies is that the researcher actively solicits the person's experiences and views and constructs the life history as a final product. Becker (1966) describes the role of the researcher in sociological life histories:

> The sociologist who gathers a life history takes steps to ensure that it covers everything we want to know, that no important fact or event is slighted, that what purports to be factual squares with available evidence and that the subject's interpretations are honestly given. The sociologist keeps the subject oriented to the questions sociology is interested in, asks him about events that require amplification, tries to make the story told jibe with matters of official record and with material furnished by others familiar with the person, event, or place being described. He keeps the game honest for us. (p. vi)

The life history has a long tradition in the social sciences and figures prominently in the work of the Chicago school in the 1920s, 1930s, and 1940s (Shaw 1931, 1966; Shaw, McKay, and McDonald 1938; Sutherland 1937; see also Angell 1945; Frazier 1978). Much of the discussion in this chapter is based on the life histories of a transsexual (Bogdan 1974); and two persons labeled mentally retarded (Bogdan and Taylor 1976, 1994).

The second type of in-depth interviewing is directed toward learning about events and activities that cannot be observed directly. In this type of interviewing, the people being interviewed are informants in the truest sense of the word. They act as observers—eyes and ears in the field—for the researcher. The role of such informants is not simply to reveal their own views, but to describe what happened and how others viewed it. Examples of this kind of interviewing include Erikson's (1976) study of a town's reaction to a natural disaster in West Virginia and Domhoff's (1975) study of power elites. Erikson's research could not have been conducted unless he happened to stumble across a natural disaster—an unlikely occurrence—whereas Domhoff probably would not have been able to gain access to intimate places frequented by the powerful.

study large #'s of people in short time (handwritten annotation)

The final type of qualitative interviewing is intended to yield a picture of a range of settings, situations, or people. Interviewing is used to study a relatively large number of people in a relatively short period of time compared to what would be required in participant observation research. For instance, several in-depth interviews with 20 teachers could probably be conducted in the same amount of time it would take to conduct a participant observation study of a single classroom. Rubin's (1976) study of working-class families, based on 100 detailed interviews with husbands and wives, and DeVault's (1991) study of mealtime routines in 15 families are good examples of this type of interviewing.

Although researchers select in-depth interviewing for different purposes, the basic interviewing techniques are similar for these different types of studies. In each case, interviewers try to establish rapport with informants through repeated contacts over time and to develop a detailed understanding of their experiences and perspectives. This chapter describes approaches and strategies for in-depth interviewing as defined here. However, many of the points in the following pages can be applied to any interviewing approach.

CHOOSING TO INTERVIEW

Every research approach has its strong points and drawbacks. We tend to agree with Becker and Geer (1957) that participant observation provides a yardstick against which to measure data collected through any other method. That is, no other method can provide the depth of understanding that comes from directly observing people and listening to what they have to say at the scene. Yet participant observation is not practical or even possible in all cases. The observer can hardly go back in time to study past events or force entry into all settings and private situations. The studies conducted by Erikson (1976) and Domhoff (1975) illustrate this point. Further, participant observation requires a commitment of time and effort that is not always warranted by the additional understanding gained as opposed to other methods. Our life histories of people labeled mentally retarded provide a ready example. Although we might take the position that the best way to construct life histories is to follow people around for a lifetime, it would be foolish to suggest this as an alternative to in-depth interviewing.

Thus no method is equally suited for all purposes. The choice of research method should be determined by the research interests, the circumstances of the setting or people to be studied, and practical constraints faced by the researcher. In-depth interviewing seems especially well suited in the following situations.

The research interests are relatively clear and well defined. Although research interests are necessarily broad and open-ended in qualitative research, the clarity and specificity of researchers' interests vary. For instance, one researcher may be generally interested in schools and teachers, whereas another may be interested in how teachers got into the profession. Interviewing is well suited for studies in which researchers have a relatively clear sense of their interests and the kinds of questions they wish to pursue. In the previously cited example, interviewing would be appropriate for studying how teachers entered the profession but less well suited for pursuing a general and unspecified interest in teachers and schools. Your prior direct experiences and reading of other qualitative studies can help you define your research interests.

Settings or people are not otherwise accessible. As noted previously, in-depth interviewing is called for when a researcher wishes to study past events or cannot gain access to a particular type of setting or people.

The researcher has time constraints. Participant observers sometimes "spin their wheels" for weeks—even months—at the beginning of the research. It takes time to locate settings, negotiate access, arrange visits, and get to know informants. Although interviewers can face similar problems, studies based on interviewing usually can be completed in a shorter period of time than those based on participant observation. Whereas the participant observer's time can be taken up with waiting for someone to say or do something, the interviewer usually collects data throughout the period spent with informants. The pressure to produce results in grant-funded studies or to write dissertations can severely limit the length of time the researcher can devote to a study. Interviewing makes the most efficient use of the researcher's limited time. Needless to say, this is not a justification for superficial or shoddy research.

The researcher is interested in understanding a broad range of settings or people. In qualitative research, an "N of 1" can be just as illuminating as a large sample (and very often more so). However, there are instances in which the researcher may want to sacrifice the depth of understanding that comes with focusing intensively on a single setting or person for the breadth that comes with studying a range of places and people.

Interviewing multiple informants lends itself to building general theories about the nature of social phenomena. Analytic induction is one method of constructing theories from qualitative data that requires a sizable number of cases (Robinson 1951; Turner 1953). Through analytic induction, Lindesmith (1968) developed a theory of opiate addiction based on interviews with a large number of opiate users.

It is also important to point out the limitations of interviewing. First, people say and do different things in different situations. Since the interview is a particular kind of situation, you cannot assume that what a person says during an interview is what that person believes or will say or do in other situations. Deutscher and colleagues (Deutscher 1973; Deutscher, Pestello, and Pestello, 1993) deal head-on with the difference between people's words and deeds. Deutscher, Pestello, and Pestello are especially critical of attitude and public opinion research in which it is assumed that people have fixed attitudes that determine what they will do in any given situation.

Deutscher, Pestello, and Pestello cite a study by Richard LaPiere (1934–1935) to illustrate the difference between what people say and what they do. In the early 1930s LaPiere accompanied a Chinese couple to hotels, auto camps, tourist homes, and restaurants across the United States. Out of 251 establishments, only 1 refused to accommodate the couple. Six months later, LaPiere sent a questionnaire to each of the establishments asking them if they would accept members of the Chinese race as guests. Of 128 establishments that replied, only 1 indicated that it would accept Chinese people! As Deutscher and his colleagues explain, the artificiality of the questionnaire and tightly controlled interview produces unreal responses.

Second, if researchers do not directly observe people in their everyday lives, they will be deprived of the context necessary to understand many of the perspectives in which they are interested. In their comparison of participant observation and interviewing, Becker and Geer (1957) list a number of shortcomings of interviews that relate to this general point: interviewers are likely to misunderstand informants' language since they do not have opportunities to study it in common usage; informants are unwilling or unable to articulate many important things, and only by observing these people in their daily lives can researchers learn about these things; interviewers have to make assumptions about things that could have been observed, and some of the assumptions will be incorrect.

Despite these limitations, few if any researchers would argue for abandoning interviewing as a basic approach for studying social life. Becker and Geer (1957, 32) state that interviewers can benefit from an awareness of these limitations and "perhaps improve their batting average by taking account of them."

It is precisely because of these limitations that we emphasize the importance of in-depth interviewing, getting to know people well enough to understand what they mean, and creating an atmosphere in which they are likely to talk freely. In addition, we always recommend that interviewers try to spend time with people "on their own turf" as they go about their day-to-day lives.

SELECTING INFORMANTS

Like participant observation, qualitative interviewing calls for a flexible research design. Neither the number nor the type of informants needs to be specified beforehand. The researcher starts out with a general idea of which people to interview and how to find them, but is willing to change course after the initial interviews.

Those new to qualitative research usually want to know exactly how many people they need to interview to complete a study. This is a difficult if not impossible question to answer prior to conducting some research. As Kvale (1996) points out:

> To the common question, "How many interview subjects do I need?" the answer is simply, "Interview as many subjects as necessary to find out what you need to know." (p. 101)

The size of the sample in an interviewing study is something that should be determined toward the end of the research and not at the beginning. In general, however, you will find that there is an inverse relationship between the number of informants and the depth to which you interview each. The greater the number of interviews with each informant, the fewer informants you will need to have enough data to write a research article, dissertation, or monograph.

The strategy of theoretical sampling can be used as a guide for selecting people to interview (Glaser and Strauss 1967). In theoretical sampling, the actual number of cases studied is relatively unimportant. What is important is the potential of each case to aid the researcher in developing theoretical insights into the area of social life being studied. After completing interviews with several informants, you consciously vary the type of people interviewed until you have uncovered a broad range of perspectives held by the people in whom you are interested. You would have an idea that you had reached this point when interviews with additional people yield no genuinely new insights.

Informants can be found in a number of ways. As discussed in the chapter on pre-fieldwork in participant observation, one of the easiest ways to build a pool of informants is *snowballing*—getting to know some informants and having them introduce you to others.

A potential drawback of the snowball technique is that it can limit the diversity of your informants. Therefore you need to be prepared to use a range of different approaches to identifying people. You can locate potential informants through the same sources the participant observer uses to gain access to private settings: checking with friends, relatives, and personal contacts; involving yourself with the community of people you want to study; approaching organizations and agencies; advertising in media sources; and announcements through the Internet. In the study of families of young children with which Taylor was involved, the researchers used a range of techniques to locate the families, including checking birth records; contacting day care centers, neighborhood centers, preschools, churches, and social clubs; distributing handouts at local stores; and, in some neighborhoods, conducting a door-to-door survey (the researchers had identification cards that indicated their affiliation with a university research project).

Life histories are written on the basis of in-depth interviews with one person or a small handful of people. Although all people have one good story to tell—their own—some people have better stories and make better research partners for the purpose of constructing a life history. Obviously, it is essential that a person have the time to devote to the interviewing. Another important consideration is people's willingness and ability to talk about experiences and articulate feelings. People simply do not have equal ability to provide detailed accounts of what they have been through and what they feel about it. Spradley (1979) also argues that strangers make better informants than friends, relatives, clients, and others with whom one has a prior relationship, although this will not always be the case.

In constructing life histories, the researcher looks for a particular type of person who has had certain experiences. For example, life histories have been written on the experiences of juvenile delinquents (Shaw 1931, 1966; Shaw, McKay, and McDonald 1938), a professional fence (Klockars 1974, 1977), a transsexual (Bogdan 1974), a professional thief (Sutherland 1937), and persons labeled mentally retarded (Bogdan and Taylor 1976, 1994). Although you might be interested in studying a certain type of person, keep in mind that people's past experiences may not have had an impact on their lives and current perspectives. What is important to you may not be important to a potential informant. Practically all youth engage in activities that someone could define as juvenile delinquency. Yet, for most youth, participation in these activities has little to do with how they view themselves. Spradley (1979) suggests that one of the requirements for good informants is "thorough enculturation"; that is, knowing a culture (or subculture, group, or organization) so well that they no longer think about it.

There are no easy steps to take to find a good informant for a life history. In this kind of research, informants are seldom *found;* rather, they emerge in the course of one's everyday activities. You just happen to stumble across someone who has an important story to tell and wants to tell it. Of course, the more involved you are in different social circles, the more likely you are to establish the contacts and reputation necessary to find a good informant.

We met Ed Murphy and Pattie Burt (the subjects of life histories of people labeled mentally retarded) through our involvement with local community groups. Ed was recommended to us as a guest speaker for a course one of us was teaching. Ed was articulate in his presentation of his experience of living at an institution and being labeled mentally retarded. In fact, the word *retarded* lost meaning as he spoke. We kept in touch with Ed after his talk at the course, running into him at a local association. About two years after we first met him, we approached him with the idea of working on his life history.

One of us met Pattie when she was living at a local institution. When she told him that she wanted desperately to leave the institution, he helped her get out. For a brief period of time, she lived with the other author and his family. We saw Pattie frequently over the next 15 months, when she was living in a series of different homes. We began interviewing her shortly after she moved to her own apartment in a nearby town.

Bogdan's life history of Jane Fry, a transsexual, came about in a similar manner. Bogdan met her when she spoke to a class taught by a colleague. Her presentation of life as a transsexual was striking in the insight it provided and the vividness of her description of her experiences. Some time after that, the author ran into Jane again at a local crisis intervention center at which she was volunteering. Through that meeting and several other encounters, he got to know her well enough to ask her about writing her life history.

APPROACHING INFORMANTS

In most in-depth interviewing, you will not know how many interviews to conduct with informants until you actually begin speaking with them. Some people will warm up only gradually; others will have a lot to say and you will want to spend quite a few sessions with them. Interviewing projects usually take anywhere from several sessions to over 25 sessions—and 50 to 100 hours of interviewing—for life histories.

Since you cannot always tell beforehand exactly how many interviews you will want to conduct, it is advisable to "come on slow" with informants initially. Tell them that you would like to set up an interview or two with them, but do not ask for a commitment to spend a lot of time being interviewed. After you have conducted a couple of interviews, you can discuss your plans more directly. We met with Ed Murphy and Jane Fry several times before we raised the possibility of writing their life histories. Interestingly enough, both had thought about writing their autobiographies previously (many people have probably thought about this at some point in their lives). Jane had even attempted to write her life history several years earlier, only to have abandoned the project after writing a few pages. Ed and Jane were both enthusiastic about the project by the end of our first serious discussions with them.

It is usually not too difficult to line up people for initial interviews, as long as they can fit you into their schedules. Most people are willing to talk about themselves. In fact, people are often honored by the prospect of being interviewed for a research project. In the family study, many parents felt honored that they were selected to participate in a university study of child rearing. Of course, it is very flattering to be asked to tell your life story. When approaching potential informants, we tell them that it seems they have had some interesting experiences or have something important to say and that we would like to sit down with them and talk about it some time. If they seem receptive to the idea, we schedule the first meeting.

If, after a couple of sessions, you decide that you will want to interview an individual for a number of sessions over time, you should try to clarify any issues that might be on the individual's mind and any possible misunderstandings. Life histories, in particular, are a collaborative endeavor. The tone you want to establish is that of a partnership rather than a researcher-subject relationship (Klockars 1977). The following issues are those that are most easily misunderstood and hence the most important to raise.

1. *Your motives and intentions.* Many people will wonder what you hope to get out of the project. They may even fear that the final product will be used to their disadvantage. If you are a social scientist, your motivation will probably have something to do with contributing knowledge to your field and professional advancement. You can discuss this with informants. Although people may not grasp your precise research interests, most will be able to understand educational and academic goals.

You probably will not be clear on whether and where the results of your study will be published. However, you should explain that you will try to have the study published in a book or journal or, in the case of students, as a dissertation or thesis. In very few instances are studies of this kind published commercially. This should be explained also. Finally, although you would not be willing to spend your time on the project unless you thought that something would come of it, you should alert informants to potential difficulties in having the study published.

2. *Anonymity.* It is usually wise to use pseudonyms for people and places in written studies. There are few legitimate research interests served by publishing people's names. The risks are substantial: embarrassment of the informant or others, legal problems, self-aggrandizement, and concealment of important details and information. Although people might want to have their names published for a variety of reasons, you should resist doing so and explain this to informants. In Jane Fry's life history, she wanted very much to see her name in print, and Bogdan initially agreed to this. However, as the interviewing progressed, it soon became apparent that this would create numerous problems and both parties agreed to the use of pseudonyms.

3. *Final say.* One way to gain informants' trust is to tell them that they will have the opportunity to read and comment on drafts of any books or articles prior to publication. Some researchers even guarantee veto power to informants over what is published. Although we are reluctant to give infor-

mants final say over the content of written materials, it strengthens the researcher's relationships with informants and the quality of the study to have informants review draft manuscripts.

4. *Money.* Money can corrupt the relationship between the interviewer and informant, turning it into an employer-employee relationship rather than a research partnership. It also raises the specter of encouraging the informant to fabricate a good story to get some money. Yet many large-scale research projects pay informants for interviews.[2] The family study paid parents nominal fees for participating in interviews. This clearly served as an inducement for some parents to stay involved in the study when they wanted to drop out. However, if people have to be paid to be interviewed, it is debatable whether they will talk candidly about anything of real importance in their lives.

Splitting book royalties with informants is a different matter than paying them for interviews. This creates a spirit of partnership in the research endeavor. Since informants usually do not have their names appear in print or receive professional credit, it is reasonable to give them a share of the proceeds from a book, although most academic books do not earn sizable royalties.

Bogdan worked out Jane Fry's royalties for *Being Different* with a lawyer. Like many subjects of life histories, she was poor at the time and received public assistance. To make sure that the royalty payments did not affect her benefits, the lawyer helped set up a special trust fund for her.

5. *Logistics.* Finally, you will have to settle on a rough schedule and a place to meet. The frequency and length of the interviews will depend on your respective schedules. You will usually need at least an hour for an interview. Anything less is too short to explore many topics. In order to preserve the flow of interviews, you should try to meet at frequent intervals. It is too difficult to pick up where you left off when you are not interviewing regularly. The length of the overall project will depend on how freely the interviewee speaks and what you hope to cover. Life histories usually take at least a few months to complete. Klockars' (1974) life history of a professional fence took 15 months of weekly or biweekly meetings (Klockars 1977). You should try to find a private place where you can talk without interruption and where the informant will feel relaxed. Many people feel most comfortable in their own homes and offices. However, in many people's homes it is difficult to talk privately. In the large-scale family study, some parents tried to listen in surreptitiously on their spouses' interviews, an obvious inhibiting factor. In our research with Ed Murphy and Jane Fry, we conducted the interviews in our private offices, located in a converted house, after working hours. We interviewed Pattie Burt at her own apartment. Nothing prevents the researcher from setting up interviews in a public restaurant or bar as long as privacy is assured.

UNDERSTANDING THE INTERVIEW IN CONTEXT

The interview is form of social interaction. It involves a face-to-face encounter between two—and sometimes more—persons, each of whom is sizing up the other and constructing the meanings of the other's words, expressions, and gestures. An understanding of the interview as a form of social interaction can help you to be a better interviewer and to make sense out of the data you collect.

In social interaction, we all attempt to manage the impressions others have of us (Goffman 1967) and we say different things depending upon the person with whom we are speaking. What informants say to interviewers will depend on how they view the interviewers and how they think the interviewers view them.

Interviews are subject to the same fabrications, deceptions, exaggerations, and distortions that characterize other conversations between persons. Benney and Hughes (1970, 137) write: "Every conversation has its own balance of revelation and concealment of thoughts and intentions."

Even when informants have come to accept and trust interviewers, what they say cannot be taken at face value as indicative of deeply held beliefs and feelings. In social interaction, meanings are not simply communicated, but constructed. Holstein and Gubrium (1995) point out that, in conventional research, subjects are viewed as "passive vessels of answers." In this view, information and attitudes exist inside of people's heads and can be elicited by asking the right questions in the right way. As Holstein and Gubrium argue, however, knowledge and social meanings are constructed during the interview process.

By virtue of being interviewed, people develop new insights and understandings of their experiences. They may not have thought about or reflected on events in which the interviewer is interested, and even if they have, they interpret things a bit differently each time. Holstein and Gubrium (1995) note that knowledge is always "knowledge-in-the making." From this perspective, informants are not merely reporters of experience, but narrators. They may tell their stories a bit differently each time and may construct the meanings of events and experiences a bit differently.

Much of human experience cannot be put easily into words (DeVault 1990). By asking questions and probing for meanings, interviewers encourage people to articulate things that they have not articulated before. As in other forms of social interaction, interviewers sometimes have to fill in the meanings that people are not able to express themselves. DeVault (1990) writes:

My procedure . . . involves noticing ambiguity and problems of expression in interview data, then drawing on my own experience in an investigation aimed at "filling in" what has been incompletely said. The point is not simply to reproduce my own perspective in my analysis; the clues I garner from this kind of introspection are only a beginning and should lead me back to hear respondents in new ways. (p. 104)

MANAGING THE INTERVIEW SITUATION

The interviewer strives to create an atmosphere in which people feel comfortable talking openly about themselves. In what kinds of situations are people most likely to express their views? In structured interviewing, the interviewer is instructed to act as a disinterested figure; the interview situation is designed to resemble laboratory conditions. Yet, as Deutscher (1973, 150) notes, people seldom express their true feelings and views under these circumstances: "Real expressions of attitude or overt behavior rarely occur under conditions of sterility which are deliberately structured for the interview situation."

In qualitative interviewing, the researcher attempts to construct a situation that resembles those in which people naturally talk to each other about important things. The interview is relaxed and conversational, since this is how people normally interact. The interviewer relates to informants on a personal level. Indeed, the relationship that develops over time between the interviewer and informant is the key to collecting data.

Certainly, there are differences between the interview situation and those in which people normally interact: interviewers sometimes hold back from expressing some of their views; the conversation is understood to be private and confidential; the flow of information is largely, though not exclusively, one-sided; and interviewers communicate a genuine interest in people's views and experiences and usually refrain from disagreeing with them. However, it is only by designing the interview along the lines of everyday conversation that the interviewer can learn about what is important to people. In fact, the interviewer has many parallels in everyday life: the good listener, the shoulder to cry on, the confidante.

Like participant observation, in-depth interviewing requires an ability to relate to others on their own terms. There is no simple formula for successful interviewing, but the following points set the tone for the atmosphere the interviewer should try to create.

BEING NONJUDGMENTAL

As informants begin to share more experiences and feelings with the interviewer, they let down their public fronts and reveal parts of themselves they ordinarily keep hidden. It is common for people to preface or conclude revelations with disclaimers and comments such as: "You must think I'm crazy for doing that," and, "I can't justify what I did, but . . ."

An important part of interviewing is being nonjudgmental. Benney and Hughes (1970, 140) write: ". . . the interview is an understanding between two parties that, in return for allowing the interviewer to direct their communication, the informant is assured that he will not meet with denial, contradiction, competition, or other harassment." In other words, if you want people to open up about their feelings and views, you have to refrain from making negative judgments about them or putting them down.

The best way to avoid the appearance of judging people is to try to accept them for who and what they are and to keep from judging them in your own mind. When you simply cannot do this, you can state your position, but gently.

During the interview, you should go out of your way to reassure people that they are "all right" in your eyes after they have revealed something personal, embarrassing, or discrediting. Communicate your understanding and empathy: "I know what you mean," "That happened to me once," "I've thought of doing that myself," and "I have a friend who did the same thing."

Of course, if people make negative judgments about things they have done in the past, it is appropriate to agree with them, but without condemning their moral character or who they are as persons.

Letting People Talk

In-depth interviewing sometimes requires a great deal of patience. Informants can talk at length about things in which you have no great interest. Especially during initial interviews, you should try to force yourself not to interrupt an informant even though you are not interested in a topic.

You can usually get a person back on track through subtle gestures, such as refraining from nodding your head or taking notes (Patton 1980), and by gently changing the subject during breaks in the conversation: "I'd like to go back to something you said the other day." Over time, informants usually learn to read your gestures and know enough about your interests to talk about some things and not others.

When people start talking about something important, let the conversation flow. Sympathetic gestures and relevant questions can keep them on a subject.

Paying Attention

It is easy to let your mind drift during extended interviews. This is especially true when you tape-record sessions and do not have to concentrate on remembering every word. Paying attention means communicating a sincere interest in what informants are saying and knowing when and how to probe and ask the right questions. As Thomas Cottle (1973b) so clearly expresses it, paying attention also means being open to seeing things in a new and different way:

> If there is a rule about this form of research it might be reduced to something as simple as pay attention. Pay attention to what the person does and says and feels; pay attention to what is evoked by these conversations and perceptions, particularly when one's mind wanders so very far away; and finally, pay attention to the responses of those who might, through one's work, hear these people. Paying attention implies an openness, not any special or metaphysical kind of openness, but merely a watch on oneself, a self-consciousness, a belief that everything one takes in from the outside and experiences within one's own interior is worthy of consideration and essential for understanding and honoring those whom one encounters. (p. 351)

BEING SENSITIVE

Interviewers always have to be attuned to how their words and gestures affect informants. They sometimes have to play dumb—what Kvale (1996, 21) refers to as "deliberate naiveté"—without being insulting. They must be sympathetic, but not patronizing. They have to know when to probe, but stay away from open wounds. They have to be friendly, but not ingratiating. Being sensitive is an attitude researchers must bring to interviewing and, for that matter, to participant observation. Robert Coles (1971b) strikes at the heart of the matter when he writes:

> Somehow we all must learn to know one another. . . . Certainly I ought to say that I myself have been gently and on occasion firmly or sternly reminded how absurd some of my questions have been, how misleading or smug were the assumptions they convey. The fact is that again and again I have seen a poor, a lowly, an illiterate migrant worker wince a little at something I have said or done, smile a little nervously, glare and pout, wonder a little in his eyes about me and my purposes, and through his grimace let me know the disapproval he surely has felt; and yes, the criticism he also feels, the sober thought-out criticism, perhaps not easily put into words . . . (p. 29)

GETTING PEOPLE TO TALK ABOUT WHAT IS IMPORTANT TO THEM

The hallmark of in-depth qualitative interviewing is learning how people construct their realities—how they view, define, and experience the world.

Presumably, researchers have some general questions to ask prior to starting the interviews. Yet they have to be careful not to push their own agendas too early in the interviewing. By asking structured or forced-choice questions initially, the researcher creates a mind-set in informants about the right or wrong things to say that can make it difficult if not impossible to get at how they really see things.

It is during the early interviews that the researcher sets the tone of the relationship with the informant. In these initial interviews, the interviewer should come across as someone who is not quite sure which questions will be most relevant to informants' experiences and who is willing to learn from the informants. Robert Coles (1971b) eloquently describes this frame of reference when he writes:

> My job . . . is to bring alive to the extent I possibly can a number of lives . . . entrusted to a person like me, an outsider, a stranger, a listener, an observer, a doctor, a curious . . . fellow who one mountaineer described as "always coming back and not seeming to know exactly what he wants to hear or know." (p. 39)

The qualitative interviewer has to find ways of getting people to start to talk about their perspectives and experiences without overly structuring the conversation and defining what the interviewee should say. Kvale (1996, 34) explains: "The interviewer leads the subject toward certain themes, but not to certain opinions about these themes."

Unlike the participant observer, the interviewer cannot stand back and wait for people to do something before asking questions. Therefore you will need to find ways to get the conversation started in the beginning. There are different ways to guide initial interviews: descriptive questioning, solicited narratives, the log-interview approach, and personal documents.

DESCRIPTIVE QUESTIONING

Probably the best way to start off interviewing informants is by asking open-ended, descriptive questions. Descriptive questions allow people to tell you about things that are important to them and the meanings that they attach to these things. In practically any interviewing, you can come up with a list of descriptive questions that will enable people to talk about topics in which you are interested without structuring exactly what the responses should be. Spradley (1979; see also McCracken 1988) refers to these as "grand-tour" questions.

The following are examples of good descriptive questions:

- "Everyone has a life story. I wonder if you can tell me a bit about your life?" (Holstein and Gubrium 1995, 60)

- "Can you tell me about . . . ?" (Kvale 1996, 133)
- "If you were to write your autobiography, what would the chapters be?"
- "I'm interested in how people become involved with. . . . Could you tell me about the first time you thought about being a . . . ?"
- "Could you tell about a typical day in your life?"
- "I'd like to know about people who are important to you. Could you start by listing people in your life?"
- "I'd like to know about your job. Would you tell me about the kinds of things you do in your work?"
- "It's been a long time since I was in elementary school. Could you tell me about things you do in school every day?"

In our life histories with people labeled retarded, we started the interviewing by asking the informants to give us chronologies of the major events in their lives. Pattie Burt listed such events as her birth, her placement in various foster homes, her institutionalization, and renting her own apartments. Ed Murphy listed the deaths of his father, mother, and sister, as well as the places where he lived.

In our interviewing with Ed Murphy, we frequently started sessions by having him list events and experiences (sometimes this took an entire session). Since Ed's institutionalization had had a profound effect on his life, we pursued this experience in great depth. For instance, we asked him to outline such things as the wards where he lived at the institution, a typical day on different wards, his friends at the institution, and his work assignments.

As informants mention specific experiences, you can probe for greater detail. It is also a good idea to take note of topics to revisit at a later time.

SOLICITED NARRATIVES

Many of the classic life histories in the social sciences have been based on a combination of in-depth interviews and narratives written by informants themselves. Shaw (1931, 1966), Shaw, McKay, and McDonald (1938), and Sutherland (1937) made extensive use of this approach in their life histories of delinquents and criminals.

Shaw and colleagues used various techniques to construct life histories of delinquents in the 1930s. Shaw (1966) reports that although the group relied heavily on personal interviews, written documents were preferred as a basis for these life histories. In *The Jack Roller,* Shaw (1966) first interviewed Stanley, the subject of the life history, to prepare a detailed chronology of his delinquent acts and experiences. Shaw then returned this chronology to Stanley to use as a guide for writing his own story. Shaw (1966, 23) writes that Stanley was instructed "to give a detailed description of each event, the situation in which it occurred, and his personal reactions to the experience." In other life histories, such as *Brothers in Crime* (1938), the only instruction Shaw and his collaborators gave their informants was that the informants were to give a detailed description of their experiences during childhood and adolescence.

Sutherland was somewhat more directive in soliciting the life history *The Professional Thief* (1937). Although he does not describe his approach in detail, he indicates that the bulk of the life history was written by the thief on questions and topics suggested by the researcher. Sutherland then met with the thief for approximately 7 hours a week for 12 weeks to discuss what the thief had written. The final life history includes the thief's original narrative, the interview material, minor passages written by Sutherland for editorial reasons, and footnotes based on a broad range of sources including interviews with other thieves and detectives.

In *Being Different*, Bogdan asked Jane Fry to write a detailed chronology of her life prior to starting the interviews. He used this chronology as a basis for his interviewing with her. Toward the end of the interviewing, he and Jane went over the chronology point by point to pick up any forgotten items.

Not all people are able or willing to write about their experiences. However, even sketchy outlines and chronologies can be used to guide openended, in-depth interviews.

THE LOG-INTERVIEW APPROACH

In the log-interview approach, informants keep a running record of their activities for a specified period of time and this is used to provide a basis for in-depth interviews. Zimmerman and Wieder (1977), who refer to this as the "diary-interview method," have described specific procedures associated with this approach.

In a study of counterculture life styles, Zimmerman and Wieder asked informants to maintain an annotated chronological log of their activities. Informants were instructed to record activities in as much detail as they could, to make entries at least daily, and to address a standard set of questions regarding each activity: Who? What? When? Where? How? Since Zimmerman and Wieder were interested in sexual activities and drug use, they instructed informants to describe these activities specifically.

Zimmerman and Wieder had two researchers review each diary and prepare a set of questions and probes to ask informants based on the narrative. They report that for every 5 to 10 pages of diary entries, the researchers generated 100 questions that involved 5 hours of interviewing.

Like solicited narratives, the log-interview approach is ill suited for informants who are not adept at recording their activities in writing. As Zimmerman and Wieder point out, daily telephone interviews and tape recording can be used as substitutes for having informants maintain written logs.

PERSONAL DOCUMENTS

Personal documents—people's own diaries, letters, pictures, records, calendars, and memorabilia—can be used to guide interviews without imposing a structure on informants. Most people store old documents and records and are willing to show at least some of these to others. If you have at least a general idea of what experiences you want to cover in the interviews, you can ask informants to see documents relating to these experiences before starting the interviews. Later in the interviewing, these materials can spark memories and help people recall old feelings.

Jane Fry kept old letters and other documents and had actually written autobiographical narratives at critical points in her life. She shared those freely with the researcher. Not only did these documents provide a framework for interviewing, they were eventually incorporated into her life history.

In Taylor's study of the Duke family, he informally interviewed Winnie, the mother, about people and events portrayed in a tattered family photo album she kept. This provided an opportunity to learn about other family members as well as about memorable events in the Duke family's life.

In some interviewing research, the interviewer has a good sense of what is on informants' minds prior to starting the interviews. For example, some researchers turn to interviewing after conducting participant observation; some also use their own experiences to guide their research. Becker's (1963) study of jazz musicians stemmed from his own experience in a band. In our research we had spent a considerable amount of time with some of our informants before we started to interview them formally. We had heard Ed Murphy talk about his life in institutions before the idea of writing his life history ever occurred to us. When researchers have a body of direct experience to build on, they can be somewhat more directive and aggressive in their initial questioning.

THE INTERVIEW GUIDE

In multiple-informant studies, some researchers use an interview guide to make sure key topics are explored with a number of informants (Kvale 1996). The interview guide is not a structured schedule or protocol. Rather, it is a list of general areas to be covered with each informant. In the interview situation the researcher decides how to phrase questions and when to ask them. The interview guide serves solely to remind the interviewer to ask about certain things.

The use of an interview guide presupposes a certain degree of knowledge about the people one intends to study. Thus an interview guide is useful when the researcher has already learned something about informants through fieldwork or preliminary interviews or other direct experience. The interview guide can also be expanded or revised as the researcher conducts additional interviews. As the researcher begins to identify themes in interview data, questions are added to the interview guide so that these areas can be covered with new informants.

An interview guide is especially useful in team research and evaluation or other funded research (Patton 1980). In team research, the guide provides a way of ensuring that all the interviewers are exploring the same general areas with informants. We have used interview guides in a research project that involved short-term, intensive field visits to a number of sites by a half dozen researchers (see Bogdan and Taylor 1990; Taylor 1982). In funded research and qualitative evaluation, the interview guide can be used to give sponsors a sense of what the researcher will actually cover with informants.

Whether or not you use a formal interview guide, it is always a good idea to try to come up with a set of open-ended, descriptive questions prior an interview. We think of these as conversation starters. Some people may not be able to relate to your initial questions ("Tell me about your life.") or may respond with terse or yes-and-no answers. If you have a set of questions in your mind, you can explore different ways of getting people to talk.

PROBING

One of the keys to successful interviewing is knowing when and how to probe. The general strategy of qualitative interviewing can be described as follows: ask open-ended, descriptive questions about general topics; wait for people to talk about meaningful experiences in their lives or what is important from their points of view; probe for details and specific descriptions of their experiences and perspectives. Throughout the interviewing, the researcher follows up on topics that have been raised by asking specific questions, encourages the informant to provide details, and constantly presses for clarification of the informant's words.

Although the tone of qualitative interviewing is conversational, probing distinguishes this kind of interviewing from everyday conversations. In normal conversation, people fill in the gaps in meaning in the other person's words. Most people share commonsense understandings and taken-for-granted meanings and assume that they know what lies behind the other person's words. As an interviewer, of course you use this stock of cultural knowledge to conduct the interview and to make sense out of what a person says. However, to be a good interviewer you must sometimes set aside what you think you know. What the other person means may be very different from what you think he or she means. Just as important, because meanings may be taken for granted, you may not be aware of them yourself. By asking the other person to explain what is meant, you try to make explicit what both of you may know but may take for granted and are ordinarily unable to articulate.

Even seemingly objective words can have different cultural meanings. Deutscher (1973) explains:

> When an American truck driver complains to the waitress at the diner about his "warm" beer and "cold" soup, the "warm" liquid may have a temperature of 50°F, while the "cold" one is 75 degrees. . . . The standard for the same objects may well vary from culture to culture, from nation to nation, from region to region and, for that matter, within any given social unit—between classes, age groups, sexes, or what have you; what is "cold" soup for an adult may be too "hot" to give a child. (p. 191)

Qualitative interviewers have to force themselves to constantly ask informants to clarify and elaborate on what they have said, even at the risk of appearing naive. Spradley (1979) comments that the interviewer has to teach the informants to be good informants by continually encouraging them to provide detailed descriptions of their experiences.

During the interview, you should continue to probe for clarification until you are sure what exactly the informant means. Rephrase what the person said and ask for confirmation; ask the person to provide examples of what he or she means; and tell the person when something is not clear to you. You should also follow up on your informant's remarks until you have a clear picture in your own mind of the people, places, experiences, and feelings in his or her life. Ask specific questions: for example,

- Can you tell me what the place looked like?
- How did you feel then?
- Can you remember what you said then?
- What were you doing at the time?
- Who else was there?
- What happened after that?

The skillful interviewer comes up with questions that will help jar a person's memory. Many past events lie hidden deep within a person's memory and remote from daily life. Try to think up questions that will bring back some of these memories: for example,

- How does your family describe you at that time?
- Do your parents ever tell stories about how you were when you were growing up?

- What kinds of stories do you tell when you get together with your brothers and sisters?

Just as the participant observer can become more aggressive in the later stages of the research, the interviewer's questioning can become more directive as he or she learns about informants and their perspectives. It is not uncommon to find that informants are unwilling or unable to talk about certain things that are obviously important to them. In our interviewing with Ed Murphy, for example, he was reluctant to talk in personal terms about being labeled mentally retarded. Instead, he talked about how the label unfairly stigmatized other mentally retarded people. In order to get Ed to speak about the experience of being labeled retarded, we came up with questions that allowed him to maintain an identity as a normal person: "You're obviously a bright guy, so why do you think you wound up at an institution for the retarded?" "A lot of kids have problems learning; how did you do in school?" There were also times during our interviewing with Ed Murphy when we confronted him with his tendency to avoid certain topics. We tried to impress upon him the importance of talking about these experiences. When he was reluctant to talk about his family, we told him something like the following: "I think it's important to know about your family life. A lot of families don't know how to deal with disabled children. I think you should try to talk about your feelings and experiences." Although Ed continued to be uncomfortable with some topics, he eventually talked about many of those he had avoided.

Like the participant observer, the interviewer also can use what Douglas (1976) calls the *phased-assertion tactic* and other aggressive questioning techniques. The phased-assertion tactic involves acting as if you are already in the know in order to gain more information.

Learning how to probe successfully in qualitative interviewing takes practice at being an active listener and recognizing potentially important themes when they are mentioned. It is not uncommon for novice interviewers to skip from topic to topic and fail to probe for details on and clarification of an informant's comments. Especially if you are new to qualitative interviewing, it is a good idea to have initial interviews transcribed as soon as possible after they are conducted. Review these carefully not only for potential themes but to assess your own skill at probing. An experienced interviewer can also be helpful in pointing out comments that you should have probed in more depth.

CROSS-CHECKS

Although qualitative interviewers try to develop an open and honest relationship with informants, they have to be alert to exaggerations and distortions in their informants' stories. As Douglas (1976) points out, people hide important facts about themselves in everyday life. Anyone may "lie a bit, cheat a bit," to use Deutscher's (1973) words. Further, all people are prone to exaggerating their successes and denying or downplaying their failures.

As emphasized throughout this book, the issue of truth in qualitative research is a complicated one. What the qualitative researcher is interested in is not truth per se, but rather perspectives. Thus the interviewer tries to elicit a more or less honest rendering of how informants actually view themselves and their experiences. Shaw (1966) explains this quite well in his introduction to *The Jack Roller:*

> It should be pointed out, also, that the validity and value of the personal document are not dependent upon its objectivity or veracity. It is not expected that the delinquent will necessarily describe his life-situations objectively. On the contrary, it is desired that his story will reflect his own personal attitudes and interpretations. Thus, rationalizations, fabrications, prejudices, exaggerations are quite as valuable as objective descriptions, provided, of course, that these reactions be properly identified and classified. (pp. 2–3)

After writing these words, Shaw quotes W. I. Thomas' (Thomas and Thomas 1928, 572) famous dictum, "If men[3] define situations as real, they are real in their consequences." In contrast to participant observers, interviewers lack the firsthand knowledge of how people act in their day-to-day lives. This can make it difficult to sort out the difference between purposeful distortions and gross exaggerations on the one hand and genuine perspectives (which are necessarily subjective and biased) on the other.

If you know a person well enough, you can usually tell when he or she is evading a subject or "putting you on." In in-depth interviewing, you spend enough time with people to read between the lines of their remarks and probe for sufficient details to know whether a story is being consciously fabricated. In his discussion of Shaw's *The Natural History of a Delinquent Career,* Ernest Burgess (in Shaw 1931) argues that the validity of a life history depends on the manner in which it was obtained:

> The validity of the statement of attitudes in the life-history seems, in my judgment, to be closely dependent upon the following conditions: (a) a document reported in the words of the person; i.e., a written autobiography or a verbatim record of an oral narrative; (b) a document representing a free, spontaneous, and detailed expression of past experiences, present aspirations, and future plans; (c) a document secured in a favorable situation where the tendencies to deception or prejudice are absent or at a minimum. (p. 240)

The researcher also has the responsibility for imposing cross-checks on the informants' stories. You should examine an informant's statements for consistency between different factual accounts of the same event or experience (Klockars 1977). In the research with Jane Fry, for example, Bogdan checked Jane's story for inconsistencies. Jane frequently skipped from one topic to another. Since she covered the same events several times over the course of the interviews, Bogdan could compare different versions given at different times.

You should also draw on as many different sources of data as possible to check out informants' statements. In the early work of the Chicago school, the researchers regularly compared informants' stories with official records maintained by police and social work agencies. Sutherland (1937) submitted the life history of a professional thief to other professional thieves and detectives to get their views on the veracity of the story. In our research we held our informants' narratives up against accounts by other knowledgeable persons and our own observations and experiences. For example, we had conducted extensive participant observation at the institutions at which Ed Murphy and Pattie Burt had lived. In constructing Jane Fry's life history, Bogdan interviewed others who had been through similar experiences. For instance, he questioned a former Navy officer on the accuracy of Jane's account of life in the Navy. In his conclusion to Jane Fry's life story, Bogdan juxtaposed Jane's accounts of experiences with psychiatric records, although his purpose was less to check out her story than to compare competing ideologies of transsexualism.

Probably the best way to deal with contradictions and internal inconsistencies is to raise the issue directly. Gently confront the person with what you believe: "Maybe you could explain something for me. One time you told me this, but what you said another time doesn't go along with that. I don't get it." Suspected lies and deceptions often turn out to be misunderstandings.

It is also important to point out that inconsistencies in a person's story are not necessarily a source of concern. As Merton and Kendall (1946) have noted, people sometimes hold logically contradictory views. Further, because people are in a constant process of constructing their stock of social knowledge and the meaning of their experiences, they can be expected to say, and believe, different things at different times and in different situations (Holstein and Gubrium 1995).

RELATIONS WITH INFORMANTS

The interviewer-informant relationship is largely one-sided. Through the relationship, the interviewer has the opportunity to conduct a study and thereby to gain the status and rewards that come with receiving a degree or publishing books or articles. It is unclear what, if anything, informants stand to gain from the relationship, other than the satisfaction that someone thinks their lives and views are important. Although informants have few tangible rewards to gain, they are asked to devote considerable time and energy to the endeavor.

Due to the one-sided nature of the relationship, interviewers often (but not always, since some people welcome an interviewer's undivided attention to their lives, experiences, or perspectives) have to work hard at maintaining informants' motivation in the interviewing. The best way to do this is to relate to informants as people and not merely sources of data.

Since informants are expected to open up during interviews—to share private and sometimes intimate aspects of themselves—there has to be some exchange in terms of what interviewers say about themselves. It is probably unwise for interviewers to hold back their feelings completely. Obviously, the interviewer should not express an opinion on every subject that comes up, especially during initial interviews. Somewhere between total disclosure and total detachment lies the happy medium that the interviewer should try to meet. The best advice is to be discreet in the interview but to talk about yourself in other situations. Researchers have to decide for themselves how they will relate to informants as fellow human beings. Our own view is that we should be willing to relate to informants in terms other than interviewer-informant. Interviewers can serve as errand-runners, drivers, baby-sitters, advocates, and—whether or not they intend to—Rogerian therapists (if you are an effective interviewer, you are bound to elicit painful memories and feelings, and you have to be prepared to deal with these). In our life history interviewing, we occasionally had lunch or dinner with our informants. This contact strengthened our relationship with them, in addition to enabling us to talk with them informally and learn about their everyday lives. In the cases of Jane Fry, a transsexual, and Ed Murphy, a man labeled retarded with minor physical disabilities, we learned a lot by just observing how people reacted to them and how they reacted in turn.

In many interviewing projects, the informant is one of society's underdogs (Becker 1966), powerless by virtue of his or her economic or social status. Researchers, in contrast, are likely to be secure in their status at universities. For this reason, researchers are in a good position to help informants lobby for their rights. When Jane Fry was discriminated against by a community college, Bogdan found a lawyer for her and put her in touch with a mental health rights group.

As with any relationship, tensions can arise between you and your informants during the course of the interviewing. It is not uncommon for rapport to wane during extended projects (Johnson 1975). Informants can get tired of answering questions or begin to see the interviewing as an imposition on their lives. You can begin to get impatient when informants are reluctant to address questions or skirt certain topics. Either of you can become bored with the endeavor.

You should try to be sensitive to your informants' low spots and feelings. When you think something is wrong, try to clear the air by expressing your concerns. Sometimes it is a good idea to take a break from the interviewing altogether.

A common problem in large studies is canceled or missed appointments. In the large-scale family study, a sizable number of parents canceled interviews at the last minute or failed to be at home at the agreed-upon time. The research team came up with a set of tactics to prevent cancellations, including phone calls on the day preceding the interviews, appointment cards, buying calendars for some families, arriving an hour early on the scheduled day, and leaving notes expressing bewilderment when families were not home. When parents repeatedly missed appointments, they were asked directly whether they wanted to continue in the study. Although these tactics reduced the number of cancellations, it became obvious that some parents simply did not want to participate in the study but, for whatever reason, were reluctant to say so. There was disagreement within the research team over what to do about these families, with some members arguing that they should be left alone if they did not want to participate and others advocating continued attempts to obtain the data. As it turned out, the study dropped many of these families from the research when continued attempts to schedule appointments failed.

TAPE-RECORDING INTERVIEWS

In the chapter on participant observation, we advised researchers to rely on their memories to record data, at least until they had developed a feel for the setting. Recording devices can make people self-conscious.

Although tape-recording can alter what people say in the early stages of the research, interviewers can usually get by with taping interviews. In interviewing, informants are acutely aware that the interviewer's agenda is to conduct research. Since the interviewees already know that their words are being weighed, they are less likely to be alarmed by the presence of a tape recorder. The interviewer often also has an extended period of time in which to get informants to relax and become accustomed to the tape recorder. In participant observation, researchers interact with a number of people, some of whom never get to know, let alone trust, the observer.

A tape recorder allows the interviewer to capture more than he or she could by relying on memory. The interviewer's data consist almost entirely of words. Unlike participant observers, interviewers cannot sit back for a while and observe during lapses in conversations. It is possible that many of the most important life histories in the social sciences would never have been written without the use of electronic recording devices. Oscar Lewis (1963,

xii) writes in his introduction to *The Children of Sanchez:* "The tape recorder, used in taking down the life histories in this book, has made possible the beginning of a new kind of literature of social realism."

The remarks should not make us lose sight of the fact that most people's memories are better than they suspect. Although we have used tape recorders in most of our interviewing, we have relied on our memories to record the substance of brief one-hour interviews. Some researchers, such as Thomas Cottle (1972), regularly conduct interviews without tape recorders.

Obviously, you should not record interviews if it makes informants ill at ease (Klockars 1977). Even if informants do not mind the fact that the interviews are being taped, try to minimize the recorder's presence. Use a small recorder and place it out of sight. The microphone should be unobtrusive and sensitive enough to pick up voices without the participants having to speak into it. Find a recorder that will accommodate long-playing tapes so that the conversation will not be interrupted often.

A few final words of caution: label each tape clearly and make sure your equipment is functioning properly before each interview. In one of our studies, we forgot to check out the tapes and recorder before some of the interviews. When we listened to the tapes later, they were barely audible. Our typist would not even try to transcribe them, and we ended up spending many hours playing and replaying them to pick up all of the data.

GROUP INTERVIEWS

One method that has become increasingly popular in the social sciences and applied research in recent years is group interviewing. In this approach, interviewers bring together groups of people to talk about their perspectives and experiences in open-ended discussions. As with in-depth interviewing, the researcher uses a nondirective approach. In group interviewing, as opposed to one-to-one interviewing, the researcher must act as a group facilitator and moderator, managing interactions between members of the group—for example, keeping people from interrupting or arguing with each other, dealing with overly talkative people who would monopolize the conversation, encouraging shy people to contribute, and so on.

Two geographers, Rowan Roundtree and Barry Gordon, employed the group interview approach to study how people define geographic space, specifically forests. Initially, Roundtree and Gordon intended to conduct observations in the field: that is, in wooded areas. This plan contained its drawbacks. Since most people go to forests to "get away from things," including other people, it would be difficult for the researchers to find people willing to be studied. Roundtree and Gordon were also interested in the definitions of people who might never have been in forests.

What the researchers decided to do instead of field interviews was to assemble groups of people, show them a set of 10 slides of forest areas, and encourage them to talk about what they had seen. The research was directed toward understanding how different people view and use forest areas.

Thomas Cottle (1973c) has used free-flowing group discussions in urban areas to examine how young people define their world. Cottle describes the approach on which his excellent paper, "The Ghetto Scientists," is based:

> It is difficult to say how many of us were speaking that afternoon in the little park near the hospital. So much was going on, like a colossal basketball game and boys darting after girls, or a pretend fight, that our population kept shifting. Still, there were always four or five young people about ten years old, who joined me on the grass alongside the basketball court and the conversation tumbled along so that we all could follow it and the newcomers could be cued in easily. The girls and boys were speaking about school, their studies, teachers, parents, and brothers and sisters, although there was an unusual side trip into politics. In times like these I wish I could be totally free to say anything to young people, young black people, in this case. It is not that I am thinking anything particular about them as much as holding back ideas that for one reason or another I feel should remain hidden. Maybe it has to do with the laziness of the day or the fact that none of the young people seem especially eager to latch onto some topic. Maybe it is the way some of us do research; entering poor areas of cities and just speaking with people, letting conversations run on without interpretation or analysis. Maybe too, some of us have a strong desire to know what these people think of us and the work we do.

A more formal approach to group interviews, known as *focus groups* (Krueger 1988; Morgan 1988), has become especially popular in applied and evaluation research in recent years. In marketing and political opinion research, for example, the focus group has become almost as commonplace as large-scale public opinion polls. In contrast to polls, focus groups are designed to explore how and why people make the decisions they do.

Focus groups are designed to use group dynamics to yield insights that might not be accessible without the kind of interaction found in a group (Morgan 1988, 12). As Rubin and Rubin (1995) write:

> In focus groups, the goal is to let people spark off one another, suggesting dimensions and nuances of the original problem that any one individual might not have thought of. Sometimes a totally different understanding of a problem emerges from the group discussion. (p. 140)

Just as one-to-one interviews must be understood as a form of social interaction, group interviews must be interpreted in terms of group dynamics. Most people cannot be expected to say the same things in a group that they might say to an interviewer in private. Group discussions can also lead to a superficial consensus in which some members defer to those who are most outspoken.

Group interviews seem most appropriate when the researcher has specific topics to explore and is not interested in private aspects of people's lives.

THE INTERVIEWER'S JOURNAL

It is a good idea to maintain a detailed journal during your interviewing. The interviewer's journal can serve several purposes. First of all, the journal should contain an outline of topics discussed in each interview. This will help you to keep track of what has already been covered in the interviewing and to go back to specific conversations when you want to follow up on something that the informant has said. In our interviewing with Ed Murphy, we neglected to do this and wasted quite a bit of time listening to tapes and reading transcripts looking for specific things.

Second, the journal takes the place of observer's comments recorded in participant observation field notes. Like the observer, you should make note of emerging themes, interpretations, hunches, and striking gestures and non-verbal expressions essential to understanding the meaning of a person's words. Holstein and Gubrium (1995, 78) recommend that the interviewer act as "an 'ethnographer of the interview,' who records for future analysis not only what is said but the related interactional details of how the interview was accomplished."

The following are examples of the kinds of comments that should be included in the journal:

- By the faces she was making, I think she was being sarcastic when she talked about her mother. She didn't seem to want to say anything really negative about her mother though.
- That's the third time she's raised that topic on her own. It must be important to her. I'll have to look into this in the future.
- I really hit a sensitive nerve when I asked him about why his wife left him. He stiffened right up and made it quite clear that he didn't want to go into this. I don't really trust the story he told me about this.
- Somehow we were both bored tonight. We just wanted to get the interview over with. Maybe this was because of the topic or maybe we were both tired today.
- I think I was a bit too aggressive tonight. I wonder if he just said those things to keep me off his back. I'll have to keep this in mind when I go over the conversation.

Notes like this will assist in guiding future interviews and interpreting data at a later time.

Finally, the journal is a good place to keep a record of conversations with informants outside of the interview situation. Ed Murphy often talked at length about important things in his life during breaks in the interviewing and informal contacts with the researchers. Such data are clearly important and should be analyzed along with those collected during the interview.

You should try to force yourself to write journal entries after each contact with informants as well as at other times when you think of something important to record. Every once in a while, look through your journal to get a sense of what you have covered and what you have learned.

In the past several chapters we have presented the strategies and tactics of the predominant qualitative research methods—participant observation and in-depth interviewing. In the next chapter we present examples of other ways in which qualitative research can be conducted. We shift our focus in this chapter from a how-to approach to a descriptive one. Our goal in this chapter is to encourage creativity and innovation in research.

NOTES

1. Many of the classic life histories prepared by the Chicago school of sociology were actually based on written documents solicited by the researchers rather than on in-depth interviewing. We discuss this later in the chapter. Also, in the Chicago school the phrase *personal documents* was used to refer to both written materials and narratives based on in-depth interviewing.

2. In addition, many of the authors or subjects of the life histories prepared by the Chicago school were paid to write their stories (see Shaw, McKay, and McDonald 1938; Sutherland 1937).

3. Yet another *sic* here. If women define situations as real, the same thing applies. To add insult to injury, Smith (1995) points out that the "Thomas Theorem," or "dictum," quoted here was originally published in a book written by both W. I. Thomas and Dorothy Swaine Thomas. Yet, classic sociology textbooks attributed this famous quote almost exclusively to W. I. Thomas. According to Smith, this reflects a professional ideology that systematically ignored the contributions of women to sociology.

CHAPTER 5

Montage: Discovering Methods

I N 1966 A team of social scientists published a book, entitled *Unobtrusive Measures: Nonreactive Research in Social Sciences,* with which they hoped to "broaden the social scientist's current narrow range of utilized methodologies and to encourage creative and opportunistic exploitation of unique measurement possibilities" (Webb et al. 1966, 1).[1] The team went on to write: "Today, the dominant mass of social science research is based upon interviews and questionnaires. We lament this overdependence upon a single, fallible method" (Webb et al. 1966, 1).

Although the authors of *Unobtrusive Measures* align themselves with quantitative research methods and a positivist world view, their plea for creativity and innovation should be heeded by qualitative researchers as well. We must guard against the overdependence cited by these researchers; that is, we must be careful not to be boxed in by a limited repertoire of research approaches.

We have concentrated thus far in this book on two research approaches: participant observation—the mainstay of qualitative methods—and in-depth interviewing, a popular tool among social researchers. Moreover, we have adopted a "how-to-do-it" approach in describing these methods. There is a danger in what we have done. We may have given the impression that subjective understanding and inductive analysis can only be pursued through tried-and-true methods.

With this thought in mind, we shift our focus in this chapter to a discussion of studies based on innovative or unconventional methods. What is to be learned from these studies is that social scientists must educate themselves on ways to study the social world. We use the term *educate* as opposed to *train* because there is an important difference between the two. As Irwin Deutscher (1973) notes, one can only be trained in something that already exists. To be educated is to learn to create anew. We must constantly create new methods and approaches. We must take to heart the words written by C. Wright Mills (1959) in his conclusion to *The Sociological Imagination:*

> Be a good craftsman: Avoid a rigid set of procedures. Above all seek to develop and to use the sociological imagination. Avoid fetishism of method and technique. Urge the rehabilitation of the unpretentious intellectual craftsman, and try to become a craftsman yourself. Let every man be his own methodologist. . . . (p. 224)

These methods are not to be copied, but rather emulated. They do not determine the range of possibilities; only our thoughts do.

The studies that follow exemplify the notion of researcher-as-innovator. Some have serious weaknesses; we mention them because of their strengths.

We do not discuss the ethical implications of the following approaches. Ethical issues have been explored in previous chapters. Some of the methods we describe kindle the fires of long-standing ethical feuds. By describing these studies, we do not necessarily endorse the ethical stances taken by the researchers.

DISRUPTING THE "COMMONSENSE WORLD OF EVERYDAY LIFE": HAROLD GARFINKEL

One hundred thirty-five people wander into stores and attempt to bargain over the prices of such common items as cigarettes and magazines. Others go out and find unsuspecting partners to play ticktacktoe: when it is their turn they casually erase their opponent's mark and move it to another square before they make their own. One person engages another in conversation and nonchalantly brings his or her face so close to the other's that their noses are almost touching. After all of these activities, the tricksters go home to write detailed notes on their encounters. All of these are strategies used by Harold Garfinkel (1967) in his influential studies in ethnomethodology. Garfinkel seems to ask himself: "What can be done to make trouble?" By producing confusion, anxiety, bewilderment, and disorganized interaction, he attempts to discover what is otherwise hidden: taken-for-granted rules of social interaction.

Garfinkel has experimented with other strategies to accomplish this goal. In one exercise, people are asked to write on one side of a sheet of paper actual conversations they have had with a friend or relative. On the other side they write what they understood the other person to have meant by each sentence. The relationships between the actual conversations and understood meanings are then examined for what they reveal about what is taken for granted, underlying assumptions, and shared meanings.

In a more provocative exercise, people are told to engage others in conversation and to insist that the others clarify the meanings of commonplace remarks. One person asked one of the experimenters, "How are you?" To this, the experimenter replied: "How am I in regard to what? My health, my finances, my schoolwork, my peace of mind, my . . . ?" The partner, red-faced and out of control, shot back, "Look! I was just trying to be polite. Frankly, I don't give a damn how you are."

Another tactic used by Garfinkel is to ask people to look at an ordinary and familiar scene in their own lives from a stranger's perspective. Thus undergraduate students are instructed to go to their families' homes and to act like boarders. Through this exercise, people become aware of things they never notice in their everyday lives, such as table manners, greetings, and other subtle conventions. In a slightly different experiment, the emphasis is placed on the reactions of others to students behaving like boarders in their own homes.

Garfinkel has created a series of strategies that allow him to explore those areas of social interaction in which he is interested. He uses his experimenters to uncover what is seen but usually unnoticed—the commonsense world of everyday life.

QUALITATIVE RESEARCH AS AUTOBIOGRAPHY

It was probably only a matter of time before qualitative researchers concerned with subjective understanding and the social construction of reality turned this focus inward. In the 1970s, the qualitative literature began to be characterized by first-person accounts of personal dilemmas confronted in the field. Johnson's *Doing Field Research* (1975) departed from the conventional research methods text by focusing on the writer's own feelings and personal trials in conducting field research. Later, Van Maanen (1982) reported on his personal experiences conducting field research among police on the beat; Taylor (1987a) described the ethical dilemmas involved in the study of institutional attendants, as illustrated in this book; Ellis (1995a) wrote about her emotional and ethical quandaries at causing pain and anger among informants who happened to read her study of life in a fishing village. Edited books (Shaffir, Stebbins, and Turowetz 1980; Shaffir and Stebbins 1991) have been published on researchers' personal reflections on the research process. Van Maanen (1988) has coined the phrase "confessional tales" to refer to this type of ethnographic writing.

In the 1990s, a new genre of qualitative reporting, encouraged by feminist and postmodern theories, has emerged in which qualitative researchers write about their personal experiences not merely as researchers but as central subjects of their studies. The use of personal experience as background information for studies is probably as old as qualitative research itself. What distinguishes this new form of ethnographic writing is that the researcher or author occupies center stage in the study being reported.

Carolyn Ellis (1991a,b, 1995a) and colleagues (Bochner, Ellis, and Tilman in press; Ellis and Flaherty 1992; Jago 1996; Ronai 1995) make the case for an "emotional sociology" based on personal narratives of the author's own experiences. In *Final Negotiations: A Story of Love, Loss, and Chronic Illness*, Ellis (1995b) tells the love story of her relationship with Gene Weinstein, who died after a long and difficult battle with emphysema. Ellis's narrative style is direct, honest, and intimate. She describes her innermost feelings as well as the most personal details of her relationship with Gene. Informed by sociological interests, but without the analysis and theorizing generally found in qualitative studies, Ellis's text draws the reader inside the experience of loving and finally losing a loved one.

Inspired by Ellis's work, Ronai (1995, in press) recounts her experiences of having a mentally retarded mother and being sexually abused by her father. Ronai (1995) uses a narrative style she refers to as a "layered account":

> A layered account is a postmodern ethnographic reporting technique that embodies a theory of consciousness and a method of reporting in one stroke. . . . The layered account offers an impressionistic sketch, handing readers layers of experience so they may fill in the spaces and construct an interpretation of the writer's narrative. The readers reconstruct the subject, thus projecting more of themselves into it, and taking more away from it. (p. 396)

Alternating between recollections of her childhood and her current feelings and interpretations, Ronai tells moving stories complete with graphic details of sexual abuse and candid admissions of being embarrassed by her mother. Hers are not sanitized accounts. She is as explicit in describing the actions of her father and mother as she is in presenting her own feelings of guilt and mixed emotions. Ronai advocates for a sociology that would broaden the range of acceptable topics and communication strategies for social science reporting.

David Karp's (1996) *Speaking of Sadness: Depression, Disconnection, and the Meanings of Illness* occupies a middle ground between conventional qualitative research and postmodern ethnography. Karp identifies with the symbolic interactionist tradition and bases much of his analysis of depression on interviews with 30 people. But there is a twist in his sociological tale. Karp uses his own long-term struggle with depression as a point of departure and a grounding for his theorizing. Thus his book begins:

> In greater or lesser degree I have grappled with depression for almost 20 years. I suppose that even as a child my experience of life was as much characterized by anxiety as by joy and pleasure. And as I look back, there were lots of tip-offs that things weren't right. (p. 3)

Karp does a masterful job of weaving together his personal experiences with the words of his informants. As Karp explains, his purpose as a sociologist is not to attempt to solve the puzzle of what causes depression, but to examine the phenomenology of being depressed—to get inside the minds of those who experience the condition. He does this by exploring the effects of depression on identity, the meanings of medication, relations with families and friends (the most devastating aspect of depression, according to Karp, is that sufferers feel disconnected from others at a time when they need human connection the most), and similar topics.

Karp's account of depression is powerful theoretically and emotionally. He leaves the reader not only with a clearer understanding of the sociological self, as previously described by Blumer, Goffman, and others, but with a personal grasp of the experience of being chronically depressed. "Someone once described social statistics," writes Karp (1996, 12), "as human beings with the tears washed away." Karp builds solid symbolic interactionist theory and does not attempt to hide the tears.

ENTERING *A WORLD WITHOUT WORDS*

There are three main subjects in the study reported in the book *A World without Words*. Two of them, Christina and Bianca, cannot speak and were born deaf, blind, and profoundly mentally retarded as a result of prenatal exposure to the German measles during the rubella epidemic of the 1960s. The third is the author, David Goode, a methodical, creative, and talented sociologist.

So that we do not mislead you by our initial description of the characters, or reinforce the predisposition you might have, this is not an ordinary study about "us" and "them." To the contrary, as in all good and powerful social science analysis of the outsider, we are confronted with the proposition that "they" are "us." Goode, by sharing the world he entered with Christina and

Bianca, brings us close to people easily dismissed as not quite human. (In philosophic debates, Christina and Bianca are the very people some authors argue do not meet the criteria of being human.) In Goode's work, "us" becomes those who share the researcher's skepticism about professional knowledge and disability labels—who understand that the initial distinction between the subjects and other human beings does not hold. "Them" becomes those who do not share this insight. While the n is tiny, the subject matter is huge—communication, what it means to have a relationship with another person, and, perhaps most ambitious, what it means when we say someone is a human being.

The reflective, elaborate, and methodologically explicit case studies of the two children form the core of Goode's study. Christina, a nine-year-old who has lived on a ward of an institution for the mentally retarded since she was six, is one of the subjects. Goode presents an interpretation of Christina's social construction of her world and documents his methods and reflection in attempting this onerous task. The second subject is Bianca—13 years old at the time of the study and nicknamed "the slug" by those in the school she attends. The focus is on communication between Bianca and her parents, with whom she has lived since birth. While the two young women are the center of the cases, the institutional staff, professionals, and parents and care-takers are included when their perspectives bear on understanding ways of constructing Christina and Bianca. We learn what others in the two girls' lives make of them and are brought close to Goode's effort to put together the puzzle for himself and us.

Goode uses multiple research techniques in inventive and creative ways. He tries all kinds of procedures with his wordless subjects—playing guitar, mimicking, jumping, swinging, rocking, wearing eye covers and ear plugs—in attempting to get data that would help him interpret what Christina and Bianca know and how he might know them. On a number of occasions, Goode spends 24 hours in continuous observation to get a more comprehensive understanding of Christina's life on the ward. He also employs audio and video taping. These less conventional research practices are anchored in countless hours of observing the subjects in their everyday activities, interviews with people who know them, and the author's deep self-reflections in attempting to break from his world and approach theirs. He shares with the reader his struggle with writing his findings, with how to use formal language to tell the story of people who are without words. The meta-tool in his arsenal is ethnomethodology. Those who have dismissed the approach as something that died in the 1960s with the peace symbol should take notice. In the hands of Goode, who comes close to stripping it from its jargon, ethnomethodology has strength and stamina and exhibits a brand of humanism that is fresh and inviting.

Part of Goode's study is a consideration of the nature of the understanding between the children who cannot hear, see, or talk and those who can, and the character of the intersubjectivity that is achieved. Goode finds communication, but only as the product of people's involvement in intense, long-term interaction. A tremendous amount of communication is not observable to people outside the intimacy of the relationship. Goode explores and explicates the ethnomethodological perspective and research technique as he practiced them and places these against the nature of other empirical work.

Following recent trends, some qualitative research historians may attempt to abduct this work to make it part of the postmodern moment. They might point to the strong presence of the author as person in the text, the dedication of the author in aligning with and giving voice to his subjects, the reflectivity, the sometimes nonlinear text, and the experimental methods. (They might overlook the fact that Goode refers to his field notes as "scientific data.") Although some might try to make a postmodernist out of Goode, there is no evidence in his references or acknowledgements that he is anything but an old-fashioned ethnomethodologist trained by Harold Garfinkel and Melvin Pollner and given guidance and led to subjects by Robert Edgerton.

Goode helps us to understand that just because someone cannot talk does not mean that person has nothing to say, or that, because someone cannot speak and is referred to as deaf, blind, and profoundly retarded, that person is not a social human being. Goode has more to teach us about than rubella syndrome children. There are lessons here about the craft of qualitative research. Goode teaches us that to think deeply about the human condition we need to observe it up close, firsthand. We need to go to dark places where people have not carried the sociological imagination, fighting the temptation to retreat to safer ground. We have to laboriously and rigorously, creatively collect data, and be open to letting it shape our thinking.

Qualitative researchers are at their best when they produce provocative and groundbreaking ethnographic work like Goode has. Goode's work is a call for others to experiment with new approaches to understanding.

PERSONAL DOCUMENTS

The use of personal documents has a proud history in social science research, stemming back to the heyday of the Chicago school (Allport 1942; Dollard 1935; Gottschalk, Kluckhohn, and Angell 1945; see also Becker 1966; Frazier 1978). Many of the classic life histories in sociology were based largely on personal documents.

The phrase *personal documents* refers to individuals' written first-person accounts of their whole lives or parts of their lives, or their reflections on a specific event or topic. The *diary* is probably the most revealing and private type of personal document. In her introduction to her famous diary, Anne Frank (1952) wrote, "I hope I shall be able to confide in you completely, as I have never been able to do in anyone else before." The diary is an excellent source of data because of its intimacy and self-reflection on the diarist's immediate experiences.

There are other types of valuable ongoing records. Travelers often maintain *logs* on their trips. Many professionals and business people keep *calendars* that contain reflections on events in addition to schedules. Some parents keep ongoing *developmental records* of the progress of their children. *Photo albums* and *scrapbooks* are other important forms of personal documents.

Private letters are a good source of information on specific events and experiences in people's lives. The soldier on the battlefield, the grandparent thousands of miles away from his or her family, the immigrant—all share their sadness and joys through letters. The classic study by Thomas and Znaniecki (1927), *The Polish Peasant in Europe and America,* was based largely on letters written to relatives overseas.

One form of private correspondence that has received considerable attention in social science research is *suicide notes* (Douglas 1967; Jacobs 1967). These notes are important for understanding not only why people decide to take their lives, but also what they intend to communicate to others by doing so.

As noted in the chapter on in-depth interviewing, solicited narratives have been used extensively in qualitative studies. The research of Shaw (1931, 1966) and colleagues, Sutherland (1937), and others was based on life histories actually written by delinquents and criminals. For a study of the life histories of German refugees, Gordon Allport (1942) ran a competition for the best essay on "My life in Germany before and after January 30, 1933." He received 200 manuscripts averaging 100 pages in length in response. In comparison with other personal documents, solicited narratives yield a relatively small amount of irrelevant and unusable data at the cost of sacrificing spontaneity.

Although there are literally millions of personal documents waiting to be found, the researcher will almost always have to search them out imaginatively and aggressively. Libraries, archives maintained by organizations, flea markets, antique shops, and historical societies are good places to start. One way to obtain documents is by placing ads in newspapers and newsletters. This is how Thomas and Znaniecki located letters for their study. Newspaper editors, columnists, celebrities, and others who receive a large volume of mail may also be willing to share it for research purposes. Finally, friends and acquaintances may be able to provide a supply of documents. Many people would rather put their letters and memorabilia to some useful purpose than burn them. Diaries are sometimes written with the expectation that someone will read them at some future time.

Personal documents are perhaps most valuable when used in conjunction with interviewing and firsthand observation.[2] While acknowledging their value, Herbert Blumer (1969) criticizes the exclusive use of personal documents on the grounds that they lend themselves more readily to diverse interpretations than do other forms of data.

ANALYZING INSANE ASYLUM POSTCARDS

On October 11, 1911, Mrs. Herman Miller walked from the front door of her home in Iowa to her roadside rural mailbox to see what the postman had brought. A picture postcard from her cousins Clara and Frank greeted her. She flipped the card over to look at the view. It was of a large, ornate institution building in attractive landscaped surrounding. The caption read *MAIN BUILDING—NORTHERN ILL. INSANE ASYLUM, ELGIN.*

Although the idea of receiving a postcard with a picture of an insane asylum seems odd today, Mrs. Miller thought nothing of it. In fact, the view (the word commonly used to refer to the picture) was so unnoteworthy that it was not even referred to in the message on the opposite side. It was just another card to add to Mrs. Miller's growing postcard collection. By 1911, postcards were widely popular, and asylum postcards[3] were a common, taken-for-granted item.

When Bogdan, who was on vacation poking around antique shops for his own enjoyment, came across the postcard, he had no idea what to make of it and did not realize that this cultural artifact would launch a more serious study. But it did. Although some qualitative research projects start with a lot of thought and careful planning, others occur serendipitously. Bogdan came across other insane asylum postcards and began collecting in earnest. First he pursued his quest at flea markets and antique shops. As he got to know more about postcard collecting, he started attending postcard shows and placing ads in postcard collectors' publications. His collection grew quickly until he had over 1600 different cards. It became his database for an interesting and unconventional study.

There were too many postcards to manage the data using a simple hand filing system; so Bogdan and a colleague used an information management software program. Although they wanted to digitalize the images and have them as part of the computerized data, this proved too labor-intensive and required too much storage space to be feasible. Instead the researchers entered all the written information they could, including descriptions of the pictures and the written messages on the cards, and began working with the material.

First, searching for a context in which to place the research, Bogdan and his colleague read widely about the history of mental hospitals. As they learned, during the period these postcards were most popular, 1905 through 1920, institutions for the mentally ill had all but deserted their original goal of cure and were largely custodial facilities. Although the conditions for the inmates varied from institution to institution and from ward to ward within the same institution, life was restrictive and barren at best and perilous at worst. The grounds and outsides of the buildings provided a serene facade for the crowded conditions and human degradation that often occurred inside.

Looking at the attractive pictures of asylums on postcards, which showed architecturally impressive buildings located in serene country settings with well-kept flower gardens and facilities, it was not a great analytic leap for the researchers to begin framing the study around the idea that postcards were propaganda for the dominant order. Although that was a feasible tack to take, and an approach consistent with current theories about analyzing visual text, it seemed too obvious and superficial. In some way the postcards might have served as propaganda, but what did the people who produced and used them think of them? The researchers delved deeper. Seeing that all the cards in the collection were designed and produced by commercial manufacturers and not by institutions or state employees, they began doing research to try to understand more about postcard production during the period in question. As they soon discovered, the primary interest of the manufacturers was to produce products people would buy. People wanted attractive views, ones that complimented the locations in which they were taken. As Bogdan and his colleague began comparing the asylum cards with the cards that depicted other places—colleges and other schools, courthouses, post offices, libraries, and resorts—they saw how the visual conventions were the same. They came to the conclusion that, although the cards might have reinforced professional authority, they looked the way they did more because they were postcard views than because they were pictures of asylums. Further, as the two researchers studied the messages on the backs of the cards, they found that most of the writing did not make reference to the picture on the other side. The messages were simple greetings. Bogdan and his colleague came to realize that they might be making more of the pictures on the asylum cards than did those who produced and used them. People of the time just took the postcards for granted. Many of the asylums were built in rural settings where there were not very many other large buildings to photograph. The researchers concluded that asylums were probably not singled out to be photographed; they were just available and were approached as any building would be. Similarly, the great majority of the people who sent the asylum cards probably did not choose them because they portrayed the asylum, but because they were available for use.

Rather than deserting the project because the data did not show what they thought it would, Bogdan and his colleague produced a paper that discussed the problems of analyzing visual material such as postcards. The authors critique researchers who jump to conclusions about what pictures mean and apply abstract theory to the visual text rather than getting at the meanings people attach to the images.

PHOTOGRAPHY AND METHODOLOGY

Photographs and other visual data can provide an excellent source for qualitative analysis (Archer 1997; Ball and Smith 1992; Gold 1997a,b; Harper 1997; Suchar 1997). The pictures people take lend insight into what is important to them and how they view themselves and others. Photographs can be analyzed the same way as any other kind of personal document or archival material. This is not the only way photography enters into qualitative research, however.

The camera can be a useful research tool in the social sciences (Dabbs 1982; Stasz 1979). Just as a tape recorder can aid in recording data, film and videotape equipment can capture details that would otherwise be forgotten or go unnoticed. As Dabbs (1982) notes:

> I have two reasons for liking these media. First, they are faithful and patient observers. They remember what they see and they can record steadily for long periods of time. Second, . . . they allow us to expand or compress time and make visible patterns that would otherwise move too slowly or too fast to be seen. (p. 38)

Ethnomethodologists have used electronic recording devices to study the mundane and taken-for-granted aspects of everyday life. Ryave and Schenkein (1974) studied the "art of walking"—how people navigate in public places—by filming eight-minute segments of videotape on a public pavement. Commenting on their use of videotape equipment, Ryave and Schenkein (1974) write:

> It is plain enough that the use of videotape affords us the opportunity to review a given instance of the phenomenon innumerable times without relying on a single observation of an essentially transitory phenomenon. In addition, . . . we require intimate study of actual instances of walking and cannot be satisfied with the study of reports on those instances. (p. 266)

David Goode (1992) "discovered" the competence of Bobby, a man with Down's syndrome, by reviewing videotapes of conversations and interactions with him. Bobby was a 50-year-old man living at a boarding home when Goode first met him. As Goode explains, Bobby was defined as "low functioning," and he left the impression of being quite incompetent. Then one day Goode and his colleagues happened to videotape an interaction between Bobby and twin sisters living at the facility. When Goode later viewed the tapes, his impressions of Bobby changed dramatically. Goode (1992) explains:

> As I watched the videotape repeatedly, an even more radical appreciation of Bobby's abilities to understand and communicate emerged. At the time of the incident and during our initial viewings of the tape, it appeared that many of Bobby's utterances were unintelligible, if not unintelligent. But after watching the tape a number of times, many "unintelligible" utterances began to sound clear to us. While it is true that persons on the tape did not seem to understand Bobby, the same persons repeatedly watching the tape could hear words where formerly they heard mumblings. . . . We began to appreciate the degree to which Bobby's not making sense to us was as much our fault as it was his. (p. 204)

By reviewing other tapes of Bobby, Goode learned that Bobby's competence was situationally determined. Whereas Bobby might seem incompetent interacting with occupational therapists, videotapes of interactions with peers at the boarding home indicated that he acted more competently and was viewed as such by them. Goode (1992, 205) writes, "It did not take long for us to understand that familiarity and intimacy were the key determinants in viewing Bobby as competent to communicate and think." Goode concludes his study by observing that identities—in this instance, the identity of a man defined as severely retarded—are socially generated.

William H. Whyte (1980) has used time-lapse photography to study small urban spaces such as parks and plazas.[4] By filming for entire days, Whyte examines what makes people use some spaces and not others. His research shows that time-lapse filming is an especially fruitful research approach.

Photographs and films can also be used as a mode of presenting and illustrating findings. Pictures take the place of words or at least convey something that words cannot. Certainly, for the reader of a qualitative study, pictures give a sense of being there, seeing the setting and people firsthand. There have also been some pieces published in sociological journals such as *Qualitative Sociology* that consist solely of pictures without commentary or analysis (see, e.g., Jackson 1978). Stasz (1979, 36) points out that "visual sociologists" can either mimic art, letting the images speak for themselves, or "aim toward the ideals of visual ethnography, where texts would accompany photographs to provide features of description and abstract generalization which cannot be handled by images alone."

Dabbs (1982) describes studies by Ziller and colleagues (Ziller and Lewis 1981; Ziller and Smith 1977) that demonstrate yet another way in which photography can be creatively used to study people's perspectives. In one study, Ziller and Lewis (1981) gave people cameras and asked them to take pictures that tell who they were. The researchers found that students with high grade averages produced more photographs in which books were prominently displayed, whereas juvenile delinquents took more pictures of people and fewer of school and home. In another study, Ziller and Smith (1977) found that when asked to describe their university, new students brought back pictures of buildings and students who had been attending the university longer turned in photos of people.

Photographers, artists, and others have long produced media forms rich in sociological understanding. Frederick Wiseman's films *Titticut Follies*, *High School, Hospital*, and others, get beneath the surfaces of places we often visit but never really see. The photos of Diane Arbus (1972) and the photographic essays of institutions for the "mentally retarded" by Blatt and Kaplan (1974) and Blatt, Ozolins, and McNally (1980) are notable for portraying the human condition.

OFFICIAL RECORDS AND PUBLIC DOCUMENTS

There is, for all practical purposes, an unlimited number of official and public documents, records, and materials available as sources of data (Hill 1993). These include organizational documents, newspaper articles, agency records, government reports, court transcripts, and a host of other materials.

Of course, researchers have analyzed official records and statistics since the beginning of the social sciences. Durkheim's (1951) classic study of suicide is a notable case in point. There have been countless studies of crime based on police records and suicide based on coroner's reports. However, the qualitative researcher brings a different perspective to reports and documents than has been common in the social sciences.

The qualitative researcher analyzes official and public documents to learn about the people who write and maintain them. Like personal documents, these materials lend insight into the perspectives, assumptions, concerns, and activities of those who produce them. Kitsuse and Cicourel (1963) point out that official statistics tell us about organizational processes rather than the criminals, deviants, or others on whom such records are kept. Similarly, Garfinkel (1967) argues that organizational records are produced for the purpose of documenting satisfactory performance of the organization's responsibilities toward its clients. Concerning psychiatric records, Garfinkel (1967) writes:

> In our view the contents of clinic folders are assembled with regard for the possibility that the relationship may have to be portrayed as having been in

accord with expectations of sanctionable performances by clinicians and patients. (p. 198)

In slightly different veins, Douglas (1967, 1971) examines commonsense understandings of why people kill themselves by analyzing coroner's records; Platt (1969) looks at definitions of juvenile delinquency around the turn of the century by reviewing official reports of charitable organizations, government reports, and other historical documents; and Ferguson (1992) analyzes constructions of people defined as "idiots"—the most severely retarded—in official state reports and institutional documents around the turn of the twentieth century.

Taylor and Bogdan (1980) examine the official goals and formal structures of total institutions for people with mental retardation through interviews with institutional officials and analysis of institutional documents. In contrast to the rational view of formal organizations, organizational goals and structures serve an important symbolic function by providing "legitimating myths" to justify the existence of an organization. Taylor and Bogdan show how institutional brochures, program descriptions, and policies must be interpreted not as describing the operation of the institutions, but in terms of presenting a preferred image of institutions and managing the impressions of external publics upon whom they depend for their existence.

Popular media forms, such as newspapers, magazines, television, movies, and radio, provide another important source of data. For example, researchers have studied societal stereotypes of the mentally ill in comic strips (Scheff 1966); images of people with disabilities in newspapers, books, and movies (Bogdan and Biklen 1977; Kriegel 1987; Longmore 1985; Zola 1992); and portrayals of sex roles in children's books.

Many official records and public documents are readily available to researchers. Public libraries, organizational archives, and historical societies are good sources for these kinds of materials. Police and agency records are usually accessible through the same means by which participant observers gain entrée into these settings. Many government reports and documents are considered public information and are available under the Freedom of Information Act. Adler (1990) provides a step-by-step guide on how information can be obtained through this law. Noakes (1995) discusses ways in which FBI files can be obtained through Freedom of Information requests. As Noakes points out, the more specific you can be in identifying the information in which you are interested, the more likely it is that you will obtain documents through this process.

The qualitative analysis of official documents opens up many new sources of understanding. Materials that are thought to be useless by those looking for objective facts are valuable to the qualitative researcher precisely because of their subjective nature.

RECONSTRUCTING THE WORLDS OF FREAKS

There are few things more offensive to present sensibilities than the practice of exhibiting people with physical differences for amusement and profit at circuses, carnivals, and amusement parks—*freak shows*. That was what Bogdan (1988) thought when he began looking into the practice. Freak shows were in their heyday in the United States from approximately 1840 until 1940, when they fell out of favor. Bogdan began searching archives in the major depositories of circus and carnival memorabilia with the intention of writing biographies of the people who were on exhibit. In the back of his mind was a project that would document the exhibits' degradation at the hands of able-bodied exploiters.

As Bogdan began going through these collections, he was surprised to be deluged with photographic images of exhibits as well as elaborate booklets describing the lives of the exhibits and providing other details about their careers. He found out that the freaks supplemented their incomes and publicized their appearances by selling booklets as mementos and that the most complete record of who was exhibited could be found in such merchandise.

At first Bogdan looked at the pictures and the pamphlets to learn about the people being exhibited. The pictures were extremely stylized, with the people dressed in divergent ways, from evening attire (tuxedos and frilly formal dresses) to loin cloths and alien costume. The booklets told, in detail, of the extraordinary lives the exhibits lived. Some were depicted as royalty from Europe, others as cannibals or savages. Looking for the truth about the lives of the exhibits in the material, Bogdan found the pictures and pamphlets unbelievable. What was going on? What was he to make out of the strange data?

Seeking a perspective from which to understand the material before him, Bogdan located candid memoirs and diaries of people who were in the circus and carnival business. He tracked down some old-timers who had worked the shows and interviewed them. In addition, he read what he could find on the culture of the amusement world. He learned that people in the world of popular entertainment, the world of which freak shows were a part, had a strained relationship with the rest of society. They saw themselves as outsiders and felt antagonism toward those they defined as being "not with it"—people who led ordinary lives outside the amusement world. These people were referred to as "townies," "suckers," and "rubes." Among circus and carnival folks it was perfectly all right to dupe the "suckers"; they had it coming. Shortchanging, rigged games of chance, picking pockets, and misrepresentation were all part of the show. Freak shows publicity reflected that. The pictures and pamphlets that Bogdan was studying were not accurate representations of the people on exhibit. They were exaggerated and fabricated presentations designed to trick patrons, to get them to step right up. Thus the wild men from Borneo, who were claimed to have been captured in Asia, were really dwarfs from Ohio. General Tom Thumb, supposedly born in England, was really the son of a poor carpenter and a barmaid and was born in Bridgeport, Connecticut.

When Bogdan understood the context of the production of the publicity photographs and booklets, he deserted the idea of writing biographies of the exhibits and began focusing on the patterns of presenting the exhibits to the public. In the book that emerged from the research, Bogdan (1988) offers a history of freak shows and the amusement culture and discusses the various modes of presenting freaks to the public. Two modes dominated: the aggrandized mode, in which the exhibit was presented as having exalted status, and the exotic mode, where the freak was presented as some strange species of human being from the nonwestern world. In the book Bogdan emphasizes that the study of the freaks is not properly directed toward the people who appeared on stage, but toward the stylized presentations that were developed in promoting these people. In addition, he points out that the people on stage did not define themselves as freaks in any derogatory sense of the term. They saw themselves as showpeople. They looked down on the people in the audience, not because they had to come gawk, but because they were gullible townies. The book ends with an examination of how people who are different are presented to the public today in such formats as charity campaigns, medical discussion, and the like.

In this chapter we have highlighted innovative approaches to the study of social life. The spirit of the studies described here is captured by Nobel Prize–winning scientist P. W. Bridgeman (quoted in Dalton 1964, 60): "There is no scientific method as such. . . . The most vital feature of the scientist's procedure has been merely to do the utmost with his mind, no holds barred. . . ."

In the preceding chapters we have discussed a broad range of ways to collect qualitative data. In the next chapter we devote attention to data analysis in qualitative research.

NOTES

1. This book has been revised and published as *Nonreactive Measures in the Social Sciences* by Webb, Campbell, Schwartz, Sechrest, and Grove (1981).
2. This is because of what Denzin (1978) refers to as the "reality-distance problem." In analyzing personal documents, the researcher is several times removed from the phenomenon in which he or she is interested.

Of course, there are many instances in which it is impossible to analyze documents in conjunction with face-to-face research approaches.

3. "Asylum postcards" was not a phrase used at the time. Bogdan coined this phrase for his study.

4. Whyte has also produced a film entitled *The Social Life of Small Urban Places,* which has been shown on public television.

CHAPTER 6

Working with Data: Data Analysis in Qualitative Research

IN THE PRECEDING chapters we discussed a variety of ways to collect qualitative data, including participant observation, in-depth interviewing, written documents, and a number of creative approaches. In this chapter we turn to a discussion of how qualitative researchers can make sense of and analyze data. We offer strategies and techniques that we have used and that you may find helpful in getting the most out of the data you have collected. We begin with a discussion of the different types of qualitative studies.

NARRATIVES: DESCRIPTIVE AND THEORETICAL STUDIES

All writing, including social science reporting, is a form of narrative. As Richardson (1990b, 20–21) writes, "Narrative is everywhere, present in myth, fable, short story, epic, history, tragedy, comedy, painting, dance, stained glass windows, cinema, social histories, fairy tales, novels, science schema, comic strips, conversation, journal articles." Both social scientists and novelists use literary devices such as metaphors to tell the story, or narrative, they wish to communicate to readers.

Although any piece of social science writing is a narrative, we can distinguish between descriptive studies, which resemble what people usually associate with literary writing, and theoretical or conceptual studies. Of course, any good qualitative study, no matter how theoretical, contains rich descriptive data: people's own written or spoken words, their artifacts, and their observable activities. In participant observation studies, researchers try to convey a sense of being there and experiencing settings firsthand. Similarly, in studies based on in-depth interviewing, researchers attempt to give readers a feeling of "walking in the informants' shoes"—and seeing things from their points of view. Thus qualitative research should provide "thick description" of social life (Geertz 1983). As Emerson (1983, 24) writes, "Thick descriptions present in close detail the context and meanings of events and scenes that are relevant to those involved in them."

Descriptive studies are communicated through the data; theoretical studies are communicated through concepts illustrated by data. The *ethnography* is probably the most well known form of descriptive study. In ethnographies, researchers try to a paint a picture of what people say and how they act in their everyday lives. Descriptive ethnographies are marked by minimal interpretation and conceptualization. The researcher tells the story not through concepts but through descriptions of events. Although researchers in descriptive studies may try to lead readers to certain conclusions by virtue of what they choose to report and how they report it, readers are free to come to their own interpretations and draw their own generalizations.

In sociology, the classic studies of the Chicago school provide some of the clearest examples of descriptive ethnography. While motivated by a keen interest in social problems, the Chicago school researchers sought to describe in graphic terms the fabric of urban life. Nels Anderson's *The Hobo* (1923) is a notable case in point. Building on his own experiences as a hobo, participant observation (before the approach was even called that), and documents, Anderson described the hobo way of life as experienced by hobos themselves: their language, favorite haunts, customs, pursuits, personalities, and ballads and songs.

Life histories, as produced by members of the Chicago school and other researchers, represent one of the purest forms of descriptive studies. In the life history, the person tells his or her story in his or her own words: "The unique feature of such documents is that they are recorded in the first person, in the boy's own words, and not translated into the language of the person investigating the case" (Shaw 1966, 1).

Life histories do not write themselves. The researcher as recorder and editor has a heavy hand in their production. In all studies, researchers present and order the data according to what they think is important. Specifically, in life histories they decide on what to include and exclude, edit the raw data, add connecting passages between remarks, and place the story in some kind of sequence. Further, in conducting their studies, researchers make decisions about what to observe, ask about, and record that determine what they are able to describe and how they describe it.

Some qualitative sociologists are experimenting with new forms of narrative. The *qualitative autobiography* described in the last chapter is one example. Here researchers tell their own personal stories and try to create in readers subjective understanding of their own experiences and emotions (Ellis and Flaherty 1992). By doing so, they blur the lines between research subject and researcher. *Drama* (Ellis and Bochner 1992; Richardson and Lockridge 1991) and *poetry* (Richardson 1992, 1994) are the most recent additions to the range of qualitative writing. Richardson, who has devoted considerable attention to the narrative production of social science, describes poetry not only as a method of representing human experience but as a device for making visible the researcher's role in constructing knowledge. Although some qualitative researchers (Schwalbe 1995, 1996) question the contribution of drama and poetry to social science knowledge, even a cursory review of major qualitative sociology journals demonstrates the growing popularity of alternative forms of social science narrative.

Most qualitative studies are directed toward building theory. The purpose of theoretical studies is the understanding or explanation of features of social life beyond the particular people and settings studied. In these studies, researchers actively interpret and point out what is important to their audience. They use descriptive data to illustrate their theories and concepts and to convince readers that what the researcher says is true.

Glaser and Strauss (1967) distinguish between two types of theory—substantive and formal (see Chapter 2). The first relates to a substantive area of inquiry, for instance, schools, prisons, juvenile delinquency, and patient care. *Formal theory* refers to a conceptual area of inquiry, such as stigma, formal organizations, socialization, and deviance. In qualitative research, most studies have focused on a single substantive area.

BUILDING THEORY

Since the publication of Glaser and Strauss' influential book, *The Discovery of Grounded Theory* (1967), qualitative researchers have discussed whether the purpose of theoretical studies should be to *develop* or *verify* social theory, or both (see for example Charmaz 1983; Emerson 1983; Katz 1983; Strauss and Corbin 1990). Glaser and Strauss argue that qualitative and other social science researchers should direct their attention to developing or generating social theory and concepts (see also Glaser 1978). Their *grounded theory approach* is designed to enable researchers to do just that. Other researchers, writing from a more positivistic stance, take the position that qualitative research, just like quantitative studies, can and should be used to develop *and* verify or test propositions about the nature of social life. The procedure of *analytic induction* has been the principal means by which qualitative researchers have attempted to do this (Cressey 1953; Katz 1983; Lindesmith 1947; Robinson 1951; Turner 1953; Znaniecki 1934). Although we question whether qualitative methods lend themselves to verification and testing, we find the logic behind both grounded theory and analytic induction useful in analyzing qualitative data.

The grounded theory approach is a method for discovering theories, concepts, hypotheses, and propositions directly from data rather than from a priori assumptions, other research, or existing theoretical frameworks. According to Glaser and Strauss (1967), social scientists have overemphasized testing and verifying theories and have neglected the more important activity of generating sociological theory:

> Description, ethnography, fact-finding, verification (call them what you will) are all done well by professionals in other fields and by laymen in various investigatory agencies. But these people cannot generate sociological theory from their work. Only sociologists are trained to want it, to look for it, and to generate it. (p. 6–7)

Glaser and Strauss propose two major strategies for developing grounded theory. The first is the *constant comparative method*, in which the researcher simultaneously codes and analyzes data in order to develop concepts. By continually comparing specific incidents in the data, the researcher refines these concepts, identifies their properties, explores their relationships to one another, and integrates them into a coherent theory.

The second strategy proposed by Glaser and Strauss is *theoretical sampling*, which was described earlier in this book. In theoretical sampling, the researcher selects new cases to study according to their potential for helping to expand on or refine the concepts and theory that have already been developed. Data collection and analysis proceed together. By studying different substantive areas, the researcher can expand a substantive theory into a formal one. Glaser and Strauss explain how their grounded theory of the relationship between nurses' estimation of the social value of dying patients and their care of patients can be elevated to a theory of how professionals give service to clients on the basis of social value.

Figure 6.1 summarizes our version of the grounded theory approach.

In generating grounded theory, researchers do not seek to prove their theories but merely to demonstrate plausible support for these theories. Glaser and Strauss (1967) argue that key criteria in evaluating theories are whether they "fit" and "work":

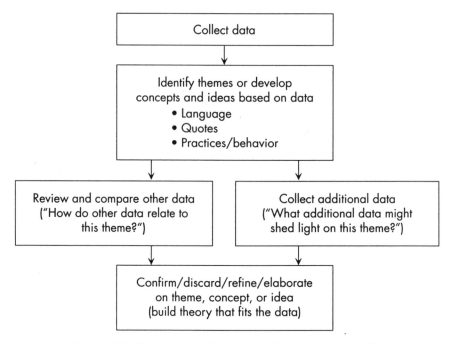

Figure 6.1   One version of the grounded theory approach.

By "fit" we mean that the categories must be readily (not forcibly) applicable to and indicated by the data under study; by "work" we mean that they must be meaningfully relevant to and able to explain the behavior under study. (p. 3)

Ultimately, for Glaser and Strauss, readers must judge the credibility of qualitative studies.

Analytic induction was developed as a procedure for verifying theories and propositions based on qualitative data. As formulated by Znaniecki in 1934, analytic induction was designed to identify universal propositions and causal laws. Znaniecki contrasted analytic induction with "enumerative induction," which provided mere correlations and could not account for exceptions to statistical relationships. The procedure was refined by Lindesmith (1947) and Cressey (1950, 1953) in their respective studies of opiate addiction and embezzlers and was used by Howard Becker (1963) in his classic study of marijuana users. Katz (1983) has characterized analytic induction, which he refers to as "analytic research," as a rigorous qualitative method for arriving at a perfect fit between the data and explanations of social phenomena.

The steps involved in analytic induction are relatively simple and straightforward (see Cressey 1950; Denzin 1978; Katz 1983):

1. Develop a rough definition of the phenomenon to be explained.
2. Formulate a hypothesis to explain that phenomenon (this can be based on the data, other research, or the researcher's insight and intuition).
3. Study one case to see the fit between the case and the hypothesis.
4. If the hypothesis does not explain the case, either reformulate the hypothesis or redefine the phenomenon.
5. Actively search for negative cases to disprove the hypothesis.
6. When negative cases are encountered, reformulate the hypothesis or redefine the phenomenon.
7. Proceed until the hypothesis has been adequately tested (according to some researchers, until a universal relationship has been established) by examining a broad range of cases.

Using this approach, Cressey (1953) arrived at the following explanation of trust violators (a revised formulation of embezzlers):

> Trusted persons become trust violators when they conceive of themselves as having a financial problem which is non-sharable, are aware that this problem can be secretly resolved by violation of the position of financial trust, and are able to apply to their own conduct in that situation verbalizations which enable them to adjust their conceptions of themselves as trusted persons with their conceptions of themselves as users of the entrusted funds or property. (p. 30)

Analytic induction has been criticized for failing to live up to the claims of its early proponents as a method for establishing causal laws and universals (Robinson 1951; Turner 1953). Turner (1953) suggests that analytic induction is fundamentally a method of producing definitions of social phenomena; hence explanations based on analytic induction may be circular.

However, the basic logic underlying analytic induction can be useful in qualitative data analysis. By directing attention to negative cases, analytic induction forces the researcher to refine and qualify theories and propositions. Katz (1983) argues:

> The test is not whether a final state of perfect explanation has been achieved but the *distance* that has been traveled over negative cases and through consequent qualifications from an initial state of knowledge. Analytic induction's quest for perfect explanation, or "universals," should be understood as a strategy for research rather than as the ultimate measure of the method. (p. 133)

In contrast to the grounded theory approach, analytic induction also helps researchers address the question of generalizability of their findings. If researchers can demonstrate that they have examined a sufficiently broad range of instances of a phenomenon and have specifically looked for negative cases, they can assert greater claims regarding the general nature of what they have found.

Our approach is directed toward developing an in-depth understanding of the settings or people under study. This approach has many parallels with the grounded theory method of Glaser and Strauss (1967). Insights are grounded in and developed from the data themselves. In contrast to Glaser and Strauss, however, we are less concerned with developing concepts and theories than with understanding the settings or people on their own terms. We do this through both description and theory. Thus sociological concepts are used to illuminate features of the settings or people under study and to aid understanding. Further, our approach probably places greater emphasis on analyzing negative cases and the context in which data are collected than does the approach of Glaser and Strauss, although our method stops short of imposing the systematic search for generalizations and universals entailed in analytic induction.

WORKING WITH DATA

All researchers develop their own ways of analyzing qualitative data. In this section we describe the basic approach we have used to make sense of descriptive data gathered through qualitative research methods.

Data analysis is probably the most difficult aspect of qualitative research to teach or communicate to others. Many people who are new to the methodology are capable of establishing rapport in the field, asking questions, and recording data, but get stuck when it comes to analyzing their data. They read the many books devoted to qualitative data analysis and still have no idea how to make sense of the data they have collected. Having read Glaser and Strauss (1967), they worry about such matters as the difference between a "category" and a "property." They want to know the simple and clear-cut procedures that will enable them to interpret their data. They spend countless hours coding and recoding their data, but come no closer to developing an understanding of the people or settings they have studied.

The reason why so many people find qualitative data analysis so difficult is that it is not fundamentally a mechanical or technical process; it is a process of inductive reasoning, thinking, and theorizing. Even Glaser and Strauss (1967, 251), who devote an entire book to analytic strategies, point out: "The root sources of all significant theorizing is the sensitive insights of the observer himself." Not all good field researchers are up to the task of significant theorizing, and no one can be trained to have sensitive insights. For many people, the ability to analyze qualitative data comes with experience, especially if they are working with a mentor who helps them learn to see patterns or themes in data by pointing these out. Perhaps the best way to learn inductive analysis is by reading qualitative studies and articles to see how other researchers have made sense out of their data. So, study up—not to find theoretical frameworks to impose on your data, but to learn how others interpret and use data. Books such as *Street Corner Society* (Whyte 1943, 1993), *Tally's Corner* (Liebow 1967), *Gender Play* (Thorne 1983), *Feeding the Family* (DeVault 1991), *Speaking of Sadness* (Karp 1996), *The Urban Villagers* (Gans 1962), *Outsiders in a Hearing World* (Higgins 1980), *Streetwise* (Anderson 1990), and *Having Epilepsy* (Schneider and Conrad 1983) are examples of insightful, clearly written studies.

Because qualitative data analysis is an intuitive and inductive process, most qualitative researchers analyze and code their own data. Unlike quantitative research, qualitative research usually lacks a division of labor between data collectors and coders. Data analysis is a dynamic and creative process. Throughout analysis, researchers attempt to gain a deeper understanding of what they have studied and to continually refine their interpretations. Researchers also draw on their firsthand experience with settings, informants, or documents to interpret their data.

Data analysis, as we see it, entails certain distinct activities. The first and most important one is ongoing discovery—identifying themes and developing concepts and propositions. It is perhaps misleading to have a separate chapter on working with data, since data analysis is an ongoing process in qualitative research. Kvale (1996, 176) refers to what he calls the "1,000-page question" often asked of qualitative researchers: "How shall I find a method to analyze the 1,000 pages of interview transcripts I have collected?" As Kvale argues, the question is posed too late. If you have collected 1000 (or fewer) pages of data and not conducted any analysis, you will be in trouble.

In qualitative research, data collection and analysis go hand in hand. Throughout participant observation, in-depth interviewing, and other qualitative research, researchers are constantly theorizing and trying to make sense of their data. They keep track of emerging themes, read through their field notes or transcripts, and develop concepts and propositions to begin to interpret their data. As their studies progress, they begin to focus their research interests, ask directive questions, check out informants' stories, and follow up on leads and hunches. In many instances researchers hold off on selecting additional settings, people, or documents for study until they have conducted some initial data analysis. Both grounded theory's strategy of theoretical sampling and analytic induction's search for negative cases require this.

The second activity, which typically occurs after the data have been collected, entails coding the data and refining one's understanding of the subject matter. Many of the steps outlined later, such as coding, occur after the data have been collected.

Some researchers prefer to distance themselves from the research prior to engaging in coding and intensive analysis. Practical considerations may also force the researcher to postpone analysis. For example, people sometimes underestimate the amount of time it takes to have taped interviews transcribed.

It is a good idea to begin coding as soon as possible after you have completed the fieldwork or collected the data. The longer you wait, the more difficult it will be to go back to informants to clarify any points or tie up loose ends. Some researchers maintain casual contact with informants throughout data analysis and even after the data have been analyzed and the study is written (see Gallmeier 1991; Miller and Humphreys 1980). Researchers may also have informants read draft reports as a check on interpretations (Douglas 1976; Lincoln and Guba 1985).

The final activity involves attempting to discount findings (Deutscher, Pestello, and Pestello 1993), that is, understanding the data in the context in which they were collected.

Discovery

In qualitative studies, researchers gradually make sense of what they are studying by combining insight and intuition with an intimate familiarity with the data. As noted earlier, this is often a difficult process. Most people inexperienced in qualitative research have difficulty recognizing patterns in their data. You must learn to look for themes by examining your data in as many ways as possible. There is no simple formula for identifying themes and developing concepts, but the following suggestions should get you on the right track.

Read and Reread Your Data
Collect all field notes, transcripts, documents, and other materials and read through them carefully. Then read through them some more. By the time you are ready to engage in intensive analysis, you should know your data inside and out.

As suggested in the chapter on fieldwork, it is always a good idea to have someone else read through your data. An outside reader can sometimes notice subtle aspects that elude the researcher.

Keep Track of Hunches, Interpretations, and Ideas
You should record any important idea that comes to you as you read through and think about your data. Keep a notebook or have a file folder handy for scribbled notes taken when an idea strikes you. In participant observation, researchers sometimes use observer's comments to note ideas and record

interpretations. As you read through your data, you can also make notations in the margins.

Look for Emerging Themes

You must force yourself to search through your data for emerging themes or patterns: conversation topics, vocabulary, recurring activities, meanings, feelings, or folk sayings and proverbs (Spradley 1980). Do not be afraid to identify tentative themes. Just do not develop a stake in any particular idea until you have had a chance to hold it up to experience and check it out.

Some patterns will stand out in your data. In Taylor's institutional study, physical restraints, pay, cleaning the ward, medications, and programming were frequent conversation topics. The attendants' vocabulary included terms such as *low grade, working boy,* and *tripping time.*

Other patterns will not be so apparent. You will have to look for deeper meanings. In his study *Stigma,* Goffman (1963) quotes a fictitious letter that is rich in sociological understanding and compassionate in human terms. This letter can be used to demonstrate how themes can be identified in data:

> Dear Miss Lonelyhearts—
>
> I am sixteen years old now and I don't know what to do and would appreciate it if you could tell me what to do. When I was a little girl it was not so bad because I got used to the kids on the block making fun of me, but now I would like to have boy friends like the other girls and go out on Saturday nites, but no boy will take me because I was born without a nose—although I am a good dancer and have a nice shape and my father buys me pretty clothes.
>
> I sit and look at myself all day and cry. I have a big hole in the middle of my face that scares people even myself so I can't blame the boys for not wanting to take me out. My mother loves me, but she crys terrible when she looks at me.
>
> What did I do to deserve such a terrible bad fate? Even if I did do some bad things I didn't do any before I was a year old and I was born this way. I asked Papa and he says he doesn't know, but that maybe I did something in the other world before I was born or that maybe I was being punished for his sins. I don't believe that because he is a very nice man. Ought I commit suicide?
>
> Sincerely yours,
> *Desperate*

Quite a few themes may be seen here. The first is despair. "Desperate" says she looks at herself and cries and asks whether she should commit suicide; the signature itself reflects this state of mind. The next theme relates to trying to find an explanation for her situation. "What did I do," she asks, "to deserve such a terrible bad fate?" She goes on to speculate about what she did in "the other world" and her father's sins. A third theme, which is somewhat more subtle, has to do with the meanings of physical stigma at different times in a person's life. "It was not so bad" when she was a little girl, but now that she has reached adolescence, when other girls have boyfriends and go out on Saturday nights, it is unbearable. A final theme relates to how "Desperate's" other qualities do not overcome the fact that she does not have a nose. That she may be a good dancer, have a nice shape, and wear pretty clothes does not get her any dates.

Construct Typologies

Typologies, or classification schemes, can be useful aids in identifying themes and developing concepts and theory. One kind of typology relates to how people classify others and objects in their lives. Taylor constructed a typology of how attendants classify residents by listing the terms used by the attendants to refer to their charges: *hyperactives, fighters, spastics, pukers, runaways, pests, dining room boys, working boys,* and *pets.*

The other kind of typology is based on the researcher's own classification scheme. In Taylor's institutional study, attendants frequently talked about the need to control residents. By examining themes in his data in light of this concept, Taylor used the phrase *control measures* to refer to the various ways attendants attempted to control residents' behavior: constant supervision of residents, restrictions on residents' freedom of movement, limiting residents' access to objects and possessions, physical restraining devices, drugging, offering residents rewards and privileges, physical force, work duty, and others.

By developing typologies, you begin to make conceptual linkages between seemingly different phenomena. This, in turn, helps you to build theory.

Develop Concepts and Theoretical Propositions

It is through concepts and propositions that the researcher moves from description to interpretation and theory. Concepts are abstract ideas generalized from observational, interview, or other data. In qualitative research, concepts are sensitizing instruments (Blumer 1969; Bruyn 1966). *Sensitizing concepts,* according to Blumer (1969, 148), provide a "general sense of reference" and suggest "directions along which to look." Blumer proceeds to explain that sensitizing concepts are communicated by "exposition which yields a meaningful picture, abetted by apt illustrations which enable one to grasp the reference in terms of one's own experience." Concepts are used to illuminate social processes and phenomena that are not readily apparent through descriptions of specific instances. Stigma is a powerful example of a sensitizing concept. When we think of stigma as a blot on one's moral character, and not merely a physical abnormality, we are better able to understand what "Desperate," quoted by Goffman (1963), experiences and to relate her experiences to those of others.

Developing concepts is an intuitive process. It can be learned, but not formally taught. However, here are some places to start. First, look for words and phrases in informants' own vocabularies that capture the meaning of what they say or do. Concepts from informants are sometimes referred to as "emic" or concrete concepts: "... the concrete concept is derived indigenously from the culture studied; it takes its meaning solely from that culture and not from the scientist's definition of it" (Bruyn 1966, 39). For example, in Taylor's study of the Duke family, people talk about themselves as being "on disability," but not as being disabled. By carefully analyzing how people used this language in different contexts, Taylor discovered that being "on disability" is contrasted with being "on welfare." It refers to the source of one's government check, but does not bring with it a potentially stigmatizing identity as a disabled or retarded person.

Second, as you note a theme in your data, compare statements and acts with one another to see whether there is a concept that unites them. Glaser and Strauss (1967, 106) point out that this comparison can usually be made from memory. In Taylor's study, attendants took precautions to avoid getting caught violating institutional rules. For example, they placed a "watchdog" at the door to warn them of the arrival of supervisors or visitors and they hit residents in such a way as not to leave marks. Taylor came up with the concept of "evasion strategies" to refer to these activities. Once he developed this concept, he noticed that other activities, such as "fudging" records, were related to these strategies.

Third, as you identify different themes, look for underlying similarities between them. When you can relate the themes in this manner, see whether there is a word or phrase that conveys how they are similar. Thus Goffman's (1959, 1961) concept of "fronts" applies equally to themes related to how institutional officials maintain grounds and how they manage media relations.

A *proposition* is a general statement grounded in the data. The statement that "Attendants use evasion strategies to avoid getting caught violating institutional rules" is a proposition. Whereas concepts may or may not fit, propositions are either right or wrong, although the researcher may not be able to prove them.

Like concepts, propositions are developed by poring over the data. By studying themes, constructing typologies, and relating different pieces of data to each other, the researcher gradually comes up with generalizations. Taylor came up with the proposition that attendants define residents according to whether the residents help or hinder the attendant's own custodial work. Whereas teachers might view people with mental retardation in terms of their learning characteristics or physicians might view them according to their medical etiologies (for example, Down syndrome, organic brain damage, fragile X syndrome), attendants' definitions of residents reflect their concern with ward order and cleanliness.

This proposition was derived from attendants' own typology of residents. By looking at attendants' terms for and comments about residents, Taylor discovered that attendants classify residents according to broad categories related to their practical, day-to-day concerns: *control problems* (residents who get into trouble); *custodial problems* (those who create cleanup work); *supervisory problems* (those who require constant surveillance); *authority problems* (those who resist attendants' authority and control); *special processing* (those who require special treatment and work); *helpers* (those who do attendants' work for them); and *pets* and *no problems* (those who do not cause any problems).

Figure 6.2 summarizes how Taylor moved from a listing of terms attendants used to a typology and then to a proposition about how attendants define residents. Of course, this figure captures the end product of Taylor's theorizing. The process began with Taylor paying attention to attendants' language and asking the question: "What do these terms have in common?" Early on in his study, Taylor came up with the following hunch: "Attendants define residents according to the problems they create for them." Yet this did not adequately capture all of the data. "Helpers" stood out as an exception; and, by examining such negative cases, Taylor refined the proposition to more accurately portray attendants' perspectives.

Read the Literature

Qualitative researchers begin their studies with minimal commitment to a priori assumptions and theory (Glaser and Strauss 1967). Toward the latter stages of your research, you will be ready to start familiarizing yourself with literature and theoretical frameworks relevant to your research.

Other studies often provide fruitful concepts and propositions that will help you interpret your data. It is not uncommon to find that the best insights come from studies of a totally different substantive area. For instance, in the study of the Duke family, some of the most useful literature came not from disability studies but from research on support networks among poor African-American mothers (see for example Stack 1974).

You should be careful not to force your data into someone else's framework. If concepts fit your data, do not be afraid to borrow them. If they do not, forget about them.

How you interpret your data depends on your theoretical assumptions. It is important to expose yourself to theoretical frameworks during the intensive analysis stage of the research. Our own theoretical framework, symbolic interactionism, leads to looking for social perspectives, meanings, and definitions. Thus the symbolic interactionist is interested in questions such as the following:

- How do people define themselves, others, their settings, and their activities?
- How do people's definitions and perspectives develop and change?

Words attendants use to refer to residents	Analysis: attendants' typology of residents	Analysis: Proposition:
"Troublemaker" "Biter" "Fighter" "Working boy" "Pet" "Runaway" "Puker" "Digger" "Smart Alec" "Working Girl" "Low grade" "Choker" "Wise Guy" "Self-Abuser" "Cripple" "Head-banger" "Aggressive" "Bucket Boy" "Soiler" "Helper" "School Boy" "Vegetable" "No Problem" "P.C." ("privileged character")	*Control problems* "Troublemaker" "Aggressive" "Fighter" *Custodial problems* "Low grade" "Soiler" "Cripple" "Vegetable" "Puker" *Authority problems* "Wise Guy" "Smart Alec" *Supervision problems* "Runaway" "Head-Banger" "Self-Abuser" "Biter" "Choker" "Digger" *Special processing* "School Boy" *No Problems* "Pet" "P.C." "No Problem" *Helpers* "Working Boy" "Working Girl" "Helper" "Bucket Boy"	Attendants define residents according to whether they help or hinder their custodial (cleaning and control) work

Figure 6.2 Analysis: constructing a typology and forming a proposition: example from a study of institutional attendants.

- What is the fit between different perspectives held by different people?
- What is the fit between people's perspectives and their activities?
- How do people deal with the discrepancy between their perspectives and activities?

Although most researchers align themselves with a specific theoretical framework, it is standard to borrow from diverse frameworks to make sense of data.

Develop Charts, Diagrams, and Figures to Highlight Patterns in the Data
Charts, diagrams, and figures can serve as useful aides in exploring patterns in your data (Spradley 1980). Sketch out potential relationships between different slices of data and see whether this helps you come up with new understandings.

In their study of staff-to-parent communication on hospital neonatal units, Bogdan, Brown, and Foster (1982) developed the diagram shown in Figure 6.3 to depict the staff's conceptual scheme of patients. Words in quotes refer to those consistently used on the units. Those without quotes are the researchers' phrases and represent categories that the staff members do not have words for but that are evident by the way they talk (e.g., "This *kind* of infant") and act. Although staff members classify infants according to their chances for survival within minutes of their arrival on the units, phrases such as "You can never really tell" dominate their communication with parents.

Early in Taylor's study of the Duke family, he noticed that Bill and Winnie make new friends easily and sometimes become close friends, even best friends, with others in a matter of weeks. Before long, however, they invariably have a falling-out with these friends and become distanced from them. A snapshot of Bill and Winnie's social relations would leave the impression of a succession of short-term, superficial relationships, as has been reported by other researchers among poor people (see for example Liebow 1967). But this would be misleading, because sooner or later the same people show up again at the Dukes' home, and Bill and Winnie become friendly with them again. The same pattern seems to repeat itself over and over again.

To try to make sense of the Dukes' social relations, Taylor charted their relationships with family members and friends with whom they had appeared to be the closest at one time or another over a period of several years. Using concentric circles to roughly approximate closeness and distance, Taylor came up with diagrams such as the one contained in Figure 6.4. This depicts Bill and Winnie's relationship with Lisa and Gary, a couple with three children, whom they have known for a number of years. Around the time Taylor first met the Dukes, Lisa and Gary were evicted from their home, and the Dukes took them in. For a while, the two families did everything

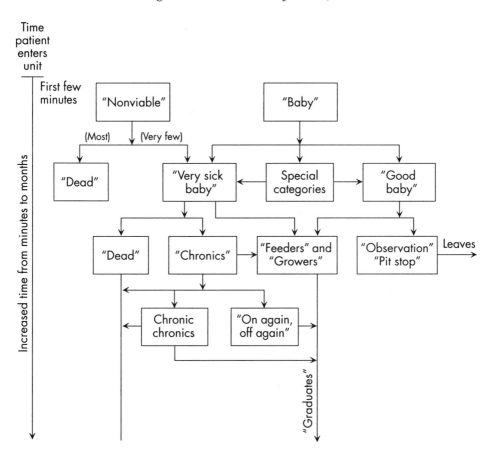

Figure 6.3 Analytical diagram: the staff's classification of infants on a neonatal unit.

together, but then Bill and Winnie had an argument with Lisa and Gary and Bill threw them out of their home. A month later, Bill and Winnie became close to Lisa and Gary again, only to have another falling-out the following month. As shown in Figure 6.4, this pattern continued for years.

On the basis of his analysis, Taylor came to understand social relations within the Dukes' social network in terms of an ebb and flow between closeness and hostility. Relations are characterized by mutual support (for example, taking in homeless people, lending money, doing favors) at one point in time, but bitter feuds (arguments, banishing people from one's home, reporting people to child abuse agencies) at another. Taylor theorized that mutual support and feuds are merely two sides of the same coin and reflect the tenuous social and economic status of the Dukes and other members of their social network.

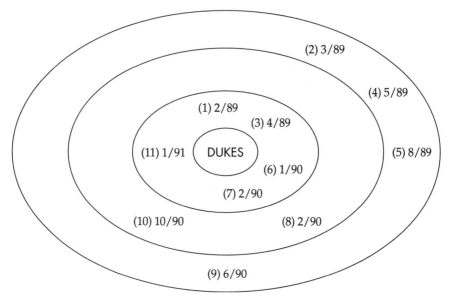

Figure 6.4   Analytic diagram: the ebb and flow of relations—
Lisa and Gary in the Dukes' network.

Proximity to the middle circle indicates closeness to the Duke family. The numbers/
dates refer to Lisa's and Gary's (another family) the closeness to or distance from the
Dukes of Lisa and Gary (another family) at different points in time.

Write Analytic Memos

Throughout the course of your study, you should stand back from your data
and write analytic memos on what you think you are learning. Charmaz
(1983) describes a process of writing, sorting, and integrating memos for
developing grounded theories. You can write memos that attempt to summarize all of the major findings of your study or that comment on specific
aspects of your study. Memo writing also provides an opportunity for you to
think about what additional data you want to collect. If you have written
memos throughout the course of your study, you will find these extremely
helpful when you sit down to write your study. In some cases, entire sections
of your study will have already been written.

Memo writing is especially useful in any kind of team or collaborative
research. Memos help keep researchers on top of what their team members
are learning and thinking.

CODING

In qualitative research, coding is a way of developing and refining interpretations of the data. The coding process involves bringing together and ana-

lyzing all the data bearing on major themes, ideas, concepts, interpretations, and propositions. What were initially general insights, vague ideas, and hunches are refined, expanded, discarded, or fully developed during this process. Here are some strategies that should help you get started in coding your data.

Develop a Story Line

We have always found it helpful to develop a story line to guide theorizing and analysis. The story line is the analytic thread that unites and integrates the major themes in a study. It is an answer to the question, "What is this a study of?"

Perhaps the best way to develop the story line is to come up with a sentence, short paragraph, or phrase that describes your study in general terms. The titles and subtitles of qualitative studies sometimes do this. For instance, the title *Making the Grade: The Academic Side of College Life* (Becker et al. 1968) tells us about the importance of grades to students; the title *Cloak of Competence: Stigma in the Lives of the Mentally Retarded* (Edgerton 1967) communicates the idea that people labeled mentally retarded try to avoid stigma; *Gender Play: Girls and Boys in School* (Thorne 1983) captures Thorne's interest in the social construction of gender on school playgrounds.

Your coding scheme should be based on what you want to write—the theory or sociological story you want to communicate. Many people start coding data without any idea of how they will write the study. As a result, the coding scheme lacks coherence and the researchers waste their time systematically coding data they will never use. When they do try to start writing, they are at a total loss on how to make disparate pieces fit together.

A story line will help you decide what concepts and themes you want to communicate in your study and how your data should be organized and coded. It is useful to think about coding in terms of writing a book (which many people will be trying to do literally). Decide on the major focus of the book, or what we have called the story line. Then, on the basis of the themes you have identified and your analytic memos, decide on what chapters should be in the book, keeping in mind that each chapter must relate to the story line. This will give you the basic structure for your coding scheme.

List All Major Themes, Typologies, Concepts, and Propositions

On the basis of your ongoing analysis, list the major themes in your data as well as your own ideas. Be as specific as possible. Some themes will be specific, and some ideas or concepts will be fully developed. Others will be tentative and vaguely formulated. For example, you may find recurring conversation topics that seem important, although you do not fully understand their meaning or significance.

After you have listed themes, see how they relate to your story line and where they fit into your hypothetical chapter outline. You will find that some themes overlap or relate conceptually and that you will be able to collapse them under broader headings. Some themes will not relate to your story line; these can be ignored. Others may seem relevant even though you are not sure where exactly they fit; you will want to code and analyze these.

At this point in your analysis, you will have a master list of coding categories. The number of coding categories will depend on the amount of data you have and the complexity of your analysis. In his job training study, Bogdan coded his data according to approximately 150 categories. Taylor used roughly 50 categories in his study of institutional attendants. His coding scheme included well-developed propositions ("attendants discount IQ as an indicator of intelligence") and topics of conversation (what attendants say about "programming").

Figure 6.5 lists the initial coding categories for Taylor's study of the Duke family, although this study continues and the coding scheme is being refined over time.

Code Your Data

Coding can be done in different ways, but it usually involves assigning a symbol or number to each coding category. Go through all field notes, transcripts, documents, and other materials indicating which data fit under which coding categories. Code both direct statements and indirect observations. For example, under the theme of *control* in the institutional study, Taylor coded both attendants' comments ("You gotta control them or they'll end up running this place") and his own observations (attendants tying residents in bed at night).

As you code your data, refine the coding scheme; add, collapse, expand, and redefine the coding categories. The cardinal rule of coding in qualitative analysis is to make the codes fit the data and not vice versa. Record any refinements in your master list of coding of categories.

You will notice that some pieces of data fit into two or more coding categories. These should be coded according to all relevant categories.

You should code both positive and negative incidents related to a theme or coding category. As Miles and Huberman (1994), using a statistical metaphor, write:

> Any given finding usually has exceptions. The temptation is to smooth them over, ignore them, or explain them away. But *the outlier is your friend*. . . . It not only tests the generality of the finding but also protects you against self-selecting biases, and may help you build a better explanation. (p. 269)

The exceptional case or negative example can help you refine your interpretations. Two related examples from the institutional study illustrate this.

LIFESTYLE

Housing
- Housing moves
- Evictions

Housekeeping

Income

Work
- Winnie's jobs

Family Purchases/Spending
- Bill's vehicles
- Sammy's vehicles

Family's Charitable Giving

Leisure/Hobbies

Family Pets

Child Rearing

DISABILITY

Disability Terms (e.g., "on disability," "retard," "crazy," "handicapped," "crippled," "medical problems")

Disability Labels from Agencies

Winnie's and Bill's Perspectives on Their Children

RELATIONS WITH FAMILY AND FRIENDS

Perspectives on Family and Friends

Family Gatherings

Relations

Favors
- Taking people in
- Debts to others

Feuds/Arguments
- Reporting others to agencies
- Bill's reports of others sabotaging his vehicles

SOCIAL SERVICES AND GOVERNMENT PROGRAMS

SSI and Social Security

Welfare

"Children's Division"

Food Banks

Disability Programs

School

Neighborhood Groups

Figure 6.5 Analysis: initial coding categories in the study of the Duke family.

In analyzing the proposition that attendants discount IQ as an indicator of intelligence, Taylor found both supportive ("You can't trust IQ") and non-supportive ("You can't teach him that much because his IQ is too low") statements. This led to a deeper understanding and more sophisticated interpretation of attendants' perspectives: attendants distrust professional techniques such as IQ testing, but they may refer to these techniques to justify their own actions.

Attendants viewed residents as severely limited in their potential for learning. "These here are all low grades" and "You can't teach them nothing" were typical comments. In reviewing his data, Taylor came across a number of statements that countered this proposition. One attendant, who usually denigrated residents' intelligence, commented on one occasion, "Yeah, they're dumb like a fox," implying that residents were smarter than they looked. Exploring the meaning of these statements, Taylor discovered that attendants described residents as "smarter than they look" when it came to scolding or punishing them. They were saying that residents "know better" than to cause problems and should be punished for their behavior. These statements were made to account for or justify attendants' treatment of residents. What initially appeared to be a contradiction was resolved through the analytic distinction between *perspectives*—how people view their world—and *accounts*—how people justify their actions to themselves and others. Although attendants may have genuinely viewed residents as severely limited intellectually, they expressed an opposite view when it was expedient to do so.

In qualitative data analysis, most researchers are not concerned with the reliability of their coding procedures as commonly thought of in quantitative research. A coding scheme can be thought of as a personal filing system. Place data in the code—or file folder, to continue the analogy—along with related data in which you see conceptual similarities. Coding is intended to help you develop insights and generate theoretical understandings, not to produce frequency counts to prove your hypotheses.

Sort the Data into the Coding Categories
Sorting data is a noninterpretative, mechanical operation (Drass 1980). Here the researcher assembles all the data coded according to each category. Before the advent of computers, qualitative researchers did this manually, which usually entailed cutting up an extra set of field notes, transcripts, and other materials and placing data relating to each coding category in a separate file folder or manila envelope. Some researchers still prefer to sort their data this way.

Today, of course, now that practically every researcher has a personal computer, computer software programs for coding qualitative data are becoming increasingly popular. A number of books are available that deal exclusively with software for qualitative data analysis (Fielding and Lee 1991; Kelle 1995; Weitzman and Miles 1995). Popular software programs for qualitative analysis include The Ethnograph (Seidel, Kjolseth, and Seymour, 1988), QUALPRO (Blackman 1993), and Q.S.R. NUDIST (Replee Pty Ltd. 1994).

As Miles and Hueberman (1994) point out, the question "What's the best program?" has no answer in the abstract. The answer depends on how comfortable you are with computers and what you want to use the software to do. Minimally, if you are using software for data analysis, you will want to be able to code and retrieve words, sentences, paragraphs, and segments of data. When you code qualitative data, whether manually or through computer software, you not only code quotes and observations but include the context (for example, your questions in addition to the informant's answers) as well. It is also useful to know what set of field notes or transcripts data came from; you should select software with this in mind. Software also exists that can enable you to develop and test propositions and conduct frequency counts.

It is easy to be enamored with computer-aided data analysis. Quantitative researchers are especially likely to use software to make qualitative data appear scientific; however, this imposes a foreign mind-set on qualitative reasoning. A word processor can make writing easier and more efficient, but it cannot make you a better writer. Computer software can serve as a useful "mechanical clerk" (Drass 1980), but there is no substitute for the researcher's insight and intuition in theorizing and interpreting data.

In his study of the Duke family, Taylor is using a different approach than either cutting up field notes or coding with computer software. Having identified the major themes in his study to date, he is going through each set of field notes and briefly, in a short phrase, noting data potentially bearing on themes (Notes #6 "threw out Lisa and Greg"; Notes #40 "Winnie helped mother move"). Then, for each theme, he is recording these brief notations found through his field notes. Thus, under the theme *disability*, Taylor has numerous pages with notations such as the following:

- #5 Bill—SSI-seizures—can't work but can drive a car
- #6 Bill, his sister, and brother institutionalized
- #7 Cindy's book, "Your handicap"
- "medical conditions"
- Winnie-sheltered workshop
- Bill—"probation"
- #11 Bill—"on disability"

Though time-consuming, this process has helped Taylor commit to memory data relating to major themes. In writing about the Duke family, he has also found it easier to work with a smaller number of pages with brief summary statements than with a mass of verbatim quotations and observations. The only hard-and-fast rule of coding is: do what makes sense to you and helps you theorize.

Compare the Data and Refine Your Analysis

Coding and sorting your data enables you to analyze together all data relevant to a theme, concept, or proposition. This is where Glaser and Strauss' (1967) constant comparative method comes into play. By comparing different pieces of data you refine and tighten up your ideas and gradually move to a higher level of conceptualization. To take a simple example, you move from quotes and observations such as "John said, 'You have to let them know who's boss' " and "Attendants keep possessions and objects locked away in a storage room to keep them from residents" to analytic propositions such as "Maintaining ward order and control is a pervasive concern among attendants." Since this is an inductive and intuitive process, there are no simple procedures or techniques for this kind of analysis. You may find it helpful to ask yourself questions like: "What do these quotes or observations have in common?" "What's going on here?" "What does this tell me about how people view their world?" "How do these themes relate to each other?" To the extent that you have written analytic memos and recorded ideas throughout your study, your task will be much easier here.

By analyzing your data in this fashion, you will likely find that some themes that were once vague and obscure will be clearly illuminated. Other concepts or ideas will not fit the data, and some propositions will not hold up. You should be prepared to discard these and develop new ones to accommodate the data.

There are no guidelines in qualitative research for determining how many instances are necessary to support a conclusion or interpretation. This is always a judgment call. The best insights sometimes come from a small amount of data. Glaser and Strauss (1967) argue that a single incident is sufficient for developing a conceptual category for grounded theory.

How you integrate data analysis and writing is a matter of personal preference. Some people prefer to conduct all of their coding, sorting, and analysis before they begin writing a single sentence. Others wait to analyze data until they are ready to write a specific section or chapter.

DISCOUNTING DATA

The final activity in qualitative analysis is what Deutscher (1973) and Mills (1940) call *discounting* the data—interpreting data in the context in which they were collected. As Deutscher (1973) points out, all data are potentially valuable if we know how to assess their credibility:

> We do, of course, routinely discount history or biography according to what we know about the author. . . . We do not discard reports merely because of biases or flaws of one sort or another. If we did, there would be no history. It is all presented by men who have some sort of stake in the matters of which they write, who are located somewhere in their own society (and tend to see the world from that perspective), and whose work is more or less open to methodological criticism. This same observation can be made of all discourse, including social science research reports. (p. 5)

All data must be discounted in this sense. You have to look at how the data were collected in order to understand them. You do not discard anything. You just interpret the data differently depending on the context.

As a check on their analysis and interpretations, Becker, Geer, and Hughes (1968) and Becker et al. (1961) systematically compare their data and provide statistical breakdowns according to such factors as volunteered versus directed statements or whether people made a statement alone or in the company of others. This probably reflects the era in which they conducted their research. In the 1950s and 1960s especially, qualitative research was strongly influenced by positivist concepts of validity and reliability, and many researchers tried to justify qualitative studies according to standards associated with quantitative research. Today, few qualitative researchers would attempt to validate their interpretations through quasi-statistics. Proof is illusive in qualitative research.

Although we believe that it is important to examine data in the context of how they were collected, an informal review should be sufficient for most researchers. There are different questions to ask about how your data were collected.

Solicited or Unsolicited Statements

Although qualitative researchers usually try to let people talk about what is on their minds, they are never totally passive. They ask certain kinds of questions and follow up on certain topics. By doing so, they solicit data that may not have emerged on their own.

You should look at whether people say different things in response to your questions than they do when talking spontaneously. Of course, you would not throw out statements simply because you elicited them. A good qualitative researcher sometimes gets people to talk about things they would otherwise keep hidden or never think to mention. Further, as DeVault (1990) points out, people are often unable to articulate some of their experiences and feelings, and the researcher must help them come up with the words. If you find that people say different things in response to direct questions than they do otherwise, then this becomes a matter for further reflection and deeper interpretation. A response to a direct question means *something*, but you cannot necessarily take it at face value. For example, the one time Taylor asked an attendant directly about abuse on his ward he roundly condemned it; yet this attendant routinely engaged in acts that could be defined as abusive. People may make certain statements because they represent the "right" thing to say, or they may think about certain acts differently in the abstract as opposed to in specific situations.

Your Role in a Setting
Most participant observers try to minimize their effects on the people they are studying until they have grasped a basic understanding of the settings. In the chapter on fieldwork we urged observers to "come on slow" during the early stages of the research. As we noted in that chapter, participant observers almost always influence the settings they study.

Especially during the first days in the field, informants may be cautious in what they say and do. They may even try to "put on" the observer. Attendants admitted to Taylor that they did many things differently when he first started to visit the ward. One attendant explained how they reacted to outsiders:

> We usually know when someone's comin'—an hour or so beforehand. They let us know when someone's coming so we can put some clothes on 'em—make sure they're not bare-assed or jerkin' off when someone comes up here. I had some visitors up here today. . . . They asked me a bunch of questions. I answered em, but I wasn't gonna overdo it. You know? I wasn't gonna tell 'em everything.

It is important to try to understand your effects on a setting. As Emerson (1981, 365) writes, the participant observer must try "to become sensitive to and perceptive of how one is perceived and treated by others." One way to do this is to look at how people reacted to you at different times in the research. In his institutional study, Taylor noticed that attendants reacted differently to him at different points in his study. Most initially seemed guarded in his presence but over time openly said and did things that they ordinarily hid from other outsiders. By comparing data collected at different points in the research, the researcher is better equipped to examine how informants' reactions to his or her presence may have influenced what they said and did.

Who Was There?
Just as an observer may influence what an informant may say or do, so too may other people in a setting. For example, attendants act differently around supervisors than they do among themselves; teachers may say something

among themselves that they would not say to their principal. You should be alert to differences between what people say and do when they are alone as opposed to when others are around. This may help you understand apparent discrepancies in your data.

Direct and Indirect Data

When you analyze your data, you code both direct statements and indirect data bearing on a theme, interpretation, or proposition. The more you have to read into your data to draw inferences based on indirect data, the less sure you can be about whether you have gotten things right (Becker and Geer 1957). Needless to say, a keen insight based on indirect inference is worth much more than a commonsense conclusion.

Who Said What, Did What?

There is a danger of generalizing about a group of people on the basis of what one or a few of them say or do. Some participant observers are so taken in by key informants, so dependent on such informants for information, that they end up with a selective view of a setting. One talkative person can produce reams of data that appear throughout the field notes or transcripts.

For this reason, you should pay attention to the sources of the data on which you base your interpretations. Key informants can provide you with critical insights, but you need to distinguish perspectives held by one person from those shared in common among members of a setting. When we write our studies, we usually try to inform readers as to who said and did what ("one informant," "some people," "most informants," and so on).

Member Checks

Some qualitative researchers use formal *member checks* to refine their interpretations and establish the credibility of their studies (Kvale 1996; Lincoln and Guba 1985; Manning 1997). Through member checks, informants may be asked not only to comment on the researcher's interpretations but to review draft case studies as well. Lincoln and Guba even recommend that researchers assemble a panel of informants to discuss draft reports at the conclusion of a research project. Writing in a different vein, some researchers associated with postmodernism, such as Richardson (1990b), advocate new forms of collaborative research in which researchers relinquish their claim to authority as all-knowing purveyors of objective truth.

Any interpretation of a social scene will be richer if you have induced members of that scene to comment on it and react to it. Even if people reject the interpretation, this can enhance your understanding of their perspectives. Though it is hardly an ethical requirement, it also seems appropriate to provide people with an opportunity to react to what has been written about them as a matter of fairness (Manning 1997).

Yet it is not always practical or desirable to solicit formal reviews of interpretations and findings. In many qualitative studies, researchers penetrate the fronts (Goffman 1959) people use to project a favorable image of themselves. Taylor analyzed the accounts attendants used to make practices that were illegal or distasteful appear morally justifiable to themselves and others. Not only would confronting attendants with this interpretation have shattered the researcher's relationships with them, it would have provoked considerable discomfort and anxiety among them. Further, Taylor's interpretations would have been dismissed in the same manner as the views of officials and professionals: "They don't know what it's really like." In some studies the researchers and subjects do not simply have different interpretations of particular views or practices; they have different worldviews.

Even when the researcher is sympathetic with the perspectives of informants, it may not warrant asking the informants to comment on the researcher's interpretations. A central focus of Taylor's Duke family study has been on the meanings of disability within their social network. People have been disproportionately labeled as disabled or mentally retarded; yet they construct identities of themselves and family members and friends as normal, nondisabled persons. They thereby avoid the social stigma associated with being mentally retarded, in particular, and create a positive social status for themselves. How deeply people hold onto these positive identities is unknown and is probably a matter that should be left unexplored. To confront the Duke family with how they are viewed in the wider society—even assuming that the sociological concept of stigma could be explained to them—would challenge how they prefer to see themselves and threaten to shake the foundations of their identities.

As with other aspects of qualitative research, the advisability of member checks can only be determined in the context of the specific situation in which a study has been conducted.

Your Own Perspective

What you see and report as findings depends on who you are and how you see the world. Findings do not exist independently of the consciousness of the observer. All observations are filtered through the researcher's selective lens. This is not to suggest that findings are solely social artifacts or products of the researcher's imagination. Just because data are never self-explanatory does not mean that anything goes. Within the researcher's theoretical perspective, stock of cultural knowledge, and particular vantage point, findings can more or less accurately reflect the nature of the world. As Richardson (1990b, 27) writes, ". . . because all knowledge is partial and situated, it does not mean that there is no knowledge or that situated knowledge is bad."

In traditional research, bias is to be avoided at all costs. It is assumed that researchers can conduct studies with no values, commitments, theoretical perspectives, or world views. In our view this is impossible.

Rather than to act as though you have no point of view, it is better to own up to your perspective and examine your findings in this light. We occasionally read studies in which researchers have an obvious "ax to grind"—pet theories to impose on the data or values commitments that prevent them from reporting, or even seeing, things that do not fit with what they believe. We also sometimes come across studies in which researchers simply confirm what they thought before they even did their studies. If you do not learn something that challenges your previously held beliefs when you do qualitative research, then you have probably done it in the wrong way.

An understanding of your findings requires some understanding of your own perspectives, logic, and assumptions. This is one of the reasons we advise researchers to record their own feelings and assumptions in observer's comments throughout their studies. Critical self-reflection is essential in this kind of research.

Mentors or colleagues usually can be helpful in challenging your findings or interpretations and helping to keep you honest.

CONSTRUCTING LIFE HISTORIES

The life history contains a description of the important events and experiences in a person's life or some major part of it in his or her own words. In constructing life histories, analysis is a process of editing and putting the story together in such a way that it captures the person's own feelings, views, and perspectives.

As a social science document, the life history should be constructed to illuminate the socially significant features of the person's life. The concept of *career* (Becker 1963; Goffman 1961; Hughes 1937) probably provides the most fruitful way of doing this. The term *career* refers to the sequence of social positions people occupy throughout their lives and the changing definitions of themselves and their world they hold at various stages of that sequence. The concept directs our attention to the fact that people's definitions of themselves and others are not unique or idiosyncratic, but rather follow a standard and orderly pattern according to the situations in which people find themselves (Goffman 1961). In putting together the life history, we try to identify the critical stages and periods in a person's life that shape his or her definitions and perspectives. For example, we can see how the meaning of being labeled mentally retarded changes as people move through infancy, early childhood, secondary age, and adulthood.

In the life history of Jane Fry, her story was organized around her career as a transsexual—that is, the chronology of experiences related to the development of her social identity as a transsexual. The story winds through her family life, high school years, life in the Navy, marriage to a woman, institutionalization as a mental patient, new life as a woman, and reflections on the future.

All analysis in qualitative research starts with becoming intimately familiar with the data. Read through all transcripts, notes, documents, and other data. Identify the major stages, events, and experiences in the person's life. The life history is constructed by coding and sorting the data according to these stages. Each stage becomes a chapter or section in the life history.

You will not be able to incorporate all of the data into the life history. Some stories and topics will not be relevant to your research interests and can be set aside. However, you should try to include all of your data that could change any interpretation of the person's life and experiences (Frazier 1978).

The final step in assembling the life history is editing the subject's accounts of his or her experiences to produce a coherent document. Since people vary in their ability to express themselves clearly, different stories will require different amounts of editing. In our interviewing with people labeled retarded, Ed Murphy was much more prone to engage in small talk and going off on tangents than was Pattie Burt, and hence Ed's story required much more editing.

As a rule, you should make the life history readable without putting words in the person's mouth or changing the meaning of his or her words.[1] You can omit repetitious phrases and words, but you should include the person's characteristic speech patterns, grammatical constructions, and mispronunciations (if you have the life history published, you will have to be firm with copy editors in this regard). You may have to add connecting passages and phrases to make the person's words understandable. Your questions will sometimes have to be incorporated into the person's answers. For example, the question, "When was the first time you heard about the state school?" and the answer, "It was about a week before I was sent there," can be combined to form the statement, "The first time I heard about the state school was about a week before I was sent there."

In most life histories, the researcher's own comments and interpretations are relegated to the introduction or conclusion. Some researchers, such as Sutherland (1937), have used footnotes to comment on or interpret their informants' words.

The preceding chapters have dealt with the logic and procedures of qualitative research methods—designing studies, collecting data, and data analysis. After researchers have collected and made sense of their data, they must decide on how to present their findings and understandings to others. Part 2 of this book is intended to aid the researcher in this endeavor. Chapter 7 provides some general guidance on writing and publishing qualitative studies, and Chapters 8 through 12 contain texts based on qualitative research.

NOTE

1. As discussed in the next chapter on writing, we advise researchers *not* to edit quotations to make them more readable in research articles. Since the life history is intended to be read as a story, albeit a sociological, anthropological, or historical one, the researcher plays a more active role in making it coherent. You do not change a person's words; you simply move them around and leave some of them out of the narrative. Of course, you should explain to readers how you have constructed the life history.

PART TWO

WRITING QUALITATIVE STUDIES

CHAPTER 7

Writing and Publishing Qualitative Studies

THIS CHAPTER DEALS with the culmination of the research process: writing books, articles, research reports, or dissertations based on qualitative studies. The purpose of research is not only to increase your own understanding of social life, but also to share that understanding with others.

Since the mid-1980s, qualitative researchers have devoted ever increasing attention to the writing process. Some researchers, such as Becker (1986) and Wolcott (1990b), have written useful books that demystify and personalize the writing of qualitative studies. We draw on some of the lessons to be learned from these books in this chapter.

Other researchers have focused on the production of qualitative texts as literary narratives. In her 1990 book *Writing Strategies: Reaching Diverse Audiences* and subsequent writings (Richardson, 1992, 1994, 1996b), Richardson has turned the social constructionist perspective inward to examine how researchers use the same literary devices (for example, metaphor and synecdoche) as writers of other forms of narrative. Richardson (1990b, 9) states: "Writing is not simply a true representation of an objective reality, out there, waiting to be seen. Instead, through literary and rhetorical devices, writing creates a particular view of reality."

According to Richardson, researchers do not merely report findings, but transform field notes, documents, interview transcripts, and other data into a form of prose.

Inspired by Richardson and postmodernist and feminist approaches generally, qualitative researchers have been experimenting with new forms of writing ethnography and qualitative research. Ellis's emotional sociology (Ellis 1991a, b; Ellis and Flaherty 1992), Ronai's (1994, in press) layered ethnographic account, and Richardson's (1992, 1996) poetry represent examples. We discussed some of these approaches in Chapter 6.

What Van Maanen (1988) calls "realist tales"—researcher accounts of social and cultural practices and perspectives—continue to be the most common form of qualitative writing. Much of our own writing falls into this category, and many of the suggestions contained in this and other chapters are designed to help people prepare this form of narrative. However, realist tales no longer constitute a monopoly in qualitative writing. "Confessional tales" and "impressionist tales," again to use Van Maanen's terminology, appear with greater frequency in the qualitative literature.

That there are new forms of reporting research and reflecting on social life is a healthy sign for the qualitative enterprise. No single form of writing should be associated with the "qualitative way." Even studies designed to paint an accurate picture of the social life of a group of people can benefit from increased sensitivity to the researcher's role in conducting the study and producing the final narrative product.

For this reason we welcome experiments with new and unconventional forms of writing qualitative work. If audiences learn something about social life from these experiments, so much the better. No one can teach anyone else how to come up with new ways of reporting and writing. And neither of us can teach literature or poetry. What we can offer are some guidelines we use in writing qualitative studies and some lessons we have learned about the writing process. In presenting these, we have one version of qualitative writing in mind; this is not the only one.

WHAT YOU SHOULD TELL YOUR READERS

As qualitative researcher, in contrast to a fiction writer, poet, or creative writer, you owe it to your readers to explain how you collected and interpreted your data. Deutcher's (1973; also see Deutscher, Pestello, and Pestello, 1993) notion of *discounting*, described in the last chapter, is relevant not only to analysis but to the writing process as well. Provide enough information about how your research was conducted to enable readers to discount your account or to understand it in the context of how it was produced. Many people tend to gloss over the specifics of their methodology. When we read their studies, we have no way of knowing whether their interpretations came from cultural knowledge, prior theoretical frameworks, direct personal experience, or actual fieldwork or interviewing. Hence we do not know how to judge the credibility of their accounts.

The controversy surrounding the popular writings of Carlos Castaneda (1968, 1971, 1972, 1974, 1977) and his dissertation in anthropology (1973) in the 1970s and early 1980s raises some interesting questions about the production of qualitative reports. Castaneda's wonderfully entertaining and in many ways insightful writings on the relative nature of reality are supposedly based on his mystical journeys with the Yaqui Indian sorcerer, don Juan. The foreword to one of the later books (Castaneda 1987, vii) reads: "My books are a true account of a teaching method that don Juan, a Mexican Indian sorcerer, used in order to help me understand the sorcerers' world."

Writer, psychologist, and self-taught anthropologist Richard de Mille (1976, 1980), joined by others, makes a convincing case that Castaneda's account is a hoax. By identifying internal inconsistencies in Castaneda's books, comparing his writings to those in philosophy and religion, and examining factual inaccuracies in his stories, de Mille concludes that what Castaneda passes off as ethnographic fieldwork is actually fiction based on library research. Castaneda has never been inclined to defend his work and has ignored requests to show field notes and other documentation to the skeptics.

Does it matter whether Castaneda's writings are grounded in fieldwork or are the product of a creative imagination? A strict postmodern stance might lead to the conclusion that it does not. If both fact and fiction are simply different forms of narrative, with neither having a superior claim to truth, then it would seem irrelevant to ask how Castaneda wrote his accounts. After all, Castaneda teaches important lessons about the nature of reality and knowledge systems.

Yet readers have a right to know what is simply a good story full of sociological insights and what is an attempt to capture a way of life more or less accurately. If we know what Castaneda (or any other writer) based his accounts on, then we will be in a better position to interpret the accounts. For example, assume that Castaneda's writings are works of fiction. Reading them conveys a clearer and more personal understanding of certain variants of European philosophy than can be achieved by wading through the original writings themselves. However, if we are informed about what Castaneda is trying to do, then we will not read his books for an understanding of Yaqui Indian belief systems or the sorcerers' knowledge of the hallucinogenic effects of different desert plants or herbs. Both fiction and traditional ethnographic reporting can be valuable, as long as we know which is which.

Although few researchers consciously fabricate their studies, it is true, as Douglas (1976, xiii) argues, that most or perhaps all qualitative accounts are "laundered": ". . . authors choose to leave certain important parts of the context out, certain details about what really happened, how they got their data or failed to do so." The trend toward candid reporting of experiences in the field started by Johnson (1975) and represented by what Van Maanen (1988) refers to as "confessional tales" is a welcome development in qualitative research. Probably no researcher will reveal to readers everything about what happened in the course of research, but the more told, the better.

Lincoln and Guba (1985) and others (Manning 1997) have proposed formal schemes for evaluating the authenticity and trustworthiness of qualitative studies. These are useful in raising some questions that can be asked about how a researcher arrived at his or her conclusions, although, as Miles and Huberman (1994) note, there are no agreed-upon canons or heuristics for evaluating a qualitative study. Each reader must necessarily judge the credibility of a qualitative study for him- or herself.

We can outline some of the information we like to have when we read a study based on qualitative methods. We find this information useful in discounting studies, to use Deutscher's (1973) term. It is not that we dismiss studies that fail to report this information; many outstanding studies have been written that provide little information about how they were conducted. However, we sometimes evaluate a study differently depending on what the researcher did in the field. For example, we tend to have more confidence in the interpretations reached by an interviewer who conducted multiple interviews with people over an extended period of time than those of a researcher who conducted one-shot interviews.

We usually look for the following information in books, monographs, and dissertations based on participant observation or qualitative interviewing. In shorter pieces and journal articles, space limitations preclude covering all of these points, at least in detail (certainly, we have not always provided all of this information in articles we have written).

1. *Methodology.* You should inform readers of the general methodology (participant observation, in-depth interviewing, documents) and specific procedures (field notes constructed from memory, audio- or videotaping) used in your study. We also like to see researchers locate their work in existing literature on qualitative research. Especially in applied fields, qualitative research has become popular in recent years, and many people are using the phrase in a way that has little in common with any published literature on the methodology. For instance, open-ended questions in a structured survey or questionnaire are sometimes referred to as producing qualitative data.

2. *Theoretical perspective.* Do you intend your study to be descriptive in nature, or has it been guided by a particular theoretical perspective (symbolic interactionism, critical ethnography, feminist theory, ethnomethodology, etc.)?

3. *Time and length of study.* You should tell readers how much time you spent in the field and over what time frame.

4. *Nature and number of informants and settings.* What kinds of settings did you study? How many? How specifically would you describe your informants?

5. *Research design.* How did you identify and select settings, informants, or documents to study? Did you use a strategy such as theoretical sampling? Did you know informants or settings beforehand?

6. *Your own frame of mind.* What was your original purpose? How did this change over time? What assumptions and allegiances did you bring into the study?

7. *Your relationship with people.* You should try to stand back from your study and describe your relationship with informants and how they saw you. Why should the reader have confidence that people acted naturally in your presence?

8. *Your analysis.* How did you analyze your data? What checks did you place on your interpretations? Did informants review drafts of your study? What did they say?

SOME TIPS ON WRITING

Some have joked that to be a social scientist is to be a poor writer (Cowley 1956). Many important ideas are obscured and many trivial ones made to sound profound through jargon and excessive verbiage (Mills 1959).

The ability to write clearly and concisely is an important skill. Like many of the other skills discussed in this book, it is learned through practice, discipline, and exposure to exemplary works. There are no quick and easy ways to become a good writer.

Writing is a deeply personal matter. As Richards (in Becker 1986) notes, it is not uncommon for people who have not had much experience publishing their work to get "stuck" when they try to write or to feel personally vulnerable about showing their writing to others. Writing can be a high-risk operation. If you experience any of these feelings, understand that other people do also.

Most people find it difficult to write at times. Even experienced and much-published writers can have problems getting started on new projects. For every person who can turn out a quick first draft, at least one other person is what Wolcott (1990b) refers to as a "bleeder." Further, we all have our own rituals and procrastination devices (Becker 1986) to avoid getting down to the task of writing.

With these thoughts in mind, we offer some suggestions you may find useful when you try to write.

Experiment with Different Ways of Writing

As Becker (1986) argues, there is no one best way to write. This is a matter of personal preference. Some writers, ourselves included, prefer to write from a detailed outline containing major and subordinate points (Wolcott 1990b). As noted in the last chapter, we let writing guide our analysis. We decide on the central story line (what Wolcott [1990b] calls "the problem problem") and then think in terms of chapters, or major sections, that relate to it.

Others follow what Becker (1986) refers to as "free-writing." The idea is to get something—anything—down on paper. Express your ideas freely; you can always edit later. Becker (1986) advises,

> Once you know that writing a sentence down won't hurt you, know it because you have tried it, you can do what I usually ask people to try: write whatever comes into your head, as fast as you can type, without references to outlines, notes, data, books or other aids. The object is to find out what you would like to say, what all your earlier work on the topic or project has already lead you to believe . . .
>
> If you write this way, you usually find out, by the time you get to the end of your draft, what you have in mind. Your last paragraph reveals to you what the introduction ought to contain, and you can go back and put it in and then make the minor changes in other paragraphs your new-found focus requires. (pp. 54–55)

In addition to this style of free-writing, Becker recommends that you take notes on what you have written, putting each idea on a file card. Then sort the cards into piles according to which seem to go together. For each pile, put a card on top that summarizes what the cards appear to have in common. Through this process an outline will emerge to guide your writing.

Decide What Audience You Wish to Reach and Adjust
Your Style and Content Accordingly

It is useful to have a specific audience or type of reader in mind when you write. One writes differently for qualitative researchers, a general social science audience, professionals in applied fields, and so on. If you are writing a dissertation, you certainly have to take into account the preferences and interests of committee members. Try to put yourself in the role of the readers: "Will they understand and appreciate what I am saying?"

Richardson (1990b) uses the term "encoding" to refer to the rhetorical function of locating writing in a particular genre (for example, popular, academic, moral, or political). Richardson (1990b, 32) writes, "Audiences have expectations regarding 'their' texts. Overall organization, code words, title, authorial designation, metaphors, images, and so on serve as signposts to potential readers."

By writing for your audience, you do not skew your findings to please readers. It is true, as Warren (1980) argues, however, that researchers take into account the anticipated reactions of colleagues, friends, journal editors, informants, and others when they prepare research reports and that this influences the body of knowledge we call science.

Decide on Your Persona

As Becker (1986, p. 33) points out, ". . . everyone writes as someone, affects a character, adopts a persona who does the talking for them." Most researchers are not conscious or explicit about the personae they adopt in their writing. They assume that as researchers they should write "classy" prose and adopt an objective, formal, and authoritative stance (for example, "This researcher concludes . . ." "It was found . . ."). This is only one of many options; the current interest in the social construction of social science narratives (Richardson 1990b) directs attention to the importance of being more conscious about persona and opens up new possibilities for experimenting with different styles of narrative reporting. Examples of different personae provided by Becker include "experiential authority" and "intimate knowledge" (details about the researcher's observations and role in the field) as well as Becker's (1986, 36–37) preferred character, the "Will Rogers," "plain folks" persona: "Shucks, you'd of thought the same as me if you'd just been there to see what I seen. It's just that I had the time or took the trouble to be there, and you didn't or couldn't, but let me tell you about it.' " Fine and Martin (1990) show how Goffman's *Asylums* is colored by sarcasm, satire, and irony and how the author takes on the persona of a partisan on the side of mental patients.

Let Your Readers Know Where You Are Going

In your final drafts, help your readers by telling them your purpose early in your writing and explain how each topic relates to this along the way. In every chapter or major section, start with a summary of what you intend to cover.

Be Concise and Direct

Use short sentences, direct words, and the active voice as much as possible. For specific rules on clear writing, skim Strunk and White's *The Elements of Style* (1979).

Social scientists have been accused of being boring writers and using complicated words when there are simple ones available. Malcolm Cowley (1956) brings home this point with the following example:

> A child says "Do it again," a teacher says "Repeat the exercise," but the sociologist says "It was determined to replicate the investigation." Instead of saying two things are alike or similar, as a layman would do, the sociologist describes them as being either isomorphic or homologous . . .

... A sociologist never cuts anything in half or divides it into two like a lay-man. Instead he dichotomizes it, bifurcates it, subjects it to a process of binary fission, or restructures it in a dyadic conformation—around a polar foci.

As you review drafts, constantly ask yourself whether you can use sim-pler, more commonly understood words to communicate your ideas.

Ground Your Writing in Specific Examples
Qualitative research should yield rich descriptions. Illustrative quotations and descriptions convey a deep understanding of what settings and people are like and provide support for your interpretations. Your account should be filled with clear examples.

Edit Early Drafts Carefully
Few people can write a polished draft the first time around. After you write a draft of an article or chapter, let it sit for a while to gain some distance. Then go back to the draft and eliminate unnecessary words, sentences, phrases, and paragraphs. Wolcott (1990b) explains that he sometimes goes through drafts in mechanical fashion and tries to eliminate one unnecessary word in every sentence and one unnecessary sentence on every page. He pays special atten-tion to unnecessary qualifiers (for example, *very, rather, really, pretty*) that many people use out of habit. Becker (1986, 5) advises going through drafts word by word, asking, "Does this need to be here? If not, I'm taking it out."

Have Colleagues or Friends Read and Comment on Your Writing
Even if someone is not familiar with your field, he or she can critique your writing in regard to clarity and logic. A good reader is someone who is not afraid to provide you with critical comments (accept them) and gets around to reading your work within a few weeks.

COMMON MISTAKES IN WRITING FROM QUALITATIVE DATA

Having read countless student research reports and dissertations as well as articles submitted for journal publication, we have come across the same mistakes or errors repeated time and time again. In this section we identify some common mistakes that you would be wise to avoid. Any knowledge-able reader will be able to identify classic works in which these mistakes are made. Goffman (1959, 1961, 1963), for example, did not follow all of the guidelines offered in this section. If you are a creative theorist capable of breaking new ground and establishing a new genre, then you do not need to follow conventions to begin with, but if you are going to try something new or different, you had better be very good at it.

1. *Letting quotes make your points.* Do not use quotes to make your points. The following is an example of what you should avoid: "The following quotes illustrate the teachers' perspectives . . ." When you quote without providing an interpretation, readers are led to believe that you are incapable of analysis. Make the point and then use a quote or description to illustrate it.

2. *Overuse of colorful quotes or examples.* Avoid using the same quote or description over and over again. In general, any specific quote should be used once and only once. Repeating quotes or examples leaves the impression that your data are thin.

3. *Changing quotes.* Unless you are writing a life history, which readers will know is constructed as a readable narrative, do not revise or edit quotes. Quotes help bring people to life. More important, revising or editing quotes can change their meanings. Field notes and transcripts are already subject to many possible distortions; do not introduce any more. If you believe that it is absolutely necessary to clarify a quote or put it into context, you can put your own comments in parentheses. When you omit words in a quote, use ellipses (. . .).

4. *Insufficient quotes.* Although we have already made the point that qualitative research accounts should be filled with quotes and rich descriptions, this bears repeating. Quotes and descriptions help readers understand how you have reached your conclusions and interpretations.

5. *Lengthy quotes and data overkill.* Most people become enamored with their own data and try to squeeze as many quotes as possible into their writing. If you include frequent lengthy quotes in your writing, most readers will stop reading them or become confused about what point you are trying to illustrate. Quotes should be concise, succinct, and crisp. Quotes should usually be no longer than several sentences. Use series of quotes sparingly.

6. *Quoting your observer's comments.* Do not quote your observer's comments from field notes unless you are the focus of the discussion (for example, an article on dilemmas in the field). Your hunches at the time you recorded data do not validate the points you are trying to make when you write.

7. *Quantitative language lapses.* Do not use *results* for *findings;* the term *results* conjures up images of an experiment. Instead of referring to *subjects* or *respondents,* refer to *informants,* or better yet, *people, students, parents,* and so on.

8. *Overstatement.* Avoid sweeping generalizations based on your study. We all tend to believe that we have discovered universal truths through our research. It is fine to believe this; just do not claim it. Qualitative methods are best suited to developing insights and understandings that apply to a particular group of people at a particular point in time, and are not well suited to reaching generalizations about a broader population. Feel free to suggest or point to general lessons, but be modest in doing this. Understatement adds to the credibility of your study. Overstatement detracts from it.

9. *Orphan findings and royalty.* All findings are somebody's findings. When you write any research piece, you are presenting *your* findings, *your* interpretations, and *your* conclusions. Do not be afraid to use *I* and *my*. Instead of saying, *It was found,* say *I found.* Do not use the "royal we" if you are writing as a single author.

10. *Cheap literary devices.* Rhetorical questions and exclamation points can be effective devices for making or drawing attention to major points. If you overuse them, however, they lose their power and begin to appear to be a substitute for explaining your point.

11. *Failing to acknowledge the contributions of others.* When you write anything, be sure to acknowledge the direct or indirect contributions of others. Specific ideas taken from anyone else, whether published or not, should be credited to that person in the text of your report or a footnote. A general acknowledgment should be included to thank others for their indirect contributions to your research. Err on the side of being generous, rather than stingy, in your acknowledgments (Wolcott 1990b).

12. *Moral superiority.* It is easy to adopt a tone of moral superiority when writing about other people's perspectives and practices. All people have illusions about themselves and can be made to look foolish. Be gentle and sensitive in your portrayal of people. Avoid gratuitous moral judgments.

PUBLISHING QUALITATIVE STUDIES

Getting your work published usually requires a major commitment of time and energy. If you are not willing to make this commitment, you are unlikely to publish your work. Publishing requires persistence and self-confidence. It is not something for people with weak egos. All authors have their work rejected at one time or another.

A small number of qualitative studies end up being published as books. If you think that your study has the potential to be published as a book (the best way to determine this is by having someone who has published a book evaluate your work), the first step is to research potential publishers to see which ones might be interested in your work. Many academic publishers (the University of California Press, Temple University Press, the University of Chicago Press, Teachers College Press) are receptive to qualitative studies. Both academic and commercial publishers sometimes sponsor series in specialty areas such as gender, race, or disability. The more you know about publishers, the better your chance of finding one that might be willing to publish your book. If possible, try to get the name of a contact at a publisher. Publishers receive a large number of unsolicited manuscripts and proposals, and it helps to be able to send something to a specific person. If you know someone who has published a book through a specific publisher, that person is a good contact. You can also check the acknowledgments in recently published books; most authors thank their editors. Many publishers have display booths at professional conferences, and you can usually make contacts this way.

Once you have identified potential publishers, develop a brief book proposal, or *prospectus.* It is usually not worth sending an entire manuscript to publishers; they will not read it. The prospectus should provide a brief overview of the book, an autobiographical statement, a table of contents, a list of competing books already published and a description of how your book is different, and a description of the potential audience or market for your book. No publisher can afford to publish a book that will not sell, so this last item is especially important. Most publishers are especially interested in books that can be used as college texts or supplemental reading in courses. Specify the kinds of courses in which your book might be used.

It is usually easier to publish an article in a professional or research journal than a book.[1] Again, you need to do your research. In addition to sociological and anthropological journals, a growing number of journals in applied fields such as education, management, disability studies, health, and social work are open to articles based on qualitative research. Skim articles published in journals in the past year or two to see whether any qualitative articles have been published; if not, then it is probably not worth your time to submit to these journals.

Since it is generally considered unethical to submit the same manuscript to more than one journal at the same time, you will need to decide where to submit your study first. (If your manuscript is not accepted by a journal, then you can submit it to another.) All journals include their editorial policy, or information for contributors. Pay careful attention to this. It will tell you such things as page limitations (do not exceed these), the number of copies to submit, and the preferred publication style of the journal (for example, Chicago Manual of Style, American Psychological Association). Manuscripts are seldom rejected solely on the basis of failure to use the recommended style. However, if your manuscript represents a substantial departure from the preferred style, this creates an unfavorable impression on the part of an editor or reviewers. It looks as though you have not taken the time to know the journal's requirements or, perhaps, as though you are submitting a manuscript that has been rejected by another journal. Some journals require authors to pay a submission fee to offset the costs of publishing the journal and will not consider manuscripts for publication unless this is paid in advance.

Publication decisions in professional and research journals are based on the peer review process. The editor, or in some journals an associate editor, selects two to five persons with knowledge or expertise in areas addressed by a manuscript to review it and provide a publication recommendation as well as comments for the author. Anyone who has had experience with journals knows that the peer review process is not infallible. Reviewers often disagree in their evaluations of manuscripts, and editors sometimes reject quality submissions.

You can maximize your chances of having a manuscript accepted for publication by anticipating the kinds of persons who might serve as peer reviewers or referees and by writing your manuscript in such a way as to guide editors in selecting the right reviewers. Journals publish a list of regular reviewers who serve on editorial boards or as consulting editors. In addition, most journals use guest reviewers to supplement their regular reviewers.

Journal editors are busy people who perform this role on top of their other responsibilities and do not have the time to read a manuscript carefully before all reviews are completed. Reviewers are typically selected on the basis of a quick skimming of a manuscript—often only the title, abstract, and possibly the reference list at the end. Editors look first to their regular reviewers or editorial board and secondarily to persons who have published related research in their own journals or related ones (journal editors generally keep on top of research published in the field).

This is where you can potentially influence the selection of reviewers. If you have familiarized yourself with the editorial board and with people who have published recent articles related to your own, you can use code words—what Richardson (1990b) calls "encoding"—in your title and abstract and list references that are likely to guide an editor to certain kinds of reviewers. You want your manuscript to be reviewed by those who will give it the most favorable reading. If your study is qualitative, you certainly want to highlight this in your title and abstract and include plenty of references to related qualitative work. Never directly suggest potential reviewers to editors; these persons will probably be excluded.

If you can anticipate the kinds of reviewers who will evaluate your manuscript, you can also take this into account in the literature you review or cite in your study. Editors and reviewers expect authors to be aware of related research and will sometimes base rejections on a failure to relate a study to the literature. If reviewers have published in the area addressed by your manuscript, you can be sure that they will look for references to their own work.

Generally, journal editors furnish one of four editorial decisions based on reviewers' recommendations (although reviewers usually provide comments to authors, most journals have them furnish their recommendations directly and confidentially to the editor): *accept; accept with revisions; do not accept, invite revision and resubmission;* and *reject* or *do not accept.* Few manuscripts are accepted as submitted, and *reject* is the most common decision. If your manuscript is not accepted and you are not invited to resubmit it, go to another journal and start all over. Most editors will not accept a resubmission of a rejected article.

An *accept with revisions* decision means that your manuscript will be accepted for publication with relatively minor changes or revisions. The editor will usually make the final decision on publication him- or herself. A *do not accept, invite revision and resubmission* decision means that the reviewers have raised some substantive concerns or questions about your manuscript and that the editor is open to seeing whether you can address them. If you submit a revised manuscript, the editor will send it back to the original reviewers, and perhaps one or two new reviewers, for their final publication recommendations. The editor may or may not tell you explicitly how a revised manuscript will be handled. Wording such as "major concerns" or "substantive revisions" generally indicates that a revised manuscript will be sent out for another round of reviews.

If you are fortunate, the editor will summarize the major areas for revision. Some editors do, and some do not. If the editor does not provide you with specific guidance for revisions, you will have to depend on the reviewers' comments and suggestions. Since reviewers often give inconsistent advice, it can be a difficult task to know which recommendations to follow.

Both an *accept with revisions* and a *do not accept, invite revision and resubmission* decision should be interpreted as expressing a positive interest in your work. Many authors, especially those who are new at trying to get their work published, are discouraged when reviewers provide critical comments about their studies and their manuscripts are not immediately accepted. In the better journals in the social sciences and applied fields, only 10 to 20 percent of manuscripts are accepted (or accepted with revisions) during the initial review process and well over 50 percent are rejected outright. So an invitation to revise and resubmit your manuscript is a sign of encouragement. If you can possibly address the reviewers' concerns, you should put the effort into making the revisions.

In evaluating revised manuscripts, both editors and reviewers look to see whether authors have made a conscientious effort to address concerns and recommendations from the initial review process. Be responsive and attend to all of the recommended changes in some way. A cover letter summarizing revisions will demonstrate your responsiveness to recommendations made previously and will be helpful to the editor and reviewers. Most editors will listen to a compelling rationale for not making recommended changes. However, do not use your cover letter to argue with the editor or reviewers or to question the review process. Any decent journal receives more quality manuscripts than there is space to publish; in most cases, you need the journal more than the editor needs your work.

Some of what we consider our best work has been rejected by publishers and journals before we found anyone interested in publishing it. Even if your book or article is rejected, use comments and suggestions to make it better. Then submit it elsewhere. Publishers and editors are not perfect. They may make mistakes, and a rejection sometimes means nothing more than a poor fit between your manuscript and the interests of a publisher or editor.

SELECTED STUDIES

Chapters 8 through 12 contain text written by us (in one case, with a colleague and former student) on the basis of the methods described in this book. These chapters are presented as examples of some of the many ways in which qualitative studies can be presented.

Chapter 8 contains an abbreviated version of a life history of a transsexual published by Bogdan in 1974. Jane Fry's story is told in her own words as communicated during tape-recorded, open-ended interviews and edited and compiled by Bogdan. Her story is permitted to speak for itself, with a minimum of interpretation by the researcher.

Chapter 9 contains a text based on Taylor's institutional study. We include this study here because we cite examples from it throughout this book. The study is largely descriptive and, as the title suggests, attempts to present how attendants view the persons under their care. Taylor conducted this study for his dissertation. The study was published 10 years afterward; this shows that it can take many years to publish articles based on a study.

Chapter 10 is based on a dissertation by Rannveig Traustadottir, a colleague and former student of ours. In this chapter Traustadottir and Taylor examine the subtle, invisible work women do to help children and adults with disabilities to form and maintain relationships with others. Traustadottir's work was based on the methods described in this book and was undertaken from a feminist standpoint.

Chapter 11 is based on Taylor's ongoing study of the Duke family, referred to in this book. This chapter reports on a relatively small slice of Taylor's study of that family, namely, relations with child protective agencies and suitability as parents. At the conclusion of the chapter, Taylor struggles with some of the policy issues surrounding child abuse and parents with disabilities.

Chapter 12 focuses on how those in close relationships with people who have severe mental disabilities think about, or construct, their disabled family members or friends. This chapter is based on a long-term applied study of agencies supporting people with severe disabilities in the community. In the course of that study, the researchers came across numerous examples of people who, in contrast to conventional wisdom, had come to like, love, and accept people who others might see as less than human. This chapter looks in depth at these persons' perspectives.

NOTE

1. Bogdan and Taylor have reviewed manuscripts for *Qualitative Sociology, Journal of Contemporary Ethnography, Social Problems, American Sociologist, Human Organization, Mental Retardation, Journal of the Asso-*

ciation for Persons with Severe Handicaps, Aggressive Behavior, Disability & Society, Journal of Disability Policy Studies, Exceptional Children, American Journal on Mental Retardation, Journal of Health and Social Behavior, and *Symbolic Interaction,* among others. Until June 2000, Taylor serves as editor of the journal *Mental Retardation.*

CHAPTER 8

The Autobiography of Jane Fry

ROBERT BOGDAN

THIS CHAPTER CONTAINS excerpts from the autobiography of a person I will call Jane Fry.[1] She is a high school dropout, a veteran of the Navy, and a former resident of five psychiatric facilities, and although she has the sexual organs of a man, she dresses and lives as a woman, and feels that she is one.

This narrative, dealing with one person's life as she tells it, is presented as more than just a story. It may be engaging, personal, moving, and enjoyable, as stories are, but its aim is one common in the social sciences: a better understanding of society, its institutions, and those who pass through them. It is a sociological autobiography; that is, it was collected and edited by one trained to ask and be concerned with sociological questions. Here, as in similar works, the sociologist partner in the enterprise guides the narrator to give details and to elaborate on areas of interest to his or her discipline. In compiling and editing as well, the concern is to present materials of sociological importance rather than to focus on materials that might serve other purposes, such as entertainment or popular market value.

This autobiography was compiled from tape-recorded interviews conducted with Jane Fry over a three-month period in 1972. The interviews lasted from one to five hours each and totaled approximately 100 hours. Over 750 pages of transcribed materials resulted from this effort.

PURGATORY: JANE FRY'S STORY

Being referred to as a "transsexual" doesn't bother me too much. I would rather be thought of as a person first, but it doesn't make me angry because that's what I am. A transsexual is a person who wishes to change sexes and is actively going about it. Which is exactly what I am doing.

I have the physical organs of a man, but I feel that I am a woman. For a long time I fought these feelings, but I don't anymore. I take female hormones and dress and live as a woman, and I have for two years. I understand my transsexualism for what it is. Basically, it boils down to this: What is a person? Is a person what he is on the inside? Or what he is on the outside? I know what I am on the inside, a female. There is no doubt there. I could spend 50 years of my life trying to change, but I doubt if that would do anything. I know what I am. I like it, and I don't want to change. The only thing I want to change is my body, so that it matches what I am. A body is like a covering; it's like a shell. What is more important? The body or the person that is inside?

I went for three years of psychotherapy and I couldn't find anything in my childhood to pin this thing down on, nothing that would be different from your background or anybody else's. Sure, if you look hard enough into my childhood you would find things, just like if I looked into yours I could find things, if I wanted to. You might say that there were psychological reasons for my state if my father was a superdrunk, or if my mother made me sleep with her, or if she wanted a girl so much she dressed me in girls' clothes; but there was nothing like that. My father said to me once that there were a few males on his side of the family way back that were fairly feminine. I don't know whether heredity is part of it or not. For sure, my father isn't feminine.

I spent three years searching for psychological reasons and other kinds of reasons, because I was expected to. I'm not interested in reasons anymore. I don't give a damn what caused it. God could have poked his finger in by belly button and said, "You're going to think of yourself as a girl," and that could have caused it. All I want to do is get it fixed. I just want to be myself. But in order to get it fixed you have to convince God knows how many people that you're sane, convince people that you really want the operation, find someone to do it, and come up with the money.

I stopped looking for reasons two years ago. Every doctor you see gives you a different explanation, and you just come to the point of knowing that they just don't know what the hell they are talking about. One thing I did learn in meeting all the doctors is that you have to give a little—pretend a little. Any one of them can kill you physically or emotionally. They can put the dampers on everything. If they decide that I am totally insane because I want to be a female, who knows what they can do. I nod when they tell me their theories now. You have got to learn to give and take, which I took some time in learning.

Before I go on and tell you about the operation and transsexualism and the hassle involved in that, let me tell you a little about the way I look at life and analyze myself. There is this story I heard once about Freud that pretty much sums it up. He was at a meeting with some colleagues, and he lit up this huge stogey. His colleagues around the table started snickering because of his writing about oral complexes and phallus symbols. Freud just looked at it and said, "Yes, gentlemen. I know this is a phallic symbol but it is also a god damned good cigar." That's a good way to look at life. If it's enjoyable, do it as long as it doesn't harm anybody, and don't worry about analyzing everything. That is my philosophy. I am the only one responsible for what I do, and as long as I don't harm another human being mentally or physically, I'm being a good person. I think that I'm a good person because I operate according to my principles. I may break the law, but I'm not breaking my law which seems like the sensible one to me. I also think people should help each other, which I try to do. I think people should help me. They shouldn't sit down and try to analyze me, or try to figure out why I am the way I am or whether I am eligible for a sex change.

There are two laws that I know of that affect transsexuals—one the police can pick you up for. It's about impersonation. I don't know the actual law, but it was put on the books in the 1700s. The reason they had it was that farmers were dressing up as Indians in order to avoid paying taxes—some would even dress as women. So they passed this law not allowing people to dress up in public and to paint their faces. That's the law they now arrest transsexuals and transvestites on.

The other law keeps surgeons from doing the operation. That one comes from England. There was a war going on there and the people were trying to get out of the draft by cutting off their fingers and toes, and they would have a surgeon do it. So the law states that no surgeon can take away any part of your body that would make you ineligible for the draft. So cutting off my genitals is making me ineligible for the draft. I think the draft board could afford to lose a few, but anyway that's the law that the surgeons are afraid of. I've heard of a couple of times where doctors were ready to perform the operation and were notified by the DA that if they did they would press charges.

The doctors usually back off. They don't want to get involved. They don't have the time to get in a test case, and most of the time they don't want that kind of publicity. The hospitals especially don't like that kind of publicity. They don't get donations, I guess, if the public finds out they are doing sexual change operations. The board of directors and contributors jumps down their throats for doing such an atrocious thing, and if the word gets out that a hospital is doing the surgery, they get besieged by transsexuals wanting to get one.

Most people don't know the difference between transvestites, homosexuals, and transsexuals, so I think I ought to clear that up before I go any further. Most people just lump them all together. I saw one Archie Bunker show on homosexuals that really pointed out how Americans think about people who have different sexual practices. People don't realize how prejudiced they are about homosexuality and transsexuality, because they aren't even at a point of knowing that it's something that you can be prejudiced about. They are so sure that the rest of the world is supposed to be the way they are that they don't even think the people who are different have an opinion. They just lump them all together as nuts or perverts. That's the way Archie was on this program.

Well, anyway, a transvestite only wants to dress like a woman. They don't want to go all the way and have an operation and live as a woman. The transsexual wants an operation. It's a difference in the way you think about yourself. The way of thinking of a transsexual is: "I am a female with a birth defect. I am a woman, but I have the organs of the other sex. I want to be a whole person again." The term is also used to refer to people who are physiologically women who want to be men. The way of thinking of a transvestite is: "I am a man, but I want to play the role of a female. I know that I am a male, but I get kicks out of dressing like a woman." The transvestite gets emotional gratification and psychological good feelings from dressing. A transsexual doesn't. There is an interest in clothing, but it's much like a woman's interest. No erotic stimulation or anything like that. Like, I am just as happy bumming around in a pair of jeans and a blouse as in some type of fancy low-cut gown with heels.

The difference between a homosexual and a transsexual or a transvestite is that the homosexual knows that he is a man, let's say, but he is sexually attracted to those of the same sex and has sex with them. He says: "I know that I am a man, but I want to have sex with a man." Some transvestites are not homosexuals, because they don't want to have sex. Transsexuals are not homosexuals because they don't want to have sex with those who are of the same sex as they are; they want sex with the opposite sex.

I used to be down on homosexuals. Homosexuals and transsexuals usually don't hit it off. I happened to relate well with a group a few years ago, and I was able to get over my prejudices and start seeing what we had in common rather what we differed over. I found it easy to relate to this group, because what we had in common was that we were suppressed. We both share some of the dangers of being brutalized because of our beliefs. We can be picked up for impersonation, or for vagrancy, or anything else they want to pick us up for. We also share being made jokes of or beat up at any time. Like, just last week I had a seizure in the middle of the street, and someone called an ambulance. The first thing that I remember was being in the ambulance strapped to a stretcher. I looked up, and there are these two guys laughing and joking. One says to me, "Don't worry, *dearie*. We've got you figured out." I was so angry I almost couldn't control myself, but that is typical of what we have to watch out for.

When you're like me, you have always got to be on your guard that you don't get into a position that is going to get you into a jam. Like, I went downtown and picketed the recruiting center as part of the antiwar demonstration. I had decided that I was going to perform an act of civil disobedience with a group if they tried to clear us out of the road. But standing around down there, all of a sudden it hit me. If I get busted and get taken to jail, they might throw every charge in the book at me if they found out I was physically a man. I have to be more careful than anybody else that goes on a march like that. I went in the front of the parade in this particular march, carrying a banner—but that wasn't too smart to do. If people were to ever find out and if it was in the papers, the reporters and the readers would zero in on the fact of what I was, and that would have blown the whole issue. Immediately, all the hard hats would go back to their favorite sayings: "Look at all those faggot queers with the long hair marching around. They got a real beauty out in front this time." People like me aren't sincere about those issues, according to them. We don't count.

It's hard for transsexuals, because you don't have many allies. I'm almost totally dependent on white, middle-class doctors to give me a fair shake. There are so few doctors that will see me, that I have to scrape to get what I want. They are in control. They told me that I have to conform to their standards or I don't get the operation.

I'm probably different from other transsexuals, but they probably think the same about themselves. One thing is that it is usually hard for transsexuals to talk about themselves, especially after the operation. I'm going to tell you a lot about myself. Talking about it opens up a lot of old wounds. I haven't had the operation, so it's a lot easier because the wounds are still in the open and I get new ones every day.

I don't think very many transsexuals have gone through three years of psychotherapy, as I have. Most phase it out after 50 sessions or so. I'm different, too, in that most transsexuals don't go to psychiatric hospitals. Why that is I don't know. Most transsexuals are also very introverted. They want to stay totally undercover, outside the public eye. They don't want to upset the apple cart. They have to keep low profiles so as to keep respectable. This is because they don't depend on each other so much as on their physicians.

Your doctor is the most important part of your life. He takes precedence over fathers and mothers, in some cases. That is the person who prescribes the hormones and may be able to help you get the operation. You've got to keep him happy. Doctors are gods to them. Which is why I don't think I get along too well with some doctors, because I don't think of them or treat them like God, not anymore anyway—I think they are as fucked up in some respects as me. When you talk to another transsexual, the first thing they will talk about is what their doctor is doing for them. I don't think it's healthy or that you can be a person, if your whole life is so dependent on someone else who can cut you off any time.

I am talking about the transsexuals I know. I haven't known that many. Maybe I've met a total of 30. There aren't too many in the United States. Dr. Benjamin's book say there are 100,000, or something like that, in the United States. Maybe I should just talk for myself.

The vast majority of transsexuals try to make it in the straight world, as the gay community calls it. The reason for that is because the operation is not very well advertised. I mean, you don't see many articles in popular magazines about it, so people don't know about it. People who are transsexuals and don't know about operations are trying to live the role that society says they have to. Like myself—everybody used to say, "You have got to be a little boy." I knew I wasn't, but they said I had to. I went into the Navy to try to be. I underwent psychotherapy, but that didn't work either. Then I heard about the operation, and that's what I have been working toward ever since.

I am presently living in purgatory. A little between heaven and hell. I am working my way upwards, slowly, but when you have to fight the whole damn system single-handed, it's hard. Usually, you look for help and people turn their backs on you. I tell them what I want, and they say, "He's really a sick person." They don't get it through their heads that they are the ones that have made me sick and are keeping me sick. Most transsexuals have had hassles, but they don't have the hassles over being a transsexual; they have them over the way society fucks over them. After it fucks over you, it asks, "What can we do to help?" So to help they stick you into an institution for the mentally ill that gives you more hassles. It's a cycle. When I went into the VA psychiatric ward, I was in hell. Now that I am getting hormone shots and living and working as a female, it's purgatory. Once I get the operation, although I know it's not going to be perfect, it will kind of be like heaven. I am not going to say that the operation is going to cure everything—I don't consider it a cure-all. I have a lot of hassles to clear up, just like most people. It's not going to be a cure-all, but it will sure as hell get rid of many of the pressures and tensions I am under.

The cost of the operation is twice what it would be if it weren't so controversial. You feel that you're being taken advantage of. The cost in Casablanca is about $8,000, and they go between $3,500 and $5,000 in other places. That is not the cost of the operation—that is just the surgeon's fees. That is not counting the anesthesiologist, the operating room, the recovery time, medication, and so on. Since when does a person get over $3,500 for less than a day's work? What they do is remove parts of their male organ and use part of it to build a vagina. The vagina has the nerve endings from the penis and scrotum, so there are sexual feelings.

There are two doctors in the world today who are working toward perfecting the male-to-female surgery. One is a doctor in Casablanca; the other is in Tijuana. They have their own clinics with operating suites and the whole things. They are both expensive. You have to deposit the right amount in their Swiss bank account prior to the operation. He gets out of paying the taxes and the hassle for taking that much through customs. These are the men who are doing most of the surgical research.

There are people in the United States doing research, but it is mostly statistical or psychological. A couple of places out West did some operations and have decided to wait between 12 and 20 years to find out the results before they do any more. Johns Hopkins did a lot, but I don't think they are doing any now either. They were supposed to be doing one every three months or so. There are other places here and there that do them, but it's hard to find out for sure who's doing them.

According to Dr. Benjamin, who studied over 100 people who had the operation, only one was considered unsatisfactory. They had all made a better adjustment to life than before the operation. The one that was unsatisfactory was a medical thing, not psychological. So the operation seems pretty fool-proof. By the way, psychotherapy has never been known to "cure" a transsexual.

The reason the cost is so high is part of the old supply and demand thing. Transsexuals need one thing, the operation, and there is only a small group of doctors who will do it. If these people stick together in the price they charge, the only thing someone can do is pay their price. You can't very well boycott or picket, or stuff like that. There is no recourse but to pay it or not get it done.

People who do the operation have this informal rule, that in order to be eligible for it you have to be living as a female for two years. That includes working as a female. You also have to have a recommendation from a psychiatrist you have been seeing for two years. They say that, if you can work as a female successfully enough to make the money, then you'll make a good adjustment after the operation. It's the kind of a situation where you're so concerned about the operation that it's hard to concentrate on working—if you had the operation, you might settle down. Besides, it's almost impossible to get any kind of job that pays enough for you to save on. The other thing is: Who is going to write you a recommendation in the first place to get a job, and what name are they going to put down, your old one or your new one? Also, what about when they ask you for your social security card and it has a man's name on it? Medicaid won't pay for it, and Blue Cross and Blue Shield get upset when you even suggest it. They consider it cosmetic surgery.

The operation is a vicious circle. I want to have the operation so bad that I am under great pressure and strain. The pressure makes it hard to find or keep a good job. The fact that you can't keep a job and that you're uptight is used as evidence that you're not sane. They tell you, "If you really wanted it, you could do it." I can see their reasoning, but I don't agree with it. I don't know what I can do about it though. They tell you getting the money is part of the therapy.

What people don't understand is that transsexuals, myself included, think of this whole operation in the same way you would think of having a wart removed, or having plastic surgery done on your nose. If you think your nose is ugly and you want it fixed, it it's bothering you, instead of worrying about it and while your head is thinking about it the way it is and all that stuff, you go out and get it fixed. That's the way I think of it, but most physicians don't. Most people are so uptight about sex in general, and about penises and vaginas, that they have to find something psychological to worry about. It's funny.

I don't know how you're taking this so far, but the majority of people hear about me and they automatically think I have problems—super head problems. Even if I don't have them, they think I'm crazy. You just try to avoid people like that. After I get to know people it works out. If I make them uptight, I leave.

People usually find out that I'm a transsexual not from me, but from my "friends." It makes me angry to have to explain it to people because, I don't know, how would you like to have to explain yourself to everyone you met? Explain how you think you're a man or a woman. Why the hell do I have to be explained? I mean to hell with the transsexualism, I'm a human being first, and female second, and a transsexual third. But people can't respond to it like that. Society doesn't want to know me as a human being. I have to be a transsexual first to do anything. It's almost, "Forget Jane Fry and let's talk about the transsexual." It's almost like when I went to get my appendix out. They were so much into looking at me as a transsexual that they didn't do anything about my appendix. When I was in the psychiatric hospitals, they concentrated so much on my being a transsexual that they weren't willing to help me with what I needed help with.

I have come to automatically distrust people because of this. I want to be accepted as a human being, and people won't do it; they make it so you can't be a human being. This combined with the operation being so hard to achieve that you have to concentrate on being a transsexual 24 hours a day instead of being a person. All your hopes ride on the operation, and that's what you keep striving for and that's what you fight for. So you think of it all the time, and people treat you like one all the time, and there you are.

It actually makes it more frustrating for me when people don't know about me before I meet them, because you have to jump over a hurdle—I have to explain more or less what I'm all about. Sometimes I blow people's minds intentionally. I get a horror or a fear reaction from people who are set in their ways, who haven't run across this kind of thing before.

Men get particularly uptight about me. They just don't know how to handle it. Some guys, the first time they see me, like all males who see a female, look at me as a female and then all of sudden they find out; it blows their image of themselves. They say to themselves, "God, I must be queer." A lot of people seem to go through that, but I don't know what to do about it. I get along with women a lot better. They don't seem so threatened.

The biggest problem I face is dealing with society in a way that it accepts me and I can accept myself. I have done that to some extent, but I feel I'm kind of doing it the easy way by living on the fringes in the freak culture. Most of my friends are either students or hang out in the university section. People are much more open in their thinking—they don't care if you're different or not. It makes life a lot easier than if I was to try, say, to play the role of the super middle-class secretary that lives in the suburbs. The majority of transsexuals do that. They are superstraight. Maybe that's easy for them, dealing with it that way, but I just couldn't make it. By living on the fringe I don't have to face the head hassles they do everyday. The majority of transsexuals don't have the time or energy left after fighting the hassles to understand what society is like. They are so busy trying to join in and at the same time fight it that they don't see what it's all about.

Being a transsexual, it seems like you're fighting all society and everybody in it. If you don't have psychological hang-ups after all that fighting, there is something wrong with you. I've got problems now, quite a few emotional hang-ups right now. It doesn't mean that I have to be locked up. I recognize them, but I also recognize the reason I got them. I spend half my time worrying about what society thinks, instead of worrying about me. So you have to end up with problems. Anybody can relate the emotional problems that I have now to my childhood and say that my transsexualism is the reason for it, but it's nothing about the transsexualism itself that causes hang-ups—it's fighting society.

This doctor told me that my father was a very violent man and in rejecting him I rejected masculinity and violence, so I had to be a female. I think that's bullshit. What he didn't stop to think was that I probably was a transsexual right from the beginning and I was so worried about the problems that it caused with others I didn't know how to relate to them. You get so wrapped up in your emotions that you can't relate.

I don't think my transsexualism is the direct cause of my emotional problems, but I have to let psychiatrists keep saying it is or else they won't treat me. I have got to get back on the road to getting my operation, so I have to see one. When I see a psychiatrist now, I just ignore it when they start rapping on about my transsexualism. If it gets too bad, I just won't see them anymore.

A lot of people can't even imagine the shit I go through. It's the same thing that they go through, except I go through it to a greater extent. They are forced to become one thing or the other; they have to conform to a certain set of standards, even though they don't think it fits them. With me it's just more obvious that's all. A normal guy, if he likes to cut flowers or want to be a hairdresser or something like that, his masculinity is questioned and he has pressure on him not to do it. Or a woman who wants to drive a truck—it's the same thing. The male/female thing is just part of it. There are other roles we play too. Masks—that's what I call them. By the time a person is 20 years old you can't see the person for the masks. If someone tries to go against the masks, they are schizophrenic or something else. That's what they are called. That's what's on my medical records.

With the masks society tries to hide human sexuality. What I mean is that society has taken and stereotyped masculinity and femininity so you don't get a full and real picture of what it is. Everybody is trying to live up to the stereotype image.

It's hard to live away from the stereotype a little, but it is a thousand times harder to go away from it as radically as I have. I am doing what most people can't even think of, going from a man to a woman. My father's first comment when I told him was, "Why can't you pick an easier one, like being a homosexual?" Which makes a good point. At least if I was a homosexual, I would be the same sex, but to do something so obvious like changing dress and everything is something that you can't hide. Women who want to go to work are thought to be crazy—if a normal person wants to change roles, he has to fight a lot, but if he wants to change sex, that's a lot more.

I guess you can think of transsexualism as more or less a mask, too. Or it can be. I'm a transsexual, but people try to force me into a stereotype—they try to exaggerate the importance of what I am. It's a part of you, granted, but they make it more a part of you that it really is. I am trying not to make it that way. I'm trying not to fall into the slot, but I'm forced into it.

THE EDITOR'S CONCLUSION

Social science holds an ever increasing position of importance in providing our definitions of reality, since the typologies, definitions, and diagnoses it creates provide sources from which individuals and groups may choose definitions for themselves and others. Social scientists must realize that they are now and will be in a position to construct the definitions of reality that form the basis of therapies and other policies. The politics of perspective will be discussed in the vocabulary that social science creates. It is important for social scientists to understand their position—that they manufacture realities. The creation of perspectives with their reifying vocabularies is not a scientific issue. It is a moral and political issue. Yet, in the age of science, morality and politics are discussed as science. Ideology—new perspectives and new definitions—will allow people who have been characterized as sick, perverted, or immoral to see themselves in new ways and to unite to make their perspectives politically viable in the arena in which reality is defined. Only when people become aware that the human situation is a matter of define or be defined will there be choice.

NOTE

1. Reprinted with permission from Robert Bogdan, *Being Different: The Autobiography of Jane Fry* (New York: John Wiley & Sons, 1974).

CHAPTER 9

"They're Not Like You and Me": Institutional Attendants' Perspectives on Residents

STEVEN J. TAYLOR

P EOPLE IN ALL settings develop definitions of objects in their world and of others with whom they interact. These definitions may be seen as general ways of thinking about objects and others that are brought into specific situations (Berger and Luckmann 1967; Douglas 1971, 177). They provide a framework for interpreting the world and, hence, a basis for action. As Herbert Blumer (1969) writes, people act toward things, as well as toward other people, on the basis of the meanings those things and people have for them.

In this chapter I examine how attendants, also referred to as direct care staff, caretakers, therapy aides, and mental hygiene assistants, define residents at public institutions for people labeled mentally retarded. The attendants at these institutions are officially responsible for the daily care of residents, maintenance of wards or living units, and, increasingly, the provision of therapeutic activities and programming (Bogdan et al. 1974).

METHODOLOGY

The study reported here[1] is based on participant observation and other qualitative research methods, specifically interviewing, conducted in the mid- to late 1970s at state-operated institutions for people labeled mentally retarded (for discussions of the methodology, see Taylor and Bogdan 1981, 1984; see also Glaser and Strauss 1967). The institutions in this study fit sociologist

Erving Goffman's (1961, xiii) definition of a total institution: "A total institution is a place of residence and work where a large number of like-situated persons, cut off from the wider society for an appreciable period of time, together lead an enclosed, formally administered round of life."

The primary data for this study come from participant observation conducted on wards or living units at four Northeastern institutions (Central, Cornerstone, Empire, and Eastern).[2] Three of these institutions are located in one state, the fourth in another; three are old facilities, established around the turn of the century, while the fourth is a new facility, constructed in the 1970s; three are located in small towns or cities, the fourth in an urban area. These institutions ranged in size from slightly over 250 residents in over 3000. However, three of the institutions have experienced significant deinstitutionalization recently.

This research began with an in-depth study of one ward at Empire State School. For a period of a year, I studied a back ward housing severely and profoundly retarded persons. During this study, I spent 110 hours of observation at the institution and recorded over 1000 pages of field notes. Later, I conducted less intensive observations at Eastern (12 hours during a multiple-day visit), Cornerstone (20 visits spread over several years), and Central (2 visits) State Schools.

This study also draws on participant observation data collected by student observers at seven additional institutions in one state. These observations were conducted during multiple-day visits to these institutions. Like Eastern, Empire, Cornerstone, and Central, these institutions vary widely in size, age, and geographical area. Although these data enable some of the findings of this study to be generalized, no conclusions are based solely on data collected by others.

In addition, I have visited over a dozen other institutions located throughout the United States. My observation at those places, as at the previously mentioned institutions, focused on ward life.

The remainder of this chapter describes attendants' definitions of the residents under their charge. I focus on the commonalities in attendants' definitions that emerged during the course of my study. Although I do not claim that the definitions described here are held by all attendants at all times, I do take the position that these are their dominant views.

DEFINITIONS OF RESIDENTS

Institutional attendants naturally develop shared definitions of those around them. In the first place, attendants, especially those on the same ward or shift, spend a great deal of time in interaction with one another. They share stories and accounts of past events. They discuss their experiences and explore the meanings of their world in a concerted way. In the second place, attendants occupy the same position in the organization of the institution. Since they perform the same tasks, undergo the same training, and encounter the same experiences, they share interests and concerns. Finally, attendants tend to have similar socioeconomic, educational, and occupational backgrounds (Bogdan et al. 1974, 148). This implies a commonality in world views as well as a basis for off-the-job relationships. The attendants often frequent the same establishments, join the same clubs. Many are related by blood or marriage. Their on-the-job and off-the-job lives tend to merge with one another; they find support for their definitions in different settings.

These definitions are handed down from attendant to attendant. Older, more experienced attendants provide new attendants with ready-made interpretations of ward life, residents, supervisors, and other aspects of the institution. They tell them what to see and how to define it. On their very first days on the ward, new attendants will be taught the "nature" of the "mentally retarded," the typical motivations of residents, and the rationales for ward practices. Within a short period of time, one will hear new attendants relate the same anecdotes related by older attendants on the ward.

Social typing, or typification, is a regular feature of everyday life. In social interaction, we perceive, or define, the other as a preconceived type of person, with characteristics and motivations that correspond to that type. This enables us to understand others, to interpret what they do, and to anticipate their actions. Psathas (1973) describes this process as follows:

> Typification consists of the equalization of traits relevant to the particular purpose at hand . . . any individual differences not relevant to this purpose are disregarded. Because of the problem-relevance of the typification, different types of the same concrete individual can be formed, dependent on the situationally determined interest. (p. 220–223)

Institutional attendants define the residents under their charge as a special type of people. First, attendants view residents as objects to be distinguished from all other people. Second, attendants lack an ability to truly empathize with residents, to look at things from their point of view, or to take their definitions into account. If residents can be seen as objects, then their perspectives may be easily ignored. Third, attendants define and label residents according to the amount of custodial work they cause or require.

Residents as Objects: "Them" and "Us"

For attendants, residents assume an objectlike quality. By this I mean that attendants lose any real sense of residents' individuality or humanity. Rather, they have stereotypic ways of thinking about residents, their characteristics, and their nature as a category of people set apart from all others. This reflects the nature of their work, total institutions, and societal definitions of mental retardation.

Attendants' work, not unlike other kinds of people work, lends itself to seeing others as objects (Perrucci 1974). Goffman (1961, 74) writes, "As materials upon which to work, people can take on somewhat the same characteristics as inanimate objects." Surgeons prefer slender to fat patients, because with fat ones instruments get slippery and there are extra layers to cut through; morticians prefer slender females to fat males, because heavy "stiffs" are more difficult to move and males must be dressed in jackets that are difficult to pull over stiffened arms and fingers (Goffman 1961, 74–75).

In the context of the total institution, attendants deal at any given time with between 15 and 75 residents who have few obvious differentiating characteristics. As Goffman (1961) has so clearly demonstrated, institutional inmates may lose many of the possessions that constitute their identify and establish their individuality. Upon commitment, residents may be stripped of such items as clothes, combs, toys, and adornments. These are stored in common rooms and distributed on special occasions and home visits. For everyday use, residents usually receive standard styles of clothing bought in large quantities. At many of these institutions, residents wear heavy institutional garb—what attendants refer to as *dope suits*. In the same vein, residents have similar hairstyles.

Like most people, perhaps, attendants subscribe to definitions of the mentally retarded as somehow less than human or as having extrahuman characteristics (Wolfensberger 1975). As Bogdan and Taylor (1976, 1982) argue, "mental retardation" is a reification or social construction which exists in the minds of those who use it to describe the cognitive states or ontological status of other people. People assume that the mentally retarded share common attributes that allow them to be unambiguously classified, as though humanity could be divided into two groups: "us" and "them," the "normal" and the "retarded" (Dexter 1967). So it is with institutional attendants.

Attendants systematically point out the differences between residents and themselves, or the "normal" and the "retarded," and disregard similarities. As the phrase *mental retardation* suggests, attendants regard residents as incompetents with severely circumscribed potential for growth or learning. Some are allegedly so "low-grade" that they can learn nothing. In reference to one particular ward, an Empire attendant asserted, "You can't change the nature of these patients. They're severely retarded and no matter what approach you try you'll never change that fact." Another remarked, "It's hard to teach them right from wrong. Their concepts of right and wrong are different from ours." Other residents, though not "low grades," are presumed capable of learning only simple tasks. As one attendant put it, "You can teach some things, but not too much. They have a plateau, and if you go beyond that it's like trying to put a cup of sugar in a spoon." Most often, attendants generalize about residents' capabilities on the basis of a few selected cases. An Eastern attendant remarked, "You can't put a retarded patient on a diet!" Other attendants point out that residents are "too retarded" to be married, to manage their own money, or to make their own decisions.

When residents do demonstrate competence or ability, attendants either choose not to see it or explain it away. They may interpret verbal and other skills as imitation as opposed to learning. For example, one attendant explained a resident's recitation of the alphabet as follows: "The only reason he can do that is that an attendant sat with him all day long and made him keep repeating it till he got it right. That's the only reason he can do all that." Or attendants may suggest that some residents "don't really belong here" or "aren't really retarded." They thus change the classification rules, rather than the nature of the classification itself. If the retarded are defined as incompetent, then a competent person cannot be retarded.

Attendants may also treat capable residents as exceptions that prove the general rule. They may emphasize and underline the exceptional nature of a resident's ability. This implies that the competent resident is a freak of some sort, and confirms the general stereotype of residents, just as sayings such as "she's really articulate for a woman," or "he's really smart for a Black" confirm the stereotypes of those groups.

Attendants also may define competence as evidence of abnormality rather than normality. They may claim that certain tasks require skills, which are actually deficiencies, which only the retarded possess. One Central attendant related, "Hell, if I was working in a factory, I could do a stocking pattern five times as fast as her (a resident), but hers would turn out better than mine because retardates continue to work on something until it's perfected if they know how to do it." In a similar vein, an Empire attendant explained, "They say the retarded make the best truck drivers 'cause they just sit there and watch the road. They're good at things as long as it's one thing at a time."

According to institutional attendants, mental retardation carries with it certain physical, as well as intellectual, characteristics. These include extraordinary strength, insensitivity to pain, and resistance to injury. Such views are related through glib savings, pseudoscientific explanations, and folktales. On any ward, one will hear stories of how residents can fall from buildings, go through windows, and slip down staircases, yet miraculously escape injury. On one ward, attendants told the following story, though none had personally witnessed the incident in question: "One kid jumped off the porch (50 feet) a while ago, but he only broke his leg. They don't get hurt like you and me." Similarly, another attendant testified, "I've never seen one of them cry. They're amazing. No matter how badly hurt they are, they just bear up under it." Still another attendant attempted to explain this phenomenon:

Retarded people have a hard time feeling pain because they're brain damaged. Their sensory receptors are not as sensitive to pain as those who aren't brain damaged. But if you want them to learn about pain, you sensitize them to it by giving them a lot of pain, like pinching them hard until they feel it.

Attendants sometimes use the term *superhuman* to describe residents' strength and other physical attributes (in contrast to the "subhuman" nature of their intelligence). One Empire attendant observed, "God may have given them no brains, but he gave them superhuman bodies. They're stronger than a regular person." Attendants may also claim that residents resist disease and live longer than other people.

Finally, attendants attribute special emotional states to the persons under their charge. As one Central attendant explained, "Of course, you know they don't have feelings like you and me." Although attendants object to the smell of certain wards, "they," the residents, allegedly don't mind it at all (or a lack of privacy and personal possessions). These views are often conveyed through comparisons of residents (including adults) with children, animals, or vegetables. As one attendant put it, "You have to think of these people as three-year-olds with men's bodies." Another remarked, "This kid is just like an animal. He protects his food and is afraid someone will steal it. He reminds me of the way a dog will stand guard over his food." Sometimes these comparisons lose their metaphoric nature. "Like" becomes "is." Attendants refer to certain residents as *animals* or *vegetables*. They refer to older men as *boys*, older women as *girls*, and all residents as *kids*. At Empire, Eastern, and Central, staff decorate adult wards with paper cutouts, cartoons, and children's pictures. Adults may be given children's toys and games.

SYMPATHY, BUT NOT EMPATHY

Although attendants may sympathize with residents, they seldom empathize with them as they would with another person. Many express fondness and affection for residents. They may feel sorry for them as well. One Central attendant stated, "It's a shame what happened to them when they were born. Their minds are horrible, you know, I mean being retarded and all." Another put it more bluntly, "The situation is awful and I hate to see them alive. Yet who should have the responsibility of taking their lives?" But sympathy and empathy represent two different mind-sets. The one requires only feelings toward another person or thing. After all, humans regularly sympathize with their pets and other animals. The other, empathy, suggests symbolic participation in another's feelings and ideas. It requires recognizing another as someone like yourself (Psathas 1973). Its absence or presence tends to structure how one person defines, understands, and acts toward another.

Attendants typically demonstrate an inability or unwillingness to empathize with residents or to understand them on their own terms. They see residents' actions as somehow caused by or symptomatic of an underlying pathological condition. Since they regard residents as nonagents of their own actions, attendants may not attempt to understand residents from their own frame of reference (Goffman 1961; Laing 1967, 110–111). Of course, these views are reflexive or self-fulfilling (Mehan and Wood 1975, 137–161). If one sees another's actions as symptomatic of an underlying condition, one will not try to understand another's perspective or the social context in which such actions take place. When viewed apart from the actor's perspective and the social context, any action appears bizarre, mysterious, and unpredictable, and provides "evidence" of the pathological state initially presumed.

Attendants' relationships with residents do not require them to take into account residents' perspectives and may actually circumscribe their ability to do so. In most social relationships, people depend on each other for instrumental or expressive rewards and must anticipate each other's goals and desires. This requires them to look at things from each other's point of view. In some relationships, however, power differentials preclude the need to take the goals or perspectives of others into account. For example, Gouldner (1965, 352) argues that the ancient Greeks tended to view their slaves as mere tools or "nonpersons." He writes, "This means, among other things, that the slave's own goals, what he wants to do, are not regarded by the master as important or problematic." Similarly, institutional attendants do not have to anticipate residents' desires or even acknowledge their definitions of the situation. They neither work for residents nor depend upon them for rewards. Rather, they work for the organization. They depend upon supervisors, not residents, for their pay, evaluations, and favorable work assignments. Residents' perspectives may be inconsequential and therefore easily ignored or disregarded.

As the preceding discussion suggests, attendants have little appreciation of how residents might view their world. To the contrary, they see residents as somewhat mysterious, unpredictable beings who are motivated, or perhaps driven, by special factors. Sometimes they subscribe to a deterministic conception of resident's behavior. "That resident always paces," said one attendant, "he doesn't know any better." At other times they blame residents for certain actions (especially when it suits their purposes to do so), and implicitly, if not explicitly, adopt a voluntaristic notion. In either case, attendants explain and understand residents' actions differently than they would the actions of a typical person.

In many instances, attendants define residents' actions as symptomatic of mental retardation, as indicated above. Although pacing, rocking, crying, head-banging, and self-abuse may be interpreted as responses to ward boredom, tension, and discomfort, if viewed from residents' perspective (Klaber and Butterfield 1968), attendants attribute such behavior to residents' nature or condition.

In other instances, attendants attribute residents' behavior to almost supernatural forces. According to folklore at most institutions, the full moon and weather changes affect residents in strange ways (Dingman, Cleland, and Swartz 1970). One attendant remarked, "Residents are always irritable in hot weather, and when there's a full moon comin', and before a storm too." Another attendant elaborated on this theme:

> Boy, you can really tell when the full moon's comin'. See how active they are? Yeah, you can always tell when it's coming. They're the same way when the weather changes too. Like the other day when we got that snow, they were really actin' up.

On women's wards, attendants often explain residents' actions and demeanor by their menstrual cycles. "A number of the more active girls have a terrible time during menstruation," stated one Cornerstone attendant. "Some really go mad."

Attendants sometimes regard what residents say or do as utterly meaningless. This is not a claim that residents have no sound or rational reasons for their actions, but that they have no reasons whatsoever. This view is generally offered in reference to allegedly violent residents (Goffman 1961, 75). For example, an Eastern attendant remarked, "Yeah, Murray can really be a handful. Like last night he started swingin' at me for no reason at all." A Cornerstone attendant echoes this sentiment regarding one of his charges: "He'll attack people for no reason." Attendants may offer this view when residents (perhaps understandably) refuse to wear soiled clothes, to be alone in the dark, or to share their few possessions.

LABELS AND TYPES

People define others according to their interest in them or what might be termed their *purpose at hand* (Heeren 1970, 47). That is, people direct their attention to those aspects of others that affect them directly. As these assume primary importance, other aspects become irrelevant. Becker et al. (1968, 109), for example, note that whenever two categories of people are engaged in a common enterprise, one is likely to view the other by the other's contribution to its success, however defined. Musicians prefer audiences that let them play as they wish; teachers prefer pupils who learn quickly.

Although institutional residents might be defined by such characteristics as family background, verbal skills, or learning ability, attendants define residents in rather limited terms. When attendants differentiate between residents, this is done on the basis of the control, daily care, and supervisory problems they present or their most superficial characteristics. For example, residents are nicknamed by their obvious quirks or special traits. Such names as "cockroach" (one who runs about), "nigger boy" (a Black resident), "belt-less" (one whose pants fall down), "midget" (a short resident), "cowboy" (one who pretends to draw pistols), "bunny rabbit" (one who allegedly resembles a rabbit), "Igor" (a large, fierce-looking resident), "monster" (an ugly resident), and "human pretzel" (a resident with spasticity) are common on institutional wards. One attendant explained how a little girl received her nickname: "Two attendants have a bet that she'll be walking in a year. They call her 'T-bone' because the bet is for a steak dinner. . . . They call her T-bone. I call her 'dog crap.' " Words like *dummy, dope, mongoloid, dumbbell,* and *idiot* are used generally to refer to different residents.

Unlike professionals, attendants do not define residents by such characteristics as nature, cause, or level or mental retardation, for these have little significance in their work or job careers. Institutional physicians see residents as *microcephalics, hydrocelphalics, Down syndromes,* and *PKUs* (among other things). Teachers see *educables, trainables,* and *subtrainables.* Administrators see the *borderlines,* the *mildly retarded,* the *moderately retarded,* the *severely retarded,* and the *profoundly retarded,* or the *Unit As, Unit Bs,* and so on, representing different *catchment areas.* Attendants, however, see *troublemakers, soilers, headbangers, working boys,* and *pets.* That is, they see different types that help or hinder their own custodial work. In a systematic way, they distinguish between control problems, custodial problems, supervisory problems, authority problems, special processing, helpers, and pets and no problems.

CONTROL PROBLEMS

On any institutional ward, attendants characterize a certain number of residents as *bastards, troublemakers, hyperactives, devils, destructives, fighters, aggressives, psychos, schizoids,* or *son-of-a-bitches.* These residents ostensibly provide control problems for attendants. Some might injure other residents. In regard to one resident, an Empire attendant explained:

> You don't want to get him going 'cause he's hard to stop. You get him mad or if another patient hits him in the back of the head, he really gets going. He can be a real son of a gun . . . if he was smart enough, he'd run this place.

A Cornerstone attendant related, "A number of these kids are capable of killing. Like that smelly redhead, Beverly." Others might even attack attendants. As one attendant warned an observer, "Don't let them behind you. You don't know what they might do. They could choke you." Another attendant expressed a similar sentiment: "He's not afraid of anybody. He'll turn on one of us. I had him cornered one time and I was scared. I didn't know what he was gonna do." According to attendants, these residents are "dangerous," "get out of hand easily," and "blow up for no reason."

CUSTODIAL PROBLEMS

Some residents present problems by virtue of the care they require. Some must be fed; others need everything done for them. Attendants label these residents by such terms as *low grades, dopes, spastics, wetters, regurgitators, cripples, dumbells, animals, vegetables, pukers, soilers,* and (sympathetically) *poor souls.* For attendants, these residents have little meaning apart from their custodial needs. One woman attendant described a young man under her care as follows:

> That's the thing. . . . That's what we call him. Look at those slanted eyes, and the hair around his eyes, mouth, chin, and cheeks. The thing is 19 years old, believe it or not. It's like this all the time, so we have to medicate it. . . . You can teach it nothing. It's just no good for nothing. It's a thing.

Attendants may also talk about caring for these residents as they would things or objects. As one put it, "It's no harder changing this kid than dressing a turkey." Or as one said to another as she began to change a resident's bed, "Roll this dumbbell over so I can change the sheets. He wet the bed again."

SUPERVISION PROBLEMS

Quite apart from control and custodial problems, certain residents create supervisory problems for attendants. These residents may run away (*runaways*), harm themselves (*diggers, head-bangers, biters, self-abusers*), eat extraneous materials, or choke on food (*chokers*). According to attendants, these residents must be carefully supervised.

AUTHORITY PROBLEMS

Some residents are defined as authority problems: *smart alecs, wise guys,* and *pests.* These residents subtly or blatantly resist attendants' authority. Some may refuse to do what they're told. Others get too close to attendants or fail to show proper deference. On one Empire ward, attendants sit on comfortable chairs, while residents use large wooden benches. When one resident happened to sit down on an attendant's chair, an attendant firmly rebuked

him: "What the hell do you think you are? An attendant or something?"
Some wise guys apparently try to trick attendants. In regard to one resident,
an attendant explained, "He's a real wise guy. They say he's legally deaf, but
he can hear. He just only hears what he wants to."

SPECIAL PROCESSING

Attendants define some residents by the special processing they receive. On
many wards, for example, attendants refer to certain residents as *dining room
boys* (those who eat in a dining room as opposed to on the ward) or *dormitory
boys* (those who sleep in a dormitory as opposed to private rooms). On other
wards, attendants may label residents as *school boys* since they attend school
during the day. These labels are used to point out the special consideration
attendants must give these residents. Dining room boys must be properly
clothed and taken to the dining room. Dormitory boys must be separated
from others at bedtime and directed into the dormitory. Schoolboys must be
dressed in the morning and escorted to the school building.

HELPERS

On all institutional wards, one will find a number of residents defined by
their contribution to ward order and maintenance. Some residents mop and
clean; others feed and dress their fellow residents; others supervise or control
their disorderly peers. Attendants label these residents *helpers, working boys,
bucket boys,* and other such terms. When, on occasion, attendants assign one
resident to care for or control another, they will label the other as so and so's
boy, wife, or *girlfriend.*

PETS AND NO PROBLEMS

Each and every ward has at least one and usually several *pets* or *p.c.'s* (*privileged characters*). As a rule, attendants grant these residents special favors and
privileges, such as later bedtimes, treats, extra coffee, and attention. On one
ward, attendants permitted their pet to hit or kick other residents without
punishment or even chastisement. In contrast to wise guys and pests, these
residents tend to be friendly, but not overbearing. They come when they're
called and leave when told to do so. In contrast to self-abusers or troublemakers, they cause few supervisory or control problems. In contrast to low
grades, they stay clean and take care of themselves. One attendant described
a 65-year-old pet: "She's very clean. She's so cute. Maybe that's why everyone takes to her so."

Sometimes attendants use the labels *dopes, dummies,* and *good boys* to refer to residents who, though having limited ability, create "no problems at all." In regard to one such resident, an attendant explained, "He's a dope. He just sits there." On any ward, attendants point to certain residents and remark, "If they were all like him [or her], we'd have no problems at all." Like pets, these residents take care of themselves, but unlike pets they have few appealing characteristics in the eyes of attendants.

As Mehan and Wood (1975, 20–23) note, attendants may define institutional residents in different ways in different times. To put it another way, attendants' definitions depend on the nature of their relationship with residents, the social context, and the concrete situation, rather than the nature of residents themselves. A resident may be seen as a dope on one ward; on another as a pet. Or a pet for some may be a troublemaker for others. Similarly, a *cripple* on a ward for ambulatory residents may be a working boy on a ward for residents confined to bed. On any given ward, attendants on different shifts define residents differently. For example, one would not find schoolboys or dining room boys during the night shift, or dormitory boys on the day shift. The same resident may be defined as one type at one time and another type at another time. Empire attendants defined one man recently transferred to their ward as a working boy since he had worked on his former ward. Although he wasn't assigned work on this ward, he retained this label until attendants learned from his records that he had been a nighttime soiler in the past. Because of this information, attendants placed the man's bed nearest the bathroom and labeled him a soiler, even though he never soiled his bed.

As attendants view residents as objects, disregard their perspectives, and define them according to their own concerns, so too do they treat the residents in ways that they themselves would not like to be treated.

CONCLUSION

Over the past two decades, institutions for the mentally retarded have come under increasing attack internationally (Biklen 1979; Blatt 1970, 1973; Blatt et al. 1977; Blatt, Ozolins, and McNally 1980; Morris 1969; Wolfensberger 1972). These attacks have resulted in significant deinstitutionalization. In the United States alone, the population of public institutions for the mentally retarded declined from approximately 195,000 in 1967 to slightly over 125,000 in 1981 (Lakin et al. 1982). Institutional officials have also sought to defend the institutional model by instituting a series of reforms. Since the early 1970s the institutions in this study have adopted new official goals, formal structures, and vocabularies (Taylor and Bogdan 1980).

Institutional attendants often have been the target of institutional reform efforts. New policies prohibiting abuse have been written; new mandates to provide programming have been handed down; new staff training programs have been implemented. Yet, at the institutions in this study, these reform efforts have not resulted in significant changes in attendants' definitions of residents. This is because those who plan new programs fail to understand the context in which they are to be implemented and how this context can circumscribe the effects of the planned change (Bogdan et al. 1974).

Total institutions by their nature isolate, segregate, and stigmatize the people they are designed to serve. When any group of people is separated from society, those who are supposed to serve them invariably view them in narrow and stereotyped terms and lose sight of their full humanity.

The idea that people labeled mentally retarded do not belong in large public institutions is gaining increasing acceptance. However, small, private facilities may be just as isolated as large public ones and may breed the same dehumanizing staff perspectives found at the institutions in this study (Bercovici 1983). Until we accept people with mental retardation as full members of our societies and provide them with opportunities for full participation, we cannot expect those we employ to serve them to respect their basic humanity.

NOTES

1. Reprinted, with revisions, from S. J. Taylor, " 'They're Not Like You and Me': Institutional Attendants' Perspectives on Residents." *Child and Youth Services* 8 (3/4), 109–125 (1987), by permission of the author.
2. The names of these institutions are pseudonyms.

CHAPTER 10

Invisible Women, Invisible Work: Women's Caring Work in Developmental Disability Services

RANNVEIG TRAUSTADOTTIR[1] AND STEVEN J. TAYLOR

SINCE THE 1970s, the field of *developmental disabilities*—the newest terminology for mental retardation and associated conditions—has been
characterized by humanistic reforms. During the early stages of the
reform efforts, attention focused on moving people with disabilities out of
total institutions, special schools, and other segregated settings (Biklen 1979).
Before long, however, leaders, advocates, and reformers realized that physical placement in communities and schools did not always, or even usually,
result in social integration (Bogdan and Taylor 1987). Many adults and children in community and regular school settings were as socially isolated as
they were in institutions and special schools. As a result, attention has shifted
to helping people with disabilities to participate in the normal life of communities, schools, and work places.

Current reform efforts focus on supporting the formation of social relationships with nondisabled persons for people with disabilities living in the
community (Smull and Bellamy 1991). In special education, the concept of
mainstreaming—selective or part-time integration—has been replaced by full
inclusion (Stainback and Stainback 1990). In the area of adult day services,
many leaders today promote the notion of *natural supports*—supportive and
assistive relationships with nondisabled coworkers—in regular work settings even for people with the most severe disabilities (Nisbet and Hagner
1988; Murphy and Rogan 1996).

These new directions in service delivery call for a new role for human services workers, teachers, and support staff (Knoll and Ford 1987). In contrast to the traditional stance, in which workers maintained "professional distance" from their "clients" and concentrated their efforts on producing behavioral or educational changes in carefully controlled environments, this new role is designed to help meet the social and human needs of people with mental retardation and related disabilities. Workers are expected to form close affective relationships with the people under their care and to assist them in becoming accepted and included in the community at large. The new role is to facilitate friendships, connections, and relationships (Amado, Conklin, and Wells 1990; Knoll and Ford 1987; Stainback, Stainback, and Wilkinson 1992).

Who will perform this new role and what will be the impact on their lives?

Because women constitute the great majority of workers in education and the human services system (Abel and Nelson 1990; Anderson et al. 1987; Hauber and Bruininks 1986; Jacobson and Ackerman 1989), they are the ones to carry out the day-to-day work of implementing this new emphasis. Despite this, very little attention has been paid to how this new role will affect women. In fact, the literature on community services, personnel preparation, and current trends rarely mentions that the majority of the workers in educational and human services systems are women.

The relative neglect of the gendered nature of human services work reflects the power of the cultural stereotype of women as caregivers (DeVault 1991). Women are seen as "natural" caregivers; it is taken for granted that women will occupy caregiving roles in the human services as well as in other spheres of life. Further, the emphasis on relationship building fits well with cultural assumptions about the nature of women. The current reforms seem to depend upon women, but women are seldom, if ever, mentioned as necessary to carry out these reforms.

This chapter looks in depth at four women—two inclusive educators, a job coach, and a personal care assistant—who perform caregiving roles with adults or children with disabilities. An understanding of the sentiments and practices of these four women may lend insight into the nature of this new role. We do not claim that these women are representative of all educators and human service workers (clearly, they are not) or that their perspectives are shared by others who hold similar positions. We do take the position that caregiving remains largely a female activity and that an examination of the work of these four women may illuminate broader issues of gender raised by current reforms in the field of developmental disabilities.

THE STUDY

This chapter is based on a larger study conducted by Traustadottir (1991a, b, 1995) of the role of women as caregivers—mothers, friends, paid support workers—for people with developmental disabilities. Although there are commonalities in how women in different types of caregiving relationships with people with disabilities approach their tasks, we focus here specifically on women as paid educators or human services workers.

Perspective and Methodology

The study was based on qualitative research methods, and specifically participant observation and in-depth interviews. Qualitative studies are flexible and open-ended (Bogdan and Biklen 1982; Taylor and Bogdan 1984). Although qualitative researchers begin their studies with a research focus and a plan of action, the research design evolves in accord with the emerging findings. The investigation began with women's everyday experiences of caring work and examined the work from the perspective of those doing it (Smith 1987). Theoretical sampling and the constant comparative method (Glaser and Strauss 1967) were used as data collection and analytic strategies. The research started with a broad focus on the caring work mothers do for their children with disabilities and the meaning attached to this work. After completing this study of mothers, Traustadottir shifted her attention to human services workers or friends who were involved in caring work and relationship building with people with disabilities.

It was not always easy to categorize women's caregiving activities in this study. As we will see, workers sometimes form close relationships with the people they care for and may come to define them as friends. Further, some of the mothers in the initial study either worked in human services or maintained independent relationships with people with disabilities. The "friends" in this study either worked in or are pursuing a degree in human services.

The study of workers and friends was conducted over a period of a little over two years. A minimum of four interviews or observations were conducted with each of the women. In one case (Lori Salerno), Traustadottir conducted more extensive interviews or observations over a period of two years. This intensive study of Lori and the man she supports (Melvin) resulted in the in-depth examination of caring practices described later in this chapter. During this phase of the research, 49 sets of field notes or transcripts representing over 1000 pages of data were collected.

Although this study was guided by a phenomenological or social constructionist perspective (Berger and Luckmann 1967; Blumer 1969), it was also informed by contemporary feminist theory (Smith, 1987, 1990a, b). Smith and others have been building a "sociology for women" that can disclose how women's everyday lives are socially organized and determined by processes that extend outside of the scope of the everyday. Smith urges us to begin with the experiences of actual women. This starting point is essential because common language, as found in theory as well as in the general culture, may not reflect women's experiences (also see DeVault 1990). For example, the categories of *work* and *leisure* are rooted in men's experiences of employment in the labor market and of the home as a place of relaxation and recreation.

THE INFORMANTS

This study is based on four women. The following provides a brief description of each.

Lori Salerno

Lori works as a personal care assistant for an older man, Melvin White, who has severe physical disabilities and lived most of his life at state institutions for people labeled mentally retarded. Lori met Mel soon after his move to a small community residence for four people with disabilities. Lori, who is in her mid-30s, has an undergraduate degree in special education and previously worked as a special educator. Lori worked as a staff member at Mel's residence for a year before becoming a personal care assistant assigned directly to him. Because of the severity of his disabilities, Mel needs assistance in doing many things, including dressing, eating, going to the bathroom, and communicating with others, and Lori helps him in these activities. Mel is a kind and gentle man, and Lori has become especially close to him and has involved him in her personal life as a friend.

Heather Williams

Heather is 25 years old and works as a job coach at a supported employment agency serving people with disabilities. This position involves helping to place and support people with disabilities in regular community jobs. Heather has an undergraduate degree in rehabilitation. One of the persons Heather works with is Al Jones, a man in his early 30s who is labeled mentally retarded. Heather knew Al before she started her current job and considers him her friend. She found employment for Al and supports him in his current job.

Elanor Baker and Johanna Matthews

Elanor and Johanna are elementary school teachers who coteach an inclusive third grade class that has six students with disabilities. Both Johanna and Elanor are in their 30s. Elanor and Johanna previously taught *special*, or segregated, classes for students with disabilities.

FACILITATING ACCEPTANCE AND INCLUSION

With the emphasis on integration and inclusion, it has become more common for children and adults with disabilities to be present in society's mainstream places. But physical presence does not automatically lead to social interaction or acceptance. Where people with disabilities have been included as active participants, there has usually been a conscious effort on someone's part to create an atmosphere that encourages their participation. In the following discussion, we consider how Lori Salerno, Heather Williams, and Elanor Baker and Johanna Matthews have attempted to create such an atmosphere to facilitate relationships between people with and without disabilities.

The first section describes how these four women understand their work and think about their roles. The second section contains an in-depth examination, based on Lori Salerno's relationship with Melvin White, of the complex nature of the work involved in supporting a person with severe disabilities.

New Roles, Relationships, and Responsibilities

Each of the women in this study is developing new ways of thinking about roles and relationships, consistent with current trends in the field of developmental disabilities. Lori Salerno, whose job entails basic physical care, has formed a close and mutually rewarding friendship with the man she supports. Heather Burgess, a job coach, tries to come up with ways to build relationships between people with disabilities and nondisabled coworkers in regular work places. Johanna Matthews and Elanor Baker define their role in an inclusive classroom as not merely teaching skills and managing behavior but as fostering relationship between students with and without disabilities as well.

The Personal Care Assistant: A Staff Person and a Friend

After almost three years of working with Melvin White, Lori Salerno has become very close to him. They have been through both hard times and good times, and this has served to strengthen their relationship. Lori's attitude toward Mel is characterized by caring and commitment. Melvin also cares deeply about Lori and regards her as his closest friend. Their relationship has little resemblance to what one typically thinks of as a client-staff relationship. A better way to describe it is as a close friendship.

Despite Melvin's severe disabilities and inability to do a number of things, he makes significant contributions to the relationship in terms of closeness, commitment, respect, support, and humor. Lori is the one who is being paid to support Melvin, and she does provide him with assistance crucial to his participation in community life. Yet Melvin has become a significant source of support in Lori's life. Lori went through a very difficult period in her personal life about a year after she started working with Mel. Not only was Melvin a very sympathetic listener who provided Lori with warmth and emotional support, he also initiated and organized support from other people and helped Lori make some of the difficult decisions she had to make through this ordeal. Lori deeply appreciates Melvin's support and how he stood by her during these difficulties. Thus, although it is quite apparent how dependent Melvin is on Lori's support, a closer look reveals a relationship that is characterized by mutuality rather than dependency.

Lori and Mel have their "routine," as they call it—they do certain things on certain days. Mornings are reserved for outings. For example, on Mondays the two go to a senior center, on Tuesdays they go swimming, and on Wednesdays they often visit Mel's old friends at the institution where he previously lived. Fridays are always open for doctor appointments or things they decide to do at the spur of the moment. Lori and Mel go out to lunch at local restaurants two or three times a week, and one of Mel's friends sometimes goes with them. Afternoons are usually spent taking care of things at Mel's home, such as laundry or calling his friends or relatives. During the summer, Melvin and Lori enjoy outdoor activities such as taking boat tours, fishing, or going to outdoor concerts. Mel and Lori seem to genuinely like each other's company and doing things together. For Lori, Mel is not merely a client; he is a friend and companion.

Inclusive Educators: Helping Kids Accept Each Other
The third-grade classroom of Johanna Matthews and Elanor Baker provides a good example of how women consciously work toward creating an atmosphere that encourages the inclusion and acceptance of people with disabilities. The classroom consists of a diverse group of 26 children: almost half are classified as minorities; they come from a range of social and economic backgrounds; they have diverse family compositions; and six have been labeled as having a disability.

Prior to coteaching this regular third-grade class, Johanna and Elanor taught students with disabilities in segregated settings. Both Johanna and Elanor moved over to regular classroom teaching in order to be able to include children with disabilities. As Elanor said, "Both of us changed settings for the ability to make integration effective." Now, after having taught in a regular classroom for four years, they have broadened their understanding of inclusion and acceptance. Instead of focusing solely on the inclusion of children with disabilities, they now see inclusion and acceptance in terms of a broad range of diversity among children, including race and class. They have also learned that children's needs are not always reflected in the disability labels. "Many of the kids who do not have labels are really needy as far as attention and more nurturing skills," Elanor said. Johanna added, "And the kids who are labeled as having disabilities are not necessarily the lowest academic kids in the class." These two teachers believe that their focus on inclusion, acceptance, and cooperation "benefits the typical kids even more than the special kids."

Elanor and Johanna try to present all the children in the classroom as positively as they can, drawing attention to each child's contributions and capabilities. Elanor explained:

> We try to make kids feel good about themselves, make them feel they are good people, and that they are good learners. That they are people, that they fit into society, that they are accepted, and that there is a place in the world for them. . . . Just making kids accept each other for who they are, and for what they are, and that still qualifies them as people in the world, and you need the diversity for fun, you know, for a healthy environment.

Through their teaching, Johanna and Elanor draw attention to and celebrate the diversity among people, and they encourage the children to view themselves and others according to what is "special and different" about them. The class has frequent and long conversations about what makes each student special and different.

Elanor and Johanna use a range of teaching strategies such as cooperative learning to make sure all the children are included. They also encourage the children to celebrate each other's successes and to recognize when they succeed together as a group. These two teachers believe that cooperation is much more constructive than competition. In a competitive atmosphere there are always losers, and the children with disabilities are the most likely candidates. Thus the emphasis on cooperation is an important component of creating an atmosphere of collaboration, acceptance, and inclusion. Elanor said that the teachers like to hear the children say, " 'Boy, *we* did good today,' not 'Boy, did *I* do good today.' " But it is not just for the sake of inclusion of children with disabilities that these two teachers emphasize cooperation. They see cooperation as a necessary thing for all children to learn, or as Johanna explained, "You have to be able to work with people to survive happily in the world."

The six children with disabilities who are in the classroom are never identified as such; "Nobody knows who the six kids are," Elanor said. Instead of being identified as disabled, the children are seen as a part of the diverse group of 26, where things that would typically be seen as weaknesses are portrayed as diversity that is acknowledged as unique and something that makes a person special, valuable, and fun. Johanna and Elanor consciously attempt to create an atmosphere that is accepting of diversity and that facilitates friendship among the students. They also help their students learn the skills needed to get along with others and be friends: "We try to help them learn how to make friends, as well as the academics." When the children move to fourth grade, Elanor and Johanna carefully plan things in such a way that each child with a disability will end up in a class with at least one of the nondisabled classmates with whom they have become friends.

The Job Coach: Facilitating Connections in the Workplace
In her role as a job coach, Heather Williams helps people with disabilities to find jobs in regular workplaces. Much of what Heather does is aimed at creating an atmosphere within the workplace that will promote the acceptance and inclusion of the worker with the disability. Heather says that one of the keys to success is maintaining a "good healthy relationship" between herself and the employer; this creates the basis for the employer's acceptance of the employee with the disability. When Heather goes to an employer, she negotiates not only for a job for the person with the disability, but also for enough flexibility within the workplace to be able to work out new arrangements if needed. Heather also tries to negotiate a job that does not isolate the person from the other workers.

After negotiating the job, Heather goes to the workplace and spends a few days learning about the job before the person with the disability starts working. As Heather said, "There is more to it than just learning the job. I'm going in and getting to know coworkers and they're getting to know me." Heather tries to create a good impression of herself, because the coworkers will transfer their likes or dislikes of Heather to the person with the disability. Before the worker with the disability comes to the workplace, Heather introduces the person to the other workers by telling them about their new colleague. She introduces the person in a positive manner to increase the likelihood of the coworkers' acceptance. Heather tries to figure out who is who in the setting—who is important and influential. She also tries to identify who will be a good contact person for the new worker. The best contact person is usually a coworker who is likely to be able to or willing to provide the person with the disability with support on the job, or a coworker who is popular or powerful within the group.

When the person with the disability starts working, Heather provides the training needed to master the job. She is careful to provide this training in such a way as to promote the acceptance of others. In addition to teaching her client to do the job, Heather also initiates that person into the social dynamics of the work place. In Heather's opinion, this part is the most important aspect of her job, and she works very hard at facilitating the acceptance of the person with the disability among the coworkers. It is not always easy to work toward the inclusion in a workplace where most of the workers have not had any previous experiences with people with disabilities. Heather explained:

You have to be pretty sensitive to the dynamics of that group and understand the personalities . . . so that you can get to know people and gain a mutual trust and comfortableness. You need to be aware of what their needs are. . . . Part of my job is to educate people, but it is in a very nonformal way. People just need time to become comfortable with a person who has a lot of different behaviors. . . . The person with the disability can usually learn the job quickly, that is usually not the major issue. The issue is that the coworkers need time to "learn" the person, so it becomes my role to pull up the slack wherever it is needed, and that is often in coworker interaction.

Heather sees her role primarily in terms of assisting the person with the disability to become a part of a working unit. In order for that to happen, it is crucial that she succeed in creating an atmosphere around the person with the disability that promotes acceptance of that person and encourages the coworkers to include him or her in the social network of the workplace. When Heather is successful in this, she said, "People become desensitized to stigma of the handicap. The person becomes another coworker and the disability is secondary, because they get to know that person for who they are."

When she believes that she has accomplished acceptance, Heather starts to fade out and her role becomes that of a supporter in what she called "a follow-along situation, maintain the employee in a coworker context."

Heather referred to her work of establishing connections between the person with the disability and the nondisabled coworkers as "working for natural supports." By natural supports, she meant: "Trying to develop coworker interaction with the new employee so that I can fade out and build in natural supports." Heather described how she does this in terms of "manipulating the dynamics" in the workplace in order to facilitate interaction between the person with the disability and the nondisabled coworkers: "I facilitate in whatever way I can . . . I may manipulate all the dynamics in the group." In order to facilitate interaction between the worker with the disability and a nondisabled coworker, Heather often asks the coworker a question. She then sits back and lets the two people carry out the interaction on their own. As Heather explained, "Each time it becomes easier for the coworker to either assist, or whatever, with the new employee."

Heather also uses another strategy she calls "disappearing" to establish supportive connections between people:

I fade at a time that I very well know that the person is going to need help. But I might make an excuse by saying to the coworker: "Could you help so and so, I really need to go to the bathroom." Or: "I have to make a phone call." And you just simply excuse yourself so that interaction is occurring. And people just get more comfortable with one another, and that is what happens in any employment situation. You know, you have a new coworker and you do things so that

that person feels comfortable and you get to know that person and feel comfortable with them. And that is what I'm doing.

Often it is the worker with the disability who initiates the interaction with the coworkers. In those instances Heather's role is to facilitate and support the interaction. Heather believes that the "coworkers need that extra insurance," and she is there to provide it, at the outset, when people may be unsure about how to act toward the person with the disability.

Although Heather calls her attempts to incorporate the worker with the disability into the social context of the workplace "working for natural supports," the connections she tries to facilitate do not come naturally. To the contrary, these have to be consciously facilitated and taught through a variety of strategies. It is Heather's hard work and conscious efforts that bring these connections about.

Not all of Heather's attempts to help people establish and maintain relationships have been as successful as she had hoped. This has been the case with Al Jones, a young man with a disability, who is one of the people for whom Heather has found employment. Besides being Al's job coach, Heather is also his best friend. Heather and Al have been friends for four years, and their friendship was established prior to Heather's current work as a job coach. Heather said,

> It is so sad, Al has no friends except me and if I don't do things with him, he doesn't do them. He may go with his family every once in a while out for dinner, but that is all.

Heather has tried very hard to assist Al in finding friends both at work and outside work:

> Al's coworkers are the most important part of his work but it doesn't go beyond work. They always invite him if they have a staff party. He is always invited. They drink and have fun, and he has fun with them. But that's it.

Heather has also tried to "hook Al up" with people outside work, but it has not worked out. She has tried to introduce him to her own friends and others in the hope that they would establish an independent relationship with him. Although her friends are friendly to Al and like to have him around, none of them have kept in contact with him independently. She has encouraged them to go places with him without her, but this does not seem to work. If Heather gets someone else involved with Al, she has to do all the planning and preparation: "Plan the time, the activity, and everything. I might as well do it myself." Heather is discouraged by this and has doubts about herself: "I wonder if I'm doing anything wrong?"

The assumption that people with disabilities will receive a considerable amount of social support through their connections with nondisabled people does not always hold. For people such as Heather who try to support relationships between people with and without disabilities, this can be frustrating.

THE ARTFUL INVISIBILITY OF CARING WORK

Caring work is complex and can involve subtle forms of support and assistance that are not readily apparent. By virtue of her close relationship with Mel, Lori Salerno has developed a sophisticated set of strategies not only to take care of his physical needs, but to facilitate interactions and relationships with others.

The assistance or support Lori provides to Mel consists of a related set of types of work: everyday practical assistance; translating conversations; facilitating interaction; and supporting him to express his desires and needs.

Everyday Practical Assistance

The most visible support Lori renders is the assistance she provides with everyday practical things. There are at least four different kinds of such practical assistance.

Physical work. The most obvious support Lori performs is pushing Mel around in his wheelchair, pulling the chair up stairs, transferring Mel in and out of the chair, and so on. This part of the support is demanding physical labor and requires a fair amount of physical strength.

Technical work. These are things like driving the agency's big van around and operating the wheelchair lift in the van. This also includes technical work and skills centered around Mel's health, such as administering medication and following the complicated Medicaid rules and regulations that govern much of Melvin's life in the community.

Personal work. Mel needs help with personal things like eating, dressing, and going to the bathroom. Some of this work requires very close personal physical contact. Melvin also needs help with other personal things, like calling his friends and family, buying clothes, selecting paint for his room, and so on.

Financial work. Lori assists Melvin in managing his spending money and overall finances. She takes him to the bank, where she aids him in making deposits and withdrawals, and helps him store some of his money in a strongbox at home. When Melvin wanted to make a will, Lori was the one who provided him with assistance in contacting a lawyer and making other arrangements.

The support Lori provides in terms of everyday practical assistance consists of hard physical labor and taking care of some of Mel's most demanding, intimate, and personal needs. If Lori were not there to take care of these things, someone else would have to assist Mel with them. This work is crucial for Mel's participation in the community. People would ordinarily find it physically difficult or embarrassing to do these things for him. When Melvin participates in social events in the community, Lori removes these difficulties and potential barriers to interaction, and people can enjoy Mel's company without having to worry about the problems related to his disabilities.

Translating Conversations

Another important function Lori fulfills is to translate for Mel. The translation goes two ways: she translates what Mel says to other people, and to Mel what other people say. Melvin is very hard to understand, and when people do not understand what he says, Lori will repeat it. In addition, because it is such an effort for Melvin to speak, Lori often adds explanations or information about what he is talking about. The second type of translating is necessary because of Melvin's hearing loss. As he has grown older, he has lost hearing and sometimes has a hard time hearing what people say. When Lori is with Melvin, she watches to see whether he can hear what people say. If he does not hear people, Lori repeats to him what was just said.

The difficulties Mel has in communicating become clear when Lori is not with him. People become uncomfortable when they do not understand what he is trying to say and find it embarrassing to have to ask him to repeat it again and again. Sometimes people pretend they understand him in order to get out of these uncomfortable situations. They also often misunderstand what Melvin says and their comments may not make sense to him. It is hard for Melvin to keep a conversation going under these circumstances.

Another difficulty that arises in situations where Lori is not with Melvin results from his hearing loss. Because Mel cannot hear well, he sometimes does not respond to comments made to him. This can create an embarrassing, confusing, and uncomfortable situation. Since Melvin looks very disabled, people sometimes assume that he is too intellectually limited to understand their questions. People may also think he does not respond to them because their questions were inappropriate or offensive. Lori takes away much of the discomfort and uncertainties surrounding conversation with Melvin and makes the communication between him and other people smooth and easy.

Lori also translates on a different level than that of just repeating words between Mel and other people. She communicates to other people what Mel wants to do, what he can and cannot do, what is safe for him to do because of his health, and so on. If Lori is not around to convey such things, people are often unsure about what Melvin wants or what is safe for him. During a visit to Melvin's sister, for example, one of his relatives offered people chocolate when Lori was out of the room. The relative asked Mel's 81-year-old sister Marie if he should give him chocolate. Marie said that she did not know whether it was safe. When she asked him if he could have chocolate, Melvin said, "Yes." Marie did not seem convinced and said something like, "You better not choke on it in my house," as she put a piece of chocolate in Melvin's mouth. When Lori returned, Marie asked her if Melvin could have chocolate. Lori said, "Oh yes, he loves chocolate, he eats it all the time." It was not until Lori convinced her that this was safe that Marie stopped being nervous about giving Melvin chocolate.

Facilitating Interaction

An important element of Lori's support is facilitating Melvin's participation in conversations and social situations. If someone does not provide this facilitation, it is nearly impossible for Melvin to participate in group conversations. Melvin's inability to participate in group conversations is mostly due to how slow his speech is, how long it takes him to prepare himself to say something, and how long it takes him to say one sentence. It is impossible for him to "jump in" or keep up with the flow of a conversation in a group. Lori is very skilled at facilitating Mel's participation, and as a team they manage to keep him a part of the conversation. Lori participates in conversations on Melvin's behalf by referring to him constantly. She tells stories about what he has done, what he said, how he acted in certain situations, what his opinion is about certain things, and so on. She also draws Melvin into the conversation by opening up an opportunity for him to add a sentence. This facilitating on Lori's behalf normalizes Melvin's participation in social situations. When Lori is talking on his behalf, Melvin participates by nodding, smiling, making faces appropriate to the topic, and keeping eye contact with the people in the group. Melvin and Lori also keep eye contact with each other while they are telling the story, and they seem to decide through this eye contact when Melvin should "jump in" and do his part of the talking. Lori plays an active role in the social situations with Mel. As his support person, she is not there in her own capacity, but to facilitate his participation. Lori's personality and the way she interacts with people is crucial for Mel's abilities to become a part of what is going on. At the same time, Lori cannot dominate the situation with her personal presence and opinions, because if she does Melvin falls in the shadow and disappears. This part of Lori's support role requires a delicate balancing act on her part.

Supporting Him to Express His Desires

Lori's role in facilitating and supporting Melvin to speak on his own behalf is the last component of her support role. Melvin lived in state institutions for over 60 years and is not used to making demands on his own behalf or having many choices. Melvin says that when he entered the institution he was determined to "have my way and I got into a lot of trouble." He explains that he changed over time and decided to "cooperate" with the staff. When Melvin moved into the community, he was not used to making choices or decisions. Melvin also reports that the staff in the apartment did not do much to encourage him to exercise decision making or to make choices. It was not until Lori started working with him that he received encouragement to make demands, choices, and decisions.

At first Melvin found it difficult to express his desires and needs. Part of the difficulty had to do with his personality. He finds it hard to deal with conflict and often keeps quiet about his wishes so that he does not upset or disagree with anyone. Melvin is also a kind and gentle person and avoids doing anything that might hurt other people's feelings. Making demands often means that he has to ask people to change the way they do things. He often assumes people will take his wishes as a criticism and be hurt. He therefore often chooses to keep quiet. A good example of this is when a new staff person at the apartment kept calling him "sweet thing" and "honey pie." Melvin did not like being addressed in this way, but he knew the woman did not have bad intentions. He was afraid that she might be hurt if he asked her to stop this. He finally got up his courage and discussed this with her, carefully explaining to her that he did not mean to hurt her, but he would appreciate if she would not call him "sweetie pie" all the time. This was the first time Melvin had the courage to address things like this and he feels very good about having done this without hurting the staff person's feelings.

Lori has played a critical role in supporting Melvin in expressing what he wants. This is something they discuss at great lengths, and Lori has explained to him that he has the right to make his own choices and to exercise control over his own life. Much of Melvin's life has been characterized by disappointments and shattered dreams. Therefore he is often afraid to make decisions to do the things he would most like to do, such visiting some of his nephews and nieces in other states. He does not want to face the disappointment if things do not work out. Lori's has encouraged him to make decisions like this. Before Lori started working with Melvin, he did not express his wishes and desires. With her encouragement, he is starting to become more outspoken.

DISCUSSION

Like other forms of women's work (Daniels 1988; DeVault 1991), the work performed by women who support people with developmental disabilities may be "invisible." It is made invisible in several ways.

First, apart from ceremonial recognition, caring work is often devalued and receives low status and low pay. The closer work is to traditional female activities such as nurturing and facilitating social connections, the more closely it is seen as an expression of women's "natural" character. Caring work is thus not seen as difficult or skillful. It is taken for granted.

Second, much of women's caring work is, as DeVault (1991) notes, "literally invisible." DeVault (1991, 56) explains how the work of managing the family meal "looks like simply enjoying the companionship of one's family" and how meal planning is largely mental work that cannot be seen. Similarly, supporting people with disabilities may be invisible in the same sense. For example, Heather Williams' work of selecting a coworker to be a "natural support" for a person with a disability looks like socializing. The work of figuring out how to make connections in the workplace or in school classes is largely mental work not apparent to others.

Third, invisibility can be built into certain kinds of activities. When the work is skillfully done, no one can see it. Lori Salerno's facilitation work with Melvin and other people enables him to converse and interact with others. As long as she does this skillfully and artfully, it is not apparent to others. It only becomes visible when people see what happens when the work is not done or is done in a clumsy way.

Fourth, caring work may bring with it emotional closeness and commitment that are easily overlooked by someone outside of a relationship. Caring for someone may result in caring about that person (DeVault 1991; Graham 1983). Thus Lori Salerno is both Melvin White's personal care assistant and his friend.

The women who form close emotional ties to the people they work with find it difficult to separate these two components of caring: the love and the work. When the workers developed such emotional closeness with a person with a disability, their caring work changed. A close emotional relationship creates a personal, intimate knowledge of the other, and this influences how the work is done.

Although it is possible to distinguish between the emotions and activities of caring, they are not easily separated in practice. Moreover, these two components of care, the work and the love, are so closely intertwined that many women find it hard to distinguish between them.

Caring work is gendered because it is the nurturing and affective aspects of the work that are invisible. These are skills associated with women. The multiple ways in which caring work is made invisible underscore the importance of reconceptualizing the concept of *work* to include the various aspects of the role of supporting people with disabilities. Bringing this work into view does not change the devaluation of these activities or the way it is organized, but may be a first step in recognizing its importance.

Disability services workers are increasingly expected to make a personal commitment to the people they support. Many do this willingly, if unconsciously. This can make it difficult to distinguish between their job and their personal life. Work done on the basis of personal commitment may no longer be defined as *work* but as *friendship*. As a result of the fluid boundaries surrounding caring work, women may experience a conflict stemming from the various demands placed upon their time, energy, and emotions.

Current reforms in the field of developmental disabilities are moving the boundaries of workers' responsibilities in a way that may increase the work they perform without compensating them for it. Most workers are women, and women are more likely to respond to the affective elements of the new roles and responsibilities.

Trends in the field may result in the recruitment of women to perform increasing amounts of caring work without being paid for it. Further, the new emphasis on natural supports and friendship may turn out to be a way of substituting volunteers for paid workers, especially at a time of declining resources for human services generally.

Without competent and skillful workers attending to the needs of others and bringing people together socially, the improved lives of people with developmental disabilities envisioned by the new reforms will not be possible. Women's contributions need to be recognized, made visible, and justly compensated. If leaders in the field of developmental disabilities continue to ignore the gendered nature of caring work, the new policies may have effects the reformers did not intend.

NOTE

1. Rannveig Traustadottir, Ph.D., is Assistant Professor at the University of Iceland, Faculty of Social Science, 101 Reykjavik, Iceland.

CHAPTER 11

"Children's Division is Coming to Take Pictures": Life in a Family with Mental Retardation and Disabilities

Steven J. Taylor

E VER SINCE THE eugenics period around the turn of twentieth century, parents who are mentally retarded have been a source of professional and public concern. Not long ago, public policy and professional opinion supported efforts to prevent people with mental retardation from bearing children through restrictive marriage laws, segregation, and involuntary sterilization (Smith 1985; Taylor and Searl 1987). With the waning of the eugenics movement and the growing popularity of the concept of normalization (Wolfensberger 1972), there is increased acceptance of the rights of adults with mental retardation to marry and bear children.

Attention has gradually shifted from the prevention of sexual expression and reproduction among people with mental retardation to questions of their parental adequacy. When the word *parent* and the phrase *mentally retarded* are paired, concern for the welfare of the children automatically arises in the minds of many child protective agencies, developmental disability agencies, and agents of the law. According to one family court judge, "(This) is a problem for a whole society. . . . The question is: how well are children cared for in the homes of parents with mental disabilities?" (Forder 1990, ix). Reflecting common professional opinion, Whitman and Accardo (1990, 203) write: "Mentally retarded adults in the community are having children and are experiencing significant problems in parenting."

This chapter[1] examines family life in a family I will refer to as the Dukes. The immediate family consists of four members—Bill and Winnie and their two children, Sammy and Cindy—but the Dukes are part of a much larger network of extended family members and friends. Each member of the Duke family has mental retardation or other disabilities, and child protective agencies have frequently intervened in the family's life.

In order to appreciate the Duke family, it is necessary to juxtapose how they look from the outside—that is, from a distance—with how they look from the inside—how they see themselves and how they look once one has gotten to know them well. At first glance, the Dukes and their kin are reminiscent of the Kallikaks (Goddard 1912), the Jukes (Dugdale 1910), or any of the other notorious families studied during the eugenics period as representing the hereditary transmission of feeblemindedness, disability, social pathology, and pauperism. Bill, Winnie, and their two children have all been diagnosed as mentally retarded or disabled by schools and human services agencies, and a sizable number of their kin and friends have been similarly diagnosed. Mental retardation, physical disabilities, mental illness or emotional disturbance, speech impediments, epilepsy, and miscellaneous medical problems are common among Bill's and Winnie's brothers and sisters, nieces and nephews, cousins, in-laws, and friends. With few exceptions, kin and friends are poor or living at the edge of poverty. The men look seedy, the women look hard, and the children look dirty. But this is only at first glance.

As I have gotten to know Bill and Winnie and their family, I have come to see them as kind, gentle, resourceful, and respectable. They have created decent lives for themselves given their circumstances and experiences. Not all of Bill and Winnie's family and friends appear as respectable as Winnie and Bill. Some drink too much, steal or have run-ins with the law, or take advantage of other members of the network. Yet, like Bill and Winnie, they are struggling to survive in a society in which they are at a distinct competitive disadvantage socially and economically.

Before examining the Duke family and their experiences, I introduce the family members and describe my study.

THE DUKE FAMILY

Bill and Winnie Duke live with their two young adult children, Sammy and Cindy, right outside of Central City, a medium-size city in the Northeast. After introducing each member of the family, I briefly describe their household, Bill's and Winnie's family backgrounds, disabilities among their friends and kin, and social relations within their network.

BILL

Bill, 45, describes himself as a "graduate of Empire State School," a state institution originally founded in 1894 as the Empire State Custodial Asylum for Unteachable Idiots. Born in a small rural community outside of Capital City, Bill was placed at the institution as an adolescent. Bill talks about his years at the institution with mixed emotions. While he says that the institution "helped me get my head together," he recalls the bitterness he felt at the time about being separated from his family.

Bill was placed on "probation" and lived for a period of time in a halfway house in Central City, approximately 150 miles from his family's home. He was officially discharged from the institution in 1971.

Bill is "on disability" and receives government Social Security and Supplemental Security Income (SSI) benefits. Shortly after his release from the institution, he held several short-term jobs, but has not worked at a regular, taxpaying job since the mid-1970s. As Bill explains,

> Last time I went to my doctor he said I couldn't work because I have seizures. Now that's something I can't understand. I can't work, but it's OK to drive a car. If you can't work, you shouldn't be able to drive a car.

Like other members of the Dukes' network of family and friends, Bill regularly goes "junking," picking up scrap metal, furniture, old appliances, bikes, and other items from the trash that he brings home, sells, or gives away. He also does odd jobs and has worked at least twice at a local garage. He worked at the garage in exchange for service and parts on his cars and also got paid a little under the table. Bill buys or trades for old cars that he drives until they no longer run or become too expensive to fix. He spends much of his time tinkering on his cars.

Bill is an avid fan of professional wrestling or, as he puts it, a "rasslin' freak." In addition to attending live events, he watches wrestling videotapes on his VCR and occasionally orders live pay-per-view wrestling on cable television. Bill also likes to fish and goes as often as he can during warm weather.

Bill takes prescription medications for seizures, diarrhea, headaches, and nerves. He has also said on various occasions that doctors have told him that he suffers from life-threatening brain tumors and lung cancer (since Bill has survived his supposedly terminal medical conditions, it is unclear whether he fully understands what doctors tell him).

WINNIE

Winnie, 43, runs the household, manages the family's finances, and negotiates relations with schools, government programs, and human service workers. Winnie was born and raised in Central City. She dropped out of school early to help raise her brother and stepbrothers and -sisters, but can read well and prides herself both on her memory and math skills.

Winnie has a speech impediment, which makes her very difficult to understand until one has known her for a while. She also has a host of medical problems. She had convulsions until she was 9 years old and has arthritis, heart problems, and a club foot. She recently went on a diet when her weight reached over 200 pounds.

When I first met the Dukes, Winnie was on public assistance, or welfare, but she was subsequently deemed eligible for SSI. She also previously received spousal benefits from Bill's Social Security. She is eligible for vocational rehabilitation because she has "a disability which results in a substantial handicap to employment," according to her individual written rehabilitation plan, and has participated in numerous job training programs. In the past several years, she has worked twice at a large sheltered workshop, Federated Industries of Central City. She took the job under the threat of losing her welfare benefits, but no longer works there because Federated ran out of work and laid off most of its clients.

Winnie frequently baby-sits for the children of family members, friends, and neighbors. She was penalized by welfare several years ago for failing to report money earned from baby-sitting a neighbor's child.

Winnie has been involved in many parenting and homemaking programs and has had a parent aide, in addition to protective service workers, assigned to the family. Winnie describes herself as a "knickknack freak" and has a large collection of statues, busts, and knickknacks of every conceivable kind.

Winnie and Bill

Winnie and Bill met when Winnie's family was living across the street from Bill's halfway house. Winnie had told her stepmother, "I'm going to meet a blue-eyed, blond-haired man who looks just like me," and she did.

When she and Bill met, Winnie recalls, "It was love at first sight." Bill's social worker posed a problem, however. Since Bill was still on "probation," his worker told him that he was not allowed to date and went to speak to Winnie to tell her to break off the relationship. Bill eventually got off "probation," and he and Winnie were married within a couple of weeks. Winnie still has her wedding dress and a wedding ring that cost $4.95.

Bill and Winnie's first child, Sammy, was born about a year later. Between the births of Sammy and Cindy, who is two and a half years younger, Winnie lost a child.

As Winnie has said to me, "You think me and Bill have a perfect marriage, but we don't." When Sammy and Cindy were young, the couple was separated, and both Bill and Winnie confess to infidelity around this time. Yet they reconciled and are looking forward to celebrating their twenty-third anniversary. Winnie points out, "We've had our ups and downs but we've been married longer than any of our brothers and sisters."

SAMMY

Sammy, 22, was born with cerebral palsy which is not currently noticeable, a cleft palate, and heart problems. According to Winnie, he has had over 90 operations for hearing, heart, and other problems. As an infant, he had a tracheostomy and was fed through a tube in his stomach. Winnie proudly recalls how she learned to handle the tracheostomy. Sammy has a severe speech impediment and is extremely difficult to understand when he talks.

Sammy dropped out of school at age 16. He was enrolled in a special education program for students with multiple disabilities, and specifically mental retardation and hearing impairments. He receives SSI, and his application for Social Security Disability benefits is under reconsideration. Winnie is the representative payee for Sammy's SSI; that is, Sammy's check comes in Winnie's name, and she must periodically report how the funds are spent.

Like his father, Sammy enjoys tinkering with bikes, cars, and just about anything else with an engine. Although he does not have a driver's license or even a learner's permit, he has owned many cars and motorcycles. Sammy collects model cars and goes to wrestling matches with his father.

Sammy has never held a regular job, although he worked for a very brief period of time at the same garage where his father worked.

Sammy is very shy and seems sullen until one has known him for a while. He has a number of friends, but spends most of the time with his family.

CINDY

Cindy, 18, has epilepsy and receives SSI. Prior to dropping out of school at age 17, she was enrolled in an intensive special education class and her federally mandated individual education plan (IEP) indicated that she is mentally retarded–mild. Both Bill and Winnie were proud of how Cindy was doing in school and were disappointed when she dropped out.

One summer while she was in high school, Cindy was placed at the Federated Industries sheltered workshop as part of a job training program. Through her school program, she had job placements at fast-food restaurants and a human services agency.

Cindy has a worker who is funded through the state office of mental retardation and developmental disabilities. I was introduced to the family by this worker.

Cindy speaks very clearly, but seems to have difficulty reading. Like Sammy, Cindy is very shy among strangers and acts withdrawn in public.

Since I started studying the Duke family, Cindy has changed from a girl to a young adult, wife, and mother. About three years ago, Bill and Winnie started to worry that Cindy was becoming sexually active. Their fears were not unfounded. Cindy became pregnant, broke up with her boyfriend, and then married a 26-year-old man, Vinnie, shortly afterward. Cindy's baby, Mikey, was born in spring 1993, and a second baby is due in summer 1994. Cindy, Vinnie, and Mikey have lived off and on with the Dukes, but currently have their own apartment not far from Winnie and Bill's home.

THE DUKE HOUSEHOLD

The Dukes moved into a mobile home in a trailer park in a small village outside of Central City in summer 1993. After less than a year there, they moved to another mobile home in the same complex. This is their eighth home in the past eight and a half years.

Prior to moving to their current trailer park, the Dukes lived in one of two parts of Central City: the North End, a lower- and working-class area identified as an ethnic community (but today diverse), and the West End, a lower-class and racially diverse area. Both parts are characterized by low-income housing, and Winnie's and Bill's family and friends in the city live in either of these two sections.

When I first met the Dukes in 1989, they were living in a small rented house in a factory and warehouse district on the North End. A railroad track ran in the front yard of the house, and slow-moving trains passed by the house two or three times a day.

Household arrangements are usually the same in most of the Dukes' homes. The master bedroom is reserved for one of their boarders or Cindy and her husband and baby; Sammy also has his own bedroom; Winnie and Bill sleep in their own room, if a bedroom is left over, or in the living room.

As the Dukes settle into each new home, it slowly begins to resemble their former homes. Floors are strewn with litter, cigarette butts, cat or dog food bowls, and sometimes machine and car parts. The ever changing living room is furnished with two or three sofas, an easy chair or two, coffee and side tables, and lamps. Just about all of the furniture comes from someone else's trash.

The old furniture stands in sharp contrast to the new television and VCR leased from rent-to-own companies. Stacks of papers are on top of the tables; a dozen prescription pill bottles are on top of the VCR. The walls are covered with brightly colored paintings and tapestries of Christ, a matador, and Elvis Presley.

Knickknack shelves are crammed full of figurines, salt and pepper shakers, religious figures, and other objects.

The Dukes' household is usually larger than their immediate family. Winnie's brother John lived with the family for over two years and as many as 10 additional adults and four children have stayed with them for weeks or even months at a time.

BILL'S FAMILY BACKGROUND

Bill comes from a large family and was one of nine children. Bill has three older sisters, a younger brother, and four younger sisters; he can name 29 nieces and nephews and nine great-nieces and nephews on his side of the family. His brother, who is divorced and has three children by his wife, has had five children with another woman, but Bill does not consider these his nieces and nephews.

Bill is proud of the fact that two of his grandparents were Indian—one Cherokee and one Mohawk—but he does not identify with Native American culture. Bill's father died a number of years ago, but his mother is still living outside of Capital City.

According to Bill, "When you talk about my family, you're talking down. I mean, down, man." Part of the folklore of Bill's family, shared by his siblings, is that his mother slept around with different men, including a milk man and the "welfare man," and that only three of his siblings can trace their paternity to their father.

Bill's mother was on welfare when her children were young. Bill's three older sisters were eventually placed in foster care and Bill, his sister Betty, and his brother were placed at Empire State School.

Bill was the first member of his family to move to Central City when he was put "on probation" by Empire State School. Three of his sisters, two nephews, and a niece subsequently moved to Central City. Bill's brother lived in Central City for a while before returning to the Capital City area.

Bill speaks of his deceased father with deep fondness and respect. He says that he did not get along with his mother for a long time, but is on good terms with her now. His mother's current boyfriend is his sister Iris's ex-husband and the brother of Bill's biological father; he refuses to call his mother's boyfriend "Dad." Bill visits his mother every couple of years.

WINNIE'S FAMILY BACKGROUND

Like Bill, Winnie comes from a very large family. She has three brothers, five stepbrothers, and three stepsisters, but it is only when explaining her family background that she distinguishes between full and step-siblings. Winnie can count 24 nieces and nephews and 6 great-nieces and nephews. Winnie's mother died when she was young and her father married her current stepmother. Her father died several years ago. Winnie's father had three brothers and one sister.

According to Winnie, her family lived all over the Central City area when she was growing up. Most of her family continues to live in Central City, but her stepmother, brother, stepbrother, and stepsister moved to Tennessee a number of years ago. Winnie's stepmother, with whom she and everyone else in her family have a stormy relationship, has moved back and forth between Central City and Tennessee several times. She currently lives in Central City. Winnie's stepsister also moved back from Tennessee. Winnie's brother John, who had lived with the Dukes at three of their former homes, moved to Tennessee in 1993.

DISABILITIES AMONG KIN AND FRIENDS

Many of the Dukes' kin and friends have been identified as mentally retarded, mentally ill, or otherwise disabled by human services agencies or government programs. Of Bill's and Winnie's 19 siblings, at least 7 have received treatment for disabilities or have been considered disabled by agencies or programs. Many of the Dukes' other relatives and friends receive SSI or have been served by sheltered workshops, developmental disability programs, or mental health agencies. To my knowledge, virtually all of the children of the Dukes' extended family members and friends have been placed in special education programs.

Within the Duke network, people do not view themselves or others as disabled or mentally retarded, except for two of Bill's nieces who have physical disabilities and are referred to as *handicapped* or *crippled*. For example, Bill describes himself as being *on disability*, but not as being *disabled* or *having a disability*; in the same manner, Winnie has referred to herself as being *on welfare*. Being *on disability* or *on welfare* simply refers to the source of one's entitlement check.

Since people do not think of themselves in terms of disability categories, it is difficult to say exactly how many have actually been defined as disabled by government programs or formal agencies. It is only when the Dukes happen to make reference to someone's SSI or placement in a disability program that one learns that a member of their social network has been defined as having a disability. Many of the Dukes' other kin and friends leave the impression of being slow or vulnerable to being defined as disabled by human services agencies.

SOCIAL RELATIONS AMONG KIN AND FRIENDS

Bill and Winnie not only come from sizable extended families, but also have a large and ever expanding network of friends and acquaintances. The

Dukes make friends easily and bring friends of friends, family of friends, and friends of family into their immediate social network.

Social relations within the Duke network are characterized by mutual support on the one hand and arguments and feuds on the other. In contrast to the conventional view of upwardly mobile American families (Mintz and Kellogg 1988), members of the Dukes' network maintain close kinship ties. Like black families headed by females (Stack 1974), the Dukes and their kin and friends depend on each other for help and assistance; mutual support networks are a means of coping with their marginal economic and social status. The Dukes, as well as their relatives and friends, take in homeless family members and friends, lend people food or money, and help each other out in other ways.

People within the Dukes' network also regularly complain about and argue with each other or become embroiled in all-out feuds. At any point, someone in the network is fighting with someone else. Hardly a month goes by when Bill and Winnie are not involved in a dispute with relatives or friends. Once an argument begins, other family members and friends are likely to be drawn into it.

Feuds can be emotionally charged and vehement, but they seldom last long. People can be bitter enemies one day and friendly to each other the next. For example, when I first met the Dukes, Lisa and Gary and their three children were staying with them because they were homeless. Bill and Winnie grew tired of Lisa and Gary and threw them out of their house. Within months, however, Lisa and Gary were once again close friends of the Dukes and frequent visitors to their home. Then another argument erupted, followed by a reconciliation a short time later. The Dukes are similarly very close to Bill's sister Betty and her family, but feud with them at least every several months.

THE STUDY

When I first heard about the Duke family, I was interested in meeting them. Cindy's worker, Mary, had casually told me about the family and how each member had a disability. Mary described how Bill referred to himself as a "graduate of Empire State School" and bought old junk cars, and how Winnie hustled money and free tickets to the Ice Capades, circuses, and other shows from the family's many workers.

Mary agreed to introduce me to the Duke family in February 1989. I have been studying them ever since that time and, to date, have completed well over 100 sets of detailed field notes based on my observations. I also talk frequently with them on the telephone.

Early on in my study, I told the Dukes that I was writing a book on families and wanted them to be in it. Bill and Winnie took the idea of a book very seriously and asked Sammy and Cindy if it was okay with them to be part of the book. By the end of this visit, it was clear that Winnie and Bill were thrilled and proud about the idea of being part of a book.

News that I was writing a book spread rapidly through the Duke network. Bill and Winnie proudly told family members and friends about the book, and people occasionally gave me advice about what I should include.

My relationship with the Duke family has evolved over time. I started out as "Mary's friend" and a teacher or professor who was writing a book. I next became the family's "lawyer." I started helping family members interpret and fill out the confusing and cumbersome paperwork they received from Social Security, welfare, and other government offices. Then one day Winnie received a copy of Cindy's individual education plan along with a list of organizations to call if parents wanted to dispute the contents of the IEP. My name and the Center on Human Policy were listed on the form. Winnie was impressed.

From there on out, Winnie and Bill referred to me as their lawyer and came to me for advice on everything ranging from Social Security, SSI, and welfare to educational programs, evictions, insurance, and a will for Bill. On numerous occasions I accompanied Winnie and Bill to the Social Security office to try to help straighten out problems with their benefits. Before long, they started referring other family members and friends to me for advice.

Today, the Dukes introduce me to others as a friend of the family. I am invited to all family gatherings, and the Dukes are disappointed if I cannot come.

My study has followed the traditional participant observation mold: hanging out with people and doing whatever they happen to be doing. I have never formally interviewed the Dukes; rather, I ask questions that seem appropriate at the time.

Especially in the beginning of my study, most of my observations occurred in the Duke home. Over the years, I have spent increasing amounts of time with the Dukes outside of their home, visiting kin or friends, attending professional wrestling matches with Bill, running errands, and accompanying Winnie to Cindy's middle school graduation. I also drove Bill and Sammy for a day-long visit to Bill's relatives outside of Capital City.

I have never been made to feel unwelcome by the Dukes. Winnie and Bill are open and honest people who never balk at answering any questions I ask and readily volunteer information about themselves and their family that most people would hide. I know more about the intimate details of the Dukes' lives than about most of my closest friends and relatives.

Throughout my study, Mary has maintained contact with Bill and Winnie and some of their relatives who have been her clients. With the Dukes' knowledge and consent, she has helped fill in gaps in my information about the family. She has also been available to confirm many of my impressions and observations.

This is a study that so far has a beginning but no end. I cannot foresee cutting off contact with the family, both because I enjoy them and because I want to see how their lives will continue to unfold.

CHILDREN'S DIVISION

To the average family, the prospect of being investigated for child abuse or neglect is frightening and shameful. For the Dukes, their kin, and their friends, it is a routine occurrence. Child abuse agencies—known as *Children's Division* or *CD* within the Dukes' network—are regularly involved with many of Bill's and Winnie's extended family members and friends, as well as their own family. Many family members have been investigated by Children's Division at one time or another and have been assigned protective workers and parent aides.

The Family History

The intervention of child welfare agencies in the Duke network extends at least as far back to Bill's family when he was a child. Bill's records at Empire State School document the state's and county's constant interventions in his family's life. As Figure 11.1 shows, Bill's case summary and abstract, compiled on his admission to Empire, describes his parents as deficient and his home environment as deplorable.

Bill, his older sister Betty, and his younger brother Joey were placed at Empire at the same time. When their mother requested that the three children return home for a summer visit, a social worker from Empire visited the home along with a county social worker. The Empire social worker reported that the family's "mountain top home was broken by the county's efforts" because of "poor supervision and unstableness displayed by the parents . . . physical abuse, incest, improper use of welfare funds and immorality." The social worker proceeded to explain, however, that the family's situation had improved considerably due to the county caseworker's efforts: "This family is being helped and studied intensively by the Commissioner of [County] to prove that if all the welfare resources in the county coordinated their services to a family of this type, much could be done to help the family situations socially and financially."

A mixed picture of Bill's parents emerges from the records at Empire State School. On the one hand, summaries characterize the family as disreputable and defective. Vague accusations that appear early in the records are passed down as fact in later entries. On the other hand, home observations, interviews with county workers and family members, and other types of firsthand information provide few specific instances of abuse or neglect. That the

William Duke, Jr.
Date of Admission (1963)   **Date of Summary** (1963)
A white male, age 15, single and Protestant, admitted . . . on a "Court Certification of Mental Defectives."

FAMILY HISTORY: Father, William Duke, Sr., born (1920), went to 5th grade in school. He is mentally retarded with an IQ 77. He is deteriorated, possibly due to alcoholism. He does not work, does not show any motivation, and shows a depressive reaction. Mother, Nancy Shenandoah Duke, born (1923), has been diagnosed as a "schizophrenic character who has not become blatantly psychotic." She has a full scale IQ. of 70.

Siblings: Pamela, born (1944). Iris, born (1945), went through 4th grade with and I.Q. just below 70, but her potential is well in the average range. She is in the defective range; diagnosis may be simply schizophrenia.

- Joseph, born (15), in 4th grade, I.Q. 58, no motivation, and fear of adult authority.
- Elizabeth (Betty), born (1952), in 3rd grade, I.Q. 61, schizophrenic reaction, preoccupied with male and female bodies, has a tremendous fear of men. Melanie, born (1956); Jean (born 1957), Sandra, Born (1961).
- Joseph and Elizabeth (Betty) were admitted to Empire State School with William.

PERSONAL HISTORY: William attained the 6th grade in school . . . He has no meaningful identification; passive aggressive personality. It was felt that he might benefit from a controlled setting such as Empire State School. The home environment is extremely poor, and there is evidence of alcoholism, incest, prostitution, pediculosis, and lack of proper nutrition and supervision.

REASON FOR ADMISSION: Because of William's inability to benefit from school, and the deplorable home situation, placement in Empire State School was recommended.

DIAGNOSIS: Mental Deficiency.

1. Familial.
2. 81-Cultural-familial mental retardation.

Figure 11.1   Excerpt of Bill's records at Empire State School:
Empire State School case summary and abstract.

family was poor, that the parents were mentally retarded or at least slow, and that Bill's mother sometimes drank excessively seem beyond dispute. Bill recalls that welfare placed his three older sisters in a "home" (presumably foster care) while he and his two siblings were sent to Empire:

> See, my mother was on P.A. [public assistance]. She was drinking real heavy then. The place we were living in didn't have electricity or a toilet. . . . We didn't even have an outhouse. You had to shit in a bucket.

According to Bill's records, charges of incest and physical abuse within the family were never substantiated upon further investigation. Perhaps the most indicting information contained in the records is that after Betty returned to the home from Empire, her mother encouraged older men to take her out in exchange for groceries or a case of beer. Bill says that his mother "sold" Betty to her first husband for a six-pack. After Betty married this 55-year-old man when she was 16, she wrote Empire asking if Bill could be released to live with her, and her home and family situation were investigated by an Empire social worker. The social worker reported that Betty's husband was kind and generous to her and that it was a good situation despite their age difference.

Every once in a while, Bill's records shed a positive light on his family. In the report on a home visit, an Empire social worker wrote, "Patient's father and mother are very fond of one another." The county public welfare department wrote Empire State School to support the return home of Bill, Joey, and Betty less than a year after they had been placed there. Bill's records also contain dozens of the original copies of letters from Bill's mother requesting that her children be permitted home for visits or released from the institution. One letter read: "We have enjoyed every minute of the times we have had them home before." Many of her requests were denied, "in view of the problems you had in supervising them before admission."

So the picture that emerges of Bill's family is that it was neither exemplary nor utterly despicable, but somewhere in between. While evidence of child abuse or neglect contained in the records is unclear and contradictory, social welfare agencies intervened in the family's life and separated the children from their parents. This pattern of agency intervention is repeated in successive generations of the Duke family.

THE CURRENT GENERATION

The Dukes have been investigated by Children's Division on at least four occasions. In at least two instances, the investigations resulted in formal intervention in the family and the assignment of parent aides.

Bill and Winnie's involvement with child protective agencies began when Sammy and Cindy were young children. Bill recalls that he was investigated for child abuse—hitting Cindy—and that he was not even living with his family at the time (this was during a two-week separation between Bill and Winnie), and Winnie says she was investigated when Cindy was hurt as a baby.

According to Winnie, she called the child protective agency and requested a parent aide when Sammy and Cindy were both young and having medical problems. I asked what the parent aide did for her and she answered, "Same thing you do. Sit here and talk. Then if they see abuse they report you to CD." When I first met the Dukes, they had a protective services worker from a private agency assigned to them (through a contract with the county).

In the late spring and early summer of 1989, Bill and Winnie were investigated by CD for "dog shit on the floor" and "no food in the refrigerator." During one of my visits around this time, I commented on how clean and tidy the Dukes' home looked. Bill explained, "Children's Division is coming to take pictures." As it turned out, Children's Division did not return until a month later. The day after this visit, Winnie showed me a Polaroid snapshot of her, Bill, Sammy, and Cindy and said:

> Children's Division is closing the case on us. The worker came here and took pictures. She said as far as she's concerned the case is closed, but it has to be approved by Capital City.

Bill and Winnie have come to expect investigations for child abuse or neglect and try to make sure that they are always covered. Shortly after the last investigation, Bill told Winnie to put some money aside to keep in the house: "That way we'll always have money for food so nobody can come in here saying we don't have food in the house." Winnie and Bill were worried about where Cindy would go on one of the occasions when they were being evicted. They were prepared to live out of a car and thought Sammy could move in with one of Winnie's brothers, but they did not know if they could find a place for Cindy to stay. Bill explained what they did:

> I did something smart. I reported us to Children's Division. I called and told them we were being evicted. . . . They said we did the right thing by calling. They said they'd have to do something about Cindy if we don't find a place, but Sammy's OK. See, he turned 18.

Recently, when Cindy was hit and bruised by a kid, Bill and Winnie reported the incident to the police so that no one would think that they abused her.

Many of the Dukes' kin and friends have regular involvements with Children's Division and child protective agencies. The Dukes' friends Lisa and

Gary were visited by a protective worker after their children contracted head lice. Children's Division was involved with the three children of Bill's brother Joey while they were living with his ex-wife and continued its involvement after the children were taken in by Bill's sister Betty. Then the agency started to question how Betty cared for her own two children. Betty bitterly complained, "First they're telling me how to raise my nieces and nephews. Now they're telling me how to raise my own kids." Betty subsequently had a protective service worker from a private child abuse agency assigned to her family. Betty's daughter by a previous marriage, Judy, lost custody of her child because she was living in a dirty and run-down home. Bill's nephew Wes was threatened by CD with having his two children taken away when he faced eviction and had nowhere to live. Children's Division has investigated at least one of Bill's other sisters and two of Winnie's brothers. Winnie reports that her cousin Earl's children were removed from his home for abuse and neglect.

People within the Duke network become involved with Children's Division and other child abuse agencies in one of three ways. First, people within the Duke network report each other to places like Children's Division when they are feuding. Everyone knows things about everyone else, so there is usually something that can be reported about kin and friends. Both the state and the county have child abuse hotlines, and anonymous allegations of abuse and neglect are investigated. Once an investigation is under way, a child abuse agency can usually uncover some shortcoming (poor housekeeping, lack of food reserves, pending eviction) among families in the Duke network.

Second, though it does not happen frequently, people have called child abuse agencies either to ask for help or to report themselves. As noted above, Winnie called an agency to get a parent aide, and Bill said, "I did something smart," when he contacted Children's Division to report that his family was being evicted. When people report themselves, it is usually in anticipation of being reported by someone else.

Third, families are reported for alleged abuse and neglect by schools and other agencies with which they are involved. Reports of child abuse and neglect are kept confidential, so it is sometimes difficult to determine who reported a family. While members of the Duke network report each other to child protective agencies, it is possible that schools and other agencies have reported families in some instances in which people accuse kin and friends of having done so. For example, when one of Bill's sisters was investigated for child abuse, she accused Bill and Winnie of reporting her, but the Dukes maintained that they had nothing to do with it.

One of Cindy's special education teachers almost reported the Dukes for child abuse, although Bill and Winnie were not aware of this. The specifics of the incident help to explain how families like the Dukes are viewed.

Cindy spent a weekend at a friend's house. When she showed up at school the following Monday morning, she was bruised. Her teacher asked Cindy how she got the bruises and became suspicious when Cindy gave her two different stories. Cindy told the teacher that she had fallen at a bowling alley and then had been hit by her friend's boyfriend. Cindy's teacher was ready to report suspected child abuse, but called Mary, Cindy's family support worker, for advice because she knew that Mary had been closely involved with the family. Mary immediately vouched for Bill and Winnie and told the teacher that she had never seen any evidence of abuse. She followed up the conversation with a letter confirming what she said on the phone. Because Mary was so certain about Bill and Winnie, the teacher decided not to report the family. As it turned out, Cindy had in fact tripped at a bowling alley and then was hit by her friend's boyfriend while she was away for the weekend (I had visited the Dukes that weekend and could verify that Cindy was not home).

THE NEXT GENERATION

Child protective agencies will undoubtedly be involved in future generations of the Duke family network. Because of Cindy's obvious intellectual limitations, it is likely that her child rearing will come under scrutiny. In fact, her first pregnancy was defined as "high risk" at the hospital where she eventually delivered. When Cindy became pregnant for the second time, according to Winnie, the hospital threatened to have her sterilized:

> The hospital told her she's going to have her tubes tied after she delivers the baby. They said if she didn't get it done on her own, they'd get a court order to do it.

Cindy and her family have lived off and on with the Dukes. Even when they are not living with Winnie and Bill, they spend a lot of time with them. Winnie instructs Cindy on child care and plays a major role in caring for the baby. The baby probably is given more juice and was started on solid food earlier (Winnie bragged that he was eating solids at three months) than child rearing books advise, but he is thriving and steadily gaining weight.

FAMILY LIFESTYLE AND PARENTING

Certainly, from the vantage point of child rearing experts, Bill and Winnie have had shortcomings as parents. This does not make them abusive or neglectful or necessarily justify intervention in the family's life.

When it comes to child rearing practices and the home atmosphere, the Dukes and many of their kin and friends depart from middle-class standards. Adults use profanity around children. Child rearing is characterized by permissiveness on the one hand and threats or yelling ("I'll smack you if you keep that up") and verbal put-downs ("stupid") on the other. Bill occasionally roughhouses with adults and children alike in ways that would be disapproved of by many people.

The Dukes' housekeeping is poor, and they often face food shortages or even a lack of housing. Each of these factors—poor housekeeping, lack of food reserves, and pending eviction—has been cited by agencies as grounds for intervention in families within the Duke network.

Looking beneath the surface, however, Winnie and Bill have been loving and caring parents. As Bill explained, "Kids need a lot of love." Even if a lack of food or a home justifies intervention by child abuse agencies (as opposed to giving families food or helping them find homes), the Dukes always find a way to eat and a place to live.

Contrary to generalizations about parents with mental retardation (Forder 1990; Whitman and Accardo 1990), the Dukes are adept at community survival skills. Despite their frequent evictions, they have never been forced to live in the streets or even in a shelter. Just as the Dukes take in homeless kin and friends, members of their social network have taken them in when they have been without a home. On one occasion when homelessness loomed as a real possibility for the Dukes, Bill and Winnie made arrangements for their children to live with different family members.

Although the Dukes sometimes lack food reserves and therefore have an empty refrigerator, they never go without food. When money is short, they first turn to family members and friends to repay past debts or to lend them food or money. If this fails, Winnie makes the rounds at community food banks and charitable organizations. When she is turned down, she contacts the family's current or former teachers, workers, or even a participant observer until she finds someone willing to help the family out. Child abuse agencies seem to look for food in the refrigerator, but the important question is whether children go hungry.

The Dukes' housekeeping is poor and is even remarked on by other members of the network. The family does not get around to dusting, washing dishes, sweeping, or scrubbing bathroom fixtures regularly, although Winnie frequently complains about all the time she spends doing housework. When, in the Dukes' previous homes, their female dog had puppies, the house occasionally smelled like animal urine. The state of the home violates aesthetic standards, but this does not make the home unhealthy or dangerous.

For all of their shortcomings in child rearing, Bill and Winnie have always looked out for the welfare of their children and do their best to impart societal values. Winnie makes sure Sammy and Cindy receive adequate medical care and visited Cindy's school program more than many parents. Both Winnie and Bill lecture their children that they should not steal, fight, use drugs, or overindulge in alcohol. Sammy did not drink a full can or bottle of beer until he was 19 years old. Notwithstanding Cindy's pregnancy, Bill and Winnie tried to curtail her sexual activity in their own way.

Profanity is common in the Duke household (although Sammy is scolded when he says *fuck* a lot), but Bill and Winnie do not discuss sex in front of children. Bill uses the term *privates* to refer to genitals when children are around. He was appalled when a friend of the family and his woman friend talked in front of Winnie's brother's two young children about having sex, and he scolded them for talking this way.

Within the Duke network, parents threaten unruly or disobedient children but do not follow through on the threats. Betty has accused Bill of slapping Sammy and Cindy on a handful of occasions. Both Bill and Winnie dispute this, and I have never witnessed anything they could be considered physically abusive. Whether or not Bill and Winnie follow the best child rearing practices, there is not the slightest evidence that they have ever abused or neglected their children.

As parents, Bill and Winnie have also helped their children construct positive identities as typical or "normal" persons. They do not view Sammy and Cindy as mentally retarded, disabled, or handicapped. For every message the children have gotten from schools or human services agencies that they have disabilities or are different from other people, they receive multiple messages that they are just like everyone else.

One day several years ago when I was visiting the Dukes, Bill was prodding Cindy to sweep the floor. Avoiding the job, Cindy would sweep for a minute or two and then sit down. After being scolded repeatedly by Bill, she laughed and said, "I'm a retard." Bill responded, "You're not a retard, you're just wise." Cindy replied, "I'll be a retard if I don't do my homework."

On another occasion, Cindy showed me a book her teacher had given her from the school library. The title was *Your Handicap: Don't Let It Handicap You.* Commenting on the book, Bill told Cindy:

> Cindy, you should read that book. You're going to be a parent some day and you could have a handicapped child. When I was at Empire there was a kid there with his head out to here (motions a very large head). He had tumors and his head just grew. He was a pretty nice kid too. You should know about handicaps so you're prepared if you have a handicapped child.

Throughout Sammy's and Cindy's childhood and young adulthood, Winnie and Bill have communicated normal expectations for them. When Sammy first turned 16, they approved when he bought his first car, even though he did not then and does not now have a driver's license. Bill and Winnie have always communicated to their children that they expected them to get married, raise their own families, and pursue careers. Winnie even talked at one point about Cindy attending college.

Winnie and Bill have given their children something that they would not receive in many families: identities as normal people who are like everyone else. In a society where having a disability, and especially an intellectual disability, is a stigmatizing and potentially discrediting characteristic (Bogdan and Taylor 1994; Edgerton 1967), this is no trivial parental contribution.

CONCLUSION

The Duke family presents complex and challenging lessons for anyone concerned about families of children with disabilities in general, and parents with mental retardation in particular. In this conclusion, I address four questions raised by this study of the Duke family.

First, do families like the Dukes need help in surviving in the community and fulfilling parental roles? The emerging ideology in family support services in the field of developmental disabilities stresses family-centered services in which the family determines the kinds of supports they receive (Center on Human Policy 1987; Taylor, Bogdan, and Racino 1991). By contrast, much of the literature and practice regarding parents with mental retardation seems to be based on the assumption that parents are inadequate and incapable of making choices about what they need (Whitman and Accardo 1990). As a consequence, services for parents with mental retardation are oriented toward training and education in parenting skills (Keltner 1994: Whitman and Accardo 1990; Whitman, Graves, and Accardo 1987).

Winnie and Bill often need help, and as a parent, Cindy will also. When viewed from the Dukes' perspective, however, what they need is assistance in dealing with government bureaucracies, schools, landlords, and sometimes even child protective agencies; emergency cash assistance; help in locating safe and affordable housing; and occasionally transportation. With the exception of the instruction Winnie received in changing Sammy's tracheostomy tube when he was an infant, the Dukes have never experienced any kind of general training or education that they found helpful or that supported their identities as competent parents.

Virtually all parents might benefit from parent education and training. No parent is perfect or knowledgeable about all aspects of child rearing. For people like the Dukes, any education or training that would challenge their definitions of themselves as loving and competent parents or place them in the role of clients with mental retardation would be a disservice to both the parents and the children. Here, the "cure" would be worse than the "disease."

A practical implication of this study is that parents with mental retardation should be approached with the same assumptions underlying family-centered support programs: Offer assistance, but help them in ways in which they want to be helped and on their own terms.

Second, when is intervention in the family life of parents with mental retardation justified? Put another way, when should public and private agencies step in to save children from abuse or neglect? The answer seems simple: when there is evidence that children are being abused or neglected.

According to Whitman and Accardo (1990, 203), "Mentally retarded parents in the community contribute more than a simple head count to the statistics for illiteracy, homelessness, child abuse, child neglect, failure to thrive, child sexual abuse, medical neglect, malnutrition, unemployment, and poverty." Statistics such as these can lead to a presumption that children of parents with mental retardation will be at risk of abuse or neglect and can be used to warrant intervention and intrusion in family life. This line of reasoning is not only flawed, but also contrary to democratic ideals. By analogy, crime statistics demonstrating a higher rate of criminal activity among certain socioeconomic or racial groups cannot be used to justify the deprivation of civil liberties among individual members of these groups.

The same standards should be applied to parents with mental retardation that are applied to all parents. Intervention in the life of any family is warranted when there is evidence of physical mistreatment, sexual abuse, hunger, malnutrition, failure to thrive, untreated medical problems, or unsafe living conditions. Yet unwanted intrusion cannot be justified on the basis of statistical risk factors in the absence of evidence of abuse or neglect.

Third, how representative is the Duke family? A related question concerns whether the experience of the Duke family has general implications for parents with mental retardation. Even if one accepts my findings and conclusions about the parental adequacy of Winnie and Bill, the generalizability of my study can be questioned.

Compared to many parents with mental retardation, Bill and Winnie have some obvious advantages. For one, despite their histories as clients of mental retardation and developmental disability agencies, they have managed to escape the social stigma associated with mental retardation and disabilities and have learned to define themselves and their children in nonstigmatizing ways. Further, they are part of a large and ever expanding social network of kin and friends that buffers them from crisis in times of economic hardship and provides support for a positive social status. Finally, they have developed survival skills that enable them to get by living on their own in the community.

Certainly, Winnie and Bill are not typical of parents with mental retardation. Like all families, the Duke family is unique. As a qualitative researcher, I cannot claim that my study is generalizable beyond the specific persons studied. The point, however, is not whether the Duke family is representative of other families, but what this particular family's experience tells us about commonsense assumptions and generalizations about parents with mental retardation. The Duke family's experience proves many commonsense assumptions, generalizations, and stereotypes wrong.

Fourth, how can abusive parents be distinguished from nonabusive ones? Child abuse or neglect is a serious matter; no one can condone the abuse or neglect of children. How are we to differentiate between parents like Winnie and Bill, who are adequate parents despite their shortcomings, and parents who are guilty of abuse and neglect?

On the basis of my intimate knowledge of the Duke family and detailed experience with them over a number of years, I have concluded that their superficial appearance is misleading and that allegations and suspicions of abuse or neglect are unfounded. For example, the Dukes' housekeeping, though substandard, has never placed the children in jeopardy. Similarly, I have evaluated the vague accusations of Bill's sister Betty that Bill hit Cindy in the context of a family feud, and I give them little weight. Cindy's worker Mary, who also knows the family well, has reached similar conclusions. Other agencies and professionals have determined that the Dukes' children were at risk of abuse and neglect and intervened in the family's life based on secondhand information about the family and brief visits to their home.

Anyone who has taken the time to get to know Bill and Winnie well can easily tell the difference between their family life and abusive and neglectful situations. And those who have not taken the time cannot. Perhaps this is the most important lesson to be learned from this study.

NOTE

1. Reprinted, with revisions, from S. J. Taylor, " 'Children's Division is Coming to Take Pictures': Family Life and Parenting in a Family with Disabilities." In *The Variety of Community Experience: Qualitative Studies of Family and Community Life*, ed. S. J. Taylor, R. Bogdan, and Z. M. Lutfiyya. (Baltimore: Paul H. Brookes, 1995), 23–45, with permission of the author and the publisher.

CHAPTER 12

The Social Construction of Humanness: Relationships with People with Severe Retardation

ROBERT BOGDAN AND STEVEN J. TAYLOR

W HILE NO ONE can dispute the fact that people with obvious disabilities often have been cast into deviant roles in society, an exclusive focus of rejection has led many sociologists to ignore or explain away instances in which rejection and exclusion do not occur. Symbolic interactionism and labeling theory, though not by nature deterministic, often have been presented in terms of the inevitability of labeling, stereotyping, stigmatization, rejection, and exclusion of people defined as deviant, including those with recognizable disabilities. According to Goffman (1963, 5), people with demonstrable stigma are seen as "not quite human" and "reduced in our minds from a whole and usual person to a tainted, discounted one." Scott (1969, 24) emphasizes how blindness is "a trait that discredits a man by spoiling both his identity and his respectability." The rejection and exclusion of deviant groups is so taken for granted that instances in which nondeviant persons do not stigmatize and reject deviant ones are often described in terms such as *denial* and *cult of the stigmatized* (Davis 1961b; Goffman 1963).

This chapter[1] is directed toward understanding the perspectives of nondisabled people who do not stigmatize, stereotype, and reject those with obvious disabilities. We look at how nondisabled people who are in caring and accepting relationships with severely disabled people (people with severe and profound mental retardation or multiple disabilities) define the other party. Although the disabled people in these relationships sometimes drool, soil themselves, or do not talk or walk—traits that most would consider highly undesirable—they are accepted by the nondisabled people as valued and loved human beings. They have moral careers that humanize rather than dehumanize (Goffman 1961; Vail 1966).

The position taken in this chapter is that the definition of a person is not determined by either the characteristics of the person or the abstract social or cultural meanings attached to the group of which the person is a part, but rather by the nature of the relationship between the definer and the defined. In taking this position, we call for a less deterministic approach to the study of deviance and suggest that people with what are conventionally thought of as extremely negatively valued characteristics can have moral careers that lead to inclusion. In a more abstract sense, this chapter suggests that the sociology of exclusion is only part of the story and that a sociology of acceptance needs to be added (Bogdan and Taylor 1987; Taylor and Bogdan 1989).

In the next section we describe our research methodology and the data on which our analysis is based. Then we discuss accepting relationships between people with severe disabilities and nondisabled people. We then turn to a discussion of the nondisabled people's definitions of their disabled partners and specifically the perspectives that sustain their belief in the humanness of the disabled people. In the conclusion, we briefly present our views on how the relationships and perspectives described in this study should be interpreted.

THE DATA

The theory presented here is grounded in over 15 years of qualitative research (Taylor and Bogdan 1984) among people defined as mentally retarded as well as staff, family members, and others who work with or relate to people so defined. Our earliest research was conducted at so-called state schools and hospitals or developmental centers for people labeled mentally retarded, in other words, total institutions (Goffman 1961). Ironically, in this research we studied the dehumanizing aspects of institutions and specifically how staff come to define the mentally retarded persons under their care as less than human (Bogdan et al. 1974; Taylor 1977, 1987a, b; Taylor and Bogdan 1980). Similarly, through life histories of ex-residents of institutions, we looked at the life experiences and perspectives of people who had been subjected to the label of mental retardation (Bogdan and Taylor 1982, 1994). This research supported the literature on stigma, stereotyping, and societal rejection of people with obvious differences.

In more recent years we have studied people with disabilities in a broad range of school (Bogdan 1983; Taylor 1982) and community settings (Bogdan and Taylor 1987; Taylor, Biklen, and Knoll 1987). For the past four years, we, as part of a team of researchers, have been conducting site visits to agencies and programs that are supporting people with severe disabilities in the community.

To date, we have visited over 20 places located throughout the country, and we continue to make visits. Each of these places is selected because it has a reputation among leaders in the field of severe disabilities for providing innovative and exemplary services. We have been especially interested in visiting agencies that support children with severe disabilities in natural, foster, and adoptive families, and adults in their own homes or in small community settings. The visits last for two to four days and involve interviews with agency administrators and staff, family members, and, if possible, the people with disabilities themselves; observations of homes and community settings are also involved. Our design calls for us to focus on at least two people with disabilities at each site. However, at most sites we end up studying the situations of six to eight individuals. During the visits, we are usually escorted by a "tour guide," typically an agency administrator or social worker, although this is not always the case. At several sites, we have been provided with the names and addresses of people served by the agency and have visited these people on our own.

Our methodological approach falls within the tradition of qualitative research (Taylor and Bogdan 1984). First of all, our interviews are open-ended and are designed to encourage people to talk about what is important to them. Second, on the basis of visits, we prepare detailed field notes, recording interviews and observations. To date, we have recorded roughly 1000 pages of field notes. Finally, our analysis is inductive. For example, the perspectives and definitions described in this paper emerged as themes in the data.

Over the course of our visits, we have probably learned something about the lives and situations of over 100 people with disabilities, or at least about the perspectives of the many nondisabled people who are involved with them. This paper focuses on the nondisabled people involved with a smaller number of people with disabilities. In the first place, we are concerned here with nondisabled people involved with people who have been labeled by professionals as severely retarded or multiply disabled, and especially people who cannot talk and whose humanness, as described later in this paper (for example, the ability to think), is often considered problematic. In the second place, we report on nondisabled people who have formed humanizing definitions or constructions of these severely disabled people. Not all of the family members, staff members, and others we have met and interviewed hold the perspectives described in this paper. Those involved with people with severe disabilities have a broad range of definitions of those people, from clinical perspectives (Goode 1984) to dehumanizing perspectives (Taylor 1987b; Vail 1966) to the humanizing perspectives described here.

The research methodology on which this chapter is based has several obvious limitations. For one, we spend relatively little time with each of the people included in this study. In contrast to other interviewing studies we have conducted, in which we spent from 25 to 50 hours or more interviewing people, the interviews in this study last from approximately 1 to 3 hours. This does not afford the opportunity to develop any level of rapport with people, to double-check stories, or to probe areas in depth. However, we have spent enough time in institutions, schools, and service settings and in interviewing people with disabilities and their families to know when people are merely reiterating formal policy or the official line.

Further, most of our data are generated from interviews and consist of verbal accounts. While we occasionally observed interactions between disabled and nondisabled people, this chapter is primarily based on what people said to us and not what we observed them do.

Thus this is a study of how nondisabled people present their disabled partners to outsiders. Depending upon one's theoretical perspective, one can view this study in terms of either accounts—how people "do" humanness in interaction with an outsider—or social meanings—how people define others in their lives as revealed by what they say in interviews. On the basis of our own theoretical framework, symbolic interactionism (Blumer 1969; Mead 1934), we are inclined to view this study in the latter way. In other words, how nondisabled people present their disabled partners in interview situations in some way reflects how they view the partners.

ACCEPTING RELATIONSHIPS

The nondisabled people described in this paper have developed accepting relationships with people with severe and multiple disabilities. An accepting relationship is defined here as one of long standing, characterized by closeness and affection, between a person with a deviant attribute—for our purposes, a severe and obvious disability—and another person. In the relationship, the deviant attribute, the disability, does not have a stigmatizing or morally discrediting character. The humanness of the person with a disability is maintained. These relationships are *not* based on a denial of the difference, but rather on the absence of impugning the other person's moral character because of the difference.

It is when these relationships are compared with staff-to-client relationships in formal organizations designed to deal with deviant populations (Higgins 1980; Mercer 1973; Scheff 1966; Schneider and Conrad 1983; Scott 1969) that they become especially interesting sociologically and important in human terms. People with the same characteristics can be defined and interacted with in one way in one situation and in a radically different way in another. As Goode (1983, 1984, 1994) points out, identities are socially produced and depend on the context in which people are viewed. The same group of people who are viewed as "not like you and me"—essentially as nonpersons—by institutional attendants (Taylor 1987b) are viewed as people "like us" by the nondisabled people in this study. Notwithstanding cultural definitions of mental retardation and the treatment of people with mental retardation in institutional settings, nondisabled people can and do form accepting relationships with people with the most severe disabilities and construct positive definitions of their humanness. While we do not claim that accepting relationships of the kind described in this study are common or representative, we do claim that such alliances exist, need to be understood and accounted for, and call into question deterministic notions of labeling, stigma, and rejection.

DEFINING HUMANNESS

Twenty-year-old Jean cannot walk or talk. Her clinical records describe her as having cerebral palsy and being profoundly retarded. Her thin, short (four feet long, forty pounds) body, atrophied legs, and disproportionately large head make her a very unusual sight. Her behavior is equally strange. She drools, rolls her head, and makes seemingly incomprehensible high-pitched sounds. But this is the way an outsider would describe her, the way we described her as sociologists encountering her for the first time.

Some scholars and professionals would argue that Jean and others like her lack the characteristics of a human being (see Frohock 1986 for a discussion). Jean and the other severely and profoundly retarded people in our study have often been the target of the indictment *vegetable*. People like those in our study have been routinely excluded from the mainstream of our society and subjected to the worst kinds of treatment in institutional settings (Blatt 1970, 1973; Blatt and Kaplan 1974; Blatt, Ozolins, and McNally 1979; Taylor 1987b).

To Mike and Penny Brown (these and the other names in this chapter are pseudonyms), Jean's surrogate parents for the past six years, she is their loving and lovable daughter, fully part of the family and fully human. Their sentiments are similar to those expressed by the other nondisabled people in our study when discussing their disabled partners. In the remainder of the chapter, we describe the perspectives of nondisabled people that underlie their relationships with disabled people and sustain their belief in the others' essential humanness. While these nondisabled people seldom use the word *humanness* in describing their partners, we use it because it captures their taken-for-granted view. The nondisabled view the disabled people as full-fledged human beings. This stands in contrast to the dehumanizing perspectives often held by institutional staff and others in which people with severe disabilities are viewed as nonpersons or subhuman (Bogdan et al. 1974; Taylor 1987b). We look at four dimensions: (1) attributing thinking to the other;

(2) seeing individuality in the other; (3) viewing the other as reciprocating; and (4) defining social place for the other. These perspectives enable the nondisabled people to define the disabled people as people "like us" despite their significant behavioral or physical differences.

Our analysis has parallels to and builds on a small number of interactionist and ethnomethodological studies of how people "do" normality or deviance (Goode 1983, 1984, 1986, 1994; Gubrium 1986; Lynch 1983; Pollner and McDonald-Wikler 1985). In contrast to some of these studies, we focus not on interactional practices that produce normality or humanness, but on the perspectives (Becker et al. 1961) associated with defining the other as human. Thus we are interested in the mental constructions made by nondisabled people of the severely disabled person. This is partially a matter of the nature of our data and partially a matter of theoretical framework.

ATTRIBUTING THINKING TO THE OTHER

The ability to think—to reason, understand, and remember—is a characteristic that is commonly thought of as defining humanness. Intelligence is what separates people from animals. Many of the disabled people in the relationships we studied are unable to talk and have been diagnosed as severely or profoundly retarded. A few accomplish minimal communication through communication boards—boards with pictures or symbols on them that the person can point to as a method of communicating. In the conventions of psychological testing, many have extremely low IQs (below 20), so low in some cases that they are considered untestable. Many give few or no obvious signs of experiencing the stimuli presented to them. Most people would say that they lack the ability to think.

At first glance, the assumption that people with severe and profound mental retardation and multiple disabilities cannot think makes sense. Upon closer examination, the question of whether or not these severely disabled people think is much more complex. The nondisabled people in this study believe and cite evidence that their disabled partners can and do think. Some people state emphatically that they know exactly what the disabled person thinks. Others report that although it is impossible to tell for sure what is going on in the other person's mind, they give the person the benefit of the doubt.

What a person thinks is always subjective and never totally accessible to others (Schutz 1967, Chapter 3). We know what other people think or experience through their ability to produce symbols through speech, writing, gestures, or body language that are meaningful to us. The severely disabled people in this study are extremely limited in their ability to move or make sounds and hence to produce symbols. Yet their inability to produce standard symbols does not prevent their nondisabled partners from attributing thinking to them.

According to the nondisabled people, thinking is different from communicating thought. From their perspective, a person can have full thinking capacity, be "intelligent," and reflective, but be locked in a body that is incapable of or severely limited in communication.

These nondisabled people hold the view that their severely disabled partners are more intelligent than they appear. Their physiology keeps them from revealing their intelligence more fully. As Gubrium (1986, 40) writes of people with Alzheimer's disease, "Yet, while the victim's outward gestures and expressions may hardly provide a clue to an underlying humanity, the question remains whether the disease has stolen it all or only the capacity to express it, leaving an unmanifested, hidden mind."

For some people, attributing thinking to a person with severe disabilities is a matter of reading into the gestures or movements he or she can make. In a case study of communication between a deaf and blind child with severe mental retardation and her parents, Goode (1994) describes how the mother, in particular, made use of nonlanguage resources and gestures to figure out what the young girl was thinking. Similarly, Gubrium (1986, 45) reports how family members or caregivers of people diagnosed as having Alzheimer's disease "sharpen their perception so that whatever clues there are to the patient's inner intentions can be captured."

In this study, the nondisabled people emphasize the significance of minor sounds and movements in attributing intelligence and understanding to the disabled people. For example, one three-year-old boy we observed is completely paralyzed. The only movements Mike makes—these are involuntary according to professionals—are slight in-and-out movements with his tongue and a slow back-and-forth rolling of his blind eyes. Mike's foster parents have been told by doctors and social workers that the boy is not able to understand or communicate, that he has no intelligence. But the parents see in his movements signs that refute the diagnosis. They describe how when certain people come into his room slight alterations in the speed of the tongue movements can be observed. They also claim that the boy, on occasion, moves his eyes toward the person in the room who is talking, an indication to them that he can hear and recognize people.

These people not only claim that their disabled partners can think, but that they can understand them and know *what* they are thinking. Since the people with severe disabilities have a limited menu of gestures and sounds, one might think that knowing what is on such people's minds is extremely difficult. For the nondisabled people in this study, this is not the case. While all of the nondisabled people acknowledged sometimes having difficulty in knowing what their partners think, they maintain that they are able to understand the partners. They say that they can read gestures and decipher signs of the inner state of the disabled people that strangers cannot see. For instance, some claim that they can understand their partners by reading their eyes.

For other people, intuition is the source of understanding people with severe disabilities and what they think. As the parent of a profoundly retarded young woman explains when asked how she knows her daughter understands: "It's just something inside me . . . I really believe that deep in my soul." Goode (1994) reports that parents and others in intimate relationships with people with severe disabilities often "just know" what the person is thinking or feeling.

Finally, some nondisabled people understand their severely disabled partners by putting themselves in their partner's position or "taking the role of the other." That is, they imagine what they would feel in the same particular situations. One foster mother says that she makes decisions about how to treat her foster daughter by pretending that she is the daughter and that she is having the daughter's experiences. She reports experiencing, vicariously, the pleasure of being taken care of by looking at what she is doing for her foster child from the child's perspective. While people acknowledge the likelihood that their assessments of the others' inner lives often may be flawed, they believe that the process brings them closer to their partners and leads them to a better understanding of what the partners are experiencing.

The nondisabled people's belief in the capacity of their severely retarded friends and loved ones to think often runs counter to professional and clinical assessments (Goode 1983; Pollner and McDonald-Wikler 1985). In some cases doctors have told the nondisabled people that their partners are brain-dead. The nondisabled people report that they have often been bombarded with specialists' judgments that, in their eyes, underestimate their partners' capabilities. They argue that specialists are not privy to long day-by-day, hour-by-hour observation of the person. Behaviors that the nondisabled people cite as indicating understanding do not occur with such frequency that the professional is likely to see them. Further, unlike the nondisabled partners in the relationships, professionals are not intimately familiar with their clients and therefore are not attuned to the subtleties of their sounds and gestures.

Also bolstering the belief that the professionals are wrong in their assessments of intelligence are numerous examples of past professional judgments that were wrong. Some people have watched their disabled companions live through predictions of early death. Others have cared for their disabled partners at home in spite of advice that such living arrangements would not be possible and that the disabled person would be destined to live his or her life in an institution.

As a foster parent of a person who was profoundly retarded told us: "They [the physicians] said she'd have to be in an institution. I said to myself 'That's all I need to hear. We'll see about that.' I knew I could take care of Amy and I have." In one family in which there are two adolescents who are severely retarded and one who is profoundly retarded, the parents told us that their foster children have been excluded from school because professionals had judged them incapable of attending. Immediately after these children were released from an institution and came to live with the family, they began attending regular school.

Whether or not people with severe disabilities, including those diagnosed as having severe and profound mental retardation, can understand and think as other people, professional assessments stand no greater claim to truth than the assessments of the nondisabled people reported in this study. Critiquing Pollner and McDonald-Wikler's (1985) account of a family's "delusional" beliefs in the competence of a severely retarded child—what they refer to as the "social construction of unreality," Goode (1994) points out that clinical and medical bodies of knowledge cannot be used to provide a standard by which to judge the legitimacy of family belief systems. Clinical perspectives are based on different ways of knowing and seeing than the perspectives of people involved in intimate relationships with people with disabilities. Further, clinical diagnoses are often proven wrong on the basis of their own criteria.

SEEING INDIVIDUALITY IN THE OTHER

Sitting in the living room of a foster home of a severely retarded young woman who had spent the majority of her life in an institution, the father described her as having very pretty hair and a great sense of humor, and as being a very appreciative person. When this young woman arrived home from school, she was dressed in a new, stylish outfit complete with Reebok running shoes. Her father told us how Monica loved to get dressed in new clothes and how the color she had on was her favorite. He told us how her hairstyle had changed from an institutional bowl cut to its present high-fashion form since she had come to live with his family. Monica had a communication board on her lap. She moved her hand, placing it in the vicinity of the picture of a radio. Her father said: "Okay, I have to start dinner and then I'll get the radio. We are having your favorite, chicken." As an aside, he said, "Monica loves to listen to music and she gets very excited when she can smell something that she likes cooking."

We have discussed how the nondisabled people in our study construct humanness by attributing thinking to their severely disabled companions. But being a person involves something more than thinking. A person is like all other people but also unique; at least in this culture, humanness implies individuality. For the people we have been studying, an important aspect of constructing humanness is seeing the others as distinct, unique individuals with particular and specific characteristics that set them apart from others. As illustrated in the story of Monica's foster father, nondisabled people in caring relationships with disabled persons see the disabled partners as having distinct personalities, particular likes and dislikes, normal feelings and motives, a distinct background—in short, a clear identity—and manage the partners' appearances to conform to these views.

Personality

The nondisabled people used a large variety of words to describe the distinctive qualities of their severely disabled partners. The adjectives *silly, fun, shy, live wire, bright, appreciative, nice, likable, calm, active, kind, gentle, wonderful, amusing, pleasant,* and *good company* fall under the broad category of *personality.* Most of the words are resoundingly positive. Occasionally one might hear phrases such as: "He's a handful," or "She gave me a lot of trouble yesterday," indicating a more critical evaluation of the partner. But even here, the tone is accepting and the comments are never indicting.

Many nondisabled people have nicknames for their disabled partners. Often the nicknames are given because they capture something unique about the partner's personality. One man who has developed a close relationship with an elderly disabled man who had spent over 50 years of his life in an institution calls the older man "Mr. Rudy." Mr. Rudy is blind and unable to talk, and only walks by leaning on a wall. The nondisabled man is not able to explain how he came up with the nickname, but he believes that *Mr. Rudy* seems to go with the man's personality. He says that Mr. Rudy has been through a lot in his life, but "He made it and still has it together." For him, the name *Mr. Rudy* for the elderly man conveys a sense of dignity.

None of these people use phrases like *profoundly retarded* or *developmentally disabled* to refer to their friend or loved one. Some feel that clinical designations are too impersonal and do not tell much about the character and personality of the person labeled. A few indicate that they believe that clinical labels define the person in terms of deficits rather than positive characteristics, and they prefer not to see their companions from this vantage point. The label can strip the person of his or her unique personality. By using a rich repertoire of adjectives and defining the partner in specific personal terms, these nondisabled people maintain the humanness of their severely disabled partners.

Likes and Dislikes

Another dimension of individuality involves being discriminating—having tastes and preferences. As illustrated in the remarks Monica's father made in describing her, the nondisabled people in this study know their partners' specific likes and dislikes and discuss them willingly. Although people with severe disabilities may be extremely limited in their activities and hence have few areas in which they can express preferences, the nondisabled people present them as having definite likes and dislikes regarding the things they do experience (Goode 1994). Music, food, colors, and individual people are commonly cited as areas where people with severe disabilities have preferences. Monica loves to listen to music, has a favorite color, and prefers to eat chicken. In one home with three disabled young people, nondisabled family members explain that one person prefers classical music, a second likes rock, and a third does not like music. In another case, a woman who has a caring relationship with a 43-year-old severely retarded woman described the woman as enjoying camping, sailing and canoeing.

By viewing the disabled person as having likes and dislikes, the nondisabled person not only confirms the partner's individuality, but often reinforces the bonds between them as well. Comments such as "She likes to eat everything we do!" and "He loves the banana bread I make," indicate that the disabled and nondisabled people share things in common.

Feelings and Motives
In everyday interaction, we attribute feelings and motives to other people's words and acts. Rather than defining the actions of the disabled people as symptomatic of an underlying pathological state (Taylor 1977), the nondisabled people in our study define them in terms of normal motives and feelings. A foster mother tells the following story about her foster child, Mike:

> Wednesday night he started to cry continuously. I got real upset and called my husband and told him to come right back. As soon as he got here he talked to Mike like he only can: "Hey bubba what's wrong with you." Mike stopped crying and I held him but then he started up again. My husband told me to give him back and he sat in the rocker and talked with Mike and he stopped again. But the minute he got ready to lay him down he started up again . . . so he (Mike) has got to know something. How would he know to cry again, that we were going to lay him down?

As the above quotation illustrates, Mike's foster mother, like the others we have studied, takes outward signs—crying, laughing, sighing—as indicators that the severely disabled person has the same feelings and motives as other people. When crying, laughing, and sighing are seen in conjunction with particular events, the events are said to have provoked them, thus revealing to the interpreters that the person is in touch with his or her surroundings and is expressing human emotion.

Life Histories
One aspect of seeing another person as an individual is constructing a biography of the person that explains who he or she is today. In interviews,

nondisabled people tell stories of the background experiences of the disabled person. The individuality and the humanness of the disabled people are communicated through biographies that are often unique and detailed. Life histories are sometimes told in two parts. The first has to do with the disabled person's experiences prior to the formation of the relationship. Especially when the person has been institutionalized, the nondisabled person describes the suffering and deprivation the partner has experienced. In recounting these experiences, the nondisabled person often puts him- or herself in the disabled person's position and imagines what it would have felt like. In some cases, the people with disabilities are presented as survivors or even heroes for having undergone their experiences. The second part of the life history relates to improvement in the lives of the disabled people, especially when they are living with the nondisabled person telling the story. For example, the nondisabled partners often point to changes in weight, behavior, skills, personality, and appearance.

Managing Appearances

The nondisabled people in this study not only see individuality in the disabled people, but activity create it by managing the appearances of the disabled people to downplay their visible differences and to accentuate their individual identities. They present a normal version of the person's self to outsiders and to themselves. By paying attention to clothing style and color and being attentive to other aspects of the person's appearance (hairstyle, nails, makeup, cleanliness, beards for men), they help construct an identity consistent with their definitions of the person. In the case of Monica, described earlier, for example, her foster parents selected clothes and a hairstyle that made her look attractive. The management of the disabled person's appearance often conforms to gender stereotypes. Many foster parents of young girls dress them in frilly, feminine dresses, complete with bows in their hair. Thus the person not only has an identity as an individual, in an abstract sense, but as a little girl, teenage boy, middle-aged woman, elderly man, and so on.

To an outsider, many of the disabled people in this study have obvious physical abnormalities, including large heads, frail bodies, bent limbs, and curved spines. However, the nondisabled people seldom mention these characteristics except when a particular condition is causing the disabled person difficulties or when recounting the negative reactions to the person's abnormalities by an outsider.

The nondisabled people often express pride in the disabled person's appearance. Regarding disabled partners who have been institutionalized, many people comment on the significant changes in their looks since leaving an institution. The change is from institutional clothing, unstyled haircuts, dirty skin, and sloppiness to a physical self closer to those of other people.

The transformation is symbolic of the disabled person's metamorphosis from dehumanized institutional inmate to family member or friend.

In dramatic contrast to total institutions, which strip people of their identities (Goffman 1961), the nondisabled people in this study see and assist in the accomplishment of individual identities for the people with disabilities with whom they are involved. Personality, likes and dislikes, feelings and motives, a biography, and appearance are all individualized aspects of a person. By highlighting the severely disabled person's personal attributes and contributing to creating them, the nondisabled people in our study maintain the humanness of their partners.

VIEWING THE OTHER AS RECIPROCATING

In order for somebody to be thought of as a full human participant in a relationship, they have to be seen as contributing something to the partnership. Exchange theorists (Blau 1964) have pointed to the tendency for close relationships to be reciprocal, with both parties defining the relationship in terms of receiving as much as they give. According to exchange theorists, people with equal resources (some combination of social worth, talent, material resources, etc.) tend to form enduring relationships. When one person does not have as much to offer, the relationship suffers from disequilibrium and this is experienced as stressful for the parties. Under these conditions the weaker partner is diminished in the other's eyes. Such formulations narrowly define the nature of the commodities exchanged and exclude the type of alliances discussed in this paper.

From the outside it might appear that the relationships in our study are one-sided (the nondisabled person giving all and receiving nothing) and, using the logic of exchange theory, doomed to stress and disintegration. After all, severely disabled people appear to have so few resources, so little of social value, talent, and material resources to exchange. This is not the way the nondisabled people in our study see their relationships or the people with disabilities. They define the person with a disability as reciprocating or giving something back, however abstract the benefit.

Joe Bain, who, along with his wife and two children, shares his home with three severely disabled young adults, tells why he has the disabled people living with them:

> . . . I am not doing what I'm doing for their benefit. They may benefit from it but I like it. It's fun, I see them as just people I enjoy to be with.

While not all of the people in this study are so exuberant, most mention deriving pleasure from their relationships because they like the disabled people and enjoy being with them. For some, the person with a disability is an important source of companionship. One person says that she does not know what she would do if she did not have her disabled loved one to take care of and to keep her company. A number of people mention how disabled people expand their lives by causing them to meet new people and to learn about aspects of their communities they had not been in touch with previously.

Companionship and new social relations are perhaps the most concrete of the benefits people talk about. Some nondisabled people are philosophical about what the person with a disability gives them. A few believe that the relationships with severely disabled partners have made them better people. The mother of a 6-year-old boy who is severely retarded and has hydrocephalus says, "He has taught me to accept people for how they are. No matter how limited you are, that everyone has within them a quality that makes them special." Another parent, this time a father whose son is severely retarded and has spina bifida, states, "He made all of our children and ourselves much more caring, much more at ease with all handicapped people."

As we have discussed in earlier sections, the nondisabled people feel that they know their severely disabled partners intimately. They understand them and know their particular likes and dislikes. Intimately knowing the individual disabled person gives the nondisabled person a feeling of being special. According to one person who has a caring relationship with a child with profound retardation:

> I think we have a very special relationship in that very often we're together alone. I feel like I'm the one person who knows him better than anyone else. I feel like I can tell if he's sick or what he needs better than anybody else.

Another benefit that some nondisabled people report receiving from their relationships is a sense of accomplishment in contributing to the disabled people's well-being and personal growth. As we discussed in the case of personal appearance, the nondisabled people see positive changes occurring in their loved one or friend. Often the progress would be considered minor by outsiders, something they would not notice or understand, but for the nondisabled person in the relationship it is significant. For example, one person who is in a relationship with a nonverbal woman describes how she had told the woman, Susan, to brush her teeth. Commenting on how when Susan came out of the bathroom she was holding a toothbrush and tooth paste with the cap stuck, she explains, "That is asking for help; that is communication. She never would have done that five years ago; she wouldn't have even gone for the toothbrush and toothpaste!" Regarding a severely disabled woman, another woman says, "She laughs, she didn't do that before. People might think it's minor, but with Jane progress is slow."

Defining Social Place for the Other

Discussions of humanness often point to the social nature of humans as being a defining characteristic. People are social beings. Humans belong to groups and are part of social networks, organizations, and institutions. Within these social groups, individuals are given a particular social place. The concept of role is often used to describe a person's social place. But social place is not merely a matter of playing a social role. It is also a matter of being defined as an integral part of the group or social unit. There is a personal dimension to roles. Roles are particularized for each social unit and personalized by each occupant. Through fulfilling particular social roles, social actors are defined as being part of humanity.

The nondisabled people described in this study define their disabled partners as full and important members of their social units and hence create a social place for them. First of all, they incorporate the disabled people in their definitions of their groups or social networks. While some of the relationships discussed in this paper involve two people, one disabled and one not, most involve the place of people with disabilities within families. In families, in particular, the disabled person is likely to be viewed as a central member. Thus the person does not simply play the role of a son or daughter, but is seen as "my son" or "my daughter." A foster parent of several children with severe disabilities, who could not have children of his own, says, "This gives us our family." In a foster family, the mother describes how her natural son sees the foster child: "He's the little brother he never had." In many cases, the family would not seem the same without the disabled person.

Second, the nondisabled people define a part for the disabled people in the rituals and routines of the social unit. In any group, members develop intertwined patterns of living. For instance, in a family, members coordinate getting up, taking showers, getting breakfast, accompanying each other on important occasions, preparing for holidays, going on vacation, having birthday parties, and so on. The inclusion of a severely disabled person in a family's or primary group's routines and rituals, in its private times and public displays, acknowledges to the members that the disabled person is one of them. The person fills a particular social place. As a foster parent of two people with severe disabilities explains:

> We bring them to all family gatherings. My sister said we could hire a babysitter and leave all of the foster children home. We said that where we go, they go. . . . The family accepts them as part of the family.

When, because of hospitalization or for other reasons, people with disabilities are missing from the social unit, other members talk about how they are missed and how things are not the same without them. The disabled people's absence interferes with normal family routines.

Primary groups belong to larger networks of human relations. When severely disabled people are integrated into primary groups and have their humanness declared there, they have a vehicle for inclusion in the social web that defines community membership. The mother of a 6-year-old profoundly retarded girl who spent most of her life in an institution said: "We take her to church, the grocery store, and everywhere we go."

CONCLUSION

The humanizing sentiments underlying the relationships described in this chapter are not unique to bonds between nondisabled and severely disabled people. They are the same sentiments described in the phenomenological literature as sustaining the perception of the social world as intersubjective (Husserl 1962; Psathas 1973; Schutz 1967). As Jehenson (1973, 221) writes, "As an actor on the social scene, I can recognize my fellow-man not as 'something,' but as 'someone,' a 'someone like me.' " So too do the nondisabled people in this study recognize people with severe disabilities as "someone like me"; that is, as having the essential qualities to be defined as a fellow human being. Disability is viewed as secondary to the person's humanness. What makes the perspectives described in this chapter striking is that they are directed toward people who have often been denied their humanity and in some instances defined as nonpersons (Fletcher 1979).

An understanding of how nondisabled people construct the humanness of severely disabled people can inform ethical debates surrounding the treatment of infants, children, and adults with severe disabilities (The Association for Persons with Severe Handicaps 1984). Whether or not people with severe disabilities will be treated as human beings or persons is not a matter of their physical or mental condition. It is a matter of definition. We can show that they are human by proving that we are capable of showing humanity to them.

It is easy to dismiss the perspectives described here. One might argue that the nondisabled people are deceiving or deluding themselves when they attribute human characteristics to people with severe and profound mental retardation and other disabilities. For example, some might consider the belief that people with severe or profound retardation can and do think to be outlandish. Yet it is just as likely that those who dehumanize people with severe disabilities, dispute their human agency, and define them as nonpersons are deceiving themselves. After all, no one can ever prove that anyone else is "someone like me" or that the assumption of common experience is anything but an illusion. What others are depends on our relationships with them and what we choose to make of them.[2]

NOTES

1. Reprinted, with revisions, from R. Bogdan and S. J. Taylor, "Relationships with Severely Disabled People: The Social Construction of Humanness." *Social Problems* 36 (2), 135–148 (1989), with permission of the authors.

2. Whether or not people with severe disabilities "really are" human is not a matter of social definition. This is a moral and philosophical question and not a sociological one.

Closing Remarks

OUR PURPOSE IN this book has been to introduce qualitative research as an approach to phenomenological understanding. Any book can take you only so far; it is up to you to carry on.

Not everyone can excel in the research approach we have described. Early practitioners suggested that the marginal person, the one caught between two cultures, has the greatest potential to become a good qualitative researcher, since he or she possesses the detachment this kind of research requires. In our experience, people with a diverse range of backgrounds and interests have become successful qualitative researchers. Yet all who do well have had an ability to relate to others on their own terms. They have also shared a passion about what they do. It excites them to be out in the world and to develop an understanding of different settings and people. For some, research becomes part of life, part of living.

Research methods can be dull and unexciting, however, if they are learned in a classroom or studied behind a desk. Qualitative research is a craft that can only be learned and appreciated through experience. It requires skills and a devotion that must be developed and nurtured in the real world.

Many, if not most, people who pursue studies in the social sciences and applied fields are not lured to these studies by the kind of work that typically appears in academic journals and publications. Although the culture of the university makes it difficult to admit, many students come with a desire to understand their world and to make it better. These "do-gooders," along with the "journalistic types," are often intimidated by the academic world. This must change if the social sciences are to play important roles in the university and the society.

Throughout this book we have described qualitative methodology as an approach to gaining basic social science knowledge and understanding. This is not the only way in which this methodology can be used.

There is a long tradition of "action research" linked to qualitative studies in the social sciences (Madge 1953; Stringer 1996). Indeed, the Chicago school researchers, led by Robert Park, sought to change conditions in urban slums through their incisive field reports and studies (Hughes 1971). On the basis of our research at state institutions for the so-called mentally retarded, we have prepared in-depth descriptive reports of institutional abuse and neglect for federal courts, the popular media, policy makers, and organizations composed of people with disabilities and their families.

Howard Becker (1966–1967) argues that researchers cannot avoid taking sides in their studies.[1] Research is never values free (Gouldner 1968, 1970; Mills 1959). When we get close to people, especially those society considers deviant, we develop a deep empathy with them. We learn that official views of morality present only one side of the picture. Becker takes the position that we should side with society's "underdogs," those who do not have a forum for their views. By presenting such people's views, we provide a balance to official versions of reality.

Becker's argument falls squarely in line with C. Wright Mills' call to action, expressed earlier in his classic book *The Sociological Imagination* (1959). For Mills (1959), the role of the sociologist, and hence the qualitative researcher, is to help people translate their "personal troubles" into "public issues":

> Whether or not they are aware of them, men in a mass society are gripped by personal troubles which they are not able to turn into social issues . . . It is the political task of the social scientist . . . continually to translate personal troubles into public issues, and public issues into the terms of their human meaning for a variety of individuals. (p. 187)

Writing from the vantage point of current theoretical interests, Richardson (1990b) continues the tradition of advocating the activist stance endorsed by Becker and the Chicago school researchers. According to Richardson (1990b), the researcher is in an ideal position to help people tell their "collective stories":

> People who belong to a particular category can develop a consciousness of kind and can galvanize other category members through the telling of the collective story. People do not even have to know each other for the social identification to take hold. By emotionally binding together people who have had the same experiences, whether in touch with each other or not, the collective story overcomes some of the isolation and alienation of contemporary life. It provides a sociological community, the linking of separate individuals into a shared consciousness. Once linked, the possibility for social action on behalf of the collective is present, and, therewith, the possibility of societal transformation. (p. 26)

For those who feel ill at ease with the strong advocacy stance adopted by Becker, Mills, Richardson, and others, qualitative evaluation research represents an alternative way of using qualitative methods to address practical issues in the day-to-day world (Guba and Lincoln 1989; Patton 1990).[2] In contrast to most forms of evaluation research, qualitative evaluation focuses on *how* things actually work as opposed to *whether* they work (Bogdan and Taylor 1990). In conducting qualitative evaluation, the researcher sets aside official goals and objectives to explore what is really happening in an organization or program.

Qualitative studies have been conducted since the beginning of what we now call the social sciences. Yet up until the past couple of decades, those who have practiced qualitative research have been few. This has changed, and interest in qualitative research continues to grow. We have reached a point where we now have many schools of thought and practice within the qualitative tradition.

We conclude by repeating our call, first issued over 20 years ago, to go to the people—for students of society to immerse themselves in everyday life and to contribute new insights and understandings. So much more remains to be learned, and many are needed to carry out the work.

NOTES

1. A refusal to take sides is often tantamount to upholding the status quo, whatever that happens to be. Those who believe that researchers can avoid values commitments should take a look at the experience of a group of social researchers who got hoodwinked into collecting intelligence information on Latin America for the U.S. military (see Sjoberg 1967). Spradley (1980) also reports one case in which the South African government used ethnographic research to attempt to make apartheid more effective.

2. In evaluation and other funded research, the researcher has to be careful not to allow sponsors or funders to exercise undue influence on how the study is conducted and how the results are analyzed and presented (see Warren 1980).

Appendix

FIELD NOTES

THIS APPENDIX CONTAINS two sets of field notes recorded by Taylor in the studies of institutional attendants and the Duke family discussed in this book. These are intended to serve as examples of how participant observation field notes can be recorded. Of course, each observer will develop his or her own style of recording field notes.

Some words of explanation about these field notes are in order. First, since these field notes were recorded during Taylor's ninth and twelfth observations, respectively, they do not describe settings as thoroughly as do earlier notes. During initial observations, settings are usually described in much greater detail. As studies progress, attention shifts to filling in gaps in descriptions of settings and documenting changes that have occurred.

Second, readers should be able to notice subtle differences in these two sets of notes. The institutional field notes, which were recorded as part of Taylor's dissertation research, are more detailed than the field notes in the study of the Duke family. Experienced researchers can probably be a bit more selective than novices in what they record. If you have analyzed qualitative data in the past, you have a clearer understanding of the kinds of data you will eventually be able to use. It should probably also be acknowledged that students working on their dissertations have fewer excuses to cut corners than tenured professors.

Readers will further note that Taylor starts the second set of field notes with a memo summarizing the session and potential themes emerging from the observation. As we have stressed throughout this book, analysis is an ongoing process in qualitative research. The sooner one begins theorizing, the better. In his preliminary analysis, Taylor has found these summary memos to be extremely useful in making sense of his data. Here too, experienced researchers probably differ from relative novices in that they feel more confident in speculating on what they are learning in the field.

Readers are invited to compare these field notes with the discussions of these studies in the text and the articles in Chapters 9 and 11. Field notes capture the flavor of participant observation research much more clearly than "how to" guidelines or analytic accounts.

FIELD NOTES: STUDY
OF INSTITUTIONAL ATTENDANTS

Steve Taylor
Field Notes #9
Friday, October 20, 1972
6:50 pm til 7:50 pm

I drive onto the grounds of the state school and proceed to the rear of the institution. The grounds are almost empty at this time of the evening, with the exception of a few people I see sitting in front of the buildings on the way in. After I park, I see a double line of people (at least 100) walking in the direction of the school building from the women's side of the institution. Although the people are too far away for me to see them clearly, I can hear women's voices.

I walk to Building 27. The small anteroom is empty and dark. To the left of the door are several rows of benches, arranged in such a way that people could look out the windows of the room.

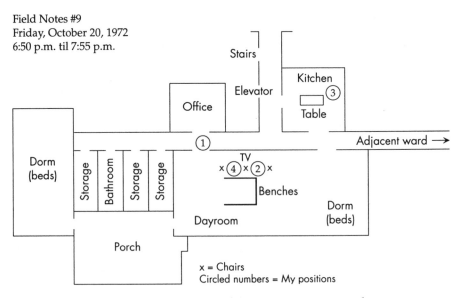

Field Notes #9
Friday, October 20, 1972
6:50 p.m. til 7:55 p.m.

Figure A.1.   A diagram of the state institution ward.

The hallway inside the building is also empty, and relatively dark, a few ceiling lights are on. I walk past the various offices off the hallway: speech and hearing, X-ray, and some others. They are all empty. I proceed to the stairway which is about three quarters of the way down the hall.

As I reach the stairway, I begin to hear some muffled voices coming from the upper floors. The smell that I first noticed when I entered the building becomes slightly stronger as I reach the stairs. (O.C. It is not as strong as it sometimes is. Perhaps this has to do with the cooler weather.) It is a funny smell—perhaps feces and urine, steamed food, and disinfectant.

I walk up the stairs which are encased in a yellow steel mesh grating. The pastel green walls are worn—paint chipped, stained. My footsteps echo as I walk the stairs. Some of the voices become louder now, especially as I go past the doors which lead to the wards on the various floors. Several windows are open on the stairway; some fresh air blows in as I pass them.

I hear a loud scream as I near the fourth floor. It echoes through the stairway.

I get to the fourth, and top, floor. The door is open. A large cartoon wall painting is in the hall as I get to the top floor. It's about five feet long and three high. Blue, orange, and yellow dominate the mural.

I turn right and walk to the central hallway, past the attendants' kitchen and the elevator.

I look down to the left as I reach the hallway. I can see an attendant at the dayroom door of the ward adjacent to Ward 83.

The woman attendant, who is heavy-set, wears a pink nurse's aide type dress and white shoes, has blonde hair and glasses, and is about 50, ignores me as I walk out into the hall. (O.C. The women on this ward neither know me nor want to know me for some reason. They appear content as long as I don't go down to visit their ward. It just occurred to me that many of the women attendants at the institution wear some kind of uniforms—pink, white, or blue—whereas only 2 of the male attendants on "my" ward, out of about the 30 who are assigned to it throughout the day, wear white uniforms. Perhaps this has something to do with how they see their jobs, or maybe it has something to do with sex-role differences. I'll have to try to question some of the attendants about this.)

I can also see a couple of residents in the dayroom of the adjacent ward. Both are boys around 14. One is naked and appears to be just walking around the room. The other is wearing some kind of gray clothes and is sitting in a chair and rocking.

As I turn right down the hall to get to Ward 83, I can hear the loud noise of the TV coming from the dayroom. The hall of 83 is empty now, as well as one of the dorms at the end of the hall. The doors to the dayroom are closed except for one halfway down the hall.

I can see Bill Kelly, a resident in his early twenties, sitting by the dayroom, half in the dayroom and half in the hall. (O.C. According to the attendants,

Kelly serves as the "watchdog." From his position, he can see anyone coming down the hall. He warns the attendants when a supervisor is coming.)

Kelly waves to me as I approach. He is smiling. Kelly is wearing gray pants made from the kind of heavy material standard on this ward, a white T-shirt, and black tennis shoes without socks. His hair appears to have been cut recently. The scars on his head stick out. (O.C. Kelly's hair, like the other residents', is never long. The residents' hair seems to be cut every few weeks. Presumably, this is to prevent parasites which would spread rapidly on this ward.)

As I get to the dayroom door, I see that all the residents are in the room. I can only see two attendants: Vince and another younger man. (O.C. It's interesting how I automatically assume that this other man is an attendant as opposed to a resident. Several hints: long hair, moustache, and glasses; cotton shirt and jeans, brown leather boots. He's also smoking a cigarette, and a resident, Bobby, is buffing his shoes with a rag. Thus this attendant's dress and appearance differ from that of the residents.) Vince, who is 21, is wearing jeans, brown leather boots, and a jersey that has "LOVE" printed on it. He has long hair, sideburns, and a moustache.

I wave to Vince. He halfheartedly waves back. (O.C. I don't think that Vince has quite gotten used to me coming.) The other attendant doesn't pay any attention to me.

Several residents wave or call to me. I wave back.

Kelly is smiling at me. (O.C. He's obviously happy to see me.) I say to Kelly, "Hi, Bill, how are you?" He says, "Hi, Steve. How's school?" "OK." He says, "School's a pain in the ass. I missed you." I say, "I missed you too."

I walk over to Vince and the other attendant. I sit down on a hard plastic rocker between Vince and the other atten., but slightly behind them. The other atten. still doesn't pay attention to me. Vince doesn't introduce me to him.

The smell of feces and urine is quite noticeable to me, but not as pungent as usual.

I am sitting in front of the TV along with the attendants and perhaps five or six residents. The TV is attached to the wall about eight feet off the floor and out of the residents' reach.

Many of the 70 or so residents are sitting on the wooden benches which are in a U-shape in the middle of the dayroom floor. A few are rocking. A couple of others are holding onto each other. In particular, Donner is holding onto the resident the attendants call "Bunny Rabbit." (O.C. Donner is assigned to "Bunny Rabbit"—to keep a hold of him to stop him from smearing feces over himself.)

A lot of residents are sitting on the floor of the room, some of these are leaning against the wall. A few others, maybe 10, just seem to be wandering around the room.

Maybe three or four residents are completely naked. I make a quick count and see that five are wearing any kind of shoes. Most of the residents are wearing their usual clothes: heavy institutional clothes or remnants of regular clothes.

Apparently, Miller and Poller are "on the bucket." Miller is sitting on one of the beds in the dormitory half of the room. His metal bucket is by his feet. Poller is sitting on the floor with his bucket not far from me.

Trach comes over to greet me. He grins, waves, and mumbles something that I can't understand. Trach has a ball of rags which he throws up into the air about five feet and catches. (O.C. There are no other things that the residents can use to throw or play with on this ward. It seems so sad that one must play with rags to have something to do.)

Bobby is still buffing the attendant's shoes. The attendant lights up a cigarette. He says to me and to Vince, "All I need is for the supervisor to come up and catch me smoking in here and letting him shine my shoes. They're not supposed to shine shoes." He says this sort of whimsically. He then goes back to watching TV. The atten. have positioned their chairs so that they can see the whole room but still watch TV.

I ask the atten., "Where are all the other guys tonight? Are a lot of them off?" (O.C. There are usually three or four attendants working on a Friday night, if not more.) Vince answers, "No, they're just out to lunch. They'll be back in a little while." (O.C. It's interesting how men who work the evening shift refer to their evening meal as lunch.)

I ask, "When's Mike coming back?" (O.C. Mike has been working on a ward downstairs for the past month since that ward is short-staffed.) Vince says, "He should be back pretty soon—maybe next week. He was up here for a little while tonight."

Vince says something about the number of residents on this ward. I can't exactly catch what he says. I ask, "Weren't they supposed to transfer some of them?" Vince says, "Yeah, but I don't know how many now. They came up here for some, but Bill wasn't here so they didn't take them."

David, a resident of about 35–40 years of age, comes over. David is shy, but friendly. He is wearing an orange jersey, jeans, no belt, and tennis shoes. His hair is short and prematurely gray. (O.C. The residents who are better dressed and wear shoes are also those who are considered more intelligent by the atten. Of course, they also tend to be the ward workers. I wonder if the clothes they receive stems from the fact that they work or that they care more about clothing than the others.)

I say to David, "Hi, David, how are you?" He says, "Just fine." Vince interrupts, "David's not going to Building 48 after all. They're going to keep him here to take care of Igor." (O.C. "Igor" is the attendants' nickname for a tall resident with hard features. They have nicknames for many of the residents. Many of these I consider dehumanizing. Somehow the atten. do not see the residents as true human beings. I noticed here how Vince talked about David in front of him but not to him. This is common. The atten. act as though the residents do not matter at times. Vince's comment reveals something very interesting—placement policies are based not on the welfare of the resident, but on his usefulness on the ward. Atten. hate to lose good workers. David takes care of another resident on a 24-hour basis.)

Bobby finishes shining the attendant's shoes. The atten. says to Bobby, "I don't have any pennies now, Bobby. I'll pay you later."

Bill, the atten. in charge, enters the room with a cup of coffee. Jim and Nick, two other atten., follow him. They all wave to me. I wave back.

Bill comes right over to me and says, "Hi, Steve. Want some coffee? Go get yourself some if you want some." I say, "Not right now, thanks, Bill. Maybe later."

Bill and the other atten. are all wearing dark pants, cotton shirts—various colors, and black tie shoes. All have relatively short haircuts and are older than the two atten. in this room. Bill's about 50 and the other two are about 30. Bill is wearing a "key caddy" from his belt. He also has a name plate on his shirt with his name on it. He is the only one on the ward to have a name plate. (O.C. It seems strange for Bill to have this name plate. The ward gets almost no visitors, and he knows all of the atten. and residents on the ward. A sign of status? It's also interesting that the older atten. seem to stick together.)

As Nick and Jim walk toward me, I see Nick try to whisper something to Jim. Jim doesn't seem to hear him, for he doesn't look at him or acknowledge him. (O.C. I wouldn't be surprised if Nick said something about me being here, like "Oh, no, he's here again.") Nick comes over to me and gives me a friendly, "Hi, Steve."

Nick and Jim leave the room again.

I notice a resident behind me and to my right who has his pants pulled down and is masturbating. He doesn't seem to be paying attention to anyone else in the room.

Miller gets up and goes over to a puddle of urine to my left. He kneels down, wipes the floor with a wet rag, wrings out the rag, and then throws it back into the bucket. He goes by me as he walks back to his chair. The smell is overpowering. Feces are floating in the water. (O.C. Miller, unlike other residents, automatically cleans up feces or urine on the floor. Many of the others wait for feces or urine to be pointed out to them.)

Miller frequently cleans up feces and urine throughout the time I am on the ward.

Bill, who has been standing near me, pulls a chair over and sits down beside Vince. (O.C. There are five plastic chairs in the room. These are used by the atten. The residents seldom try to sit in any of them. When they do, they are castigated by the atten.)

A resident named Jim is sitting on the floor in front of all of us. Jim is in his late teens and is wearing gray pants and shoes, but nothing else. The new atten. says, "Hello Jim, hello, Jim. O.K. O.K." He says it in a mocking tone. Jim repeats him, "Hello, Gem. O.K. O.K." The atten. says, "O.K., Gem, O.K. O.K." Jim repeats him again. The atten. then says, "Fuck you, Gem, Fuck you." Jim waves his arms around, swatting the air. The atten. all laugh. Bill, laughing, looks over at me, as though to share the laughter. I smile. (O.C. Situations like this are always difficult. I feel guilty smiling, but somehow feel that I don't want to seem like I'm putting the atten. down.)

The new atten. turns around to Bobby. He says, "Fuck you, Bobby," and sticks his middle finger up vigorously. Bobby returns the gesture, laughing. (O.C. Bobby cannot hear, according to the atten., but is quite intelligent.)

This same atten. begins to sing. (O.C. He seems to be joking around.) "It's beginning to look a lot like Christmas. Bill says, "You're a little early, aren't you?" He says, "Nah, it'll be Christmas any time now."

Vito, about 21, comes running over to me. He has cerebral palsy and is crippled on the left side of his body. Vito says to me, "Hi, Steve." I say, "Hi, Vito, how are you?" he smiles.

Vito walks over behind Bill and starts to rub his back. Bill screams at him, "Get the hell outta here, Vito. I don't want my back rubbed."

Bill points to the new atten. and says, "Go rub his back, Vito." The atten. says, "He won't rub my back 'cause of what I did to him that one night. Remember?" (O.C. The atten. says it in such a way that I don't think I should pursue the matter—too sensitive at this time. I don't want to seem like a snooper.)

The atten. then says to Vito, "What's the matter Vito? Don't you want to rub my back? Don't you like me?" (O.C. He says this mockingly.) Vito is behind me so I can't see his face, but the atten. says, "Why not, Vito? Come on, rub my back." Vito goes over to him and begins to rub his back.

Vince asks me, "Has Vito ever rubbed your back." Then he says to Vito, "Come rub Steve's back." I say, "Yeah, he's rubbed my back." Vince says to Vito, "That's O.K., Vito. Never mind," and then to me, "Oh, then you know what he's like. He really rubs hard."

One of the residents wanders over to the dayroom door. Bill yells at him, "Bates, get away from that door."

The new atten. points to Trach's ball of rags and says, "Give that to me." Trach gives it to him. He throws the rags at the resident by the door and hits him in the back. The resident runs away from the door.

Miller is behind me and is wiping up a puddle of urine. A resident near us pulls his pants to his knees and crouches on the floor. Vince yells to Miller, "Miller, get up. Hurry! Take him to the bathroom. Hurry up before he goes on the floor!" Miller grabs the resident's hand and leads him out of the room.

Vito is still rubbing the new attendant's back. This atten. asks Vince, "Should I pay him for the backrub?" Vince says, "I usually give him a nickel if he does a good job. He doesn't deserve it if he rubs too hard."

Bill says something about the trouble he's having trying to keep residents from "pissing and shitting on the floor." He then says something to the effect, "These patients here are low grades."

Bill continues, "I'd love to be able to train them. I really would. But you can't do it. Not here you can't." Bill points to a resident who is a couple of feet away from us and says, "This isn't bad. You can teach him something." He points to Vito and says, "This one isn't bad either. You can teach them something. I mean, you can teach them so much. There's a limit. They have a borderline. You can do so much with 'em, but that's all. They have a borderline and you can't go beyond on them. They can talk so you can tell 'em what to do. If they can talk you can do somethin' with'em. They can comprehend."

Bill continues, "See, if they can talk, you can do something with 'em. You can tell them to do something, and they'll do it. Most of these here you can't talk to. They only listen to two things." Bill pauses, makes a fist, and says, "This," he makes a slapping motion and says, "Or this."

Bill stands up and asks me, "You want some coffee, Steve? Come on." Bill starts for the door. I stand up and follow him. We walk out of the room and down the hall to the kitchen.

Both of us take a cup and get coffee from a percolator in the room. Bill walks over to a refrigerator in the room and takes out a large carton of milk. He pours some into his coffee and then hands it to me. We sit down at a table in the kitchen. There are five loaves of bread and a box of green bananas on a table by the refrigerator.

Bill lights a cigarette, sits back, and says, "The supervisor just told us that we have to start taking the low grades to a special dance just for low grades. So this Tuesday we have to take them. What we have to do is dress them all up in their own clothes and then one employee has to take them over to the dance and stay with them the whole night. How are we going to do that? We don't have enough employees. We'll get them all dressed up and start taking them over and then one will shit his pants and we'll have to bring them all back."

I ask Bill, "Well, why are they having this special dance?" He says, "I'll tell ya why. It's because they get federal grants for having so many patients in the program. That's why they have so many programs around here. (O.C. From Bill's perspective there are too many programs. Yet very few residents actually receive programming.) See, they get state grants, county grants, and federal grants. They may have the program anyway, but the government gives them more money if they have more patients in it. They had record hops before. They had one employee to run the hi-fi. What they did was add more patients to get the federal grant. Where's the money going? There's still that one employee running the hi-fi. What they did was add more patients to get the federal grant. The money ain't goin' to the patients and it ain't goin' to the employees so where's it goin'? Well, I know where it's goin' and I think you know too—it's goin' to graft. The people runnin' this place are gettin' rich on graft. The people above them know it, but they don't care."

Bill goes on, "I'll tell ya, I know there's graft around here. Every year around January they start cuttin' down on food. See, the year starts in April so January's the end of the year for money. So they start scrimpin'."

I say, "Well, it's not even January and you don't have enough stuff here." Bill says, "That's right. They don't give us enough disinfectant. That's why I have to buy it myself—with my own money. Hell, in 29—the medical building—they have all they need. That's 'cause they get all the visitors there. Nobody comes here, but these are the buildings that need it the most."

I ask Bill, "Where were you before you came up here?" He says, "I was downstairs before. I was second in charge. The charge down there didn't care about nothin'. He never cleaned the place. He said if the place was dirty he wouldn't get any visitors and I guess he was right. I was second charge and every time the charge was off I cleaned the whole place. Then the supervisor told me he wanted me to be charge up here."

Bill goes on, "You see, they knew I was clean. They knew I'd keep this place clean. That's why they wanted me up here. This place was the dirtiest place in the world. The charge up here didn't care. He just put his watchdogs at the door and played cards. I got this place clean too. I just can't stand filth. So now that I'm up here they won't give me the things I need to keep this place clean."

I say, "You must get discouraged." Bill says, "Sure I get discouraged. They won't give us any disinfectant or anything. The state don't care what we take home to our kids. Well, I care. I'm not takin' home hepatitis or somethin' to my kids. I'm gonna keep this place clean. I just can't stand filth."

Bill stands up quickly and says, "If I don't take a leak now, I'm gonna piss my pants. I'll be back in a second. Go ahead, have another cup of coffee." Bill hurries out of the room.

(O.C. Bill has given me important insights into how he defines his supervisors and his job. I'll have to follow up on this graft and this cleanliness thing.)

I pour myself another cup of coffee and sit alone for a couple of minutes.

Bill returns and immediately begins to speak, "Everybody is here for one reason and one reason only—money. That's right. They're all here for money. That's why they took this job. That's why I took this job. I'm 50 years old now and when I came here I was 40. Who's gonna hire you at 40? Nobody wants a guy who's 40 years old."

I ask Bill, "Do you have a problem keeping good men? I mean, is there a lot of turnover?" He answers, "No, I have good employees now. They'll do what I say. They're clean like I am."

Bill continues, "My wife's a supervisor, but she lets people take advantage of her." I ask, "Where does she work—over on the other side?" He answers, "Yeah, over in 18." I ask, "Isn't 18 the children's building?" He says, "Yeah, my wife has them until 12 to 16—whenever they mensurate [*sic*]. When they mensurate [*sic*] they put them in another ward. There are only three employees on my wife's ward, and on weekends they only have two. My wife's supervisor was makin' them work eight and a half hours without lunch on weekends. Can you believe that?" (O.C. I am amazed at how many atten. have relatives working at the institution. The institution almost makes this a company town.)

Jim comes into the room with a box and different slips of paper. These are for a lottery on the World Series. Bill fills out a slip and gives Jim one dollar. Jim leaves after some small talk about baseball.

Bill stands up, goes over to the sink, and washes out his coffee cup. I do the same. We walk back to the dayroom. We had spent about 25 minutes in the kitchen.

Jim and Nick are in the dayroom now and are sitting in front of the TV. Vince and the other atten. are in the dayroom too. Bill walks around the room. I sit down beside Vince.

A resident walks up behind me and stands there. Vince looks at him and screams, "Harris, get out of there. Leave him alone." Vince says to me, "Don't ever let them behind you. You don't know what they might do. They could choke you. One time, Bobby got a kid in a choke hold and wouldn't let go. Nobody could get him off either." (O.C. I've never seen a resident attack or strike an atten. Neither have I ever seen Bobby hurt anyone.)

Bill leaves the room.

Nick and Jim talk about snowmobiles and watch TV.

Vince asks me, "Have you ever seen Frankie tie shoes?" I answer, "No," and he says, "You should see him. He really does it different." Vince looks around the room and calls, "Hey Frankie, come here." Frankie ignores Vince. Instead, he kicks a resident who is sitting on the floor. The resident doesn't do anything. Vince calls to Frankie again. Frankie comes over this time. Frankie is a heavy-set man in his early twenties. He is not wearing shoes but has on institutional clothing.

Vince says to Frankie, "Tie Steve's shoes, Frankie." Frankie unties my shoes and then methodically ties them again without even looking at them.

Vince says to Frankie, "Tie my shoes, Frankie." Vince is wearing boots which do not have shoelaces. Frankie doesn't respond to Vince.

The new atten. says, "Hey Frankie," makes a fist, and points to a young black resident who is sitting against the wall and near the TV. Frankie walks over to the resident and punches him in the head. The resident cringes and runs away toward the dormitory part of the room. Frankie wanders away also. The atten. don't pay attention to what Frankie did. (O.C. There are three black residents on the ward. The atten. all seem to be racist by their behavior toward these residents and by how they refer to them.)

Vince points a puddle of urine out to Miller. Miller goes over to it and wipes it up.

I ask Vince, "What did Miller do to get on the bucket?" He answers, "He didn't do anything. He doesn't mind being on the bucket. He knows that if he's on the bucket he'll get extra food. We give extra food to whoever is on the bucket. Miller knows that so he doesn't mind. Some of the other ones aren't that smart, but Miller is."

Vince starts to talk to the new atten. about baseball.

I decide to leave. I say to Vince, "Well, I think I'd better get home now. I'll be seeing you." He says, "O.K., I'll see you later." I wave goodbye to the other atten. and to some of the residents. I leave the room. I walk past the office in the hall.

Bill is sitting at the desk in the office. He is filling out some kind of chart. I say, "I'm leaving now, Bill." He says, "O.K., Steve, take it easy. Stop up any time." I leave the ward and the building.

As I walk to my car, a man comes up to me. (O.C. I assume that he is a resident by his clothes—old and baggy, his hair, and the way he speaks.) He says, "I don't have a day off until Sunday. I work all the time." He walks with me. He points to a tree and says, "My brother cut a branch off that tree. He works here. I have another brother who works here too. One at home too."

We get to the parking lot. He asks, "Which one is your car?" I point to it and say, "That one." He says, "I see it. You need someone to wash it? I'll wash it for you some time. It'll only cost you a quarter. I do a good job." I say, "O.K., I'll be seeing you." He walks away. I walk to my car. The man comes back over to me, and says, "I work over in Building 22. Come get me if you want your car washed—inside and out." I say, "O.K.," and leave the institution. (O.C. It was important to this man for me to believe that he was an employee and not a resident here. This probably has something to do with the stigma of being "retarded.")

FIELD NOTES: STUDY OF THE "DUKE" FAMILY

CONFIDENTIAL

FIELD NOTES #12

"YOU'RE NOT A RETARD, YOU'RE JUST WISE"

Steve Taylor
Observation: Winnie and Bill's Home
Time: 3:15–5:40 p.m.
Date: Thursday, May 18, 1989
Notes Recorded: May 19

Memo:

I had planned to interview Winnie today about her family. The last time I was here she showed me a picture with her brothers and sisters. I had told her that the next time I visited I wanted to have a pen and paper so I could write down everyone's names; otherwise I would forget them. I brought a couple pads of paper and plenty of pens today in anticipation of the interview. I left them in the car and planned to go out and get them. I had decided that I first wanted to see what was happening before I walked into the home with paper and pens.

As it turned out I didn't interview Winnie. First, she wasn't there until about 4:30. Second, she said that she didn't know where the picture was. I could have interviewed her anyway, but actually I'm glad I didn't.

While I was there I felt a little frustrated because things hadn't gone as planned and also because I ended up spending a lot of time watching TV, especially cartoons. I often feel that the visit is not that productive while I am there. It is only after I get home that I appreciate the significance of the observation. This happened with this visit.

I am still doing p.o.—participant observation—here and am glad that I am. I have to force myself to be patient and not rush into more formal interviewing, although I still want to do this. It is important to go with the flow, try to blend into the woodwork, and get a sense of what things are like naturally in the home. In terms of gathering basic information—for example, specifics on Winnie's brothers and sisters, p.o. is very "inefficient." It takes a long time to get just a little bit of information and it is impossible to remember all of the specific things that are said to me (although, I generally remember the kinds of things I forget or didn't understand at the time). But through p.o. I learn things that would be impossible to get in any other way: how people naturally act in the home and how they see themselves and each other.

The title of these notes—"You're not a retard, you're just wise"—is an example of the kind of thing that I would only get hanging out at the home. This is what Bill said to Cindy after she said in a joking kind of way, "I'm a retard." And then she said, "I'll be a retard if I don't do my homework." I need to ponder this interaction and interpret it in light of other data. But I think I stumbled upon something centrally important today about the meaning of labels and stigma. Here's how I'm making sense of it now: in terms of this social network, stigma is what you feel when you come into contact with the outside world, but it is not necessarily something you carry around inside of you. Cindy is labelled "retarded" and has been called a "retard." Yet within the family and network, this is not how she views herself or is viewed by others. The fact that she could joke about this and then Bill could turn it around and "normalize" her behavior by saying in effect that she was acting like a "wise ass" (the clear meaning of his comment, said the way any parent would scold an adolescent) indicates to me that she doesn't feel stigma within the home and family.

Many other interesting things happened during this observation. First, I had to laugh to myself when Winnie confused Sweden with Lake City. This seems to suggest that a foreign country is outside of the realm of her experience. Second, I also get a chuckle out of all the talk about spring cleaning. The place is as dirty as ever, although it's possible that the upstairs has been cleaned. Third, Tom is still living there and Bill and Winnie seem to feel comfortable with him, especially since he contributes money and food stamps to the household. Fourth, since we spent so much time watching TV, I had the opportunity to concentrate on what the living room looks like and also to play back in my mind things that I saw or heard. I would estimate that at least half of the time I was there, nothing was happening except passive TV watching. This is why I was able to stay almost two and one-half hours and not feel totally overwhelmed. Finally, Bill has another old car. As I read through my notes, it will be interesting to see how many cars and trucks he has over a period of a year or so.

It's a good use of my time to jot down these hunches as I go, but I'd better get on with the notes.

New Car

I drive To Winnie's and Bill's, pull up across the street, park, get out of my car and cross the busy street. I notice two cars in the driveway. One is the blue station wagon Bill has had for a while; the other is a blue Pontiac LeMans that is new here. The front door is open. I walk up the two steps and come into the living room.

I see Donnie, the nephew, on the sofa on the left; Bill on the sofa on the right; and Cindy and Sammy. The stereo is playing. I say, "Hi, how you doing? (To Bill) I thought you'd be fishing today." Bill says, "No, I've been too busy today to go fishing." I go over towards the bench. Bill says, "Cindy said that was you, but I said, 'Naw,' but she was right."

Bill gets up and says, "I got a new car. Come on." We go outside to the Pontiac. The front of the car is resting on a stack of old tires.

Bill says, "I just bought it from a guy for two and a quarter. He was ready to start taking out the windshield and junk it and I told him to sell it to me." I say, "It looks like it's in great shape." He says, "Yeah, the body's in great shape."

Bill goes to the driver's side, leans in the window, puts the key in the ignition, turns it, and the car starts right up. I say, "Boy that sounds good." Bill says, "Yeah," and then turns it off.

He says, "I've got to fix the brakes on it before I drive it. I'll drive my other one until I get this one fixed" He also mentioned something about work that needs to be done on the other car. I ask, "What year is this?" Bill says, "78. (Looking at sticker) No, let me see, 79."

Bill gets a tire iron from the back of the car and says, "I'll show what's wrong with the brakes." The tire iron is one of those that's crossed, with four wrenches. I say, "That's a nice tire iron. That makes it a lot easier." Bill says, "I paid a lot for it when I bought it, but it's worth it."

Bill takes the tire off and points to the brakes and shows how they are worn. "I won't drive it until I fix the brakes. I'm not going to take a chance on getting into an accident with my family. I could feel it pulling when I drove it home." He puts the tire back on.

I notice that one of the tires the car is sitting on is a small emergency spare. I say, "What's that, one of those emergency spares?" Bill says, "Yeah, I got it from a car I had. I don't need any more tires. I got enough of them around here." (O.C. In addition to the four tires the car is sitting on, I notice another couple on the side of the yard.)

Then Bill says something about the engine, pops the hood, and shows it to me.

He closes the hood and then points to the front of the car. He says, "That's all plastic. If you run into anything that wouldn't hold up."

I ask, "You know a lot about cars. Where did you learn it all?" Bill answers, "From my father, my brother. Just working on them." I say, "I don't know anything about cars. I never learned when I was young and it seems like the kind of thing that's hard to learn once you get older." Bill says, "You could learn. You're not too old." I laugh and say, "Well, I'm not over the hill anyway."

Bill says, "As soon as I get this car running, I'm taking it to Capital City."

I say to Bill, "Where's Tom today? He's been here the last couple times I was here." Bill says, "He's working today. Welfare makes him work 12 days a month. He gets paid $34. His mother just had a had a stroke and fell and hit the side of her head. She's in the hospital." I say, "That's too bad."

I say, "Tom seems like a nice guy." Bill says, "Yeah he is. I don't mind helping him out letting him stay here. We can use the help too. He gives us food stamps. He just gave Winnie $50 and then he gave her another $25. He helps me work on the cars too." I say, "You don't mind helping people out if they appreciate it." Bill says, "Yeah."

Bill says, "I'll let you know when me and Tommy are going to pull an engine if you want to see that." I say, "Sure. I'd like to see that."

I say, "By the way, do you ever seen Lisa and Gary anymore?"

Bill answers, "I guess they had a falling out with Betty and Charles. They don't want to see nothing of them. They stopped by here for about 5 minutes last night, but we don't want to have anything to do with them."

Cindy leans out of the front door and says to me, "What's your name again?" I say, "Steve." She says, "Steve, do you want to buy a burger buck. It's only a dollar. Mary bought one." I say, "Well, then, get Mary to buy another from you." Bill laughs at this.

Bill and I wander back to the front door.

Bill says, "The landlord is putting a whole new electrical system in and he's digging that up too (points to a septic tank vent in the front yard). He was over here this morning. He's getting a back hoe in here to dig that up. The drain is backing up on us. Winnie went over there this morning and told him unless he fixed this place up she was going to report him to the Board of Health. He said he's been out of town and didn't know anything about it. He said, 'No problem. I'll fix the place up.' I'm glad. I like this place. I didn't want to have to move. I want to fix up this yard."

Bill continues, "A guy's going to help me finish off the sheetrock in the living room, sand it down, and paint it. We'll have this place all fixed up."

I say, "So you have a septic system here, huh? That's unusual for the city." Bill says, "Yeah, it's clogged up (says something about how they're going to dig it up). He told me not to lift any engines from that tree until he gets it fixed." I say, "Yeah, it could probably cave in, right?" He says, "Yeah, right over there, it's probably rotted away."

Looking around the front yard, I notice by the house behind some old shrubs, a shoe, an ashtray stand, a jockey-type lantern holder.

Many cigarette butts and scraps of paper are scattered in front of the house. Bike parts are in the front yard.

I say, "Is Cindy home early from school today?" Bill says, "No, she skipped school today. Winnie got her up this morning at 7:00 and then we went back to bed. Cindy was still here at 8:15 and said she missed her bus. I said, 'I don't know how you could miss your bus. You were up at 7:00.' "

Bill says, "I got 3,000 worms now I'm selling."

I ask something about fishing and then say, "I guess it's too hot to go fishing on a day like this." (O.C. It is a beautiful warm day.) Bill says, "No, you can still catch some fish. The guy I go with is getting old and his arm was hurting so we didn't go."

Bill continues, "I've been too busy to go fishing anyway. I want to work on this car and I've been helping Winnie out with the spring cleaning. I've been trying to get Cindy off her ass to help but she's too lazy."

Cindy comes out by the door eating a sandwich that looks like it has ham in it. She tears off a piece and hands it to Bill who gives it to one of the dogs.

Bill points to the dryer I brought last week. "I haven't touched that yet. I've been too busy."

Bill calls in the house, "Cindy, I want you to sweep that floor. I already told your mother you did it, so you'd better do it before she gets home." Cindy doesn't do anything.

About a minute later, Bill says, "Cindy, sweep that floor!"

Sammy comes out with part of a bike frame and a can of spray paint. Bill says, "Don't spray that around the car. Do that down in the basement." Sammy leaves and comes back a minute later. "The can broke." The bike part is painted a bright red. Donnie is there and says, "That's the same color as a fire engine."

Bill calls in the house, "Cindy, I told you to sweep that floor. Right now."

While we are standing outside, the stereo is turned up, playing country music.

I hear Cindy yell from inside the house, "Dad, tell Donnie he'd better stop it or else!" Bill says, "Cut it out, Donnie."

Cindy comes to the front door. She is holding a very large glass filled with a blue liquid. Bill says, "What's that?" Cindy says, "Blueberry Kool-Aid." Bill says, "Let me try some." He takes a sip and says something to the effect that it tastes terrible. He offers me some. "Want to try it?" I say, "No thanks."

Babe the dog is by the door. I say, "It looks like Babe's expecting any time." Bill says, "Yeah, I was going to give her a bath yesterday, but I decided not to because she's pregnant."

Bill says to me, "Want to come in?" I say, "Sure." We go back into the house.

Cindy and the Floor

As we enter, Bill says to Cindy, "Clean off those sofas so he can sit down." Bill goes over to a sofa—the one on the right, picks up a pile of clothes and moves it to the other sofa. Cindy picks up some notebooks and other books and places them on the coffee table by the sofa where I am. He also clears off a seat on the far sofa where he ends up sitting. I say to Cindy, "Is that your homework, huh?" She says, "Yeah."

Bill turns on the TV.

Bill says, "Cindy, I told you I want this floor swept. I told your mother you already did it so you'd better get it done." Bill takes a broom. "Here sweep it like this."

Cindy takes the broom and sweeps a little bit.

Bill says, "Oh, I've got something to show you." He leaves the room. Cindy sits down in the chair and sweeps the floor from there. She says, laughing, "I'll sweep the floor sitting down." I say, "Sure, and we'll pick the chair up and carry you around so you can sweep the whole floor."

Bill comes back in holding a cb radio. He hands it to me, "I just bought this. I got this, an antenna and a mount for $137. I'll tell you, if you ever want a cb, go to Radio Shack."

I look at it. I say, "This really looks like a good cb. Have you tried it out yet?" He says, "Yea, I like to listen to the truckers and people talking. I really like on the thruway. (To Sammy) How many times have we used it. Two right?" We talk a bit about cb's. I notice different buttons on it. I ask, "Now what are these for?" Bill says, "You can program it to get certain stations. I have to take it in and have them do it. I don't know how to program it."

Bill says, "One of Winnie's brothers offered me $25 for it. It cost $137 and he offered me $25. Can you believe that?"

I hold the cb looking at it and admiring it for about 5 minutes. Then I hand it over towards Bill. Cindy is between us.

Bill says, "Cindy, take it from him. Be careful with it. Don't drop it. It's not even a month old." She takes it and hands it to Bill.

Bill says, "Sammy, take this and put it on top of the refrigerator." He gives it to Sammy and Sammy leaves.

Bill says, "Cindy, sweep this floor. Come on. Your mother's going to kick your ass when she gets home."

Cindy doesn't do anything.

Between the time I arrive and 4:30, Bill tells Cindy to sweep the floor at least 15 times. Several times she makes a half-hearted effort. (O.C. It's interesting how Bill and Winnie will threaten the kids, but never do anything when the kids don't pay attention.)

We sit and watch TV. First, Alvin and the Chipmunks cartoon is on. Then "Duck Tales," another cartoon. Then "Batman." Then "Leave it to Beaver."

While we are watching there is relatively little conversation. During commercials I ask Bill questions. Otherwise I just sit back and observe. (O.C. I'm struck by what a nice day it is outside, but we're here inside. Also, while Bill talks about how busy he's been he's not doing anything.)

Since we are hanging out, I get the chance to observe the room.

The room is still very dirty. The floor has a lot of dog hair, scraps of paper, and other stuff. Each of the sofas are covered at least partially with a bedspread. Piles of clothes, newspapers, a phone book, and other things are on the sofas. All three of the tables in the room are covered with things. There is more than I can begin to note. For example, on the table across from me I notice three coffee cups, an empty cigarette pack, an empty milk carton, and other stuff. The guinea pig (O.C. I called it a hamster last week) is in a small aquarium on top of the stereo. It is larger than last week and really looks squeezed in. The picture of Betty's family that I noticed before is now hung in the doorway leading to the next room. The two table lamps look in pretty good shape and are matching. There's a plate with food, mostly bread, on the bench. A new knick knack book case, full of knick knacks, is in the room. New curtains, white with flowers, are on the window. Familiar pictures and knick knacks are on the wall. Two large, 2–3' high, statues are by the stereo speakers. One is of St. Francis and one is the Virgin Mary. A large ceramic cat is on one of the stereo speakers. (O.C. I can't believe how this room changes all of the time. I really have to pay attention to note the changes in the room. The curtains looked different, and when I got home I compared them to pictures I have, which confirmed that they were "new.")

Bill is wearing light colored blue jeans, which are dirty, a flannel shirt with a jersey underneath, a belt, and black work boots. His hair and beard are growing back.

Sammy is wearing jeans, tennis shoes with white socks, and a jersey. When he is standing he sometimes pulls his jersey up exposing his stomach. He has long blond hair. A hair brush is stuck into his back pocket.

Donnie is wearing jeans and a rock star jersey. He is heavy, and has short light hair and freckles. His stomach is often hanging out beneath his jersey.

Cindy is barefoot and has extremely dirty feet, with dirt caked around her toenails. She is wearing a t-shirt and blue jeans.

(O.C. I feel embarrassed to even say this, but her jersey and jeans accentuate her body. In the short time I've known her, she seems to be maturing. There is a coy, self-conscious sexuality about her, that Mary has also noticed. The image she projects is that of a Lil' Abner type hillbilly's daughter. If I were not studying the family, I would probably unconsciously notice that she was growing up, just as Sammy is beginning to get a little facial hair. As an observer, however, I'm trying to get a sense of how people view each other and notice Cindy's conspicuous sexual maturity, even though I feel that I shouldn't notice it or record it. With some of the scruffy looking men I've met around here, I feel a bit concerned about her and how she seems flirtatious around men. I'm partially reassured because both Bill and Winnie care about their children, and Bill has mentioned in the past that he doesn't trust certain of Winnie's brothers around Cindy.)

Bill and I smoke cigarettes. While "Alvin" is on, the TV shows a banner with writing on. I remember the words "senior" and then "Alvin." Cindy tries to read it, but doesn't get it all. Bill says, "No that says, ——, Alvin," but he leaves out the "senior."

A commercial comes on and then an ad for the upcoming Batman program. Bill says, "That Batman's an asshole. I don't like that. I like that program on at 5:30. What is that?" A pause and then Sammy says, "Webster." Bill says, "Yeah, Webster, I like that program. I like —— and —— too (other sitcoms, perhaps "Happy Days")."

I ask Bill, "So you think you'll be going to Capital City soon?" He says, "Yeah, I have to go there to pick up my birth certificate. I have a check waiting for me but I can't get it without my birth certificate." I say, "You have to go all the way there? You'd think they could mail it." He says, "No, I have to go pick it up." TV watching.

Bill gets up and goes over by the door. Donnie says or does something to Cindy. Cindy says, "Stop it, Donnie!" Bill gives Donnie a soft cuff on the back of the head, "Cut it out, Donnie." Bill sitting again.

Bill says something to me about the movies that have been on Channel 68 this week. He says, "I've seen them all, the Fly, the Thing. Cat People's on tonight." TV watching.

Cindy says to Sammy, "I know who stole your bike, Robert and Paul." Sammy says, "That's not true, Robert's my friend, Paul's that asshole's friend." There's other talk about bikes. (O.C. Sammy is still hard for me to understand, especially from across the room.)

Donnie has a pocket knife and is playing with it. Bill says, "Donnie, put that knife away. You can't play with it here. Your mother will be getting home from work in a half hour. You can leave in a little while."

TV watching.

Babe the dog is there. Bill says, "Hi, Ma, how you doin'? Your momma will be home in a little while."

Bill says to Donnie, "OK, you can go home now." Donnie says, "Bye, Uncle Bill," and leaves. He does not say good-bye to anyone else. Bill goes outside with him. I see Donnie ride his bike down the street.

TV watching. Commercial. I ask Bill, "Donnie's your nephew, right?" He says, "Yea." I say, "Your sister's kid right?" He says, "Yeah, my sister Iris."

I ask, "That's the sister who's moving to Capital City, right?" Bill says, "No, Iris and Don are staying here. They got it worked out with their landlord. They owe him $289 and they can't pay it, but they worked it out. They're going to pay him $100 one week, $100 the next week, and then $89. He said, 'Fine, you can stay then.' "

I say, "Now where did you tell me you were born?" Bill says, "———." I say, "That must be a small town. I've never even heard of it." Bill says, "Yeah, it is. It's right outside of ah, ah, Berlin."

Bill says to Cindy, again (O.C. This has been constant), "Cindy, I want you to sweep that floor now. Come on." She takes the broom and goes over by the door and starts sweeping. She sweeps a dust cloud of dirt, dog hair, and debris towards me (O.C. Gasp. It really is filthy). Bill says, "Cindy, sweep it all this way (pointing to the next room)." Before long she is sitting on the floor.

TV watching—"Duck Tales." Everyone seems to pay attention to this, laughing at the cartoon.

Bill says, "Cindy, I told you. I want this floor cleaned."

Cindy gets up and takes the broom and starts sweeping. She says, "I'm a retard." (O.C. She says this in a joking way, acting silly just as when she was sweeping sitting down earlier.) Bill says, "You're not a retard, you're just wise." (O.C. This is said as "wise ass," or "smart alec.") Cindy says, "I'll be a retard if I don't do my homework." She sweeps another minute and then stops.

TV watching—"Batman."

WINNIE'S HOME

I look out the door and see Winnie coming down the street, walking on this side of the road on the road itself. (O.C. I want to try to capture what one sees here.) Winnie is wearing purple pants and a yellow t-shirt. She is pushing a black baby carriage.

She is very pigeon toed and walks a bit bent over with her hips sticking out. Her walk looks labored as she places one leg in front of the other. (O.C. She looks very conspicuous and would strike one as being disabled in some way.)

I watch as Winnie comes in the door. It is a bit after 4:30. Winnie comes in, looking very tired, and says, "Hi, Steve." I say, "Hi, Winnie, how are you." She says, "Tired!" She comes over to the sofa to the left and plops down.

Winnie starts talking to Bill. Because she is across the room and apparently tired, I can't understand her as well as usual, but she seems to be talking about Betty and Charles and Gary and Lisa. She tells Bill something about a broken engine block on Betty's and Charles's car. She also says something about Lisa and Gary and money. She also says, "Kathy was wearing shorts and showing off her sexy legs." (O.C. The nature of her conversation is that of reporting on what's going on at Betty's.)

She looks over to the stereo speakers, "What's that?" Bill gets up, "That's blueberry Kool-Aid. Try some." He takes it and gives her some and she makes a face. He then gives some to Sammy. Then he says, "Cindy, go get some more." She leaves the room and comes back with more.

Sammy takes it and goes outside. Cindy does too. They're yelling at each other, playing. I can't see them from where I am sitting. Cindy comes running into the house. Bill says, "I think she got him." Sammy comes in, a bit wet. Bill says, "She did." There's some chasing around between Cindy and Sammy.

Winnie says to me, "Steve, would you like two kids?"

Cindy runs outside. Winnie yells, "Cindy get in here." Bill laughs pointing out the door. Cindy comes back in and the back of her pants are dirty.

Cindy runs out again. She comes back a minute or two later and goes over to Winnie. She holds up the bottom of her foot to show a cut. Winnie says, "Go clean it off." Cindy goes into the next room and comes back with a wet towel. She sits in the chair and wraps the towel around one of her filthy feet.

More TV watching.

A commercial comes on. Sammy, who is sitting on the sofa by Winnie, looks at me and says, "What did you say?" I had said nothing. I say, "I didn't say anything." Bill laughs and says, "He didn't say anything! Now he's hearing things."

Winnie asks me, "Have you been watching the monster movies on Channel 68 this week?" I say, "Yeah, I saw the Fly." Bill says, "I'm going to videotape Cat People tonight. Tomorrow night is Bigfoot and I'm going to videotape that too. Firestarter's coming up too."

Winnie says to me, "Did you get your wife something for mother's day?" I say, "Mother's day? I didn't buy her anything. She's not my mother." (Joking tone.) Winnie says, "She's a woman. Mother's day is for women." I say, "No, it's not. It's just for mothers. What about father's day? I think she should buy me something for father's day."

Somebody says something about the dogs. Winnie says to Bill, "Rainbow jumped up on Steve's leg last week and got his pants dirty. I bet he had to change them as soon as he got home." I say, "It didn't bother me."

TV watching as "Leave it to Beaver" comes on.

Winnie says, "Are you all packed and ready for your trip to Lake City (pause), I mean, Sweden?" (O.C. Incredible.) I say, "No not yet, I haven't even started packing." She said, "Oh, you'll wait til the last minute?" I say, "Yea."

Winnie says to Bill, "He's going to Sweden. That's half way around the world."

She says, "How are you getting there? Flying?" I say, "Yeah." She says, "That's not for me. I wouldn't fly over there. Not after Flight 103. I'd go to Florida or somewhere."

Winnie says, "When you go away, have somebody drive your car and stop by your house. Find somebody you trust. You'll have to have somebody take care of your dogs anyway. Make sure it looks like somebody's living there. You better call the Post Office too. You should tell the police you're going away so they can keep an eye on your place."

"Leave it to Beaver" is about Beaver doing well on a test, being shunned by friends, and his parents looking at a special school for him. Sammy, Cindy, and Bill have an exchange about this, with Sammy saying, "What did Beaver do?" and Bill saying, "He was smart," and Cindy saying, "He got a 100 on a test."

Sammy has his bike part. The wheels from the bike are on the sofa. Bill says to Winnie, "He ran out of money so he didn't finish painting it." Winnie says to Sammy, "What happened to your change from the cans and bottles?" Sammy says, "I spent it all."

Winnie a little later says, "I had some money yesterday, but I spent it all."

Winnie says, "The party's all set for June 10. We're celebrating Babe's puppies and a surprise. I can't tell you what it is because it's a surprise."

Winnie says to me, "Steve, do you want a burger buck?" I say, "No thanks, Winnie, Cindy already asked me. I think she should try to sell more to Mary."

Winnie asks me, "Steve, do you like wrastlin'?" I say, "Sure, but I haven't gone in a long time." Winnie says, "There's a big match at the War Memorial on June 26." Bill says, "I'm going to that one no matter what. I'll walk there if I have to."

Somebody says, "Dean's here." Bill gets up and goes outside. He comes back a couple minutes later. Winnie asks, "Are you going fishing?" Bill says, "No, not today, maybe tomorrow. Dean says he's going out to get drunk. He's already half pie-eyed. He stopped at a bar for one beer and had a lot more. I'm not riding with him." Bill leaves the room and comes right back, "I'm not riding with anybody's who's drunk." Winnie says, "I don't blame you." Bill goes out the door again.

I ask Winnie, "So how's R.B. doing, Winnie?" She says, "Alright."

I ask, "So you went to Betty's to do your laundry?" She says, "Yeah, our plumbing's not working so we can't use the washer and dryer. The water from the washing machine goes right out in the back yard. We could have it go right outside, but it's hooked to the sink." (O.C. I don't quite get this, but this is what she says.)

Winnie says, "I still have three more loads to do." I say, "When you have a family you end up with a lot of laundry." She says, "You do when you have one kid who takes off her dirty clothes and throws them in with clean clothes and another one who's almost an adult who takes his dirty clothes and throws them into a corner in his room."

Sammy has two wrenches and is using them to take brackets off of the bike part he painted. He is muttering and seems upset, saying, "Fuckin' . . . fuck . . . fuck. I'm throwing this out." He gets up, walks to the door, and throws the bike part out toward the street.

He comes back and says, "I'm going to steal a bike. I know where one is. I'm going to steal it." (O.C. He says this like a frustrated child.)

Cindy says something to the effect that Sammy can have her bike and she'll borrow it when she needs it.

Sammy says, "I'm stealing that bike." Winnie says, "Go ahead and you'll end up in jail." (Not being able to resist) I say, "Yeah, we'll all visit you in jail, Sammy." Sammy looks at me and says, in a semi-sarcastic, but not mean or defiant tone, "Thanks." I say, "Tom seems like a nice guy." Winnie says, "Yeah, he is. He helps Bill out with his cars. His mother's in the hospital. She had a stroke and fell and hit the side of her face. She was alone in her apartment and nobody could get an answer on the phone. So they got a key from her landlord and found her and took her to the hospital."

I ask, "How do you know Tom anyway?" Winnie says, "I've known him for a long time. Let's see, about 18 years."

I say, "You sure do have a lot of family and friends, Winnie." She says, "Yeah, I have a lot of friends. I'm still friends with my best friend when I was growing up. I see her all the time. We've been friends since I was one month old. I know her husband, her three children, and her brothers and sisters."

Quiet for a while. I say to Winnie, "You look tired today, Winnie." She says, "I'm always tired."

I look out and see Tom walking down the street toward the house. He first goes over to where Dean is parked and then comes in the house. I say, "Hi, Tom," and he says, "Hi."

He goes through the room and into the next and I hear the bathroom door close. He comes out a minute later.

He sits down in the living room where Bill had been sitting.

Winnie says, "So how was your day?" He says, "I spent it at the hospital with my mother. My brother showed up too. My sister from Northville is coming down. You've met her haven't you?" Winnie says, "Yeah."

Tom says, "I told them at work that my mother had a stroke and they told me to go ahead and go to the hospital. I had to have them sign for me at the museum, and then take that to the County Center and have them sign it and then go back to the museum at the end of the day to have it signed."

Bill is outside the house now. Dean apparently has gone. Tom goes outside.

I partially see a man from one of the next door houses outside. He is older and is wearing suspenders. Then he leaves. I stand up and say, "Well, Winnie, I'd better be going now. I might be by next week, but I might not. I might be too busy packing. If I don't see you next week, I'll see you on June 10. Now what time is that?" Winnie says, "7:00." I say, "OK." Winnie gets up and walks with me to the door. She says, "Have a nice vacation, Steve." I say, "Thanks." She says, "Now remember. Don't take cash, take American Express, ah, ah." I say, "Traveler's checks?" She says, "Yeah, traveler's checks." I say, "Good idea."

As we get to the door, I say, "Maybe I'll see what these guys are doing before I go." I step outside. Bill and Tom are on the other side of the car, sitting on the ground.

I notice the red compact new looking car parked in the driveway next door. I see the older guy in suspenders and an older woman two houses down. Another car pulls up next door and Whitney, the girl next door, gets out. I hear her yell, "Grandpa" to the older guy next door. Looking at the house next door, I notice that there is no trash or garbage around. The side door of the house faces Winnie's and Bill's side door. Looking to the back yards, I notice that the grass is cut next door, but not Winnie's and Bill's. (O.C. Bill says that the neighbors are his friends and Whitney is described as Cindy's best friend, but these people seem like they're from a different world than Winnie and Bill.)

I stand by Bill and Tom. They are talking about the brake: ". . . shoe . . . caliper . . . Now how does that come off." Bill yells into the house, "Winnie, get me my Allen wrenches."

Tom is wearing jeans, work boots, a jersey, and a clean, white corduroy short-sleeved shirt. He has a hat on that has a picture of men fishing and the words, "Quick . . . Throw It Back." (O.C. I believe I've seen Bill wearing this hat in the past.) I get to study his tattoos. He has many on both arms and hands: a large, multi-colored bird on his right forearm; a "D" and an "N" on two fingers; a "MOM"; a cross; what looks like lettering that has been gone over (O.C. A girlfriend's name?); and others.

Tom says to Bill, "My mother can't move anything on her left side." Bill doesn't respond and talks about the brakes. (O.C. So much for social-emotional support in the network.)

I say to Tom, "Yeah, I hear your mother's in the hospital." He says, "Yeah, she should be released Monday. They're still doing tests though. They injected blue dye into her and they're running some other tests."

About two minutes after Bill called to her, Winnie comes back with a small one. Bill and Tom say, "That's too small." Bill tries it, but it is too small. Bill says, "Send Cindy up to Betty's and Charles' to borrow one from them. She'd better hurry. They'll be going junking at 6:00." Winnie yells, "Cindy, Cindy." Cindy does not appear. Either Winnie volunteers to go up or Bill asks her to. I say, "Well, I'd better be going now. I'll see you. Good luck, guys."

I cross the street and get in my car. Tom has gone over and sat on the front steps. I get back out of my car and walk over to Tom.

I yell, "Hey Tom, ask Winnie if she wants a ride over?" He yells back, "Just a second," and turns to the house. Just then Cindy comes out, gets on her bike, and starts riding. Winnie appears and yells, "Cindy's going." I wave, get back in my car, and drive away.

Bibliography

Abel, E. K., and M. K. Nelson, eds. *Circles of Care: Work and Identity in Women's Lives.* Albany, NY: State University of New York Press, 1990.

Adams, R. N., and J. J. Preiss, eds. *Human Organization Research.* Homewood, IL: Dorsey Press, 1960.

Adler, A. R. *Using the Freedom of Information Act: A Step by Step Guide.* Washington, DC: American Civil Liberties Union, 1990.

Adler, P. A., and P. Adler. *Membership Roles in Field Research.* Newbury Park, CA: Sage Publications, 1987.

Adler, P. A., P. Adler, and J. M. Johnson. "Street Corner Society Revisited: New Questions about Old Issues." *Journal of Contemporary Ethnography* 21 (1): 3–10, 1992.

Agar, M. "Text and Fieldwork: Exploring the Excluded Middle." *Journal of Contemporary Ethnography* 19 (1): 73–88, 1990.

Agar, M. H. *The Professional Stranger: An Information Introduction to Ethnography.* New York: Academic Press, 1980.

———. "Whatever Happened to Cognitive Anthropology: A Partial Review." *Human Organization* 41 (1982): 82–86.

———. "Ethnography and Cognition." In *Contemporary Field Research,* edited by R. M. Emerson, 68–77. Boston: Little, Brown, 1983.

Alasuutari, P. *Researching Culture: Qualitative Method and Cultural Studies.* Thousand Oaks, CA: Sage Publications, 1995.

Allport, G. *The Use of Personal Documents in Psychological Science.* New York: Social Science Research Council, 1942.

Allport, G., J. S. Bruner, and E. M. Jandorf. "Personality Under Social Catastrophe: An Analysis of 90 German Refugee Life Histories." *Character and Personality* 5 (10): 1–22, 1941.

Altheide, D. L. "Leaving the Newsroom." In *Fieldwork Experience: Qualitative Approaches to Social Research,* edited by W. B. Shaffir, R. A. Stebbins, and A. Turowetz, 301–310. New York: St Martin's Press, 1980.

Amado, A. N., F. Conklin, and J. Wells. *Friends: A Manual for Connecting Persons with Disabilities and Community Members.* St. Paul, MN: Human Service Research and Development Center, 1990.

American Sociological Association. *Code of Ethics.* Washington, DC: American Sociological Association, 1989.

Anderson, B. G. *First Fieldwork: The Misadventures of an Anthropologist.* Prospect Heights, IL: Waveland Press, 1990.

Anderson, D., K. C. Lakin, R. H. Bruininks, and B. K. Hill. *A National Study of Residential and Support Services for Elderly Persons with Mental Retardation* (Report No. 22). Minneapolis: University of Minnesota, Department of Educational Psychology, 1987.

Anderson, E. *Streetwise: Race, Class, and Change in an Urban Community.* Chicago: University of Chicago Press, 1990.

Anderson, N. *The Hobo.* Chicago: University of Chicago Press, 1923.

Angell, R. *The Family Encounters the Depression.* New York: Charles Scribner's Sons, 1936.

———. "A Critical Review of the Development of the Personal Document Method in Sociology 1920–1940." In *The Use of Personal Documents in History, Anthropology, and Sociology,* edited by L. Gottschalk, D. Kluckhohn, and R. Angell. New York: Social Science Research Council, 1945.

Angell, R. D., and R. Friedman. "The Use of the Documents, Records, Census Materials, and Indices." In *Research Methods in the Behavioral Sciences,* edited by L. Festinger and D. Katz, 300–326. New York: Henry Holt, 1953.

Angell, R. D., and R. H. Turner. "Comment and Reply on Discussions of the Analytic Induction Method." *American Sociological Review* 19 (1954): 476–478.

Appell, G. *Ethical Dilemmas in Anthropological Inquiry: A Case Book.* Waltham, MA: Crossroads, 1978.

Arbus, D. *Diane Arbus.* New York: Aperture Monographs, 1972.

Archer, D. "Unspoken Diversity: Cultural Differences in Gestures." *Qualitative Sociology* 20 (1): 79–105, 1997.

Arensberg, C. M. "The Community-Study Method." *American Journal of Sociology* 60 (1954): 109–124.

Argyris, C. "Diagnosing Defenses Against the Outsider." *Journal of Social Issues* 8 (3): 24–34, (1952).

Arrington, R. "Time Sampling in Studies of Social Behavior." *Psychological Bulletin* 40 (1943): 81–124.

Asad, R., ed. *Anthropology and the Colonial Encounter.* London: Ithaca Press, 1973.

Asher, R. M., and G. A. Fine. "Fragile Ties: Shaping Research Relationships with Women Married to Alcoholics." In *Experiencing Fieldwork: An Inside View of Qualitative Research,* edited by W. B. Shaffir and R. A. Stebbins, 196–205. Newbury Park, CA: Sage Publications, 1991.

Association for Persons with Severe Handicaps. *Legal, Economic, Psychological, and Moral Considerations on the Practice of Withholding Medical Treatment from Infants with Congenital Defects.* Seattle, WA: Association for Persons with Severe Handicaps, 1984.

Atkinson, P. *Understanding Ethnographic Texts.* Newbury Park, CA: Sage Publications, 1992.

Babchuck, N. "The Role of the Researcher as Participant Observer and Participant-as-Observer in the Field Situation." *Human Organization* 21 (3): 225–228, 1962.

Back, K. W. "The Well-Informed Informant." *Human Organization* 14 (4): 30–33, 1956.

Bader, C. "Standardized Field Practice." *International Journal of Opinion and Attitude Research* 2 (1948): 243–244.

Bain, R. "The Impersonal Confession and Social Research." *Journal of Applied Sociology* 9 (1925): 356–361.

Bain, R. K. "The Researcher's Role: A Case Study." *Human Organization* 9 (1): 23–28, 1950.

Baldamus, W. "The Role of Discoveries in Social Science." In *The Rules of the Game: Cross-Disciplinary Essays on Models in Scholarly Thought,* edited by T. Shanin, 276–302. London: Tavistock, 1972.

Ball, D. "An Abortion Clinic Ethnography." *Social Problems* 5 (14): 293–301, 1966–1967.

Ball, M. S., and G. W. H. Smith. *Analyzing Visual Data.* Newbury Park, CA: Sage Publications, 1992.

Banaka, W. H. *Training in Depth Interviewing.* New York: Harper & Row, 1971.

Barber, B. "Research on Human Subjects: Problems of Access to a Powerful Professional." *Social Problems* 21 (summer 1973): 103–112.

Barnes, J. A. "Some Ethical Problems in Modern Field Work." *British Journal of Sociology* 14 (June 1963): 118–134.

Bartlett, F. C. "Psychological Methods and Anthropological Problems." *Africa* 10 (1937): 401–420.

Barton, A. H., and P. F. Lazarsfeld. "Some Functions of Qualitative Analysis in Social Research." *Frankfurter Beitrage zur Soziologie* 1 (1955): 321–361.

Bateson, G. "Experiments in Thinking About Observed Ethnological Materials." *Philosophy of Science* 8 (1941): 53–68.

Beals, R. L. "Native Terms and Anthropological Methods." *American Anthropologist* 59 (1957): 716–717.

———. *Politics of Social Research.* Chicago: Aldine, 1968.

Becker, H. S. "The Career of the Chicago Public School Teacher." *American Journal of Sociology* 57 (March 1952): 470–477.

———. "The Teacher in the Authority System of the Public School." *Journal of Educational Sociology* 27 (November 1953): 128–141.

———. "A Note on Interviewing Tactics." *Human Organization* 12 (4): 31–32, 1954.

———. "Interviewing Medical Students." *American Journal of Sociology* 62 (1956): 199–201.

———. "Problems of Inference and Proof in Participant Observation." *American Sociological Review* 23 (1958): 652–660.

———. "Notes on the Concept of Commitment." *American Journal of Sociology* 66 (July 1960): 32–40.

———. *Outsiders: Studies in the Sociology of Deviance.* New York: Free Press, 1963.

———. "Problems in the Publication of Field Studies." In *Reflections on Community Studies,* edited by A. J. Vidich, J. Bensman, and M. R. Stein, 267–284. New York: John Wiley & Sons, 1964.

———. Introduction to *The Jack-Roller,* by C. Shaw. Chicago: University of Chicago Press, 1966.

———. "Whose Side Are We On?" *Social Problems* 14 (Winter 1966–1967): 239–247.

———. *Sociological Work: Method and Substance.* Chicago: Aldine, 1970.

———. *Writing for Social Scientists: How to Start and Finish Your Thesis, Book, or Article.* Chicago: University of Chicago Press, 1986.

———. *The Other Side.* New York: Free Press, 1967.

Becker, H. S., and J. W. Carper. "The Development of Identification with an Occupation." *American Journal of Sociology* 61 (January 1956a): 289–298.

———. "The Elements of Identification with an Occupation." *American Sociological Review* 21 (June 1956b): 341–438.

Becker, H. S., and E. Friedson. "Against the Code of Ethics." *American Sociological Review* 29 (1964): 409–410.

Becker, H. S., and B. Geer. "Participant Observation and Interviewing: A Comparison." *Human Organization* 16 (3): 28–32, 1957.

———. "The Fate of Idealism in Medical School." *American Sociological Review* 23 (February 1958a): 50–56.

———. " 'Participant Observation and Interviewing': A Rejoinder." *Human Organization* 17 (2): 39–40, 1958b.

———. "Latent Culture: A Note on the Theory of Latest Social Roles." *Administrative Science Quarterly* 5 (September 1960a): 304–313.

———. "Participant Observation: The Analysis of Qualitative Field Data." In *Human Organization Research,* edited by R. N. Adams and J. J. Preiss, 267–289. Homewood, IL: Dorsey Press, 1960b.

Becker, H. S., B. Geer, and E. Hughes. *Making the Grade: The Academic Side of College Life.* New York: John Wiley & Sons, 1968.

Becker, H. S., B. Geer, E. C. Hughes, and A. L. Strauss. *Boys in White: Student Culture in Medical School.* Chicago: University of Chicago Press, 1961.

Becker, H. S., and I. L. Horowitz. "Radical Politics and Sociological Research: Observations on Methodology and Ideology." *American Journal of Sociology* 78 (July 1972): 48–66.

Becker, H. S., and A. L. Strauss. "Careers, Personality and Adult Socialization." *American Journal of Sociology* 62 (November 1956): 253–263.

Becker, H. S., et al., eds. *Institutions and the Person: Essays Presented to Everett C. Hughes.* Chicago: Aldine, 1968.

Becker, M., et al. "Predicting Mother's Compliance with Medical Regimens." *Journal of Pediatrics* 81 (1972): 843–854.

Beecher, H. K. *Research and the Individual: Human Studies.* Boston: Little, Brown, 1970.

Beezer, R. H. *Research on Methods of Interviewing Foreign Informants* (George Washington University Human Resources Research Office Technical Report No. 30.) Washington, DC: George Washington University Human Resources, 1956.

Begley, S., and A. Rogers. " 'Morphogenic Field Day': A PC Academic Journal Falls for a Physicist's Parody of Trendy-Left Social Theory." *Newsweek,* 3 June 1996, 37.

Bendix, R. "Concepts and Generalizations in Comparative Sociological Studies." *American Sociological Review* 28 (1963): 532–539.

Bennett, C. C. "What Price Privacy?" *American Psychologist* 22 (1967): 371–376.

Bennett, J. W. "The Study of Cultures: A Survey of Technique and Methodology in Field Work." *American Sociological Review* 13 (1948): 672–698.

Benney, M., and E. C. Hughes. "Of Sociology and the Interview." In *Sociological Methods: A Sourcebook,* edited by N. K. Denzin, 175–181. Chicago: Aldine, 1970.

Bensman, J., and A. Vidich. "Social Theory in Field Research." *American Journal of Sociology* 65 (1960): 577–584.

Bercovici, S. "Qualitative Methods and Cultural Perspectives in the Study of Deinstitutionalization." In *Deinstitutionalization and Community Adjustment of Mentally Retarded People,* edited by R. H. Bruininks, C. E. Meyers, B. B. Sigford, and K. C. Lakin. Washington, DC: American Association on Mental Deficiency, 1981.

Bercovici, S. M. *Barriers to Normalization*. Baltimore: University Park Press, 1983.

Berger, P. "On Existential Phenomonology and Sociology (II)." *American Sociological Review* 31 (April 1966): 259–260.

Berger, P. L., and T. Luckmann. *The Social Construction of Reality*. Garden City, NY: Doubleday, 1967.

Berk, R. A., and R. A. Adams. "Establishing Rapport with Deviant Groups." *Social Problems* 18 (Summer 1970): 102–117.

Bernard, J. "Observation and Generalization in Cultural Anthropology." *American Journal of Sociology* 50 (1945): 284–291.

Bernard, H. R., and J. S. Pedraza. *Native Ethnography: A Mexican Indian Describes his Culture*. Newbury Park, CA: Sage Publications, 1989.

Berreman, G. D. "Ethnography: Method and Product." In *Introduction to Cultural Anthropology: Essays in the Scope and Methods of the Science of Man*, edited by J. A. Clifton, 337–373. Boston: Houghton Mifflin, 1968.

Bevis, J. C. "Interviewing with Tape Recorders." *Public Opinion Quarterly* 13 (1950): 629–634.

Bickman, L., and T. Henchy, eds. *Beyond the Laboratory: Field Research in Social Psychology*. New York: McGraw-Hill, 1972.

Bierstedt, R. "A Critique of Empiricism in Sociology." *American Sociological Review* 24 (1949): 584–592.

Biklen, D. "The Case for Deinstitutionalization." *Social Policy* 10 (1979): 48–54.

Bittner, E. "The Concept of Organization." *Social Research* 31 (1964): 239–255.

———. "Objectivity and Realism in Sociology." In *Phenomenological Sociology: Issues and Applications*, edited by G. Psathas, 109–125. New York: John Wiley & Sons, 1973.

———. "Realism in Field Research." In *Contemporary Field Research*, edited by R. M. Emerson, 149–155. Boston: Little, Brown, 1983.

Blackman, B. I. *QUALPRO Text Database and Productivity Tools: User's Manual, Version 4 for IBM and PC Compatibles*. Tallahassee, FL: Impulse Development, 1993.

Blatt, B. *Exodus from Pandemonium*. Boston: Allyn & Bacon, 1970.

———. *Souls in Extremis*. Boston: Allyn & Bacon, 1973.

Blatt, B., D. Biklen, and R. Bogdan, eds. *An Alternative Textbook in Special Education*. Denver: Love, 1977.

Blatt, B., R. Bogdan, D. Biklen, and S. Taylor. "From Institution to Community: A Conversion Model." In *Educational Programming for the Severely and Profoundly Handicapped*, edited by E. Sontag, J. Smith, and N. Certo. Reston, VA: Council for Exceptional Children, 1977.

Blatt, B., and F. Kaplan. *Christmas in Purgatory: A Photographic Essay on Mental Retardation*. Syracuse, NY: Human Policy Press, 1974.

Blatt, B., A. Ozolins, and J. McNally. *The Family Papers: A Return to Purgatory*. New York: Longman, 1979.

Blau, P. *Exchange and Power in Social Life*. New York: John Wiley & Sons, 1964.

Blauner, R., and D. Wellman. Toward the decolonization of social research. In *The Death of White Sociology*, edited by J. Ladner. New York: Vintage Books, 1973.

Bloor, M. J. "On the Analysis of Observational Data: A Discussion of the Worth and Uses of Inductive Techniques and Respondent Validation." *Sociology* 12 (1978): 545–552.

———. "Notes on Member Validation." In *Contemporary Field Research*, edited by R. M. Emerson, 156–172. Boston: Little, Brown, 1983.

Blum, F. H. "Getting Individuals to Give Information to the Outsider." *Journal of Social Issues* 8 (3): 35–42, 1952.

Blumer, H. *An Appraisal of Thomas and Znaniecki's "The Polish peasant in Europe and America."* New York: Social Science Research Council, 1939.

———. "Sociological Analysis of the 'Variable.' " *American Sociological Review* 21 (December 1956): 683–690.

———. "Sociological Implications of the Thought of George Herbert Mead." *American Journal of Sociology* 71 (March 1966): 535–544.

———. "Society as Symbolic Interaction." In *Symbolic Interaction*, edited by J. Manis and B. Mentzer. Boston: Allyn & Bacon, 1967.

———. *Symbolic Interactionism: Perspective and Method.* Englewood Cliffs, NJ: Prentice-Hall, 1969.

Boas, F. *Handbook of American Indian Languages* (Bureau of American Ethnology Bulletin 40). Washington, DC: Bureau of American Ethnology, 1911.

Bochner, A., C. Ellis, and L. Tillman. "Relationships as Stories." In *Handbook of Personal Relationships*, edited by S. Duck. Sussex, UK: John Wiley & Sons, in press.

Bodemann, Y. M. "A Problem of Sociological Praxis: The Case for Interventive Observation in Field Work." *Theory and Society* 5 (1978): 387–420.

Boelen, W. A. M. "Street Corner Society: Cornerville Revisited." *Journal of Contemporary Ethnography* 21 (1): 11–51, 1992.

Bogdan, R. "A Forgotten Organization Type." Doctoral dissertation, 1971.

———. *Participant Observation in Organization Settings.* Syracuse, NY: Syracuse University Division of Special Education and Rehabilitation, 1972.

———. *Being Different: The Autobiography of Jane Fry.* New York: John Wiley & Sons, 1974.

———. "Interviewing People Labeled Retarded." In *Fieldwork Experience: Qualitative Approaches to Social Research*, edited by W. B. Shaffir, R. A. Stebbins, and A. Turowetz, 235–243. New York: St Martin's Press, 1980.

———. "Does Mainstreaming Work? Is a Silly Question." *Phi Delta Kappa* 64 (1983): 427–428.

———. *Freak Show: Presenting Human Oddities for Amusement and Profit.* Chicago: University of Chicago Press, 1988.

Bogdan, R., and D. Biklen. "Handicapism." *Social Policy* 7 (4): 14–19, 1977.

Bogdan, R., and S. K. Biklen. *Qualitative Research for Education: An Introduction to Theory and Methods.* Boston: Allyn & Bacon, 1992.

Bogdan, R., M. A. Brown, and S. B. Foster. "Be Honest but Not Cruel: Staff/Parent Communication on a Neonatal Unit." *Human Organization* 41 (1): 6–16, 1982.

Bogdan, R., and S. Taylor. "The Judged, Not the Judges: An Insider's View of Mental Retardation." *American Psychologist* 31 (1): 47–52, 1976.

Bogdan, R., S. Taylor, B. de Grandpre, and S. Haynes. "Let Them Eat Programs: Attendants' Perspectives and Programming on Wards in State Schools." *Journal of Health and Social Behavior* 15 (June 1974): 142–151.

Bogdan, R., and S. J. Taylor. *Introduction to Qualitative Research Methods: A Phenomenological Approach to the Social Sciences.* New York: John Wiley & Sons, 1975.

———. *Inside Out: The Social Meaning of Mental Retardation.* Toronto: University of Toronto Press, 1982.

———. "Toward a Sociology of Acceptance: The Other Side of the Study of Deviance." *Social Policy* 18 (2): 34–39, 1987.

———. "Looking at the Bright Side: A Positive Approach to Qualitative Research." *Qualitative Sociology* 13 (2): 183–192, 1990.

———. *The Social Meaning of Mental Retardation: Two Life Stories.* New York: Teachers College Press, 1994.

Bogdan, R., et al. "Simplistic Answers to the Problems of Inequality: Teacher Meets Technology." In *Introduction to Qualitative Research Methods: A Phenomenological Approach to the Social Sciences,* edited by R. Bogdan and S. J. Taylor, 187–196. New York: John Wiley & Sons, 1975.

Bonacich, P. "Deceiving Subjects: The Pollution of our Environment." *American Sociologist* 5 (February 1970), 45.

Bonaparte, M. A. "A Defense of Biography." *International Journal of Psycho-Analysis* 5 (20): 231–240, 1939.

Booth, W. C., G. G. Colomb, and J. M. Williams. *The Craft of Research.* Chicago: University of Chicago Press, 1995.

Bowers, R. V. "Research Methodology in Sociology: The First Half-Century." In *Method and Perspective in Anthropology,* edited by R. F. Spencer, 251–270. Minneapolis: University of Minnesota Press, 1954.

Braginsky, D., and B. Braginsky. *Hansels and Gretels.* New York: Holt, Rinehart & Winston, 1971.

Brajuha, M., and L. Hallowell, "Legal Intrusions and the Politics of Fieldwork: The Impact of the Brajuha Case." *Urban Life* 14 (1986): 457–478.

Bromley, D. G., and A. D. Shupe, Jr. "Evolving Foci in Participant Observation: Research as an Emergent Process." In *Fieldwork Experience: Qualitative Approaches to Social Research,* edited by W. B. Shaffir, R. A. Stebbins, and A. Turowetz, 191–202. New York: St Martin's Press, 1980.

Brookover, L. A., and K. W. Black. "Time Sampling as a Field Technique." *Human Organization* 25 (1966): 64–70.

Bruininks, R. H., C. E. Meyers, B. B. Sigford, and K. C. Lakin, eds. *Deinstitutionalization and Community Adjustment of Mentally Retarded People.* Washington, DC: American Association on Mental Deficiency, 1981.

Bruyn, S. T. *The Human Perspective in Sociology: The Methodology of Participant Observation.* Englewood Cliffs, NJ: Prentice Hall, 1966.

Brymer, R. A., and B. Faris, "Ethical and Political Dilemmas in the Investigation of Deviance: A Study of Juvenile Delinquency." In *Ethics, Politics, and Social Research,* edited by G. Sjoberg, 297–318. Cambridge, MA: Schenkman, 1967.

Buckner, H. T. "Organization of a Large Scale Field Work Course." *Urban Life and Culture* 2 (3): 361–379, 1973.

Bulmer, M. "Concepts in the Analysis of Qualitative Data: A Symposium." *Sociological Review* 27 (1979): 651–677.

———. *The Chicago School of Sociology: Institutionalization, Diversity, and the Rise of Sociological Research.* Chicago: University of Chicago Press, 1984.

Burchard, W. W. "Lawyers, Political Scientists, Sociologists—And Concealed Microphones." *American Sociological Review* 23 (1958): 686–691.

Burgess, E. W. "What Social Case Records Should Contain to be Useful for Sociological Interpretation." *Social Forces* 6 (1925): 524–532.

———. "Statistics and Case Studies as Methods of Sociological Research." *Social Forces* 12 (1927): 103–120.

———. "Research Methods in Sociology." In *Twentieth Century Sociology,* edited by G. Gurvitch and W. Moore, 20–41. New York: Philosophical Library, 1945a.

———. "Sociological Research Methods." *American Journal of Sociology* 50 (1945b): 474–482.

Burgess, R. G., ed. *Field Research: A Sourcebook and Field Manual.* London: George Allen & Unwin, 1982.

———. "Sponsors, Gatekeepers, Members, and Friends: Access in Educational Settings." In *Experiencing Fieldwork: An Inside View of Qualitative Research,* edited by W. B. Shaffir and R. A. Stebbins, 43–52. Newbury Park, CA: Sage Publications, 1991.

Burr, A. R. *The Autobiography: A Critical and Comparative Study.* New York: Houghton Mifflin, 1909.

Camilleri, S. F. "Theory, Probability, and Induction in Social Research." *American Sociological Review* 27 (1962): 170–178.

Campbell, D. T. "The Informant in Qualitative Research." *American Journal of Sociology* 60 (1955): 339–342.

———. "Factors Relevant to the Validity of Experiments in Social Settings." *Psychological Bulletin* 54 (1957): 297–312.

———. "Systematic Error on the Part of Human Links in Communication Systems." *Information and Control* 1 (1959): 334–369.

Cannel, C. F., and M. Axelrod. "The Respondent Reports on the Interview." *American Journal of Sociology* 62 (1956): 177–181.

Caplow, T. "The Dynamics of Information Interviewing." *American Journal of Sociology* 62 (1956): 165–171.

Carey, A. "The Hawthorne Studies: A Radical Criticism." *American Sociological Review* 32 (3): 403–416, 1967.

Carroll, J. "Confidentiality of Social Science Research Sources and Data: The Popkin Case." *Political Science* 6 (1973): 11–24.

Cartwright, D., and J. R. P. French, Jr. "The Reliability of Life History Studies." *Character and Personality* 8 (1939): 110–119.

Cassell, J. "Risk and Benefit to Subjects of Fieldwork." *American Sociologist* 13 (1978): 134–143.

———. "Ethical Principles for Conducting Fieldwork." *American Anthropologist* 82 (1980): 28–41.

Cassell, J., and M. Wax. "Ethical Problems of Fieldwork." *Social Problems* 27 (1980): 259–264.

Castaneda, C. *"The Teachings of don Juan: A Yaqui Way of Knowledge.* Los Angeles: University of California Press, 1968.

———. *A Separate reality: Further Conversations with don Juan.* New York: Simon & Schuster, 1971.

———. *Journal to Ixtlan: The Lessons of don Juan.* New York: Simon & Schuster, 1972.

———. *Sorcery: A Description of Reality.* Ann Arbor, MI: University Microfilms, 1973.

———. *Tales of Power.* New York: Simon & Schuster, 1974.

———. *The Second Ring of Power.* New York: Simon & Schuster, 1977.

———. *The Power of Silence: Further Lessons of don Juan.* New York: Simon & Schuster, 1987.

Cavan, R. S. "Interviewing for Life-History Material." *American Journal of Sociology* 35 (1929–1930): 100–115.

Cavan, S. "Seeing Social Structure in a Rural Setting." *Urban Life and Culture* 3 (October 1974): 329–346.

Center on Human Policy. *Families for All Children*. Syracuse, NY: Center on Human Policy, September 1987.

Chapin, F. S. *Field work and Social Research*. New York: Century, 1920.

Charmaz, K. "The Grounded Theory Method: An Explication and Interpretation." In *Contemporary Field Research*, edited by R. M. Emerson, 109–126. Boston: Little, Brown, 1983.

Chesler, M., and R. Schmuck. "Participant observation in a superpatriot discussion group." *Journal of Social Issues* 19 (2): 18–30, 1963.

Chrisman, N. J. (1976). "Secret Societies and the Ethics of Urban Fieldwork." In *Ethics and Anthropology: Dilemmas in Fieldwork*, edited by M. A. Rynkiewich and J. P. Spradley. New York: John Wiley & Sons, 1976.

Christie, R. M. "Comment on Conflict Methodology: A Protagonist Position." *Sociological Quarterly* 17 (1976): 513–519.

Cicourel, A. *Method and Measurement in Sociology*. New York: Free Press, 1964.

———. *Cognitive Sociology: Language and Meaning in Social Interaction*. New York: Free Press, 1974a.

———. "Interviewing and Memory." In *Pragmatic Aspects of Human Communications*, edited by C. Cherry. Dordrecht, The Netherlands: D. Reidel, 1974b.

Cicourel, A., and J. Kitsuse. *The Educational Decision-Makers*. Indianapolis: Bobbs-Merrill, 1963.

Clarke, J. "Survival in the Field: Implications of Personal Experience in Fieldwork." *Theory and Society* 2 (1975): 95–123.

Clifford, J. *The Predicament of Culture*. Cambridge, MA: Harvard University Press, 1988.

Coffey, A., and P. Atkinson. *Making Sense of Qualitative Data: Complementary Research Strategies*. Thousand Oaks, CA: Sage Publications, 1996.

Cole, S. *The Sociological Method*. 2nd ed. Chicago: Rand McNally, 1976.

Coleman, J. S. "Relational Analysis: The Study of Social Organizations with Survey Methods." *Human Organization* 17 (4): 28–36, 1958.

Coles, R. *Children of Crisis*. Boston: Little, Brown, 1964.

———. *The South Goes North*. Boston: Little, Brown, 1971a.

———. *Migrants, Sharecroppers, Mountaineers*. Boston: Little, Brown, 1971b.

Colfax, D. J. "Pressure Toward Distortion and Involvement in Studying of Civil Rights Organization." *Human Organization* 25 (Summer 1966): 140–149.

Collier, J., Jr. *Visual Anthropology: Photography as a Research Method*. New York: Holt, 1967.

Colvard, R. "Interaction and Identification in Reporting Field Research: A Critical Reconsideration of Protective Procedures." In *Ethics, Politics and Social Research*, edited by G. Sjoberg, 319–358. Cambridge, MA: Schenkman, 1967.

Comte, A. *The Positive Philosophy*. Translated by Harriet Martineau. London: George Bell & Sons, 1896.

Conklin, H. C. "Lexicographical Treatment of Folk Taxonomies." In *Cognitive Anthropology*, edited by S. A. Tyler, 41–59. New York: Holt, Rinehart & Winston, 1969.

Cook, P. H. "Methods of Field Research." *Australian Journal of Psychology* 3 (2): 84–98, 1951.

Cooley, C. H. *Human Nature and the Social Order.* New York: Charles Scribner's Sons, 1902.

Cooper, K. J. "Rural-Urban Differences in Responses to Field Techniques." *Human Organization* 18 (3): 135–139, 1959.

Coser, L. A., J. A. Roth, M. A. Sullivan, Jr., and S. A. Queen. "Participant Observation and the Military: An Exchange." *American Sociological Review* 24 (1959): 397–400.

Coser, R. L. "Comment." *American Sociologist,* 13 (1978): 156–157.

Cottle, T. J. *The Abandoners: Portraits of Loss, Separation, and Neglect.* Boston: Little, Brown, 1972.

———. *The Voices of School: Educational Images Through Personal Accounts.* Boston: Little, Brown, 1973a.

———. "The Life Study: On Mutual Recognition and the Subjective Inquiry." *Urban Life and Culture* 2(3): 344–360, 1973b.

———. "The Ghetto Scientists." Unpublished paper, 1973c.

Coulon, A. *Ethnomethodology.* Newbury Park, CA: Sage Publications, 1995.

Coulter, J. "Decontextualized Meanings: Current Approaches to Verstehende Investigations." *Sociological Review* 19 (1971): 301–323.

Cowley, M. "Sociological Habit Patterns in Linguistic Transmogrification." *The Reporter* (September 20, 1956): 170–175.

Craig, K. H. "The Comprehension of the Everyday Physical Environment." In *Environmental Psychology,* edited by H. M. Proshansky, W. H. Ittelson, and L. E. Rivlin. New York: Holt, Rinehart & Winston, 1970.

Cressey, D. *Other People's Money: A Study in the Social Psychology of Embezzlement.* Glencoe, IL: Free Press, 1953.

———. "Limitations on Organization of Treatment in the Modern Prison." In *Crime and Justice in Society,* edited by R. Quinney. Boston: Little, Brown, 1969.

Cressey, D. R. "Criminal Violations of Financial Trust." *American Sociological Review* 15 (1950): 733–748.

Cressey, P. G. *The Taxi-Dance Hall.* Chicago: University of Chicago Press, 1932.

Creswell, J. W. *Research Design: Qualitative and Quantitative Approaches.* Thousand Oaks, CA: Sage Publications, 1994.

Crossley, R., and A. McDonald. *Annie's Coming Out.* New York: Penguin, 1980.

Dabbs, J. M., Jr. "Making Things Visible." In *Varieties of Qualitative Research,* edited by J. Van Maanen, J. M. Dabbs, Jr., and R. R. Faulkner, 31–64, Beverly Hills, CA: Sage Publications, 1982.

Dalton, M. *Men Who Manage.* New York: John Wiley & Sons, 1961.

———. "Preconceptions and Methods in 'Men Who Manage.' " In *Sociologists at Work,* edited by P. E. Hammond, 50–95. New York: Basic Books, 1964.

Daniels, A. *Invisible Careers: Women's Civic Leaders from the Volunteer World.* Chicago: University of Chicago Press, 1988.

Daniels, A. K. "The Low-Caste Stranger in Social Research." In *Ethics, Politics, and Social Research,* edited by G. Sjoberg, 267–296. Cambridge, MA: Schenkman, 1967.

Davis, F. "Comment on Initial Interaction of Newcomers in Alcoholics Anonymous." *Social Problems* 8 (4): 364–365, 1961a.

———. "Deviance Disavowal: The Management of Strained Interaction by the Visibly Handicapped." *Social Problems* 9 1961b: 120–132.

———. "The Martian and the Convert: Ontological Polarities in Social Research." *Urban Life and Culture* 2(3): 333–343, 1973.

———. "Stories and Sociology." *Urban Life and Culture* 3 (October 1974): 310–316.

Dean, J. P. "Participant Observation and Interviewing." In *An Introduction to Social Research,* edited by J. T. Doby, 225–252. Harrisburg, PA: Stackpole, 1954.

Dean, J. P., R. L. Eichhorn, and L. R. Dean. "Observation and Interviewing." In *An Introduction to Social Research.* 2nd ed., edited by J. T. Doby, 274–304. New York: Appleton-Century-Crofts, 1967.

Dean, J. P., and W. F. Whyte. "How Do You Know If the Informant is Telling the Truth?" *Human Organization* 17 (2): 34–38, 1958.

Dean, L. R. "Interaction, Reported and Observed: The Case of One Local Union." *Human Organization* 17 (3): 36–44, 1958.

Deegan, M. J., and J. S. Burger. "George Herbert Mead and Social Reform." *Journal of the History of the Behavioral Sciences* 14 (1978): 362–372.

———. "W. I. Thomas and Social Reform: His Work and His Writings." *Journal of the History of the Behavioral Sciences* 17 (1981): 114–125.

DeLaguna, F. "Some Problems of Objectivity in Ethnology." *Man* 57 (1957): 179–182.

de Mille, R. *Castaneda's Journey: The Power and the Allegory.* Santa Barbara, CA: Capra Press, 1976.

———. *The don Juan papers: Further Castaneda Controversies.* Santa Barbara, CA: Ross-Erikson, 1980.

Denzin, N. "On the Ethics of Disguised Observation." *Social Problems* 15 (1968): 502–504.

———, *Sociological Methods: A Sourcebook.* Chicago: Aldine, 1970.

———. "The Logic of Naturalistic Inquiry." *Social Forces* 50 (1971): 166–182.

———. *The Research Act: A Theoretical Introduction to Sociological Methods.* 2nd ed. New York: McGraw-Hill, 1978.

———. *Interpretive Biography.* Newbury Park, CA: Sage Publications, 1989a.

———. *Interpretive Interactionism.* Newbury Park, CA: Sage Publications, 1989b.

———. "Whose Cornerville Is It, Anyway?" *Journal of Contemporary Ethnography* 21 (1): 120–132, 1992.

———. "The Facts and Fictions of Qualitative Inquiry." *Qualitative Inquiry* 2 (2): 230–241, 1996.

———. "Whose Sociology Is It? Comment on Huber." *American Journal of Sociology* 102 (5): 1416–1429, 1997.

Denzin, N. K., and Y. S. Lincoln. "Transforming Qualitative Research Methods: Is It a Revolution?" *Journal of Contemporary Ethnography* 24 (1995): 349–357.

———, eds. *Handbook of Qualitative Research.* Thousand Oaks, CA: Sage Publications, 1994.

Deutscher, I. "Words and Deeds: Social Science and Social Policy." *Social Problems* 13 (Winter 1966): 233–254.

———. "Looking Backward: Case Studies on the Progress of Methodology in Sociological Research." *The American Sociologist* 4 (February 1969): 34–42.

———. *What We Say/What We Do: Sentiments and Acts.* Glenview, IL: Scott, Foresman, 1973.

Deutscher, I., F. P. Pestello, and H. F. G. Pestello. *Sentiments and Acts.* New York: Aldine de Gruyter, 1993.

DeVault, M. L. "Talking and Listening from Women's Standpoint: Feminist Strategies for Interviewing and Analysis." *Social Problems* 37 (1): 96–116, 1990.

———. *Feeding the Family: The Social Organization of Caring as Gendered Work.* Chicago: University of Chicago Press, 1991.

———. "Ethnicity and Expertise: Racial-Ethnic Knowledge in Sociological Research." *Gender & Society* 9 (5): 612–631, 1995.

———. "In Defense of Textual Experimentation: A Response to Michael Schwalbe." *Qualitative Sociology* 19 (4): 529–531, 1996.

Dewey, J. *Human Nature and Conduct.* New York: Modern Library, 1930.

Dexter, L. A. "Role Relationships and Conceptions of Neutrality in Interviewing." *American Journal of Sociology* 62 (1956): 153–157,

———. "The Good Will of Important People: More on the Jeopardy of the Interview." *Public Opinion Quarterly* 28 (1964): 556–563.

———. "On the Politics and Sociology of Stupidity in Our Society." In *The Other Side,* edited by H. S. Becker, 37–49. New York: Free Press, 1967.

———. *Elite and Specialized Interviewing.* Evanston, IL: Northwestern University Press, 1970.

Diesing, P. *Patterns of Discovery in the Social Sciences.* Chicago: Aldine-Atherton, 1971.

Dingman, H. F., C. C. Cleland, and J. D. Swartz. "Institutional 'Wisdom' as Expressed through Folklore." *Mental Retardation* 8 (1970): 2–8.

Dingwall, R. "Ethics and Ethnography." *Sociological Review* 28 (1980): 871–891.

Dollard, J. *Criteria for the Life History.* New York: Social Science Research Council, 1935.

Domhoff, G. W. *The Bohemian Grove and Other Retreats.* New York: Random House, 1975.

Dorn, D. S., and G. L. Long. "Brief Remarks on the Association's Code of Ethics." *American Sociologist* 9 (February 1974): 31–35.

Douglas, J. D. *The Social Meaning of Suicide.* Princeton, NJ: Princeton University Press, 1967.

———. *Observations of Deviance.* New York: Random House, 1970a.

———. *American Social Order: Social Rules in a Pluralistic Society.* New York: Free Press, 1971.

———. *Investigative Social Research: Individual and Team Field Research.* Beverly Hills, CA: Sage Publications, 1976.

———. Douglas, J. D. *Creative Interviewing.* Beverly Hills, CA: Sage Publications, 1985.

———, *Understanding Everyday Life: Toward the Reconstruction of Sociological Knowledge.* Chicago: Aldine, 1970b.

Douglas, J. D., and J. M. Johnson, eds. *Existential Sociology.* New York: Cambridge University Press, 1977.

Drass, K. A. "The Analysis of Qualitative Data: A Computer Program." *Urban Life* 9 (3): 332–353, 1980.

Dugdale, R. L. *The Jukes.* New York: Putnam, 1910.

Durkheim, E. *The Elementary Forms of Religious Life.* New York: Free Press, 1915.

————. *The Rules of Sociological Method*. New York: Free Press, 1938.

————. *Suicide: A Study of Sociology*. Translated and edited by George Simpson. New York: Free Press, 1951.

Duster, T., D. Matza, and D. Wellman. "Field Work and the Protection of Human Subjects." *American Sociologist* 14 (1979): 136–142.

Earle, W. *The Autobiographical Consciousness: A Philosophical Inquiry into Existence*. Chicago: Quadrangle, 1972.

Easterday, L., D. Papademas, L. Schorr, and C. Valentine. "The Making of a Female Researcher: Role Problems in Fieldwork." *Urban Life* 6 (1977): 333–348.

Eaton, J. W., and R. J. Weil. "Social Processes of Professional Teamwork." *American Sociological Review* 16 (1951): 707–713.

Edgerton, R. B. *The Cloak of Competence: Stigma in the Lives of the Mentally Retarded*. Berkeley, CA: University of California Press, 1967.

Eggan, R. "Social Anthropology and the Method of Controlled Comparison." *American Anthropologist* 56 (1954): 743–763.

Eisner, E. W., and A. Peshkin, eds. *Qualitative Inquiry in Education: The Continuing Debate*. New York: Teachers College Press, 1990.

Elementary and Secondary Education Act. Public Law 92-232, Title VI, 1965.

Ellis, C. *Fisher Folk: Two Communities on Chesapeake Bay*. Lexington, KY: The University Press of Kentucky, 1986.

————. "Emotional Sociology." In *Studies in Symbolic Interaction. Vol. 12*, edited by N. K. Denzin. Greenwich, CT: JAI Press, 1991a.

————. "Sociological Introspection and Emotional Experience." *Symbolic Interaction* 14 (1991b): 23–50.

————. "Emotional and Ethical Quagmires in Returning to the Field." *Journal of Contemporary Ethnography* 24 (1): 68–98, 1995a.

————. *Final Negotiations: A Story of Love, Loss and Chronic Illness*. Philadelphia: Temple University Press, 1995b.

Ellis, C., and A. P. Bochner. "Telling and Performing Personal Stories: The Constraints of Choice in Abortion." In *Investigative Subjectivity: Research on Lived Experience*, edited by C. Ellis and M. G. Flaherty, 79–101. Newbury Park, CA: Sage Publications, 1992.

Ellis, C., and M. G. Flaherty, eds. *Investigative Subjectivity: Research on Lived Experience*. Newbury Park, CA: Sage Publications, 1992.

Elsner, H. *Robert E. Park: The Crowd and the Public, and Other Essays*. Chicago: University of Chicago Press, 1972.

Emerson, R. M. "Observational Field Work." *Annual Review of Sociology* 7 (1981): 351–378.

————, ed. *Contemporary Field Research*. Boston: Little, Brown, 1983.

Emerson, R. M., R. L. Fretz, and L. L. Shaw. *Writing Ethnographic Fieldnotes*. Chicago: University of Chicago Press, 1995.

Epstein, A. L., ed. *The Craft of Social Anthropology*. New York: Barnes & Noble, 1967.

Erikson, K. T. "A Comment on Disguised Observation in Sociology." *Social Problems* 14 (1967): 366–373.

————. *Everything in Its Path*. New York: Simon & Schuster, 1976.

————. "Commentary." *The American Sociologist* 26 (2): 4–11, 1995.

Etzioni, A. "Two Approaches to Organizational Analysis: A Critique and Suggestion." *Administrative Science Quarterly* 5 (1960): 257–278.

Evans-Pritchard, E. E. *Social Anthropology and Other Essays.* New York: Free Press, 1964.

———. "Some Reminiscences and Reflections on Fieldwork." In *Witchcraft, Oracles and Magic among the Azande* (Abridged). Oxford, UK: Clarendon Press, 1976.

Faulkner, R. "Improvising on a Triad." In *Varieties of Qualitative Research,* edited by J. Van Maanen, J. M. Dabbs, Jr., and R. R. Faulkner, 65–102. Beverly Hills, CA: Sage Publications, 1982.

Feldman, M. S. *Strategies for Interpreting Qualitative Data.* Thousand Oaks, CA: Sage Publications, 1995.

Ferguson, P. M. *Abandoned to their Fate: Social Policy and Practice toward Severely Retarded People in America, 1820–1920.* Philadelphia: Temple University Press, 1992.

Ferguson, P. M., D. L. Ferguson, and S. J. Taylor, eds. *Interpreting Disability: A Qualitative Reader.* New York: Teachers College Press, 1992.

Festinger, L., and D. Katz, eds. *Research Methods in the Behavioral Sciences.* New York: Holt, 1953.

Festinger, L., H. Riecken, and S. Schacter. *When Prophecy Fails.* Minneapolis: University of Minnesota Press, 1956.

Fetterman, D. M. *Ethnography in Educational Evaluation.* Beverly Hills, CA: Sage Publications, 1984.

———. *Ethnography: Step by Step.* Newbury Park, CA: Sage Publications, 1989.

Feyerabend, P. K. *Against Method: Outline of an Anarchistic Theory of Knowledge.* Atlantic Highlands, NJ: Humanities Press, 1975.

Fichter, J. H., and W. L. Kolb. "Ethical Limitations on Sociological Reporting." *American Sociological Review* 18 (1953): 544–550.

Fielding, N. G., and R. M. Lee. *Using Computers in Qualitative Research.* Thousand Oaks, CA: Sage Publications, 1991.

Filstead, W., ed. *Qualitative Methodology: Firsthand Involvement with the Social World.* Chicago: Markham, 1970.

Fine, G. A. "Cracking Diamonds: Observer Role in Little League Baseball Settings and the Acquisition of Social Competence." In *Fieldwork Experience: Qualitative Approaches to Social Research,* edited by W. B. Shaffir, R. A. Stebbins, and A. Turowetz, 117–131. New York: St Martin's Press, 1980.

Fine, G. A., and D. D. Martin. "A Partisan View: Sarcasm, Satire, and Irony as Voices in Erving Goffman's Asylums." *Journal of Contemporary Ethnography* 19 (1): 89–115, 1990.

Fine, G. A., and K. L. Sandstrom. *Knowing Children: Participant Observation with Minors.* Newbury Park, CA: Sage Publications, 1988.

Fletcher, J. F. *Humanhood: Essays in Biomedical Ethics.* Buffalo, NY: Prometheus Books, 1979.

Forcese, D. P., and S. Richer. *Social Research Methods.* Englewood Cliffs, NJ: Prentice Hall, 1973.

Forder, A. C. Foreword to *When a Parent is Mentally Retarded,* edited by B. Y. Whitman and P. J. Accardo, ix–xii. Baltimore: Paul H. Brookes, 1990.

Form, W. H. "The Sociology of Social Research." In *The Organization, Management, and Tactics of Social Research,* edited by R. T. O'Toole. Cambridge, MA: Schenkman, 1971.

Foucault, M. *Power/Knowledge*. New York: Pantheon, 1980.

Fox, J., and R. Lundman. "Problems and Strategies in Gaining Access in Policy Organizations." *Criminology* 12 (1974): 52–69.

Frake, C. O. "The Ethnographic Study of Cognitive Systems." In *Anthropology and Human Behavior*, edited by T. Gladwin and W. C. Sturtevant, 72–85. Washington, DC: Anthropological Society of Washington, 1962a.

———. "Cultural Ecology and Ethnography." *American Anthropologist* 64 (1962b): 53–59.

———. "A Structural Description of Subanun 'Religious Behavior.' " In *Explorations in Cultural Anthropology*, edited by W. H. Goodenough, 111–129. New York: McGraw-Hill, 1964a.

———. "Notes on Queries in Ethnography." *American Anthropologist* 66 (1964b): 132–145.

———. "Plying Frames Can Be Dangerous: Some Reflections on Methodology in Cognitive Anthropology." *The Quarterly Newsletter of the Institute for Comparative Human Development* 1 (1977): 1–7.

———. "Ethnography." In *Contemporary Field Research*, edited by R. M. Emerson, 60–67. Boston: Little, Brown, 1983.

Francis, R. G. *The Rhetoric of Science*. Minneapolis: University of Minnesota Press, 1961.

Frank, A. *The Diary of a Young Girl*. New York: Doubleday, 1952.

Frazier, C. E. "The Use of Life-Histories in Testing Theories of Criminal Behavior: Toward Reviving a Method." *Qualitative Sociology* 1 (1): 122–142, 1978.

Freakley, M. "Contingency and Case Study: Lessons from Natural History." *International Journal of Qualitative Studies in Education* 9 (2): 225–235, 1996.

French, J. R. P., Jr. "Experiments in Field Settings." In *Research Methods in the Behavioral Sciences*, edited by L. Festinger and D. Katz, 98–135. New York: Holt, 1953.

French, K. S. "Research Interviewers in a Medical Setting: Roles and Social Systems." *Human Organization* 21 (3): 219–224, 1962.

Frenkel-Brunswik, E. "Mechanisms of Self-Description." *Journal of Social Psychology* 5 (10): 409–420, 1939.

Friedenberg, E. Z. "The Films of Frederick Wiseman." *The New York Review of Books* 17 (October 21, 1971): 19–22.

Friedman, N. *The Social Nature of Psychological Research: The Psychological Experiment as a Social Interaction*. New York: Basic Books, 1967.

Frohock, F. M. *Special Care*. Chicago: University of Chicago Press, 1986.

Gallaher, A., Jr. "Plainville: The Twice Studied Town." In *Reflections on Community Studies*, edited by A. J. Vidich, J. Bensman, and M. R. Stein, 285–303. New York: John Wiley & Sons, 1964.

Galliher, J. F. "The Protection of Human Subjects: A Reexamination of the Professional Code of Ethics." *American Sociologist* 8 (1973): 93–100.

———. "Professor Galliher Replies." *American Sociologist* 9, (1974): 159–160.

———. "The ASA Code of Ethics on the Protection of Human Beings: Are Students Human Too?" *American Sociologist* 10 (1975): 113–117.

———. "Social Scientists' Ethical Responsibilities to Superordinates: Looking Upward Meekly." In *Contemporary Field Research*, edited by R. M. Emerson, 300–312. Boston: Little, Brown, 1983.

Gallmeier, C. P. "Leaving, Revisiting, and Staying In Touch: Neglected Issues in Field Research." In *Experiencing Fieldwork: An Inside View of Qualitative Research*, edited by W. B. Shaffir and R. A. Stebbins, 224–231. Newbury Park, CA: Sage Publications, 1991.

Gans, H. *The Urban Villagers*. New York: Free Press, 1962.

———. "The Participant-Observer as a Human Being: Observations on the Personal Aspects of Field Work." In *Institutions and the Person*, edited by H. S. Becker, B. Greer, D. Riesman, and R. S. Weiss, 300–317. Chicago: Aldine, 1968.

———. *The Levittowners*. New York: Random House, 1969.

Gardner, B. B., and W. F. Whyte. "Methods for the Study of Human Relations in Industry." *American Sociologist Review* 11 (1946): 506–512.

Garfinkel, H. "Conditions of Successful Degradation Ceremonies." *American Journal of Sociology* 59 (1956): 420–424.

———. *Studies in Ethnomethodology*. Englewood Cliffs, NJ: Prentice Hall, 1967.

Geer, B. "First Days in the Field." In *Sociologist at Work*, edited by P. E. Hammond, 322–344. New York: Basic Books, 1964.

Geer, B., J. Haas, C. Vivona, S. Miller, C. Woods, and H. S. Becker. "Learning the Ropes: Situational Learning in Four Occupational Training Programs." In *Among the People*, edited by I. Deutscher and E. Thompson. New York: Basic Books, 1966.

Geertz, C. "From the Native's Point of View: On the Nature of Anthropological Understanding." In *Meaning in Anthropology*, edited by K. H. Basso and H. A. Selby, 221–237. Albuquerque, NM: University of New Mexico Press, 1976.

———. "Thick Description: Toward an Interpretive Theory of Culture." In *Contemporary Field Research*, edited by R. M. Emerson, 37–59. Boston: Little, Brown, 1983.

Georges, R. A., and M. O. Jones. *People Studying People: The Human Element in Fieldwork*. Berkeley, CA: University of California Press, 1980.

Giallombardo, R. *Society of Women: A Study of a Woman's Prison*. New York: John Wiley & Sons, 1966.

Gilligan, C. *In a Different Voice: Psychological Theory and Women's Development*. Cambridge, MA: Harvard University Press, 1982.

Glaser, B. G. "The Constant Comparative Method of Qualitative Analysis." *Social Problems* 12 (1965): 436–445.

———. *Theoretical Sensitivity*. Mill Valley, CA: Sociology Press, 1978.

———. *Emergence vs. Forcing: Basics of Grounded Theory Analysis*. Mill Valley, CA: Sociology Press, 1992.

———, ed. *Organizational Careers*. Chicago: Aldine, 1968.

Glaser, B. G., and A. Strauss. *The Discovery of Grounded Theory: Strategies for Qualitative Research*. Chicago: Aldine, 1967.

Glazer, M. *The Research Adventure: Promise and Problems of Field Work*. New York: Random House, 1972.

Goddard, H. H. *The Kallikaks: A Study in the Heredity of Feeblemindedness*. New York: Macmillan, 1912.

Goffman, E. *The Presentation of Self in Everyday Life*. Garden City, NY: Doubleday, 1959.

———. *Asylums: Essays on the Social Situation of Mental Patients and Other Inmates*. Garden City, NY: Doubleday, 1961.

———. *Stigma: Notes on the Management of Spoiled Identity*. Englewood Cliffs, NJ: Prentice Hall, 1963.

————. *Interaction Ritual.* Garden City, NY: Doubleday, 1967.

————. *Relations in Public.* New York: Harper & Row, 1971.

Gold, D. "Comment on 'A Critique of Tests of Significance.' " *American Sociological Review* 24 (1959): 328–338.

Gold, R. "Janitors versus Tenants: A Status-Income Dilemma." *American Journal of Sociology* 57 (1952): 486–493.

Gold, R. L. "Roles in Sociological Field Observation." *Social Forces* 36 (1958): 217–223.

Gold, S. J. "Introduction." *Qualitative Sociology* 20 (1): 3–6, 1997a.

————, ed. "Visual Methods in Sociological Analysis [Special Issue]." *Qualitative Sociology* 20 (1), 1997b.

Golde, P., ed. *Women in the Field.* Chicago: Aldine, 1970.

Goldner, F. H. "Role Emergence and the Ethics of Ambiguity." In *Ethics, Politics, and Social Research,* edited by G. Sjoberg, 245–266. Cambridge, MA: Schenkman, 1967.

Goode, D. A. "Kids, Culture and Innocents." *Human Studies* 9 (1986): 83–106.

————. "Who is Bobby? Ideology and Method in the Discovery of a Down's Syndrome Person's Competence." In *Health Through Occupation,* edited by G. Kielhofner, 237–255. Philadelphia: Davis, 1983.

————. "Socially Produced Identities, Intimacy and the Problem of Competence among the Retarded." In *Special Education and Social Interests,* edited by S. Tomlinson and L. Barton, 228–248. London: Croom-Helm, 1984.

————. "Who is Bobby? Ideology and Method in the Discovery of a Down Syndrome Person's Competence." In *Interpreting Disability: A Qualitative Reader,* edited by P. M. Ferguson, D. L. Ferguson, and S. J. Taylor, 197–212. New York: Teachers College Press, 1992.

————. *A World without Words: The Social Constructions of Children Born Deaf and Blind.* Philadelphia: Temple University Press, 1994.

Goode, E. "The Ethics of Deception in Social Research: A Case Study." *Qualitative Sociology* 19 (1): 11–33, 1996.

Goode, W. "Community within a Community: The Professions." *American Sociological Review* 22 (1957): 194–200.

————. "Encroachment, Charlatanism, and the Emerging Professions: Psychology, Sociology, and Medicine." *American Sociological Review* 25 (1960): 903.

Goode, W. J., and P. K. Hatt. *Methods in Social Research.* New York: McGraw-Hill, 1952.

Goodenough, W. H. "Cultural Anthropology and Linguistics." *Georgetown University Monograph Series on Language and Linguistics* 9 (1957): 167–173.

————. *Culture, Language, and Society.* Reading, MA: Addison-Wesley Modular Publications, 1971.

Gorden, R. L. "Dimensions of the Depth Interview." *American Journal of Sociology* 62 (1956): 158–164.

Gottschalk, L., C. Kluckhohn, and R. D. Angell. *The Use of Personal Documents in History, Anthropology and Sociology.* New York: Social Science Research Council, 1945.

Goulder, A. W. *Enter Plato.* New York: Basic Books, 1965.

————. "The Sociologist as Partisan: Sociology and the Welfare State." *The American Sociologist* 3 (1968): 103–116.

————. *The Coming Crisis of Western Sociology.* New York: Basic Books, 1970.

Graham, H. "Caring: A Labour of Love." In *A Labour of Love: Women, Work and Caring,* edited by J. Finch and D. Groves, 13–30. London: Routledge & Kegan Paul, 1983.

Green, P. "The Obligations of American Social Scientists." *Annals of the American Academy of Political and Social Science* 394 (1971): 13–27.

Griffin, C. "The Researcher Talks Back: Dealing with Power Relations in Studies of Young People's Entry in the Job Market." In *Experiencing Fieldwork: An Inside View of Qualitative Research,* edited by W. B. Shaffir and R. A. Stebbins, 109–119. Newbury Park, CA: Sage Publications, 1991.

Gross, N., and W. Mason. "Some Methodological Problems of Eight Hour Interviews." *American Journal of Sociology* 59 (1953): 197–204.

Guba, E. G., and Y. S. Lincoln. *Fourth Generation Evaluation.* Thousand Oaks, CA: Sage Publications, 1989.

Gubrium, J. F. "The Social Preservation of Mind: The Alzheimer's Disease Experience." *Symbolic Interaction* 9 (1986): 37–51.

———. *Analyzing Field Reality.* Newbury Park, CA: Sage Publications, 1988.

———. "Recognizing and Analyzing Local Cultures." In *Experiencing Fieldwork: An Inside View of Qualitative Research,* edited by W. B. Shaffir and R. A. Stebbins, 131–142. Newbury Park, CA: Sage Publications, 1991.

Gullahorn, J., and G. Strauss. "The Field Worker in Union Research." *Human Organization* 13 (3): 28–32, 1954.

Gurney, J. N. "Female Researchers in Male-Dominated Settings: Implications for Short-Term versus Long-Term Research." In *Experiencing Fieldwork: An Inside View of Qualitative Research,* edited by W. B. Shaffir and R. A. Stebbins, 53–61. Newbury Park, CA: Sage Publications, 1991.

Gurwitsch, A. *Studies in Phenomenology and Psychology.* Evanston, IL: Northwestern University Press, 1966.

Gusfield, J. G. "Field Work Reciprocities in Studying a Social Movement." *Human Organization* 14 (3): 29–34, 1955.

Gussow, Z. "The Observer-Observed Relationship as Information About Structure in Small-Group Research: A Comparative Study of Urban Elementary School Classrooms." *Psychiatry* 27 (1964): 230–247.

Haas, J., and W. Shaffir. "Fieldworkers' Mistakes at Work: Problems in Maintaining Research and Researcher Bargains." In *Fieldwork Experiences: Qualitative Approaches to Social Research,* edited by W. B. Shaffir, R. A. Stebbins, and A. Turowetz, 244–256. New York: St Martin's Press, 1980.

Habenstein, R. *Pathways to Data: Field Methods for Studying Ongoing Organizations.* Chicago: Aldine, 1970.

Hader, J. J., and E. C. Lindeman. *Dynamic Social Research.* London: Kegan Paul, 1933.

Haley, A. Epilogue to *The Autobiography of Malcolm X,* by Malcolm X. New York: Grove Press, 1966.

Hall, E. T. *The Silent Language.* New York: Doubleday, 1959.

Hamel, J., S. Dufour, and D. Fortin. *Case Study Methods.* Newbury Park, CA: Sage Publications, 1993.

Hammond, P. E., ed. *Sociologists at Work: The Craft of Social Research.* New York: Basic Books, 1964.

Hannerz, U. *Soulside: Inquiries into Ghetto Culture and Community,* 1969.

———. *Exploring the City: Inquiries toward an Urban Anthropology.* New York: Columbia University Press, 1980.

Haring, D. G. "Comment on Field Techniques in Ethnography, Illustrated by a Survey in the Ryuke Islands." *Southwestern Journal of Anthropology* 10 (1954): 255–267.

Harper, D. "Visualizing Structure: Reading Surfaces of Social Life." *Qualitative Sociology* 20 (1): 57–78, 1997.

Harrell-Bond, B. "Studying Elites: Some Special Problems." In *Ethics and Anthropology: Dilemmas in Fieldwork*, edited by M. A. Rynkiewich and J. P. Spradley. New York: John Wiley & Sons, 1976.

Harvey, S. M. "A Preliminary Investigation of the Interview." *British Journal of Psychology* 28 (1938): 263–287.

Hauber, F. A., and R. H. Bruininks. "Instrinsic and Extrinsic Job Satisfaction among Direct-Care Staff in Residential Facilities for Mentally Retarded People." *Educational and Psychological Measurement* 46 (1986): 95–105.

Hay, D. "My Story." *Mental Retardation* 32 (1982): 11–16.

Heap, J. L., and P. A. Roth. "On Phenomenological Sociology." *American Sociological Review* 38 (1973): 354–367.

Heeren, J. "Alfred Schutz and the Sociology of Common-sense Knowledge." In *Understanding Everyday life: Toward the Reconstruction of Sociological Knowledge*, edited by J. D. Douglas, 45–56. Chicago: Aldine, 1970.

Henry, J., and M. Spiro. "Psychological Techniques in Projective Tests in Field Work." In *Anthropology Today*, edited by A. Koreber, 417–429. Chicago: University of Chicago Press, 1953.

Henry, R., and S. Saberwal, eds. *Stress and Response in Field Work*. New York: Holt, Rinehart & Winston, 1969.

Heron, J. *Qualitative Inquiry: Research into the Human Condition*. Thousand Oaks, CA: Sage Publications, 1995.

Herskovits, M. J. "The Hypothetical Situation: A Technique of Field Research." *Southwestern Journal of Anthropology* 6 (1950): 32–40.

———. "Problems of Method in Ethnography." In *Method and Perspective in Anthropology*, edited by R. F. Skinner. Minneapolis: University of Minnesota Press, 1954.

Hertz, R., and J. B. Imber. "Fieldwork in Elite Settings: Introduction." *Journal of Contemporary Ethnography* 22 (1993): 3–6.

Hewitt, J. P., and R. Stokes. "Disclaimers." *Sociological Review* 40 (1975): 1–11,

Heyns, R. W., and R. Lippitt. (1954). "Systematic Observational Techniques." In *Handbook of Social Psychology*. Vol. 1, edited by G. Lindsey, 370–404.) Cambridge, MA: Addison-Wesley, 1954.

Higgins, P. *Outsiders in a Hearing World*. Berkeley, CA: Sage Publications, 1980.

Hill, M. R. *Archival Strategies and Techniques*. Newbury Park, CA: Sage Publications, 1993.

Hoffman, N., I. L. Horowitz, and L. Rainwater. "Sociological Snoopers and Journalistic Moralizers: Comment—An Exchange." *Trans-action* 7 (7): 4–10, 1970.

Hoffmann, J. E. "Problems of Access in the Study of Social Elites and Boards of Directors." In *Fieldwork Experience: Qualitative Approaches to Social Research*, edited by W. B. Shaffir, R. A. Stebbins, and A. Turowetz, 45–56. New York: St Martin's Press, 1980.

Holstein, J. A., and J. F. Gubrium. *The Active Interview*. Thousand Oaks, CA: Sage Publications, 1995.

Homans, G. C. *Social Behavior: Its Elementary Forms*. New York: Harcourt Brace, 1961.

———. "Contemporary Theory in Sociology." In *Handbook of Modern Sociology*, edited by R. E. L. Foris, 951–977. Chicago: Rand McNally, 1964.

Honigmann, J. J. "The Personal Approach in Cultural Anthropological Research." *Current Anthropology* 17 (1976): 243–251.

Horowitz, I. L. "The Life and Death of Project Camelot." *Trans-action* 3 (7): 44–47, 1965.

———, ed. *The Rise and Fall of Project Camelot*. Cambridge, MA: MIT Press, 1967.

Horowitz, I. L., and L. Rainwater. "Journalistic Moralizers." *Trans-action* 7(7): 5–8, 1970.

Horton, J. "Time Cool People." *Trans-action* 4(5): 5–12, 1967.

Huber, J. "Symbolic Interaction as a Pragmatic Perspective: The Bias of Emergent Theory." *American Sociological Review* 38 (1973): 274–284.

Huber, J., and J. Mirowsky. "Of Facts and Fables: Reply to Denzin." *American Journal of Sociology* 102(5): 1423–1429, 1997.

Hughes, E. C. "Institutional Offices and the Person." *American Journal of Sociology* 63 (1937): 404–413.

———. "Institutions and the Person." In *Principles of Sociology*, edited by A. L. McClung. New York: Barnes & Noble, 1951.

———. *Men and Their Work*. New York: Free Press, 1958.

———. *The Sociological Eye: Selected Papers*. Chicago: Aldine, 1971.

Humphreys, L. "Tearoom Trade: Impersonal Sex in Public Places." *Trans-action* 7 (3): 10–25, 1970.

———. *Tearoom Trade*. Enlarged ed. Chicago: Aldine, 1975.

Husserl, E. *Ideas*. London: George Allen & Unwin, 1962.

Hyman, H. H., W. J. Cobbs, J. J. Feldmen, C. W. Hart, and C. H. Stember. *Interviewing in Social Research*. Chicago: University of Chicago Press, 1954.

Hyman, J. J. "Do They Tell the Truth?" *Public Opinion Quarterly* 8 (1944): 557–559.

Hymes, D. H. "The Ethnology of Speaking." In *Anthropology and Human Behavior*, edited by T. Gladwin and W. C. Sturtevant. Washington, DC: Anthropological Society of Washington, 1962.

———. "Introduction: Toward Ethnographies of Communication." *American Anthropologist* 66 (1964): 1–34.

Jackson, J. B. "Killing Time: Life in the Arkansas penitentiary." *Qualitative Sociology* 1 (1): 21–32, 1978.

Jackson, J. E. " 'Deja Entendu': The Liminal Qualities of Anthropological Fieldnotes." *Journal of Contemporary Ethnography* 19 (1): 8–43, 1990.

Jacobs, G., ed. *The Participant Observer*. New York: Braziller, 1970.

Jacobs, J. "A Phenomenological Study of Suicide Notes." *Social Problems* 15 (1967): 60–72.

Jacobson, J. W., and L. J. Ackerman. *The Operation of Group Homes: Day-to-Day Issues Important to Staff*. Albany, NY: New York State Office of Mental Retardation and Developmental Disabilities, 1989.

Jago, B. J. "Postcards, Ghosts, and Fathers: Revisiting Family Stories." *Qualitative Inquiry* 2 (4): 495–516, 1996.

James, W. *The Meaning of Truth: A Sequel to Pragmatism*. Ann Arbor, MI: University of Michigan Press, 1970.

Janes, R. W. "A Note on Phases of the Community Role of the Participant Observer." *American Sociological Review* 26 (1961): 446–450.

Janowitz, M. Introduction to *On Social Organization and Social Personality*, by W. I. Thomas. Chicago: University of Chicago Press, 1966.

Jehenson, R. "A Phenomenological Approach to the Study of the Formal Organization." In *Phenomenological Sociology*, edited by G. Psathas, 219–250. New York: John Wiley & Sons, 1973.

Johnson, J. C. *Selecting Ethnographic Informants*. Newbury Park, CA: Sage Publications, 1990.

Johnson, J. M. *Doing Field Research*. New York: Free Press, 1975.

Jorgensen, D. L. *Participant Observation: A Methodology for Human Studies*. Newbury Park, CA: Sage Publications, 1989.

Josselson, R., A. Lieblich, R. Sharabany, and H. Wiseman. *Conversation as Method: Analyzing the Effects of Growing Up Communally on Later Relationships*. Thousand Oaks, CA: Sage Publications, 1997.

Junker, B. H. *Field Work: An Introduction to the Social Sciences*. Chicago: University of Chicago Press, 1960.

Kahn, R. L., and C. F. Cannell. *The Dynamics of Interviewing*. New York: John Wiley & Sons, 1957.

Kahn, R. L., and F. Mann. "Developing Research Partnerships." *Journal of Social Issues* 8 (3): 4–10, 1952.

Kames, D. H. "Legitimating Myths and Educational Organization." *American Sociological Review* 42 (1977): 208–219.

Kaplan, I. M. "Gone Fishing, Be Back Later: Ending and Resuming Research among Fishermen." In *Experiencing Fieldwork: An Inside View of Qualitative Research*, edited by W. B. Shaffir and R. A. Stebbins, 232–237. Newbury Park, CA: Sage Publications, 1991.

Karp, D. A. "Observing Behavior in Public Places: Problems and Strategies." In (Eds.), *Fieldwork Experience: Qualitative Approaches to Social Research*, edited by W. B. Shaffir, R. A. Stebbins, and A. Turowetz, 82–97. New York: St Martin's Press, 1980.

———. *Speaking of Sadness: Depression, Disconnection, and the Meanings of Illness*. Oxford, UK: Oxford University Press, 1996.

Karp, I., and M. B. Kendall. "Reflexivity in Field Work." In *Explaining Human Behavior: Consciousness, Human Action and Social Structure*, edited by P. F. Second. Beverly Hills, CA: Sage Publications, 1982.

Katz, D. "Psychological Barriers to Communication." *Annals of the American Academy of Political and Social Science* 250 (1947): 17–25.

Katz, J. "A Theory of Qualitative Methodology: The Social Science System of Analytic Fieldwork." In *Contemporary Field Research*, edited by R. M. Emerson, 127–148. Boston: Little, Brown, 1983.

Kay, P. "Comment on B. N. Colby, 'Ethnographic Semantics: A Preliminary Survey.'" *Current Anthropology* 7 (1966): 20–23.

———. "Some Theoretical Implications of Ethnographic Semantics." In *Current Directions in Anthropology, Part 2*. Bulletins of the American Anthropological Association 3, 1970.

Kelle, U., ed. *Computer-aided Qualitative Data Analysis: Theory, Methods, and Practice*. Thousand Oaks, CA: Sage Publications, 1995.

Kelman, H. C. "Human use of Human Subjects: The Problem of Deception in Social Psychological Experiments." *Psychological Bulletin* 67 (1967): 1–11.

Keltner, B. "Home Environments of Mothers with Mental Retardation." *Mental Retardation* 32 (2): 123–127, (1994).

Kimmel, A. J. *Ethics and Values in Applied Social Research.* Newbury Park, CA: Sage Publications, 1988.

Kirk, J., and M. L. Miller. *Reliability and Validity in Qualitative Research.* Beverly Hills, CA: Sage Publications, 1986.

Kitsuse, J. "Societal Reaction to Deviant Behavior." *Social Problems* 9 (3): 247–256, 1962.

Kitsuse, J., and A. V. Cicourel. "A Note on the Uses of Official Statistics." *Social Problems* 11 (1963): 131–139.

Klaber, M. M., and E. C. Butterfield. "Stereotyped Rocking—A Measure of Institution and Ward Effectiveness." *American Journal of Mental Deficiency* 73 (1968): 13–20.

Kleinman, S. "Learning the Ropes as Fieldwork Analysis." In *Fieldwork Experience: Qualitative Approaches to Social Research,* edited by W. B. Shaffir, R. A. Stebbins, and A. Turowetz, 171–184. New York: St Martin's Press, 1968.

———. "Field-workers' Feelings: What We Feel, Who We Are, How We Analyze." In *Experiencing Fieldwork: An Inside View of Qualitative Research,* edited by W. B. Shaffir and R. A. Stebbins 184–195. Newbury Park, CA: Sage Publications, 1991.

Klockars, C. B. *The Professional Fence.* New York: Free Press, 1974.

———. "Field Ethics for the Life History." In *Street Ethnography,* edited by R. S. Weppner, 201–226. Beverly Hills, CA: Sage Publications, 1977.

Klockars, C. B., and R. W. O'Connor, eds. *Deviance and Decency: The Ethics of Research with Human Subjects.* Beverly Hills, CA: Sage Publications, 1979.

Kluckhohn, C. "Participation in Ceremonies in a Navajo Community." *American Anthropologist* 40 (1938): 359–369.

———. "Theoretical Basis for an Empirical Method of Studying the Acquisition of Culture by Individuals." *Man* 39 (1939): 98–103.

———. "The Participant Observer Technique in Small Communities." *American Journal of Sociology* 46 (1940): 331–343.

Knoll, J., and A. Ford. "Beyond Caregiving: A Reconceptualization of the Role of the Residential Service Provider." In *Community Integration for People with Severe Disabilities,* edited by S. J. Taylor, D. Biklen, and J. Knoll, 129–146. New York: Teachers College Press, 1987.

Knopp Biklen, S. *School Work: Gender and the Cultural Construction of Teaching.* New York: Teachers College Press, 1995.

Knupfer, A. M. "Ethnographic Studies of Children: The Difficulties of Entry, Rapport, and Presentations of Their Worlds." *International Journal of Qualitative Studies in Education* 9 (2): 135–149, 1996.

Kobben, A. J. "New Ways of Presenting an Old Idea: The Statistical Method in Social Anthropology." *Journal of the Royal Anthropological Institute of Great Britain and Ireland* 82 (1952): 129–146.

Kolaja, J. "Contribution to the Theory of Participant Observation." *Social Forces* 35 (1956): 159–163.

Kotarba, J. A. (1980). "Discovering Amorphous Social Experience: The Case of Chronic Pain." In *Fieldwork Experience: Qualitative Approaches to Social Research,* edited by W. B. Shaffir, R. A. Stebbins, and A. Turowetz, 57–67. New York: St Martin's Press, 1980.

Kriegel, L. "The Cripple in Literature." In *Images of the Disabled, Disabling Images*, edited by A. Gartner and T. Joe, 31–46. New York: Praeger, 1987.

Krueger, E. T. "The Value of Life History Documents for Social Research." *Journal of Applied Sociology* 9 (1925): 196–201.

Krueger, R. A. *Focus Groups: A Practical Guide for Applied Research*. Newbury Park, CA: Sage Publications, 1988.

Kuhn, M. "Major Trends in Symbolic Interaction in the Past Twenty-five Years." *Sociological Quarterly* 5 (1964): 61–84.

Kvale, S. *Interviews: An Introduction to Qualitative Research Interviewing*. Thousand Oaks, CA: Sage Publications, 1996.

Labovitz, S., and R. Hagedorn. *Introduction to Social Research*. New York: McGraw-Hill, 1971.

Laing, R. D. *The Politics of Experience*. New York: Ballantine, 1967.

Lakin, K. C., R. H. Bruininks, D. Doth, B. Hill, and F. Hauber. *Sourcebook on Long-Term Care for Developmentally Disabled People*. Minneapolis: University of Minnesota, Department of Educational Psychology, 1982.

Lang, K., and G. E. Lang. "The Unique Perspective of Television and Its Effect: A Pilot Study." *American Sociological Review* 18 (1953): 3–12.

Langness, L. L. *Life History in Anthropological Science*. New York: Holt, 1965.

LaPiere, R. T. "Attitudes and Actions." *Social Forces* 13 (1934–1935): 230–237.

Lasswell, H. D. "The Contributions of Freud's Insight Interview to the Social Sciences." *American Journal of Sociology* 45 (1939): 375–390.

Lazarsfeld, P. F. "The Art of Asking Why." *National Marketing Review* 1 (1935): 26–38.

———. "The Controversy over Detailed Interviews—An Offer for Negotiation." *Public Opinion Quarterly* 8 (1944): 38–60.

———. "Evidence and Interference in Social Research." In *Evidence and Inference*, edited by D. Lerner, 107–138. New York: Free Press, 1959.

———. *Qualitative Analysis: History and Critical Essays*. Boston: Allyn & Bacon, 1972.

Lazarsfeld, P. F. and B. Allen. "Some Functions of Qualitative Analysis in Sociological Research." *Sociologica* 1 (1955): 324–361.

Lazarsfeld, P. F., and W. S. Robinson. "The Quantification of Case Studies." *Journal of Applied Psychology* 24 (1940): 817–825.

Lazarsfeld, P. F., and M. Rosenberg, eds. *The Language of Research*. New York: Free Press, 1955.

Lemert, E. *Social Pathology*. New York: McGraw-Hill, 1951.

Lesser, A. "Research Procedure and Laws of Culture." *Philosophy of Science* 6 (1939): 345–355.

Letkemann, P. "Crime as Work: Leaving the Field." In *Fieldwork Experience: Qualitative Approaches to Social Research*, edited by W. B. Shaffir, R. A. Stebbins, and A. Turowetz, 292–300. New York: St Martin's Press, 1980.

Lewis, O. "Controls and Experiments in Field Work." In *Anthropology Today*, edited by A. L. Kroeber, 452–475. Chicago: University of Chicago Press, 1953.

———. *Five Families*. New York: John Wiley & Sons, 1962.

———. *The Children of Sanchez*. New York: Vintage Books, 1963.

————. *Pedro Martinez*. New York: Random House, 1964.

————. *La Vida*. New York: Vintage Books, 1965.

Leznoff, M. "Interviewing Homosexuals." *American Journal of Sociology* 62 (1956): 202–204.

Liazos, A. "The Poverty of the Sociology of Deviance: Nuts, Sluts, and Perverts." *Social Problems* 29 (1972): 103–120.

Lieblich, A., and R. Josselson, ed. *The Narrative Study of Lives*. Vol. 5. Thousand Oaks, CA: Sage Publications, 1997.

Liebow, E. *Tally's Corner*. Boston: Little, Brown, 1967.

Lincoln, Y. S., and N. K. Denzin. "The Fifth Moment." In *Handbook of Qualitative Research*, edited by N. K. Denzin and Y. S. Lincoln, 575–586. Thousand Oaks, CA: Sage Publications, 1994.

Lincoln, Y. S., and E. G. Guba. *Naturalistic Inquiry*. Beverly Hills, CA: Sage Publications, 1985.

Lindeman, E. C. *Social Discovery*. New York: Republic, 1924.

Lindesmith, A. *Opiate Addiction*. Bloomington, IN: Principia Press, 1947.

————. *Addiction and Opiates*. Chicago: Aldine, 1968.

Lindesmith A., S. K. Weinberg, and W. S. Robinson. "Two Comments and Rejoinder to 'The Logical Structure of Analytic Induction.' " *American Sociological Review* 17 (1952): 492–494.

Lipetz, B. "Information Storage and Retrieval." *Scientific American* 215 (3): 224–242, 1966.

Littrell, W. B. "Vagueness, Social Structure, and Social Research in Law." *Social Problems* 21 (1973): 38–52.

Lofland, J. "Reply to Davis—Comment on 'Initial interaction.' " *Social Problems* 8 (4): 365–367, 1961.

————. *Doomsday Cult: A Study of Conversion, Proselytization, and Maintenance of Faith*. Englewood Cliffs, NJ: Prentice Hall, 1966.

————. *Analyzing Social Settings*. Belmont, CA: Wadsworth, 1971.

————. "Editorial Introduction—Analyzing Qualitative Data: First Person Accounts." *Urban Life and Culture* 3 (1974): 307–309.

————. *Doing Social life: The Qualitative Study of Human Interaction in Natural Settings*. New York: John Wiley & Sons, 1976.

————. "Analytic Ethnography: Features, Failings, and Futures." *Journal of Contemporary Ethnography* 24 (1): 30–67, 1995.

Lofland, J., and L. H. Lofland. *Analyzing Social Settings*. 3rd ed. Belmont, CA: Wadsworth, 1995.

Lohman, J. "The Participant Observer in Community Studies." *American Sociological Review* 2 (1937): 890–897.

Lombard, G. F. F. "Self-Awareness and Scientific Method." *Science* 112 (1950): 289–293.

Longmore, P. K. "Screening Stereotypes: Images of Disabled People in Television and Motion Pictures." *Social Policy* 16 (1): 31–37, 1985.

Lopata, H. Z. "Interviewing American Widows." In *Fieldwork Experience: Qualitative Approaches to Social Research*, edited by W. B. Shaffir, R. A. Stebbins, and A. Turowetz, 68–81. New York: St Martin's Press, 1980.

Lowie, R. H. *The History of Ethnological Theory*. New York: Farrar & Rinehart, 1937.

Lundberg, G. A. "Case Work and the Statistical Method." *Social Forces* 5 (5): 61–65, 1926.

Lyman, S. M., and M. B. A. Scott. *Sociology of the Absurd.* New York: Appleton-Century-Crofts, 1970.

Lynch, M. "Accomodation Practices: Vernacular Treatments of Madness." *Social Problems* 31 (1983): 152–164.

MacAndrew, C. "The Role of 'Knowledge at Hand' in the Practical Management of Institutionalized 'Idiots.' " In *Sociobehavioral Studies in Mental Retardation,* edited by R. K. Eyman, C. E. Myers, and G. Tarjan, 123–133. Los Angeles: American Association on Mental Deficiency, 1973.

Madge, J. *The Tools of Social Science.* London: Longmans, Green, 1953.

Maines, D. R., W. B. Shaffir, and A. Turowetz. "Leaving the Field in Ethnographic Research: Reflections on the Entrance-Exit Hypothesis." In *Fieldwork Experience: Qualitative Approaches to Social Research,* edited by W. B. Shaffir, R. A. Stebbins, and A. Turowetz, 261–280. New York: St Martin's Press, 1980.

Malcolm X. *The Autobiography of Malcolm X.* New York: Grove Press, 1966.

Malinowski, B. *Argonauts of the Western Pacific.* London: Routledge, 1932.

———. *A Diary in the Strict Sense of the Term.* New York: Harcourt, Brace and World, 1967.

Manis, J., and B. Meltzer, eds. *Symbolic Interaction.* Boston: Allyn & Bacon, 1967.

Mann, F. "Human Relations Skills in Social Research." *Human Relations* 4 (4): 341–354, 1951.

Manning, K. "Authenticity in Constructivist Inquiry: Methodological Considerations without Prescription." *Qualitative Inquiry* 3 (1): 93–115, 1997.

Manning, P. K. "Observing the Police: Deviants, Respectables and the Law." In *Research on deviance,* edited by J. Douglas. New York: Random House, 1972.

———. "The Researcher: An Alien in the Police World." In *The Ambivalent Force.* 2nd ed., edited by A. Neiderhoffer and A. Blumberg. Chicago: Dryden Press, 1976.

Marshall, C., and G. B. Rossman. *Designing Qualitative Research.* Newbury Park, CA: Sage Publications, 1989.

Mason, J. *Qualitative Researching.* Thousand Oaks, CA: Sage Publications, 1996.

McCall, G., and J. L. Simmons, eds. *Issues in Participant Observation.* Reading, PA: Addison-Wesley, 1969.

McCall, M. "Who and Where are the Artists?" In *Fieldwork Experience: Qualitative Approaches to Social Research,* edited by W. B. Shaffir, R. A. Stebbins, and A. Turowetz, 145–157. New York: St Martin's Press, 1980.

McCartney, J. L. "On Being Scientific: Changing Styles of Presentation of Sociological Research." *American Sociologist* 5 (1970): 30–35.

McCracken, G. *The Long Interview.* Newbury Park, CA: Sage Publications, 1988.

McEwen, W. J. "Forms and Problems of Validation in Social Anthropology." *Current Anthropology* 4 (1963): 155–169.

McGinnis, R. "Randomization and Inference in Sociological Research." *American Sociological Review* 22 (1957): 408–414.

McHugh, P. *Defining the Situation.* Indianapolis: Bobbs-Merrill, 1968.

McKeganey, N. P., and M. J. Bloor. "On the Retrieval of Sociological Description: Respondent Validation and the Critical Case of Ethnomethodology." *International Journal of Sociology and Social Policy* 1 (1981): 332–354.

McKinney, J. C. *Constructive Typology and Social Theory.* New York: Appleton-Century-Crofts, 1966.

Mead, G. H. *Mind, Self and Society.* Chicago: University of Chicago Press, 1934.

———. *The Philosophy of the Act.* Chicago: University of Chicago Press, 1938.

Mead, M. "More Comprehensive Field Methods." *American Anthropologist* 35 (1933): 1–15.

Mead, M., and R. Metruay. *The Study of a Culture at a Distance.* Chicago: University of Chicago Press, 1953.

Mehan, H., and H. Wood. *The Reality of Ethnomethodology.* New York: John Wiley & Sons, 1975.

Melbin, M. "An Interaction Recording Device for Participant Observers." *Human Organization* 13 (2): 29–33, 1954.

Mensh, I. N., and J. Henry. "Direct Observation and Psychological Tests in Anthropological Field Work." *American Anthropologist* 55 (1953) 461–480.

Mercer, J. *Labeling the Mentally Retarded.* Berkeley, CA: University of California Press, 1973.

Merton, R. K. *Social Theory and Social Structure.* Revised ed. New York: Free Press, 1957.

Merton, R. K., and P. Kendall. "The Focused Interview." *American Journal of Sociology* 51 (1946): 541–557.

Mey, H. *Field-Theory: Study of Its Applications in the Social Sciences.* Translated by Douglas Scott. New York: St Martin's Press, 1972.

Miles, M. B., and A. M. Huberman. *Qualitative Data Analysis: An Expanded Sourcebook.* 2nd ed. Thousand Oaks, CA: Sage Publications, 1994.

Miller, B., and L. Humphreys. "Keeping in Touch: Maintaining Contact with Stigmatized Subjects." In *Fieldwork Experience: Qualitative Approaches to Social Research,* edited by W. B. Shaffir, R. A. Stebbins, and A. Turowetz, 212–222. New York: St Martin's Press, 1980.

Miller, G., and R. Dingwall, eds. *Context and Method in Qualitative Research.* Thousand Oaks, CA: Sage Publications, 1997.

Miller, S. M. "The Participant Observer and 'Over-rapport.'" *American Sociological Review* 17 (1952): 97–99.

Mills, C. W. "Situated Actions and Vocabularies of Motive." *American Sociological Review* 5 (1940): 904–913.

———. *The Sociological Imagination.* London: Oxford University Press, 1959.

Miner, H. "Body Ritual Among the Nacirema." *American Anthropologist* 58 (1956): 503–507.

Mintz, S., and S. Kellogg. *Domestic Revolutions: A Social History of American Family Life.* New York: The Free Press, 1988.

Mishler, E. G. "Meaning in Context: Is There Any Other Kind?" *Harvard Educational Review* 49 (1979): 1–19.

Moore, J. W. "Social Constraints on Sociological Knowledge: Academics and Research Concerning Minorities." *Social Problems* 21 (1973): 65–77.

Morgan, D. L. *Focus Groups as Qualitative Research.* Newbury Park, CA: Sage Publications, 1988.

Morgan, G., ed. *Beyond Method: Strategies for Social Research.* Newbury Park, CA: Sage Publications, 1983.

Morris, P. *Put Away.* New York: Atherton, 1969.

Morse, J. M. "Designing Funded Qualitative Research." In *Handbook of Qualitative Research*, edited by N. K. Denzin and Y. S. Lincoln, 220–235. Thousand Oaks, CA: Sage Publications, 1994.

Murdock, G. P. "The Processing of Anthropological Materials." In *Anthropology Today*, edited by A. L. Kroeher, 476–487. Chicago: University of Chicago Press, 1953.

Murphy, S., and P. Rogan. *Closing the Shop*. Baltimore, MD: Paul H. Brookes, 1996.

Myers, V. "Toward a Synthesis of Ethnographic and Survey Methods." *Human Organization* 36 (1977): 244–251.

Nader, L. "Perspectives Gained from Fieldwork." In *Horizons of Anthropology*, edited by S. Tax, 148–159. Chicago: Aldine, 1964.

———. "Up the Anthropologist—Perspectives Gained from Studying Up." In *Reinventing Anthropology*, edited by D. Hymes, 284–311. New York: Vintage Books, 1969.

Naroll, R. *Data Quality Control*. New York: Free Press, 1962.

———. "Native Concepts and Cross-cultural Surveys." *American Anthropologist* 69 (1967): 511–512.

Naroll, R., and F. Naroll. "On Bias of Exotic Data." *Man* 25 (1963): 24–26.

Nash, D. "The Ethnologist as Stranger: An Essay in the Sociology of Knowledge." *Southwestern Journal of Anthropology* 19 (1963): 149–167.

Nash, D., and R. Wintrob. "The Emergence of Self-consciousness in Ethnography." *Current Anthropology* 13 (1972): 527–542.

National Commission for the Protection of Human Subjects of Biomedical and Behavioral Research. *The Belmont Report: Ethical Principles and Guidelines for the Protection of Human Subjects of Research*, 1978.

Nejelski, P., and K. Finster Buch. "The Prosecutor and the Researcher: Present and Prospective Variations on the Supreme Court's Branzburg Decision." *Social Problems* 21 (1973): 3–21.

Nejelski, P., and L. M. Lerman. "A Research-Subject Testimonial Privilege: What to Do Before the Subpoena Arrives." *Wisconsin Law Review* (1971): 1085–1148.

Newcomb, T. M. "An Approach to the Study of Communicative Acts." *Psychological Review* 60 (1953): 393–404.

Nisbet, J., and D. Hagner. "Natural Supports in the Workplace: A Reexamination of Supported Employment." *Journal of The Association for Persons with Severe Handicaps* 13 (4): 260–267, 1988.

Nisbet, R. A. *The Sociological Tradition*. New York: Basic Books, 1966.

Noakes, J. A. "Using FBI Files for Historical Sociology." *Qualitative Sociology* 18 (2): 271–286, 1995.

Oeser, O. A. "Methods and Assumptions of Field Work in Social Psychology." *British Journal of Psychology* 27 (1937): 343–363.

Oleson, V. "Feminisms and Models of Qualitative Research." In *Handbook of Qualitative Research*, edited by N. K. Denzin and Y. S. Lincoln, 158–174. Thousand Oaks, CA: Sage Publications, 1994.

Oleson, V. L., and E. Whittaker. "Role-making in Participant Observation: Process in the Researcher-Actor Relationship." *Human Organization* 26 (1967): 273–281.

Orlandella, A. R. "Boelen May Know Holland, Boelen May Know Barzini, but Boelen 'Doesn't Know Diddle about the North End!' " *Journal of Contemporary Ethnography* 21 (1): 69–79, 1992.

Orlans, H. "Ethical Problems in the Relations of Research Sponsors and Investors." In *Ethics, Politics and Social Research,* edited by G. Sjoberg, 3–24. Cambridge, MA: Schenkman, 1967.

Orne, M. T. "On the Social Psychology of the Psychological Experiment." *American Psychologist* 17 (1962): 776–783.

Osgood, C. "Informants." In *Ingalik Material Culture,* edited by C. Osgood, 50–55, Yale University Publications in Anthropology No. 22. New Haven, CT: Yale University, 1940.

Paget, M. A. "Performing the Text." *Journal of Contemporary Ethnography* 19 (1): 136–154, 1990.

Palmer, V. M. *Field Studies in Sociology: A Student's Manual.* Chicago: University of Chicago Press, 1928.

Park, R. *Principles of Human Behavior.* Chicago: Zalaz, 1915.

———. "Murder and the Case Study Method." *American Journal of Sociology* 36 (1930): 447–454.

Parsons, T. *The Social System.* Glencoe, IL: Free Press, 1951.

Passin, H. "Tarahumara Prevarication: A Problem in Field Method." *American Anthropologist* 44 (1942): 235–247.

Patton, M. Q. *Qualitative Evaluation and Research Methods.* 2nd ed. Thousand Oaks, CA: Sage Publications, 1990.

Patton, R. *Qualitative Evaluation Methods.* Beverly Hills, CA: Sage Publications, 1980.

Paul, B. "Interview Techniques and Field Relationships." In *Anthropology Today,* edited by A. L. Kroeber, 430–451. Chicago: University of Chicago Press, 1953.

Payne, S. L. *The Art of Asking Questions.* Princeton, NJ: Princeton University Press, 1951.

Pearsall, M. "Participant Observation as Role and Method in Behavioral Research." *Nursing Research* 14 (1965): 37–47.

Pepinsky, H. E. "A Sociologist on Police Patrol." In *Fieldwork Experience: Qualitative Approaches to Social Research,* edited by W. B. Shaffir, R. A. Stebbins, and A. Turowetz, 223–234. New York: St Martin's Press, 1980.

Perrucci, R. *Circle of Madness.* Englewood Cliffs, NJ: Prentice Hall, 1974.

Perske, R. *Mental Retardation: The Leading Edge.* Washington, DC: President's Committee on Mental Retardation, 1978.

Phillips, D. L. *Knowledge from What? Theories and Methods in Social Research.* Chicago: Rand McNally, 1971.

Pitt, D. C. *Using Historical Sources in Anthropology and Sociology.* New York: Holt, Rinehart & Winston, 1972.

Platt, A. M. *The Child Savers: The Invention of Delinquency.* Chicago: University of Chicago Press, 1969.

Platt, J. "On Interviewing One's Peers." *British Journal of Sociology* 32 (1981): 75–91.

Polansky, N., W. Freeman, M. Horowitz, K. Irwin, N. Papania, D. Rapaport, and F. Whaley. "Problems of Interpersonal Relation in Research on Groups." *Human Relations* 2 (1949): 281–292.

Pollner, M., and R. M. Emerson. "The Dynamics of Inclusion and Distance in Fieldwork Relations." In *Contemporary Field Research,* edited by R. M. Emerson, 235–252. Boston: Little, Brown, 1983.

Pollner, M., and L. McDonald-Wikler. "The Social Construction of Unreality: A Case Study of a Family's Attribution of Competence to a Severely Retarded Child." *Family Process* 24 (1985): 241–254.

Polsky, N. *Hustlers, Beats and Others*. Garden City, NY: Doubleday, Anchor Books, 1969.

Polya, G. *Patterns of Plausible Inference*. Princeton, NJ: Princeton University Press, 1954.

Ponsansky, N. A. *English Diaries*. London: Methuen, 1923.

Posner, J. "Urban Anthropology: Fieldwork in Semifamiliar Settings." In *Fieldwork Experience: Qualitative Approaches to Social Research*, edited by W. B. Shaffir, R. A. Stebbins, and A. Turowetz, 203–211. New York: St Martin's Press, 1980.

Prus, R. "Sociologist as Hustler: The Dynamics of Acquiring Information." In *Fieldwork Experience: Qualitative Approaches to Social Research*, edited by W. B. Shaffir, R. A. Stebbins, and A. Turowetz, 132–144. New York: St Martin's Press, 1980.

———. *Symbolic Interaction and Ethnographic Research: Intersubjectivity and the Study of Human Lived Experience*. Albany, NY: University of New York Press, 1996.

Psathas, G. *Phenomenological Sociology: Issues and Applications*. New York: John Wiley & Sons, 1973.

———. *Conversation Analysis: The Study of Talk-in-Interaction*. Thousand Oaks, CA: Sage Publications, 1995.

Punch, M. *The Politics and Ethics of Fieldwork*. Beverly Hills, CA: Sage Publications, 1986.

Radin, P. *The Method and Theory of Ethnology*. New York: McGraw-Hill, 1933.

Rainwater, L., and D. J. Pittman. "Ethical Problems in Studying a Politically Sensitive and Deviant Community." *Social Problems* 14 (1967): 357–366.

Reck, A. J., ed. *George Herbert Mead: Selected Writings*. Indianapolis: Bobbs-Merrill, 1964.

Record, J. C. "The Research Institute and the Pressure Group." In *Ethics, Politics and Social Research*, edited by G. Sjoberg, 25–49. Cambridge, MA: Schenkman, 1967.

Reinharz, S. *On Becoming a Social Scientist: From Survey Research and Participant Observation to Experimental Analysis*. San Francisco: Jossey-Bass, 1979.

———. *Feminist Methods in Social Research*. London, New York: Oxford University Press, 1992.

Reiss, A. J., Jr. "Some Logical and Methodological Problems in Community Research." *Social Forces* 33 (1954): 52–54.

———. "The Sociological Study of Communities." *Rural Sociology* 24 (1959): 118–130.

Replee Pty Ltd. *QSR Nud*ist Version 3.0: User Guide*. Victoria, Australia: Replee Pty, 1994.

Reynolds, P. D. "On the Protection of Human Subjects and Social Sciences." *International Social Science Journal* 24 (1972): 693–719.

Rice, S. A. "Contagious Bias in the Interview: A Methodological Note." *American Journal of Sociology* 35 (1929): 420–423.

Richards, T. J., and L. Richards. "Using Computers in Qualitative Research." In *Handbook of Qualitative Research*, edited by N. K. Denzin and Y. S. Lincoln, 445–462. Thousand Oaks, CA: Sage Publications, 1994.

Richardson, J. T., M. W. Stewart, and R. B. Simmonds. "Researching a Fundamentalist Commune." In *Understanding the New Religions*, edited by J. Needleman and G. Baker. New York: Seabury Press, 1978.

Richardson, L. *The New Other Woman: Contemporary Single Women in Affairs with Married Men*. New York: Free Press, 1985.

———. "Narrative and Sociology." *Journal of Contemporary Ethnography* 19 (1): 116–135, 1990a.

———. *Writing Strategies: Reaching Diverse Audiences*. Newbury Park, CA: Sage Publications, 1990b.

———. "Trash on the Corner: Ethics and Technography." *Journal of Contemporary Ethnography* 21 (1): 103–119, 1992.

———. "Writing: A Method of Inquiry." In *Handbook of Qualitative Research*, edited by N. K. Denzin and Y. S. Lincoln, 516–529. Thousand Oaks, CA: Sage Publications, 1994.

———. "Ethnographic Trouble." *Qualitative Inquiry* 2 (2): 227–229, 1996a.

———. "A Sociology of Responsibility." *Qualitative Sociology* 19 (4): 519–524, 1996b.

Richardson, L., and E. Lockridge. "The Sea Monster: An Ethnographic Drama and Comment on Ethnographic Fiction." *Symbolic Interaction* 14 (3): 335–340, 1991.

Richardson, S. A. "Training in Field Relations Skills." *Journal of Social Issues* 8 (1952): 43–50.

———. "A Framework for Reporting Field Relations Experiences." In *Human Organization Research*, edited by R. N. Adams and J. H. Preiss, 124–139. Homewood, IL: Dorsey Press, 1960.

Richardson, S. A., B. S. Dohrenwend, and D. Klein. *Interviewing: Its Forms and Functions*. New York: Basic Books, 1965.

Richter, C. P. "Free Research versus Design Research." *Science* 118 (1953): 91–93.

Riecken, H. W. "The Unidentified Interviewer." *American Journal of Sociology* 62 (1956): 210–212.

Riemer, J. W. "Varieties of Opportunistic Research." *Urban Life* 5 (4): 467–478, 1977.

Ries, J. B., and C. G. Leukefeld. *Applying for Research Funding: Getting Started and Getting Funded*. Thousand Oaks, CA: Sage Publications, 1995.

Riesman, D., and M. Benney. "The Sociology of the Interview." *Midwest Sociologist* 18 (1956): 3–15.

Rist, R. "On the Relations among Education Research Paradigms: From Disdain to Détente." *Anthropology and Education* 8 (2): 42–50, 1977.

———. "Influencing the Policy Process with Qualitative Research." In *Handbook of Qualitative Research*, edited by N. K. Denzin and Y. S. Lincoln, 545–557. Thousand Oaks, CA: Sage Publications, 1994.

Roadberg, A. (1980). "Breaking Relationships with Research Subjects: Some Problems and Suggestions." In *Fieldwork Experience: Qualitative Approaches to Social Research*, edited by W. B. Shaffir, R. A. Stebbins, and A. Turowetz, 281–291. New York: St Martin's Press, 1980.

Robbins, T., D. Anthony, and T. E. Curtis. "The Limits of Symbolic Realism: Problems of Empathetic Field Observation in a Sectarian Context." *Journal of the Scientific Study of Religion* 12 (1973): 259–271.

Robinson, W. S. "The Logical Structure of Analytic Induction." *American Sociological Review* 16 (1951): 812–818.

Rock, P. *The Making of Symbolic Interactionism*. Totowa, NJ: Roman & Littlefield, 1979.

Rogers, C. R. "The Non-directive Method as a Technique for Social Research." *American Journal of Sociology* 50 (1945): 279–283.

Rogers, C. R., and F. J. Roethlisberger. "Barriers and Gateways to Communication." *Harvard Business Review* 30 (4): 46–52, 1952.

Ronai, C. R. "The Reflective Self through Narrative: A Night in the Life of an Erotic Dancer/Researcher." In *Investigating Subjectivity: Research on Lived Experiences,* edited by C. Ellis and M. G. Flahery, 102–124. Newbury Park, CA: Sage Publications, 1994.

———. "Multiple Reflections on Child Sex Abuse: An Argument for a Layered Account." *Journal of Contemporary Ethnography* 23 (4): 395–426, 1995.

———. "On Loving and Hating My Mentally Retarded Mother." *Mental Retardation,* in press.

Ronai, C. R., and C. Ellis. "Turn-ons for Money: Interactional Strategies of the Table Dancer." *Journal of Contemporary Ethnography* 18 (3): 271–298, 1989.

Rose, A. "A Research Note on Interviewing." *American Journal of Sociology* 51 (1945): 143–144.

———. "A Systematic Summary of Symbolic Interaction Theory." In *Human Behavior and Social Processes,* edited by A. Rose. Boston: Houghton Mifflin, 1962a.

———, (ed). *Human Behavior and Social Processes.* Boston: Houghton Mifflin, 1962b.

Rose, D. *Living the Ethnographic Life.* Newbury Park, CA: Sage Publications, 1990.

Rosenhan, D. L. "On Being Sane in Insane Places." *Science* 179 (4070): 250–258, 1973.

Rosenthal, R. *Experimenter Effects in Behavioral Research.* New York: Appleton-Century-Crofts, 1966.

Roth, J. "Comments on Secret Observation." *Social Problems* 9 (1962): 283–284.

———. *Timetables.* Indianapolis: Bobbs-Merrill, 1963.

———. "Hired Hand Research." *The American Sociologist* 1 (1966): 190–196.

———. "Turning Adversity to Account." *Urban Life and Culture* 3 (1974): 347–361.

Rothman, D. J., and S. M. Rothman. *The Willowbrook Wars.* New York: Harper & Row, 1984.

Roy, D. "Efficiency and 'the Fix': Informal Intergroup Relations in a Piecework Machine Shop." *American Journal of Sociology* 60 (1952a): 225–260.

———. "Quota Restriction and Goldbricking in a Machine Shop." *American Journal of Sociology* 57 (1952b): 427–442.

———. "Work Satisfaction and Social Reward in Quota Achievement: An Analysis of Piecework Incentives." *American Sociological Review* 18 (1953): 507–514.

———. "Banana Time: Job Satisfaction and Informal Interaction." *Human Organization* 18 (1959–1960): 158–168.

———. "The Role of the Researcher in the Study of Social Conflict: A Theory of Protective Distortion of Response." *Human Organization* 24 (1965): 262–271.

Rubin, H. J., and I. S. Rubin. *Qualitative Interviewing: The Art of Hearing Data.* Thousand Oaks, CA: Sage Publications, 1995.

Rubin, L. B. *Worlds of Pain: Life in the Working-Class Family.* New York: Basic Books, 1976.

Ruebhausen, O. M., and O. G. Brim, "Privacy and Behavioral Research." *American Psychologist* 21 (n.d.): 423–437.

Ryave, A. L., and J. N. Schenkein. "Notes on the Art of Walking." In *Ethnomethodology,* edited by R. Turner. Baltimore: Penguin, 1974.

Rynkiewich, M. A., and J. P. Spradley, eds. *Ethics and Anthropology: Dilemmas in Field-work*. New York: John Wiley & Sons, 1976.

Sacks, H. (1992). *Lectures on Conversation*. Vols. 1 and 2. Oxford, UK: Blackwell, 1992.

Sagarin, E. "The Research Setting and the Right Not to Be Reached." *Social Problems* 21 (1973): 52–64.

Sanday, P. R. "The Ethnographic Paradigm(s)." *Administrative Science Quarterly* 24 (1979): 527–538.

Sanders, C. R. "Rope Burns: Impediments to the Achievement of Basic Comfort Early in the Field Research Experience." In *Fieldwork Experience: Qualitative Approaches to Social Research*, edited by W. B. Shaffir, R. A. Stebbins, and A. Turowetz, 158–170. New York: St Martin's Press, 1980.

Sanders, W. B., ed. *The Sociologist as Detective: An Introduction to Research Methods*. New York: Praeger, 1974.

Sawyer, E. "Methodological Problems in Studying So-called 'Deviant' Communities." In *The Death of White Sociology*, edited by A. J. Ladner. New York: Vintage Books, 1973.

Schatzman, L., and A. L. Strauss. *Field Research: Strategies for a Natural Sociology*. Englewood Cliffs, NJ: Prentice Hall, 1973.

Scheff, T. J. "Control over Policy by Attendants in a Mental Hospital." *Journal of Health and Human Behavior* 2 (1961): 93–105.

———. *Being Mentally Ill*. Chicago: Aldine, 1966.

Schneider, E. V. "Limitations on Observation in Industrial Sociology." *Social Forces* 28 (1950): 279–284.

Schneider, J. W., and P. Conrad. *Having Epilepsy: The Experience and Control of Illness*. Philadelphia: Temple University Press, 1983.

Schuler, E. "Toward a Code of Ethics for Sociologists: A Historical Note." *American Sociologist* 3 (1969): 316–318.

Schur, E. M. *Labeling Deviant Behavior: Its Sociological Implications*. New York: Harper & Row, 1971.

Schutz, A. *Collected Papers: The Problem of Social Reality*. Vol. I, edited by M. Natanson. The Hague: Martinus Nijhoff, 1962.

———. *Collected Papers: Studies in Social Theory*. Vol. II, edited by M. Natanson. The Hague: Martinus Nijhoff, 1966.

———. *The Phenomenology of the Social World*. Evanston, IL: Northwestern University Press, 1967.

Schwab, W. B. "Looking Backward: An Appraisal of Two Field Trips." *Human Organization* 24 (1965): 372–380.

Schwalbe, M. "The Responsibilities of Sociological Poets." *Qualitative Sociology* 18 (4): 393–413, 1995.

———. "Rejoinder: This is Not a World." *Qualitative Sociology* 19 (4): 539–541, 1996.

Schwartz, G., and D. Merten. "Participant Observation and the Discovery of Meaning." *Philosophy of the Social Science* 1 (1971): 279–298.

Schwartz, H., and J. Jacobs. *Qualitative Sociology: A Method to the Madness*. New York: Free Press, 1979.

Schwartz, M. S., and C. G. Schwartz. "Problems in Participant Observation." *American Journal of Sociology* 60 (1955): 343–354.

Schwartzman, H. B. *Ethnography in Organizations*. Newbury Park, CA: Sage Publications, 1993.

Scott, M. B., and S. M. Lyman. "Accounts." *American Sociological Review* 33 (1968): 46–62.

Scott, R. *The Making of Blind Men*. New York: Russell Sage Foundation, 1969.

Scott, R. W. "Field Work in a Formal Organization: Some Dilemmas in the Role of Observer." *Human Organization* 22 (2): 162–168, 1963.

———. "Field methods in the study of organizations." In *Handbook of Organizations*, edited by J. G. March. Chicago: Rand McNally, 1965.

Seashore, S. E. "Field Experiments with Formal Organizations." *Human Organization* 23 (2): 164–178, 1964.

Seidel, J. V., R. Kjolseth, and E. Seymour. *The Ethnograph: A User's Guide (Version 3.0)*. Amherst, MA: Qualis Research Associates, 1988.

Sells, S. B., and R. M. W. Travers. "Observational Methods of Research." *Review of Educational Research* 40 (1945): 394–407.

Selltiz, C., M. Jahoda, M. Deutsch, and S. W. Cook. *Research Methods in Social Relations*. Revised ed. New York: Holt, 1959.

Shaffir, W. B. "Managing a Convincing Self-presentation: Some Personal Reflections on Entering the Field." In *Experiencing Fieldwork: An Inside View of Qualitative Research*, edited by W. B. Shaffir and R. A. Stebbins, 72–81. Newbury Park, CA: Sage Publications, 1991.

Shaffir, W. B., and R. A. Stebbins, eds. *Experiencing Fieldwork: An Inside View of Qualitative Research*. Newbury Park, CA: Sage Publications, 1991.

Shaffir, W. B., R. A. Stebbins, and A. Turowetz, eds. *Fieldwork Experience: Qualitative Approaches to Social Research*. New York: St Martin's Press, 1980.

Shaw, C. "Case Study Methods." *The American Sociological Society* 21 (1927): 149–157.

———. *The Natural History of a Delinquent Career*. Chicago: University of Chicago Press, 1931.

———. *The Jack Roller*. 2nd ed. Chicago: University of Chicago Press, 1966.

Shaw, C., N. D. McKay, and J. F. McDonald. *Brothers in Crime*. Chicago: University of Chicago Press, 1938.

Sherman, E., and W. J. Reid, eds. *Qualitative Research in Social Work*. New York: Columbia University Press, 1994.

Shibutani, T. "Reference Groups as Perspectives." *American Journal of Sociology* 40 (1955): 562–569.

———. *Human Nature and Collective Behavior: Papers in Honor of Herbert Blumer*. Englewood Cliffs, NJ: Prentice Hall, 1970.

Sieber, S. D. "The Integration of Fieldwork and Survey Methods." *American Journal of Sociology* 78 (1973): 1335–1359.

Sjoberg, G. "Project Camelot: Selected Reactions and Personal Reflections." In *Ethics, Politics and Social Research*, edited by G. Sjoberg. Cambridge, MA: Schenkman, 1967.

Sjoberg, G., and P. J. Miller. "Social Research on Bureaucracy: Limitations and Opportunities." *Social Problems* 21 (1973): 129–143.

Sluyter, C. V. "The Unit Management System." *Mental Retardation* 14 (3): 14–16. 1976.

Smigel, E. "Interviewing a Legal Elite: The Wall Street Lawyer." *American Journal of Sociology* 64 (2): 159–164, 1958.

Smith, D. E. *The Everyday World as Problematic: A Feminist Sociology.* Boston: Northeastern University Press, 1987.

———. *The Conceptual Practices of Power: A Feminist Sociology of Knowledge.* Boston: Northeastern University Press, 1990a.

———. *Texts, Facts, and Femininity: Exploring the Relations of Ruling.* London: Routledge, 1990b.

Smith, H. T. "A Comparison of Interview and Observation Methods of Studying Mother Behavior." *Journal of Abnormal and Social Psychology* 57 (1958): 278–282.

Smith, J. D. *Minds Made Feeble: The Myth and Legacy of the Kallikaks.* Austin, TX: PRO-ED, 1985.

Smith, R. S. "Giving Credit Where Credit is Due: Dorothy Swain Thomas and the 'Thomas Theorem.' " *The American Sociologist* 26 (4): 9–28, 1995.

Smull, M. W., and G. T. Bellamy. "Community Services for Adults with Disabilities: Policy Challenges in the Emerging Support Paradigm." In *Critical Issues in the Lives of People with Severe Disabilities,* edited by L. H. Meyerl, C. A. Peck, and L. Brown, 527–536. Baltimore: Paul H. Brookes, 1991.

Snow, D. A. "The Disengagement Process: A Neglected Problem in Participant Observation Research." *Qualitative Sociology* 3 (1980): 100–122.

Snow, D., and C. Morrill. "Reflections on Anthropology's Ethnographic Crisis of Faith." *Contemporary Sociology* 9 (1993): 8–11.

———. "Ironies, Puzzles, and Contradictions in Denzin and Lincoln's Vision for Qualitative Research." *Journal of Contemporary Ethnography* 24 (3): 358–362, 1995.

Spector, M. "Learning to Study Public Figures." In *Fieldwork Experience: Qualitative Approaches to Social Research,* edited by W. B. Shaffir, R. A. Stebbins, and A. Turowetz, 98–110. New York: St Martin's Press, 1980.

Spencer, G. "Methodological Issues in the Study of Bureaucratic Elites: A Case Study of West Point." *Social Problems* 21 (1973): 90–103.

Spencer, R. F., ed. *Method and Perspective in Anthropology.* Minneapolis: University of Minnesota Press, 1954.

Spradley, J. P. *The Ethnographic Interview.* New York: Holt, Rinehart & Winston, 1979.

———. *Participant Observation.* New York: Holt, Rinehart & Winston, 1980.

Stack, C. *All Our Kin: Strategies for Survival in a Black Community.* New York: Harper & Row, 1974.

Stainback, S., and W. Stainback. *Understanding and Conducting Qualitative Research.* Reston, VA: Council for Exceptional Children, 1988.

———. *Support Networks for Inclusive Schooling.* Baltimore, MD: Paul H. Brookes, 1990.

Stainback, W., S. Stainback, and A. Wilkinson. "Encouraging Peer Supports and Friendships." *Teaching Exceptional Children* 24 (2): 6–11, 1992.

Stake, R. E. *The Art of Case Study Research.* Thousand Oaks, CA: Sage Publications, 1995.

Stanley, B. H., J. E. Sieber, and G. B. Melton, eds. *Research Ethics: A Psychological Approach.* Lincoln, NE: University of Nebraska Press, 1996.

Stanton, A., and M. Schwartz. *The Mental Hospital.* New York: Basic Books, 1954.

Stasz, C. "Text, Images and Display Conventions in Sociology." *Qualitative Sociology* 2 (1): 29–44, 1979.

Stavrionos, B. K. "Research Methods in Cultural Anthropology in Relation to Scientific Criteria." *Psychological Review* 57 (1950): 334–344.

Stone, G. P. "Appearance and the Self." In *Human Behavior and Social Processes: An Interactionist Approach,* edited by A. M. Rose. Boston: Houghton Mifflin, 1962.

Stone, P. J., R. F. Bales, J. Z. Namenwirth, and D. M. Ogilivie. "The General Inquirer: A Computer System for Content Analysis and Retrieval Based on the Sentence as a Unit of Information. *Behavioral Science* 7 (1962): 1–15.

Stone, P. J., D. C. Dunphy, M. S. Smith, and D. M. Ogilivie. *The General Inquirer: A Computer Approach to Content Analysis.* Cambridge, MA: MIT Press, 1966.

Stouffer, S. A. *Social Research to Test Ideas.* New York: Free Press, 1962.

Strauss, A. *The Social Psychology of George Herbert Mead.* Chicago: University of Chicago Press, 1956.

———. *Qualitative Analysis for Social Scientists.* Cambridge, UK: Cambridge University Press, 1987.

Strauss, A., and J. Corbin. *Basics of Qualitative Research: Grounded Theory, Procedures, and Techniques.* Newbury Park, CA: Sage Publications, 1990.

———. "Grounded Theory Methodology: An Overview." In *Handbook of Qualitative Research,* edited by N. K. Denzin and Y. S. Lincoln, 273–285. Thousand Oaks, CA: Sage Publications, 1994.

———, ed. *Grounded Theory in Practices.* Thousand Oaks, CA: Sage Publications, 1997.

Strauss, A., and Schatzman, L. "Social Class and Modes of Communication." *American Journal of Sociology* 60 (4): 329–338, 1955.

Strauss, A., L. Schatzman, R. Bucher, D. Ehrlich, and M. Sabshin. *Psychiatric Ideologies and Institutions.* New York: Free Press, 1964.

Strickland, D. A., and L. E. Schlesinger. " 'Lurking' as a Research Method." *Human Organization* 28 (1969): 248–250.

Stringer, E. T. *Action Research: A Handbook for Practitioners.* Thousand Oaks, CA: Sage Publications, 1996.

Strunk, W., Jr., and E. B. White. *The Elements of Style.* 3rd ed. New York: Macmillan, 1979.

Stryker, S. "Symbolic Interaction as an Approach to Family Research." *Marriage and Family Living* 21 (1959): 111–119.

Sturtevant, W. C. "Studies in Ethnoscience." *American Anthropologist* 66 (1964): 99–131.

Suchar, C. S. "Grounding Visual Sociology Research in Shooting Scripts." *Qualitative Sociology* 20 (1): 33–56, 1997.

Sudnow, D., ed. *Studies in Social Interaction.* New York: Free Press, 1972.

Sullivan, H. S. "A Note on Implications of Psychiatry, the Study of Interpersonal Relations, for Investigations in Social Sciences." *American Journal of Sociology* 42 (1937): 848–861.

Sullivan, M. A., Jr., S. A. Queen, and R. C. Patrick, Jr. "Participant Observation as Employed in the Study of a Military Training Program." *American Sociological Review* 23 (1958): 660–667.

Sutherland, E. *The Professional Thief.* Chicago: University of Chicago Press, 1937.

Sykes, G. M., and D. Matza. "Techniques of Neutralization: A Theory of Delinquency." *American Sociological Review* 22 (1957): 664–670.

Szasz, T. *Ideology and Insanity.* Garden City, NY: Doubleday, Anchor Books, 1970.

Tax, S., ed. *Horizons of Anthropology.* Chicago: Aldine, 1964.

Taylor, S. J. "Attendants' Perspectives: A View From the Back Ward." Paper presented at the 97th annual meeting of The American Association of Mental Deficiency, 1973.

———. *The Custodians: Attendants and Their Work at State Institutions for the Mentally Retarded*. Ann Arbor, MI: University Microfilms, 1977.

———. "From Segregation to Integration: Strategies for Integrating Severely Handicapped Students in Normal School and Community Settings." *Journal of The Association for the Severely Handicapped* 8 (3): 42–49, 1982.

———. "Observing Abuse: Professional Ethics and Personal Morality in Field Research." *Qualitative Sociology* 10 (3): 288–302, 1987a.

———. " 'They're Not Like You and Me': Institutional Attendants' Perspectives on Residents." *Children and Youth Services* 8 (3/4): 109–125, 1987b.

———. "Leaving the Field: Research, Relationships, and Responsibilities." In *Experiencing Fieldwork: An Inside View of Qualitative Research*, edited by W. B. Shaffir and R. A. Stebbins, 238–247. Newbury Park, CA: Sage Publications, 1991.

———. " 'Children's Division is Coming to Take Pictures': Family Life and Parenting in a Family with Disabilities." In *The Variety of Community Experience: Qualitative Studies of Family and Community Life*, edited by S. J. Taylor, R. Bogdan, and Z. M. Lutfiyya, 23–45. Baltimore: Paul H. Brookes, 1995.

Taylor, S. J., D. Biklen, and J. Knoll, eds. *Community Integration for People with Severe Disabilities*. New York: Teachers College Press, 1987.

Taylor, S. J. and R. Bogdan. "Defending Illusions: The Institutions Struggle for Survival." *Human Organization* 39 (3): 209–218, 1980.

———. "A Qualitative Approach to the Study of Community Adjustment." In *Deinstitutionalization and Community Adjustment of Mentally Retarded People*, edited by R. H. Bruininks, C. E. Meyers, B. B. Sigford, and K. C. Lakin, 71–81. Washington, DC: American Association on Mental Deficiency, 1981.

———. *Introduction to Qualitative Research Methods: The Search for Meanings*. 2nd ed. New York: John Wiley & Sons, 1984.

———. "On Accepting Relationships Between People with Mental Retardation and Non-disabled people: Towards an Understanding of Acceptance." *Disability, Handicap & Society* 4 (1): 21–36. 1989.

Taylor, S. J., R. Bogdan, and Z. M. Lutfiyya, eds. *The Variety of Community Experience: Qualitative Studies of Family and Community Life*. Baltimore: Paul H. Brookes, 1995.

Taylor, S. J., R. Bogdan, and J. A. Racino, eds. *Life in the Community: Case Studies of Organizations Supporting People with Disabilities*. Baltimore: Paul H. Brookes, 1991.

Taylor, S. J., and S. J. Searl. (1987). "The Disabled in America: History, Policy, and Trends." In *Understanding Exceptional Children and Youth*, edited by P. Knoblock, 5–64. Boston: Little, Brown, 1987.

Thomas, J. *Doing Critical Ethnology*. Newbury Park, CA: Sage Publications, 1993.

Thomas, W. I. *The Unadjusted Girl*. Boston: Little, Brown, 1931.

Thomas, W. I., and D. S. Thomas. *The Child in America*. New York: Alfred A. Knopf, 1928.

Thomas, W. I., and F. Znaniecki. *The Polish Peasant in Europe and America*. New York: Alfred A. Knopf, 1927.

Thorne, B. "Political Activist as Participant Observer: Conflicts of Commitment in a Study of the Draft Resistance Movement of the 1960s." *Symbolic Interaction* 2 (1979): 78–88.

———. " 'You're Still Takin' Notes.' Fieldwork and Problems of Informed Consent." *Social Problems* 27 (1980): 284–297.

————. "Political Activist as Participant Observer: Conflicts of Commitment in a Study of the Draft Resistance Movement of the 1960s." In *Contemporary Field Research*, edited by R. M. Emerson, 216–234. Boston: Little, Brown, 1983.

————. *Gender Play: Girls and Boys in School*. New Brunswick, NJ: Rutgers University Press, 1994.

Thrasher, F. *The Gang*. Chicago: University of Chicago Press, 1927.

————. "How to Study the Boys' Gang in the Open." *Journal of Educational Psychology* 1 (1928): 244–254.

Tibbitts, H. G. "Research in the Development of Sociology: A Pilot Study of Methodology." *American Sociological Review* 27 (1962): 892–901.

Tiryakian, E. "Existential Phenomenology and Sociology." *American Sociological Review* 30 (1965): 674–688.

Tizard, J. "The Role of Social Institutions in the Causation, Prevention, and Alleviation of Mental Retardation." In *Social-Cultural Aspects of Mental Retardation*, edited by H. C. Haywood, 281–340. New York: Appleton-Century-Crofts, 1970.

Traustadottir, R. "The Meaning of Care in the Lives of Mothers of Children with Disabilities." In *Life in the Community: Case Studies of Organizations Supporting People with Disabilities*, edited by S. J. Taylor, R. Bogdan, and J. A. Racino, 185–194. Baltimore: Paul H. Brookes, 1991a.

————. "Mothers Who Care: Gender, Disability, and Family Life." *Journal of Family Issues* 12 (2): 211–228, 1991b.

————. "A Mother's Work is Never Done: Constructing a 'Normal' Family." In *The Variety of Community Experience: Qualitative Studies of Family and Community Life*, edited by S. J. Taylor, R. Bogdan, and Z. M. Lutfiyya, 47–65. Baltimore: Paul H. Brookes, 1995.

Trice, H. M. "The Outsider's Role in Field Study." *Sociology and Social Research* 41 (1): 27–32, 1956.

Trice, H. M., and P. Roman. "Delabeling and Alcoholics Anonymous." *Social Problems* 17 (4): 538–546, 1969–1970.

Trow, M. "Comment on 'Participant Observation and Interviewing: a Comparison.' " *Human Organization* 16 (3): 33–35, 1957.

Truzzi, M., ed. *Subjective Understanding in the Social Sciences*. Reading, MA: Addison-Wesley, 1974.

Turner, R., ed. *Ethnomethodology*. Baltimore: Penguin, 1974.

Turner, R. H. "The Quest for Universals in Sociological Research." *American Sociological Review* 18 (1953): 604–611.

Vail, D. *Dehumanization and the Institutional Career*. Springfield, IL: Charles C. Thomas, 1966.

Van Maanen, J. "Watching and Watchers." In *Policing*, edited by P. K. Manning and J. Van Maanen. Pacific Palisades, CA: Goodyear, 1978.

————. "Notes on the Production of Ethnographic Data in an American Police Agency." In *Law and Social Inquiry*, edited by R. Luckham. Uppsala, Sweden: Scandinavian Institute of African Studies, 1981.

————. "Fieldwork on the Beat." In *Varieties of Qualitative Research*, edited by J. Van Maanen, J. M. Dabbs, Jr., and R. R. Faulkner, 103–151. Beverly Hills, CA: Sage Publications, 1982.

———. "The Moral Fix: On the Ethics of Fieldwork." In *Contemporary Field Research*, edited by R. M. Emerson, 269–287. Boston: Little, Brown, 1983.

———. *Tales of the Field: On Writing Ethnography*. Chicago: University of Chicago Press, 1988.

———. "Great Moments in Ethnography: An Editor's Introduction." *Journal of Contemporary Ethnography* 19 (1): 3–7, 1990a.

———. "Playing Back the Tape: Early Days in the Field." In *Experiencing Fieldwork: An Inside View of Qualitative Research*, edited by W. B. Shaffir and R. A. Stebbins, 31–42. Newbury Park, CA: Sage Publications, 1991.

———., ed. "The Presentation of Ethnographic Research [Special Issue]." *Journal of Contemporary Ethnography* 19 (1): 1990b.

———., ed. *Representation in Ethnography*. Thousand Oaks, CA: Sage Publications, 1995.

Van Maanen, J., J. M. Dabbs, Jr., and R. R. Faulkner, eds. *Varieties of Qualitative Research*. Beverly Hills, CA: Sage Publications, 1982.

Vaughan, T. R., & Sjoberg, G. "Comment." *American Sociologist* 13 (1978): 171–172.

Vaz, K. M., ed. *Oral Narrative Research with Black Women*. Thousand Oaks, CA: Sage Publications, 1997.

Vidich, A. J. "Methodological Problems in the Observation of Husband-Wife Interaction." *Marriage and Family Living* 28 (1955a): 234–239.

———. "Participant Observation and the Collection and Interpretation of Data." *American Journal of Sociology* 60 (1955b): 354–360.

———. "Boston's North End: An American Epic." *Journal of Contemporary Ethnography* 21 (1): 80–102, 1992.

Vidich, A. J., and J. Bensman, "The Validity of Field Data." *Human Organization* 13 (1): 20–27, 1954.

———. *Small Town in Mass Society*. Princeton, NJ: Princeton University Press, 1958.

———. "The Springdale Case: Academic Bureaucrats and Sensitive Townspeople." In *Reflections on Community Studies*, edited by A. J. Vidich, J. Bensman, and M. R. Stein. New York: John Wiley & Sons, 1964.

Vidich, A. J., and G. Shapiro. "A Comparison of Participant Observation and Survey Data." *American Sociological Review* 20 (1955): 28–33.

Volkart, E. H., ed. *Social Behavior and Personality: Contributions of W. I. Thomas to Theory and Research*. New York: Social Science Research Council, 1951.

Von Hoffman, N. "Sociological Snoopers." *Transaction* 7 (7): 4–6, 1970.

Waitzkin, H., and J. D. Stoeckle. "The Communication of Information about Illness." *Advances in Psychosomatic Medicine* 8 (1972): 180–215.

Wald, A. *Sequential Analysis*. New York: John Wiley & Sons, 1947.

Walker, A. L., and C. W. Lidz. "Methodological Notes on the Employment of Indigenous Observers." In *Street Ethnography*, edited by R. S. Weppner, 103–123. Beverly Hills, CA: Sage Publications, 1977.

Wallace, S. *Skid Row as a Way of Life*. New York: Harper Torchbooks, 1968.

Warren, C. A. B. "Data Presentation and the Audience: Responses, Ethics, and Effects." *Urban Life* 9 (1980): 282–308.

———. *Gender Issues in Field Research*. Newbury Park, CA: Sage Publications, 1988.

Warren, C. A. B., and P. K. Rasmussen. "Sex and Gender in Field Research." *Urban Life* 6 (1977): 349–370.

Warwick, D. P. "Tearoom Trade: Means and Ends in Social Research." *The Hastings Center Studies* 1 (1973): 27–38.

———. "Who Deserves Protection?" *American Sociologist* 9 (1974): 158–159.

———. "Social Scientists Ought to Stop Lying." *Psychology Today* 8 (1975): 38–40, 105–106.

Wax, M. "On Misunderstanding Verstehen: A Reply to Abel." *Sociology and Social Research* 51 (1967): 323–333.

———. "Tenting with Malinowski." *American Sociological Review* 37 (1972): 1–13.

———. "Paradoxes of 'Consent' to the Practice of Fieldwork." *Social Problems* 27 (1980): 272–283.

———. "On Fieldworkers and Those Exposed to Fieldwork: Federal Regulations and Moral Issues." In *Contemporary Field Research,* edited by R. M. Emerson, 288–299. Boston: Little, Brown, 1983.

Wax, M., and J. Cassell, eds. *Federal Regulations: Ethical Issues and Social Research.* Boulder, CO: Westview Press, 1979.

Wax, M., and L. J. Shapiro. "Repeated Interviewing." *American Journal of Sociology* 62 (1956): 215–217.

Wax, R. H. "Field Methods and Techniques: Reciprocity as a Field Technique." *Human Organization* 11 (3): 34–37, 1952.

———. "Twelve Years Later: An Analysis of Field Experience." *American Journal of Sociology* 63 (1957): 133–142.

———. *Doing Fieldwork: Warnings and Advice.* Chicago: University of Chicago Press, 1971.

———. "Gender and Age in Fieldwork and Fieldwork Education: No Good Thing Is Done by Any Man Alone." *Social Problems* 26 (1979): 509–522.

Webb, E. J., D. T. Campbell, R. D. Schwartz, and L. Sechrest. *Unobtrusive Measures: Nonreactive Research in Social Sciences.* Chicago: Rand McNally, 1966.

Webb, E. J., D. T. Campbell, R. D Schwartz, L. Sechrest, and J. Grove. *Nonreactive Measures in the Social Sciences.* 2nd ed. Boston: Houghton Mifflin, 1981.

Webb, S., and B. Webb. *Methods of Social Study.* New York: Longmans, Green, 1932.

Weber, M. *The Theory of Social and Economic Organization.* New York: Oxford University Press, 1947.

———. *The Methodology of the Social Sciences,* edited by E. A. Shils and H. A. Finch. New York: Free Press, 1949.

———. *From Max Weber: Essays in Sociology.* Translated and edited by H. Gerth and C. Wright Mills. New York: Oxford University Press, 1958.

———. *Economy and Society.* New York: Bedminster Press, 1968.

Weis, R. S. "Alternative Approaches in the Study of Complex Situations." *Human Organizations* 25 (1966): 108–206.

Weiss, C., ed. *Evaluating Action Programs.* Boston: Allyn & Bacon, 1972.

Weitzman, E. B., and Miles, M. B. *Computer Programs for Qualitative Data Analysis: A Software Sourcebook.* Thousand Oaks, CA: Sage Publications, 1995.

West, C., and D. H. Zimmerman. "Doing Gender." *Gender and Society* 1 (2): 125–151, 1987.

West, W. G. "Access to Adolescent Deviants and Deviance." In (Eds.), *Fieldwork Experience: Qualitative Approaches to Social Research,* edited by W. B. Shaffir, R. A. Stebbins, and A. Turowetz, 31–44. New York, St Martins's Press, 1980.

Whitman, B. Y., and P. J. Accardo, eds. *When a Parent is Mentally Retarded*. Baltimore: Paul H. Brookes, 1990.

Whitman, B. Y., B. Graves, and P. J. Accardo. "The Mentally Retarded Parent in the Community: Identification Method and Needs Assessment Survey." *American Journal of Mental Deficiency* 91 (6): 636–638, 1987.

Whyte, W. F. *Street Corner Society: The Social Order of an Italian Slum*. Chicago: University of Chicago Press, 1943.

———. "Observation Field Methods." In *Research Methods in Social Relations*. 1st ed., Vol. II, edited by M. Vahoda, M. Deutsch, and S. W. Cook, 493–513. New York: Holt, 1951.

———. "Interviewing for Organizational Research." *Human Organization* 12 (2): 15–22, 1953.

———. *Street Corner Society: The Social Order of an Italian Slum*. 2nd ed. Chicago: University of Chicago Press, 1955.

———. "On Asking Indirect Questions." *Human Organization* 15 (4): 21–23, 1957.

———. "Interviewing in Field Research." In *Human Organizational Research*, edited by R. N. Adams and J. J. Preiss, 352–374. Homewood, IL: Dorsey Press, 1960.

———. *Street Corner Society: The Social Structure of an Italian Slum*. 3rd ed. Chicago: University of Chicago Press, 1981.

———. *Learning From the Field: A Guide from Experience*. Beverly Hills, CA: Sage Publications, 1984.

———. "In Defense of 'Street Corner Society.' " *Journal of Contemporary Ethnography* 21 (1): 52–68, 1992.

———. *Street Corner Society: The Social Structure of an Italian Slum*. 4th ed. Chicago: University of Chicago Press, 1993.

———. "Qualitative Sociology and Deconstructionism." *Qualitative Inquiry* 2 (2): 220–226, 1996.

———. "Whyte's Response: Facts, Interpretations, and Ethics in Qualitative Inquiry." *Qualitative Inquiry* 2 (2): 242–244, 1996b.

Whyte, W. F., and K. K. Whyte. *Learning from the Field: A Guide from Experience*. Beverly Hills, CA: Sage Publications, 1984.

Whyte, W. H. *The Social Life of Small Urban Spaces*. Washington, DC: The Conservation Foundation, 1980.

Wieder, D. L. *Language and Social Reality: The Case of Telling the Convict Code*. The Hague: Mouton, 1974.

Williams, T. R. *Field Methods in the Study of Culture*. New York: Holt, 1967.

Wilson, J. "Interaction Analysis: A Supplementary Field Work Technique Used in the Study of Leadership in a 'New Style' Australian Aboriginal Community." *Human Organization* 21 (4): 290–294, 1962.

Wilson, T. P. "Conceptions of Interaction and Forms of Sociological Explanation." *American Sociological Review* 35 (1970): 697–710.

Wirth, L. *The Ghetto*. Chicago: University of Chicago Press, 1928.

Wiseman, J. P. "The Research Web." *Unborn Life and Culture* 3 (1974): 317–328.

Wolcott, H. F. "Making a Study 'More Ethnographic.' " *Journal of Contemporary Ethnography* 19 (1): 44–72, 1990a.

———. *Writing Up Qualitative Research*. Newbury Park, CA: Sage Publications, 1990b.

————. *Transforming Qualitative Data: Description, Analysis, and Interpretation.* Thousand Oaks, CA: Sage Publications, 1994.

————. *The Art of Fieldwork.* Walnut Creek, CA: Altamira Press, 1995.

Wolf, K. K. "A Methodological Note on the Empirical Establishment of Cultural Patterns." *American Sociological Review* 10 (1945): 176–184.

Wolfensberger, W. *Normalization: The Principle of Normalization in Human Services.* Toronto: National Institute of Mental Retardation, 1972.

————. *The Origin and Nature of Our Institutional Models.* Syracuse, NY: Human Policy Press, 1975.

Yablonsky, L. "Experiences with the Criminal Community." In *Applied Sociology,* edited by A. Gouldner and S. M. Miller. New York: Free Press, 1965.

————. "On Crime, Violence, LSD, and Legal Immunity of Social Scientists." *American Sociologist* 3 (1968): 148–149.

Yancey, W. L., and L. Rainwater. "Problems in the Ethnography of the Urban Underclass." In *Pathways to Data: Field Methods for Studying Ongoing Social Organizations,* edited by R. Habenstein, 245–269. Chicago: Aldine, 1970.

Yin, R. K. *Case Study Research: Design and Methods.* 2nd ed. Thousand Oaks, CA: Sage Publications, 1994.

Young, F. W., and R. C. Young. "Key Informant Reliability in Rural Mexican Villages." *Human Organization* 20 (3): 141–148, 1961.

Zelditch, M., Jr. "Some Methodological Problems of Field Studies." *American Journal of Sociology* 67 (1962): 566–675.

Zetterberg, H. L. *On Theory and Verification in Sociology.* Revised ed. Totowa, NJ: Bedminster Press, 1963.

Ziller, R. C., and D. Lewis. "Orientations: Self, Social and Environmental Precepts through Auto-photography." *Personality and Social Psychology Bulletin* 7 (1981): 338–343.

Ziller, R. C., and D. E. Smith. "A Phenomenological Utilization of Photographs." *Journal of Phenomenological Psychology* 7 (1977): 172–185.

Zimmerman, D. H., and D. L. Wieder. "Ethnomethodology and the Problem of Order: Comment on Denzin." In *Understanding Everyday Life,* edited by J. Douglas. Chicago: Aldine, 1970.

————. "The Diary: Diary-Interview Method." *Urban Life* 5 (4): 479–498, 1977.

Znaniecki, F. *The Method of Sociology.* New York: Farrar & Rinehart, 1934.

Zola, I. K. " 'Any Distinguishing Features?' The Portrayal of Disability in the Crime-Mystery Genre." In *Interpreting Disability: A Qualitative Reader,* edited by P. M. Ferguson, D. L. Ferguson, and S. J. Taylor, 233–250. New York: Teachers College Press, 1992.

Zorbaugh, H. *The Gold Coast and the Slum.* Chicago: University of Chicago Press, 1929.

Author Index

Subject Index